LARRY
CONRAD
OF
INDIANA

LARRY CONRAD OF INDIANA

A BIOGRAPHY

Raymond H. Scheele

PUBLISHED IN COOPERATION
WITH THE
IUPUI OFFICE
OF SERVICE LEARNING AND
STUDENT VOLUNTARY SERVICE

INDIANA UNIVERSITY PRESS / BLOOMINGTON & INDIANAPOLIS

© 1997 by Raymond H. Scheele

The paper used in this publication meets the minimum requirements of American National Standard for Information Sciences—Permanence of Paper for Printed Library Materials, ANSI Z39.48-1984.

Manufactured in the United States of America

Library of Congress Cataloging-in-Publication Data

Scheele, Raymond H.
Larry Conrad of Indiana : a biography / Raymond H. Scheele.
p.   cm.
"Published in cooperation with the IUPUI Office of Service Learning and Student Voluntary Service."
Includes index.
ISBN 0-253-33329-6 (cloth : alk. paper)
1. Conrad, Larry Allyn, 1935–1990. 2. Politicians—Indiana—Biography. 3. Indiana—Politics and government. 4. United States—Politics and government—1945–1989. I. Indiana University–Purdue University Indianapolis. Office of Service Learning and Student Voluntary Service.   II. Title.
F530.22.C66S34   1997
977.2'043'092—dc21
[B]   97-9968
1   2   3   4   5   02   01   00   99   98   97

Dedicated to the Memory of my Parents
Glenn E. and Alice M. Scheele

Larry Conrad, IUPUI, and The Center on Public Service and Leadership

LARRY CONRAD WAS AN EXCEPTIONAL MAN. IN LIFE, HE WAS AN INSPIRATION TO A GENERATION OF HOOSIERS WHO KNEW HIM AND TO OTHERS WHO KNEW ABOUT HIM. IT IS THUS IMPORTANT THAT THROUGH THIS BIOGRAPHY THE EXAMPLE OF HIS LIFE'S WORK BE KEPT ALIVE IN OUR MEMORIES AND IN OUR EXPECTATION OF WHAT IS POSSIBLE IN INDIANA.

INDEED, IT WAS LARRY CONRAD'S UNASSUMING DEDICATION OF HIS TALENT AND ENERGY TO THE COMMON GOOD OF THE WHOLE COMMUNITY—NOT JUST CERTAIN PEOPLE OR PARTICULAR PLACES—WHICH MADE HIM AT ONCE SUCH A SPECIAL INDIVIDUAL AND YET A REPRESENTATIVE OF ALL OF US. COMMUNITY SERVICE AND LEADERSHIP WERE ORDINARY AND COMMON TO LARRY CONRAD. THEY WERE NATURAL AND DAILY HABITS, AND HE EXPECTED THE SAME FROM EVERYONE HE MET. IN INDIANA'S HISTORY AND IN THE LIVES OF ITS LEADING CITIZENS, THIS UNCOMMON COMMITMENT TO COMMUNITY AND TO THE COMMON GOOD HAS BECOME A LEGACY WE ALL SHARE.

BECAUSE WE CANNOT TAKE SUCH DEDICATION AND PERSONAL ENGAGEMENT FOR GRANTED, THE WORK OF THE CENTER ON PUBLIC SERVICE AND LEADERSHIP AT INDIANA UNIVERSITY PURDUE UNIVERSITY–INDIANAPOLIS IS DEDICATED TO PREPARING FUTURE GENERATIONS OF ORDINARY LEADERS LIKE LARRY CONRAD. AS A GRADUATE OF THE INDIANA UNIVERSITY SCHOOL OF LAW-INDIANAPOLIS AND A LONG TERM MEMBER OF THE COMMUNITY BOARD OF ADVISORS, LARRY CONRAD SERVED IUPUI AS A DISTINGUISHED ALUMNUS AND FRIEND. IN TURN, IUPUI WILL SERVE INDIANA THROUGH THE EDUCATION AND PREPARATION OF STUDENTS WHO HAVE AS DEEP AN UNDERSTANDING AS LARRY CONRAD OF THE VALUE OF SERVICE TO THE COMMUNITY OF WHICH THEY ARE A PART. OUT OF A SHARED VISION FOR THE FUTURE OF INDIANA, THE CENTER ON PUBLIC SERVICE AND LEADERSHIP IS PROUD TO SPONSOR THE PUBLICATION OF THIS BIOGRAPHY.

PREFACE

This is the story of Larry Allyn Conrad, son, husband, father, campaign manager, Capitol Hill staffer, secretary of state of Indiana, candidate for governor, and "mover and shaker" in the Hoosier State.

Larry A. Conrad was in the middle of many major events at the local, state, national, and international levels. Rising from modest beginnings in Laconia, Indiana, he was fully engaged in his adult life with the massive currents and shifts that were occurring in the lives of people in our country and the world. He was at the center of some of these, and at the periphery of many others. He wrote the Twenty-fifth Amendment to the U.S. Constitution. Although he never won Indiana's highest office, he was the causal agent in reforming Indiana's Democratic party. After surviving one of the most vicious political attacks in Indiana history, he democratized the oldest political party in the state. After leaving public office in 1978, he became one of the leading figures in the movement to revitalize Indianapolis.

This story explains these many momentous events through the eyes, and contributions, of Larry A. Conrad. The focus is his adult life, roughly from 1960 to his death in 1990.

I first met Larry Conrad in the spring of 1973, when I invited him to be a speaker at a banquet in Schererville, Indiana. From that evening on, he was an inspiration to me. I spent thousands of hours trying to get him elected, and I stayed in touch with him for the rest of his life. When episodes are described in this book without a footnote or citation, it is because I was an eyewitness. Because of my long association with Larry Conrad, this biography, by nature, is a sympathetic work. As a political scientist, however, I always have tried to check my viewpoint with an eye to fairness and accuracy—something Larry Conrad too always insisted on.

I last saw Larry Conrad in May 1990, in a restaurant in Muncie, Indiana. Larry and his wife, Mary Lou, along with former senator Birch Bayh, my wife and I, and Dr. and Mrs. Robert T. Perry met the evening before Bayh was to receive an honorary degree from Ball State University. The evening was filled with stories from the eight campaigns in which these two men were candidates. Some of those stories are in these pages.

That night, as on all occasions when one was with Larry Conrad, a delightful and animated atmosphere surrounded everyone. There was laughter; but not in response to jokes. The conversation was in stories, and his stories were told as great pictures are painted; the observer sees the whole scene forming, and, at times, senses he is even part of the painting. I have strived to make this story of his life as compelling as the stories he told throughout his life. He is deserving of that effort.

Larry Conrad was a lawyer. But it was history, not the details of the law, that informed his mind. And the great historical events and patterns of life on this planet were the raw data he used to tease, inspire, cajole, entertain, inform, teach, and unite others. In his brief life of fifty-five years he did this to thousands of people. Those closest to Larry Conrad still listen to him. Many of the people I talked with in researching his life and times grew emotional while speaking of Larry. Some had to stop and regain their composure before continuing. To this day, in their minds, Larry Conrad is still reminding them to "do something"; and that "something" should not be watching "prime-time television." It is to do something purposeful—something meaningful—something grand—to break down barriers between people and weave those threads that connect one human to another.

Larry Conrad led not only by holding high offices in government and business. He led by example. In conducting over 100 interviews for this book, I was never able to elicit a memory of Larry Conrad denigrating another person. During his political years he harshly criticized the public policies of Republican candidates, but such pronouncements were never personal attacks on the men in office.

Any author incurs massive debts. In most cases these debts are not monetary, but personal. This biography was the inspiration of Mary Lou Conrad. Her willingness, and that of her children and grandchildren, to share memories and personal thoughts have made this story possible. I have been provided an unusual insight into their family and their lives that I will forever appreciate.

To those men and women who allowed me to question them about events of decades ago, I extend my gratitude. Not only were the close friends and political allies of Larry Conrad free and open in their recollections and opinions, but, somewhat surprisingly, so too were the many men and women who fought fiercely against Conrad's political career— both Democrats and Republicans. This fact is a significant statement about Indiana politics and the men and women who engage in it. With very few exceptions, there is a bond among these people that sustains the hard-fought and ferocious wars of Indiana politics. This bond resonates throughout our state and nation, making the men and women who survive the Hoosier political wars some of America's best political leaders.

I would like to single out some who have directly contributed to my efforts. Thomas P. Wolfe, Instructor of English at California State University–Northridge, never met Larry Conrad, but he patiently corrected my grammar and, at times, severely criticized my analogies and similes. He could do so, for our friendship has lasted over forty years. Where I did not take his advice, I did so at my peril. Wylie Spurgeon, former editor of the *Muncie Star*, detected several errors in my first drafts. His encyclopedic knowledge of Indiana has vastly improved the accuracy of this story. Robert F. Wagner, who served as Larry Conrad's campaign manager in 1974 and 1976, read several chapters and spent many hours with me reliving the political days. Robert Boxell, one of Larry's closest friends and co-workers, also commented extensively on the first few chapters and clarified many events. Finally, Claudia Prosser, Larry Conrad's aide-de-camp and comrade-in-arms, continually allowed me to interrupt her personal and professional life with questions. Of course, any errors, of either commission or omission, are mine alone.

I owe special thanks to my colleagues and students at Ball State University. To have the resources of a large university immediately available eases the mental anguish that accompanies any research project. On dozens of occasions I called on my colleagues across campus to answer a technical question or discuss the significance of a particular event. Because the thousands of documents, diaries, and letters pertaining to Conrad have not been yet catalogued, my office became, in effect, the repository of the "Conrad papers." These now are housed in the university library at IUPUI. While sorting through these materials, several graduate assistants assisted in researching and organizing them, including Erik Estep, Billy Linville, Jeffrey Mast, Keith Stouder, and Stephen Wages. Two persons in the office of the Department of Political Science at Ball State University deserve special mention. While writing this biography I also was serving as chair of the department. Sharon McShurley, the administrative coordinator, withstood my many frustrations and neglect of administrative duties, and ensured the smooth functioning of the department. Stephanie Painter, the department secretary, provided invaluable help in preparing the manuscript.

My wife, Marci D. Scheele, read every word many times. She was the first to question whether it was the "right word" in the "right place." She tolerated my endless Saturdays and Sundays "working on Larry." This story would never have been concluded without her constant encouragement and support. My three children, Laura, Stephen, and Robert, saw little of me for over three years. I assuaged my conscience by noting that they were either in college or at work, many miles from Muncie. Now, perhaps, we can have a family vacation.

Preface

This book is dedicated to my parents, Glenn E. and Alice M. Scheele. Until their passing in 1991, they nurtured and succored me through all the good and bad times of my life. In a sense, they still do. They were always there reminding me to think about the greater events happening in our world while remaining aware of the duties, responsibilities, and fun within our family. In a very real way, they have written this story of a man with very similar values.

LARRY
CONRAD
OF
INDIANA

1

I am not a prophet nor the son of a prophet.

—*Larry A. Conrad*

THE MODERN WORLD has no prophets. We have pretenders. Modern skeptics have another word for those men and women who claim divine insight into future events that others cannot see: soothsayer; or even fortune teller.

In the world of religious faith, many prophets exist. John the Baptist. Muhammad. They speak to a future life, beyond this vale of tears. But in the secular world where men and women spend their allotted time, there are only spokesmen. These people are public people. They are politicians. In America that means you find such spokesmen in Washington, D.C., in the thousands of small towns and great cities, and in the fifty state capitals. Larry Allyn Conrad, from a small Indiana town, to Washington, D.C., and back to Indianapolis, was such a politician. He was a spokesman for change, and his words and his actions were to forever change the United States Constitution, recast the Democratic party in Indiana, and reshape the landscape and rebuild the reputation of the city of Indianapolis.

Except for an occasional cheer for a college team, Americans do not usually think in terms of their states. But this has not always been so. For most of America's history, it was the state in which one was born or lived that focused one's identity and loyalty. In April 1861, Robert E. Lee left his mansion in Arlington, Virginia, crossed the Potomac into Washington, and met with President Abraham Lincoln's emissary, who offered him the general command of the Union Army. Lee agonized, then said no, declaring that his first loyalty was to Virginia.[1]

Today, that is incomprehensible. On all serious matters we are Americans, not Virginians or Hoosiers or even Texans. We eat the same food from the same restaurants; we watch the same television show on the same network on the same evening; we drive the same highways, with only the signs informing us we have entered another state.

But our minds have retained a vestigial role for our states. There is a vernacular in all states, and when you talk to Hoosiers you use certain words and phrases and they nod knowingly. To others, these words are devoid of meaning or have completely different connotations. "The region." "The race." "The snakepit." "The circle." "The sectionals." "Qualifications." "The lake." "The river."

These words were part of Larry Conrad's life, and he was to become one of the most skillful of all Hoosiers in weaving them into the context of Indiana life in the twentieth century.

The "region" is northwest Indiana, particularly Lake County—and people from the "region" (the "region rats") are proud of being nearly from Chicago.

The "race" is not the Kentucky Derby, but the "greatest spectacle in racing," the Indianapolis 500. At the "race" the "snakepit" is located on "the first turn" in the "infield" of the "track" where the heaviest partying takes place on "race day."

The "circle" is not the "oval," but the roundabout in downtown Indianapolis, where the Soldiers and Sailors Monument is located. This has been called the second ugliest monument in the world, which may explain why it is covered by Christmas lights six weeks a year.

The "sectionals" are not living-room furniture, but the first round of high school basketball games where opponents are determined by the "draw" at "tourney-time" in March, when there is always a blizzard.

"Qualifications" have nothing to do with one's job. They are the two weekends in "the month of May" at the "track" where the thirty-three-car "field" is set for the "race" unless there is a "bump" of somebody on the "bubble" or a car has "hit the wall" on "carburetion day," which is the Thursday before "the race."

The "lake" is the most prominent of the great lakes: Lake Michigan. Indiana has less shoreline on the Lake than any of the other adjacent states.

The "river" is not the Wabash. It is the Ohio, and it paints the map picture of the southern edge of Indiana.

When the river leaves Cincinnati, continuing its over 800- hundred-mile trek to the Mississippi, it greets Indiana at Dearborn County, just outside Lawrenceburg. From there it flows westerly to Aurora where it takes a looping, nearly two-mile southeasterly swing to Rising Sun. There it drifts back southwest, then, abruptly, due east, back south, and then, with a 90-degree curve, west. It moves lazily along these miles, forming the southern borders of Switzerland and eastern Jefferson counties until it hits the huge bluffs upon which Madison, Indiana, sits. There the water must turn, not slowly, but sharply. It rushes directly south, and at some slight twists it even turns southeast until it curves westerly again and moves on toward the Falls of the Ohio. It is forty-two miles, as the river runs, from Madison to the Falls. These Falls, actually a series of shallow rapids, created the need for Louisville, Kentucky. Frontiersmen and tradesmen had to landfall on the southern bank, above the rapids, and carry their canoes and boats along the shoreline to reenter below the rapids. Louisville became a major trading port, providing services and goods to the landed travelers. In the spring of 1778, it was at Louisville that George Rogers Clark and his 176 men encamped while traveling downriver from Fort Pitt, through the Shawnee, to Illinois to take the French garrison at Kaskaskia before marching on to Vincennes.[2]

"From George Rogers Clark taking Vincennes, to Mad Anthony Wayne defeating the Miami and the Shawnee at Fort Wayne—from the northeast to the southwest—our land has been tamed by the fighters of the ages," Larry Conrad would shout as he "rattled the rafters" during his standard stump speech.

Below the Falls of the Ohio the river spreads out like a giant pond, moving slowly southeast. Thirty-four miles downriver, just south of Laconia, Indiana, the river does a dipsy-doodle, turning abruptly south and then back again to the northwest, forming a little nipple on the map of Harrison County. On the far side of this nipple the river slows and widens and the depth narrows. On the north bank is Mauckport, and it is a perfect place to ford the river.

About mid-morning on July 8, 1863, as the summer sun began burning the mist from the river, 2,400 men on the Kentucky side began loading themselves, their horses, wagons, and four cannons onto two commandeered steamboats to cross to Indiana. These were Morgan's Raiders, and this was the major Confederate invasion of Indiana.[3]

Word had reached the residents of Harrison County that Rebel leader John Hunt Morgan and his men were coming and, under the cover of the morning mist, they prepared to halt the invasion by pulling an old cannon to the riverbank to fire on the two steamboats. This "Home Guard" was under the command of Captain Harvey Huffman, Larry Conrad's great-grandfather.[4] The Hoosiers opened their rifle fire just as Morgan commenced his river crossing, then fired the cannon, which was wide of the steamers. Larry Conrad, in a college term paper, described what happened next:

> Morgan ordered two of his parrot guns, one near the water's edge, and one near the Brandenburg court house to return the fire of the Hoosiers. The heavy fire compelled the militia to fall back, minus their cannon, to

a ridge five or six hundred yards from the river, and parallel to it. Immediately Morgan ordered [two regiments] across, without horses, to drive
the militia back. Having crossed, the two regiments formed under the
bluff bank and assaulted the ridge. After a short skirmish, the militia fell
back toward Corydon, along the Mauckport Road.[5]

Morgan's men continued their crossing and by midnight the Raiders
were on the north shore. The next day they set out for Corydon, fourteen
miles to the north-northeast. Corydon was the county seat of Harrison
County and had been the first state capital of Indiana.

The Home Guards had managed to construct a barricade of logs and
fence rails across the road south of town, and about 400 men ringed the
Old Capitol. Morgan's men galloped into Corydon with their rifles blaz-
ing, and the Hoosiers scattered and ran. The dug-in defenders of the Old
Capitol returned fire for about thirty minutes before surrendering. The
Raiders looted the stores and stole the money from the county treasury
before leaving town, heading north toward Salem, taking their captive,
Captain Huffman, with them.

Morgan's Raiders were marauders, not occupiers, and word spread
quickly that they were on their way to pillage and sack every town in their
path. They moved fast. They were prepared to ride as many as twenty-one
hours a day, and they had mastered the art of sleeping in the saddle. They
lived off the land, pillaging several miles either side of their route, collecting food and fresh horses. Before entering Salem, Morgan returned Captain Huffman's sword and released him, on foot, to return to Corydon.[6]
After sacking Salem, Morgan turned east, and during the night of July 13,
the Raiders reached the Indiana-Ohio border. They entered Ohio, burning
the bridge over the Whitewater River to delay the pursuing Union troops.[7]

Seventy-two years after Morgan's Raiders landed in Mauckport, Indiana, just six miles east of there, in a small white house in the small town of
Laconia, a woman named Ruby Conrad went into a very difficult labor. On
February 8, 1935, Larry Allyn Conrad was born. The baby was the first
child of Ruby and her husband, Marshall, and was Harvey Huffman's
great-grandson.

"I was born in the red clay country, down on the river, way down there
in Harrison County," Conrad would say in his standard political speech.
And red clay country it is.

Some three hundred millennia before Larry Conrad, or Morgan's Raiders, a huge glacier moved down from the north, scraping all of northern
Indiana. The ice known as the Illinois Glacier stopped just north of where
Bloomington, Indiana, is today and separated, shooting its icy tentacles
south to both the left and the right. When the ice receded it deposited the
glacial till all over Indiana except on that untouched part. On the geolo-
gist's map it looks like a slice out of a pie, that unglaciated land in southern
Indiana stretching from Laconia north to Bloomington. The soil in this slice

is red. It is colored by the iron minerals of the original Midwest. You can dig through the red clay in Harrison County and hit bedrock, sometimes within two feet. But up north, up where the Illinois and, later, the Wisconsin Glacier scraped the land and dumped the gravel and the dirt of Canada, you can dig for sixty or seventy feet or more before hitting bedrock.

Laconia, Indiana, was not in the middle of that deep, fertile soil of the Midwest. And in the middle of the Great Depression, in the year of Conrad's birth, times were not easy in southern Indiana. There was no steady work in Laconia and only with the assistance of relatives and friends could families make it. Fortunately, there were many Conrad family members in Harrison County.

Ruby Rooksby Conrad had ten brothers and sisters who were bound together in keeping the homestead functioning. They lived on a ten-acre farm outside of Elizabeth, Indiana, just northeast of Laconia. Her father, Lonnie McDade Rooksby, was a "huckster." Ruby herself described his work as "buying wholesale and selling at retail." He would load his canvas covered wagon with staples and wares and journey to the river bottom where he would sell, trade, and barter. He would provide the "store-boughts" in exchange for fresh produce, eggs, butter, chickens, and animal furs. He would then, in turn, barter or sell these items at the marketplaces in New Albany and Louisville. With whatever profit he derived, he would purchase groceries and dry goods which he would use to replenish the shelves in his small general store back in Elizabeth.[8]

Lonnie McDade Rooksby's life was spent in his wagons. On Monday mornings he would leave the general store before dawn for the trip to the river bottom. He always carried at least two lanterns with him to light his way and to keep his feet warm on the cold winter mornings. Returning late Monday evening, he would repack the wagon and leave again on Tuesday, around noon, for other stops in Harrison County. On Thursday morning he repacked the wagon again for the trip to the marketplaces in New Albany and Louisville. He would return to Elizabeth late on Saturday or early Sunday morning.

While Ruby's father was peddling his wares, his wife, True Curry Huffman Rooksby, along with her mother, Louisa Huffman, and the older children, tended the farm and the general store. True Curry Huffman Rooksby had no memory of her father, Captain Harvey Huffman. She was born August 12, 1883, and her father died about two years after her birth. Her mother, Louisa, obviously favored True over her brothers and sisters and moved permanently to the small farm where she became the "chief cook, house attendant and child attender," while her daughter ran the general store and her son-in-law was traveling the red clay roads of south central Indiana.

The Rooksby general store outside of Elizabeth became the meeting place for neighbors throughout the township. Particularly on Sunday mornings, when Lonnie was back from the marketplaces, customers and neighbors would gather around the wood-burning stove at the general store "to talk about the times, politics and business."

When Ruby was fifteen, the family moved to Laconia, which was then known as Davidson. Ruby remembered the move: "Another grocery store, much larger, was being erected before we moved to the new location. Moving day was great excitement, as this was an entirely new experience for us. We moved only a distance of seven or eight miles, but it seemed far away from our friends and playmates. We soon made new friends and adjusted to another one room country school. We attended Laconia High School and the younger siblings attended Laconia Elementary after Center, the one room school, was phased out."[9]

One of Ruby's new friends was a native of Laconia: Marshall Conrad, who was two years older than Ruby. Through Ruby's high school years, their friendship progressed to romance.

The large Rooksby clan had an unshakable belief in education. It was expected that all the children would not only graduate from high school, but attend college or a trade school. Ruby's older sister, Violet, attended Indiana State College in Terre Haute as well as Central Normal College in Danville, Indiana, where she obtained her teaching degree. In fact, the small normal college in Danville was attractive to the Rooksbys because they had an aunt living in Danville who would keep an eye on the young nieces and nephews.[10] When Ruby graduated from high school she moved to Danville to attend the normal college. It was not surprising that Marshall Conrad was persuaded to make the trek northward to Danville to enroll in college. He wanted to be with Ruby. Ruby loved being with Marshall. He always had a smile on his face. His animated gestures punctuated his jokes and stories. A short man with rounded jowls, he was quick-minded and delighted in making others laugh.

After two years at Central Normal, Ruby and Marshall received their associate degrees and Ruby was certified to teach elementary school. Their love had grown in college, and on May 7, 1930, as the Depression deepened, Ruby Rooksby and Marshall Conrad were married in the Presbyterian church in New Albany, Indiana.

Marshall worked at various odd jobs in and around Laconia during the 1930s, but by the winter of 1937 he had run out of work. Ruby began searching for a teaching position. In early 1938 she found a teaching job in Borden, Indiana, about twenty-seven miles, as the eagle flies, to the northeast, in Clark County. That summer the Conrads moved into a one-room apartment on the second floor of a white frame house in Borden. They paid six dollars a month rent to Faith and Zenos Johnson, the homeowners who lived downstairs with their three-year-old son, Larry Lee Johnson. To distinguish the boys, Faith Johnson and Ruby Conrad took to calling them by their middle names as well, so for the mothers it became "Larry Allyn" and "Larry Lee." To the Conrads and the Johnsons, Borden seemed like a good place to raise their boys and, relatively speaking, it promised economic prosperity. Just two years before, in 1936, State Road 60 was opened, connecting Borden to the factories of Jeffersonville and Louisville to the south. The local Borden Cabinet Company maintained steady employment even during the roughest days of the Depression and it wasn't long before Marshall Conrad went to work there.

But Borden is one of those little towns that drive mapmakers crazy. This is because Borden, Indiana, is not Borden, Indiana; it is New Providence, Indiana. If you drive north from the river on Route 60 you will see the large green sign: "Welcome to Borden—A Small Town with a Big Future." You will drive past the post office that says "Borden, Indiana," but on the official state highway map when you find Borden's location you see the name "New Providence."

The Borden family founded the town and called it New Providence, because they were from Providence, Rhode Island. When a descendent, William Borden, died in 1906, the citizens decided to honor him by naming the town Borden. They changed the name by changing the signs. The post office has the name Borden on it and uses a "Borden" cancellation mark, but all the property deeds and official records refer to New Providence. The residents once voted to change the name to Borden, but a quirk in the state law required a majority of all registered voters, not just those who voted. In May of 1993 the local senior citizens who were gathered at their luncheon at the local museum said that their state senator was going to amend the law to make it easier to officially change to Borden, but eighty-three-year-old Harry Jackson did not think it was a pressing matter. "We've been this way since aught-six," Jackson said, "and besides, I can't remember the name of the state senator anyway."[11]

Larry Allyn and Larry Lee spent their waking hours together. They played all the imaginative games young children invent and they roamed the woods and small hills surrounding Borden. Larry Lee's Dad bought him a fifteen-year-old standardbred trotter named Old Blacky. The boys would ride her through the gullies and along the ridges. The Monon railroad tracks ran directly through town and the big black steam engines pulling dozens of cars came screaming through several times a day, kicking up dust, scaring the cats and dogs, and fascinating all the little kids. Faith and Ruby constantly warned the boys to stay away from the tracks, telling them that a fast-moving train would suck them under the steel wheels.

Just down the railbed, in Mr. McKinley's front yard, a thirty-inch drainage culvert ran under the tracks. Larry Allyn imagined the two of them crawling into that culvert, sitting under the tracks and letting the old Number 6 rumble overhead as it headed south for Louisville. Then they could tell their parents they had been "run over" by the train. After crawling in the culvert and discovering that they could look up through huge holes in the rusted metal and see the ties and rails, they still agreed it was going to be strong enough to protect them.

One sunny summer afternoon they heard that faraway whistle of Number 6. They stared at each other with wide eyes, dashed to the culvert, crouched low, and crawled in. They didn't wait long. The noise was deafening. The ground began heaving and shaking as the train raced toward the culvert. When the huge steam locomotive hit overhead, hot water and steam poured through the rusted culvert onto the heads of the boys. Red hot cinders and sparks careened through the cracks, singeing their hair and pockmarking their necks and arms.

Time passes slowly for eight-year-olds, and it seemed forever before the caboose crossed the culvert. The two Larrys finally crawled slowly from under the tracks. They stood up and stared at one another with lingering fear still in their eyes. Larry Allyn finally said, "Let's not tell our Moms about this."[12]

But most secrets of young boys in small towns do not stay secret for long. Everybody knows everybody, and Ruby Conrad knew the boys well. She was their first grade teacher. She watched them closely every day at school as they moved from one grade to the next.

The art of transmitting enthusiasm and knowledge to another has never been distilled into a formula. Among the hundreds of thousands of school teachers in America, some appear to have been "chosen" to teach. They possess that rare combination of human elements that stirs the impulse of curiosity in others. They awaken that quality that so often lies dormant in mankind. They are the natural-born teachers.

Ruby Rooksby Conrad was one of the chosen. Rooted in the homespun verities of southern Indiana, she viewed even the most recurring and routine chores as adventures. Her enthusiasm, her humor, her patience, were infectious. "She was a magician, making anything and everything interesting," Mary Lou Conrad remembers.[13]

Larry Allyn and Larry Lee entered Ruby's first grade classroom in September of 1941, just three months before Pearl Harbor. "We played a lot of war games in school. We always played America versus the Germans or the Japanese. Even in school we would draw pictures of airplanes in dogfights and the Japanese planes would be spiraling down in smoke," Larry Lee Johnson recalls.[14]

With the war effort fueling the economy, jobs finally became plentiful in the Greater Louisville area. Marshall Conrad worked variously at International Harvester in Louisville, JeffBoat in Jeffersonville, and the Army Ordnance Depot in Charlestown. In the spring of 1945 he was offered a war-related job in Tennessee, and when school ended the Conrads packed their bags and left Indiana. But not for long, because when the war ended in August, Marshall Conrad's job also ended. Through Marshall's sister

Hallie, Ruby found out about a teaching position in Daleville, Indiana, just outside of Muncie. She was hired just before the start of school. The Conrads repacked their belongings and moved back to Indiana. They rented a small frame house on Highland Avenue in Muncie, sharing it with a woman who was the truant officer for the public schools. Although Marshall was also certified to teach, he obtained a higher paying job as an over-the-road truck driver. He and Ruby began closely budgeting their money to save for a down payment on a house.

The young boys in the neighborhood entertained themselves with sports and improvised games. Once again, Larry was one of the leaders. In those days, Muncie had a Class D professional baseball team affiliated with the Cincinnati Reds. Larry became the envy of the neighborhood boys when he won the job of batboy for the team. He also inspired his friends to play ice hockey, a sport to which young Hoosier boys were not automatically attracted. "He got us engaged in ice hockey," remembers Joe Beck, who lived across the street. "We got some old skates and sticks and in the winter we formed teams and flailed one another with our bodies and sticks."[15]

The Conrads settled in to Muncie, but did not forget Borden and Laconia. Each summer, and sometimes on holidays, Ruby would take Larry Allyn to Borden for a stay of a week or so, or Faith would bring Larry Lee to Muncie to visit.

"We both looked forward to our visits. We were close. Even closer than some brothers. When we would think up things to do, it was usually Larry's idea. Even when I was real young I knew he was something special and that he would be famous some day," Johnson says.[16]

It was the freedom of those southern Indiana hills and the unconditional love and support of his parents—and the friends and neighbors of Borden—that formed those elements of character in the young Conrad. His young mind was free to imagine and invent ways to entertain himself and his friends. The gentle proddings of Ruby ensured that he knew of the wider world, and Marshall's lively stories imbued the household with fun and humor. For the rest of his life Larry Conrad would return to Laconia and Borden, not only on his many visits, but also in his mind.

In March of 1963, shortly after he had moved into his Capitol Hill office where he was legislative assistant to Senator Birch Bayh, he wrote to Larry Lee to tell him about the ways of Washington and the great men in the Senate, like Hubert Humphrey and Richard Russell. His mind went back to "those Indiana hills and hollers"; those "old days when we had the good times, the times that count, the times that once gone cannot be regained, the times no one can take away nor can we keep except in memory. I have pity for many of the people here who were deprived of those times. They think they know the universe whilst in truth they have not lived at all."[17]

Like any boy in Indiana, by the time Larry Allyn was a teenager, he was hooked on basketball. But he had no height, and his frame held some of that pudginess that slowed him a step or two against the thin six-footers. Muncie had one dominant high school, Muncie Central, and the basketball coach had his pick from nearly all the Muncie boys who grew up dribbling balls and setting screens. But how could you be in high school in Indiana and not be on the basketball team? Conrad figured it out.

The Muncie Central Bearcats had a student manager who would hang around the gym during practice, making sure the towels and the water jugs were in the right place. He would pick up the balls and equipment after practice and lock them in the equipment room. He ran errands for Coach Jay McCreary. And he got to travel with the team. Most important of all, if he did his job well, he earned his letter jacket.[18]

Do the job well? Conrad turned the job of student manager into an art form. During games he would sit on a basketball in front of the Bearcat bench, following the action and taking notes.[19] He became the official team statistician and the unofficial team historian. How many rebounds did Tom Raisor have? Larry Conrad knew the answer—for both this year and last. The Bearcat stats would roll out of his mind and through his lips as quickly as you could ask him a question. His answers were laced with humor and anecdotes, as though he were a play-by-play announcer. And everybody wanted to know the answers, because Hoosier Hysteria was at its height in Muncie after the Bearcats won their fourth state title in 1952. Everybody was talking basketball and they all went to Conrad for the facts. Before long the other students began calling him "Bearcat" as he walked through the hallways in his purple and white letter jacket reeling off facts, statistics, and stories.

His initiative and organizing abilities also found an outlet in student politics. When school opened in September of 1951, Conrad became the campaign manager for a "ticket" of class officers. He distributed campaign cards in the hallways and, for the first time, delivered a speech before a large audience, urging his fellow students to vote for Tom Raisor for junior class president.[20]

Conrad's body and mind were growing at the same pace. Like a locomotive picking up speed, he used what he read and what he saw to fuel his actions and his plans. His grades were always above average, but he was not a studious pupil. What he read he absorbed, especially anything dealing with sports, history, or politics. "He had a very good mind for history—he'd read something once and remember it," Johnson says.[21]

Although he was in grade school during World War II, the Civil War was his war. He felt linked to that maddening time by birth. The hoofprints of Morgan's Raiders in Harrison County were indelible in Conrad's mind. Whenever he wrote a term paper on American history it was on the Civil War and, if possible, on Morgan's raid. His early readings and writings focused on the Confederate side. He was captivated by those Rebel leaders who, without sufficient equipment or men, made up the difference with courageous commitment, brilliant tactics, and unrelenting perseverance. One of the first things he did when he moved to Washington, D.C., in 1963 was take his three-year-old son, Jeb, to Manassas where they ran around the battlefield and "shot a thousand Yankees."[22]

Television came to Muncie early in 1949, when Conrad was fourteen. Marshall was one of the first in the neighborhood to buy one of the small black and white television sets. Now Larry could sit in his own living room and "see baseball games and about anything."[23]

Part of that "anything" was news and current events.

By the time Senator Estes Kefauver launched televised hearings on organized crime in 1952, the Conrads had bought a small white frame house on Rex Street in Muncie, about five blocks from Ball State Teachers College. It was on that early television set that Conrad had his first sight of a Senate committee in action. He was mesmerized by the proceedings. Eleven years later Senator Kefauver would die of a massive heart attack. His death would touch Conrad personally—and it also would fundamentally alter his career. But at seventeen years of age, the Kefauver hearings represented something new to Conrad. Indeed, the outer world was increasingly a part of his world. The Korean War was raging, and the draft was sweeping young men into war once again. Conrad read about baseball stars like Ted Williams shipping off to war, and he had friends who had just graduated from Muncie Central who were drafted.

For Conrad and his classmates, his senior year was a decision year. He was going to college—of this there was no doubt. Ruby had forever stressed to him the importance of higher education, and Larry took it as an article of faith that he would go on to college. He wanted to attend Indiana University in Bloomington, but it was too expensive to live away from home. And Ball State Teachers College was within walking distance of his house.

In March of 1953 Conrad went to the local National Guard Armory to talk to the recruiter about the army. The local unit had openings, and he signed up, just four months before the Korean armistice was signed. He considered himself lucky that he didn't have to join the regular army right away. Within the next few weeks he was reporting regularly to the armory and was assigned duties of a clerk and orderly until summer camp.

With his military obligation resolved, he now turned his attention toward college, and became incensed when he heard that his best friend, Larry Lee, was thinking about not going on. He could not understand why anyone would forsake an opportunity to attend college. "If I were you I'd think it over before I acted!" Conrad wrote to his friend. To entice Larry Lee, Conrad suggested that "maybe if you did decide to go you could come up here with me. We could stay at our house as I have my room to myself."[24]

Larry Lee acquiesced, and moved in with the Conrads in the fall of 1953. Larry Allyn got Larry Lee signed up in his national guard unit, and they pledged the same fraternity, Sigma Phi Epsilon.

On campus, Conrad's uninhibited manner was reflected in his dress. He wore his Muncie Central letter jacket to his classes every day, with the collar turned up. With a lock of hair curling down his forehead and a long key chain hanging from his pants pocket, his high school nickname of "Bearcat" stayed with him. In fact, so many of the male students wore their high school letter jackets that the Ball State administration, in an effort at dissolving old loyalties, decreed that the jackets could not be worn unless the letter was removed. Most of the men ignored the rule, including Conrad. He was particularly proud of Muncie Central because it appeared the Bearcat basketball team would win another state championship in 1954. But the Bearcats ran into the Indians from Milan, led by Bobby Plump.[25]

Larry Allyn and Larry Lee were glued to the black and white TV in the living room of the Rex Street house in March of 1954 when Plump held the ball for that last shot, which fell at the buzzer. "Larry just wilted when Bobby Plump made that shot," Johnson recalls. The next Monday, on campus, everybody was teasing Conrad about the loss. Johnson remembers one student running up to Larry holding up two fingers on one hand and five on the other, yelling "Bobby Plump, two-five," referring to Plump's number twenty-five.[26]

But the defeat of his beloved Bearcats was only a temporary disappointment. The give-and-take of the teasing seemed to stimulate him and improve his self-confidence. He reveled in the banter. He overcame his fear of public speaking, and any other inhibitions dissolved in those late teenage years. He delighted in being the center of attention, whether in class or at a fraternity party. "He got his sense of humor from his Dad," Johnson maintains, "and he was like a magnet; he could have been a stand-up comic. He could mimic Jonathan Winters, and look more like him than Winters himself."[27] He would weave historical facts into stories, planting "punch lines" throughout. It was in these years that his verbal skills were honed to pinpoint sharpness, presaging his later years when Democrats throughout Indiana would pack union halls and church basements to hear Larry Conrad "peel the paint from the walls."

He also sharpened his organizational skills. He could envision what he wanted in fraternity shows, and took over the production of all the fraternity events. He invented elaborate props and scenes, once producing a thick fog from massive amounts of dry ice and strategically placed fans. These Conrad productions became the talk of the campus, and were forerunners of the extravaganzas he would stage three decades later.

During his second year at Ball State something happened that was to profoundly affect him for the rest of his life. It happened in English literature class. He met Mary Lou Hoover.

A Biography

If you have seen a serious composer at work, you have witnessed all the aspects of music come together in glorious sound. This act of creation is god-like, providing mankind those grand musical scores that permit a peek into our own souls. The personification of this majesty is in witnessing the young child being raised up; first as an improvised rhapsody, filled with energy but randomly off-key; then, in those teenage years, a melody is detected. In early adulthood, some individuals combine the chords of these melodies into a wonderful harmony. Then you just await experience, and all the movements of a symphony will be heard.

By the time Mary Lou Hoover was a teenager in Fort Wayne, Indiana, her actions, manners, and values were already a rhapsody undergoing constant improvisation, but pleasing to those all around. One could hear the melody within, and the hint of harmony. By the time she graduated from Fort Wayne Snider High School in 1953 she had the physical and personal scorings that were to define her for the rest of her life. Physically, she was tall and slender, with a wide mouth and a glistening smile. She seemed to have been kissed by some good fairy and imbued with such movement and power of character that all could see that her inner strength could support more than just one person.

It was the early fifties in America, and, other than the fear of communism, all was right in Indiana and America. With less than 7 percent of the world's population, Americans produced nearly 50 percent of the world's goods and services. Japan and the nations of Europe were crawling from the ashes of World War II, with the assistance of American dollars and under the watchful eye of occupying troops. For the first time in America's history, young women were able to naturally assume they could and should go to college. The war years proved to all that women were more than appendages of men. When nearly fifteen million Americans pulled on their uniforms "for the duration of the war" and disembarked for the distant battlefields, the women left behind took their places in the factories and the stores. Nearly one-third of all the workers on the production lines manufacturing B–29's were women. Their role in America, like so many other things, would never be the same again.

Mary Lou Hoover wanted to teach music, and Ball State Teachers College was just down the highway, in Muncie. The piano was her instrument and she knew from an early age that she possessed musical talent. In her college curriculum she had other courses, as well, including a major in library science. It was in her second year that she enrolled in English literature.

"I sat in the second row, on the left. Larry was in the third row, on the right," Mary Lou recalls, "and we would look at one another in class. We knew each other because he had dated my sorority sister. She told him she was interested in one of his fraternity brothers and he said he wanted to go out with me. They set up our first date."[28]

Mary Lou was intrigued by this uninhibited young man who sported pegged pants, a turned-up collar, and a swinging key chain in one pocket. His sense of personal freedom and his self-confidence around his peers were manifested in his casual dress and flamboyant manners. "I found him fascinating," she says. "He was kind of 'hoody' and we didn't have 'hoods' like that in my high school in Fort Wayne."[29]

On her nineteenth birthday, Thursday, October 28, 1954, Mary Lou accepted a "Coke date" with Larry Conrad. Since another man had already asked her out, she scheduled Larry for a late "second date." She made sure the other man took her home immediately. When Conrad arrived in his father's car, they drove to a local drive-in restaurant. After that evening she never dated another man. It was Mary Lou and Larry.

That Christmas he asked her to go steady. The next Christmas holiday they were pinned. The Christmas after that they were engaged, with Larry asking the question: "Will you share the rest of your life with me?" Mary Lou's answer was "Yes," and on December 28, 1957, they were married in the First Presbyterian Church in Fort Wayne. They honeymooned in Florida, driving there via Lookout Mountain, Tennessee, where Larry explored the Civil War battlefield.[30]

Larry Conrad loved Mary Lou. But it was difficult for him to express such emotions to others. He intellectualized emotions and feelings, and he found it difficult to act on them alone. They were to be pondered, and analyzed. On explaining marriage, he knew there was a fundamental difference between man and woman. In a letter to Larry Lee just prior to Johnson's marriage in 1960, a young Conrad explained to him that "the woman is a strange creation. She seeks the nest, peace and affection, much like the homing pigeon. Whilst the nature of man tends to cater to roving, fighting, drinking, political brawling, and absence from the nest. There is, in all cases, a difficult adjustment to make when persons are suddenly thrust together, making it necessary to accept constantly the ideology of one another."

By this time Conrad had worked enough in a law firm—and seen enough divorces—to be able to reflect on what makes marriages go bad. "Basic differences percentage-wise usually arise either from misunderstandings or from failure of the persons to evaluate and recognize the feelings of one another. The ultimate is consideration of the other person." At age twenty-five, married just twenty-seven months, his thinking about love and marriage turned to one's beliefs and one's honor: "When the marriage vows are repeated, dwell upon those words, 'honor, cherish and love.'"[31]

His commitment to Mary Lou was dug into the bedrock of his values. But while falling in love, other thoughts were churning in his mind. What was he preparing for? What was to be his career?

Since his days of watching the Kefauver hearings and campaigning for his high school classmates, Conrad had been fascinated by government and politics. In his undergraduate years he talked to his mother and Mary Lou about pursuing a political career. By his senior year at Ball State, he had made up his mind. A law degree was the best route to politics. But he had not studied much in college and he began to worry about his ability to handle law school. His grades were largely C's and B's, with a smattering of A's. He hoped they were good enough for law school, but he could not be certain. He decided to obtain a teaching degree at Ball State, just in case he either did not gain admittance to or complete law school.

In the spring of 1957, Larry and Mary Lou graduated together. There was another special person marching down the aisle that day at Ball State: Larry's mother, Ruby. She had decided to complete her higher education by taking the last two years at Ball State. She timed her coursework to ensure she was in the same class as her son and future daughter-in-law.

After graduation, Conrad received the good news. He had been accepted in night law school at Indiana University in Indianapolis.

For the first time in his life, in law school, Conrad had to actually study. The carefree days of undergraduate life were over. He took a clerk position with a downtown Muncie law firm during the day and drove to Indianapolis for classes at night.

Larry and Mary Lou were now living in a house trailer in a trailer park at 8810 Pendleton Pike on the northwest side of Indianapolis. Mary Lou had secured a teaching position in the Lawrence Township school district in Marion County. With her parents' help, she had purchased the house trailer during the summer of 1957 and lived there with her former college roommate, who also taught in Indianapolis. After Larry and Mary Lou were married that December, the trailer became their first home. Mary Lou's roommate found another apartment in Indianapolis.

These first months of married life were full of first jobs, studying law, a few beer and pizza parties, and friends. On race day, Larry and Mary Lou always had the party. They mailed invitations to all their college friends, who would drive from all over the state to join them on race day.

As the young married couple continued to work for the future, Mary Lou learned she was pregnant. On October 26, 1959, at Ball Memorial Hospital in Muncie, she gave birth to their first child, Jeb Allyn Conrad, named after James Ewell Brown (Jeb) Stuart, the Confederate general. After Jeb's birth, Mary Lou quit teaching and, like so many young couples, they relied on their parents, especially Ruby and Marshall, for help. "Mary is sure shot by the end of the day, keeping Jebbo content," Conrad wrote to Larry Lee in February of 1960. "She says this parent business is not what it is cracked up to be. These last 2 weeks we have been in Muncie (five live cheaper than two when Marshall buys the food!)."[32]

Conrad's values were now fully formed. His early years in southern Indiana had provided him with the internal security that comes from a close family as well as a sense of adventure from roaming the "hills and hollers" of Harrison County. His high school and college years built his self-confidence. He had come to respect, and even admire, the institutions created by man. He was caught up in those pursuits—such as basketball, auto racing, and politics. These pursuits captivated Hoosiers, and captured Larry Conrad. He thoroughly enjoyed other people, and delighted in entertaining them. To his many friends he provided encouragement and unquestioned support. He was all Hoosier, enjoying those special things that makes Indiana distinct.

In the fall of 1960, Conrad's formal education was coming to a close. Knowing that a very important phase of his life was soon to begin, he was proud to say that, upon graduating in January of 1961, he would soon be a lawyer. But a big hurdle remained: the bar exam.

The aspiring Indiana lawyers gathered for the exam in the House chamber of the Indiana General Assembly on Thursday morning, March 16, 1961. When Conrad entered the chamber, an outgoing, well-dressed man strolled up to him, stuck out his hand and said, "Hi, Larry." That man felt at home in that House chamber. He was the minority leader for the House Democrats and a former Speaker of the House. He also was there to take the exam, for the second time.[33] Conrad smiled, shook his hand, and said, "Why, it's Birch Bayh."

2

FOR OVER A YEAR, Birch Evans Bayh, Jr., had been planning to run for the Indiana Senate seat. The Republican incumbent, Homer E. Capehart, was completing his third term in 1962. Immediately after taking the bar exam, Bayh began traveling the state nearly full-time, securing political commitments.[1]

On October 19, 1961, Birch Bayh officially announced his candidacy for the U.S. Senate in a news conference in the Claypool Hotel in downtown Indianapolis. His wife, Marvella, was there, along with their five-year-old son, Birch Evans Bayh III.

What officially started that day in the Claypool was a campaign that was to transform Indiana politics for the rest of the century. It was the political equivalent of an earthquake, reshaping the landscape of the eleventh most populous state. The aftershocks radiated from Indianapolis to Washington, D.C., and in six years the American people would be reading a new amendment in their Constitution, written by Larry Conrad.

Senator Capehart's major concern in early 1961 was not Birch Bayh but his own Republican party. Throughout the 1950s, the Indiana Republican party was being whipsawed by its own leaders. William Ezra Jenner, a right-wing isolationist, held the other Senate seat. A staunch defender of Senator Joseph McCarthy, Jenner had managed to exert control over the Indiana Republican party even though he was opposed at nearly every turn by Homer Capehart. By the mid-fifties their disagreements had turned into a personal feud, with Jenner calling Capehart a "New Deal sonofabitch" for Capehart's support of President Eisenhower. In the closing days of the 1956 campaign, when Capehart was seeking his third term, Jenner told Indiana Republican leaders that he would rather belong "to a losing Republican party which is faithful to the Constitution than to a winning Republican party which makes deals with those who would betray America." He then predicted the defeat of Capehart on election day.[2]

Capehart, however, won that third term, and Harold Handley, the Republican candidate for governor, defeated Ralph Tucker, the Democratic nominee and the mayor of Terre Haute. But shortly into Handley's term there was more bad news for the Republicans. The highway scandals left over from Governor Craig's Republican administration, where Handley had served as lieutenant governor, resulted in several indictments and convictions of Republicans who were accused of bribery and kickbacks.

In October of 1957, the mercurial Senator Jenner abruptly announced he would not seek reelection in 1958. Governor Handley, in firm control of the Republican organization, decided to seek the open seat, much to Capehart's chagrin. The Democrats nominated first-term Evansville Mayor Rupert Vance Hartke, and in a surprising turnabout, Hartke buried Handley by 242,000 votes—a genuine landslide.

Two years later, in 1960, when the Republicans also lost the governor's office, it was clear that their internecine party wars and a rapidly changing Hoosier population were taking a toll on the Indiana Republican party:

> The state Republican machine, so efficient and sleek in 1952, was unraveling at the seams through much of the 1950's. . . . The GOP percentage of the off-year election vote slid from 56.2 in 1946 to 53.9 in 1950 to 51.4 in 1954 and a disastrous 44.2 in 1958. The Republican primary vote declined and was surpassed by the Democrats in 1958, and the rural, conservative counties on which the GOP still relied so heavily counted for less and less in the total vote picture; by 1960, 25 percent of Indiana's people lived in just two urban counties; 40 percent in only five counties, and 60 percent in just fourteen out of the state's ninety-two counties. . . . The bedrock of the old GOP power base was gone.[3]

Capehart now seized control of the Republican State Central Committee. He named a new chairman: Thomas Gallmeyer of Fort Wayne. In what proved to be a major error, he turned his reelection campaign over to the demoralized party organization.[4]

Indiana Democrats, on the other hand, were in the ascendancy. Hartke had won the Senate seat in 1958, and their Matthew E. Welsh was the new governor. Nationally, the young president, John F. Kennedy, was reinvigorating the Great Party of the Democracy.

Conrad and Bayh already knew one another when they sat down in the House chamber to take the bar exam in 1961. They had met the previous year at a Young Democrats dinner in Muncie, where Bayh and Matt Welsh were the featured speakers. They also had studied together when they both enrolled in a preparation course for the bar exam.[5]

Conrad was impressed with Bayh. Bayh was young, good-looking, personable, and quick-minded. Conrad discussed Bayh with his friend, Robert (Bob) Boxell, the president of the Young Democrats of Delaware County. It had been Boxell's idea to hold the Young Democrats dinner in 1960, and he had invited Bayh to speak.

Conrad and Boxell first met early in 1960. They were introduced by mutual friends at a meeting at a private home in Muncie. The purpose of the meeting was to "talk politics," and several topics were on the table, including the upcoming dinner, the statewide Young Democrats, the local Delaware County political organization, and the state and national races in 1960. Charlie Richmond, a former Muncie police officer and long-time local politician, recalls the meeting well: "Conrad and Boxell may not have caught on that some of us were more interested in taking over the local party organization than in doing anything statewide. Eventually, we gained control of the Delaware County Democrat Party, but it was years later and it was Jerry Thornburg and Rip Nelson who became county chairmen, and those two were not there."[6]

Boxell pushed ahead with the plans for the dinner, which was to be at the Delaware Hotel in downtown Muncie. When the night arrived, the place was packed. People were standing along the walls and in the doorways. It was a smashing success. Both Bayh and Welsh spoke to the cheering crowd, and the Young Democrats raised enough money to contribute dollars directly to the Delaware County Central Committee, a feat never before accomplished.

Boxell achieved his goal, and Matt Welsh remembered that dinner. After he was elected governor, Welsh said he wanted Boxell to take over the statewide organization.[7]

From an early age, Bob Boxell had but two passions in life: baseball and politics. And he has managed to make a living from each. When Boxell was growing up in Muncie in the 1930s and '40s, there was only one game being played by American boys: baseball. It was still the genuine "pastime" of America, before the superbowls and the stretched-out NBA playoffs. There were only sixteen major league teams, and the teams "out west" were in St. Louis. About 400 men played in the big leagues in the summertime, compared to 700 now. But the relentless search for talent was the same. Each major league club supported as many as six minor league teams, and small towns like Pocatello, Idaho, had professional baseball.

Baseball scouts look for that young man who can do five things: run, hit, hit with power, catch, and throw. When you find one of these men you have a potential hall-of-famer: A Willie Mays. Or a Mickey Mantle.

Unless, of course, you need a pitcher. Then you'll begin with just one thing: the fast ball. The other qualities, such as control, fielding, a curve, or a change-up, are secondary. The pitcher needs the live arm.

Bob Boxell was fast. He proved it at Muncie Central High School, where he threw four no-hitters. And he had other qualities scouts love. He threw left-handed, and southpaws are always in short supply. He had a decent curve. Only five-nine, he did not dominate the mound, but he was broad at the shoulders and sat atop a pair of powerful thighs that propelled him past the front edge of the mound as he came around in full stride.

A scout for the Pittsburgh Pirates liked what he saw in Boxell. Upon Boxell's graduation from high school in 1949, he was signed to a $6,000 contract and sent to San Bernardino, California, for rookie camp. "I wondered who else in the world had any money, because I had it all," Boxell recalls. "And here I was, with all this money, and headed for California. It was the first time I had ever been on a train."

After his rookie season, the Pirates assigned Boxell to Bartlesville, Oklahoma. Mickey Mantle had played in that league the previous year, as a shortstop. In 1951, it was Wausau, Wisconsin. "I had been told I had the dangerous combination," Boxell says, "I threw left and hit right." He was up to bat when he was hit by a pitch, on his left arm, just above the elbow. That one pitch was to end Boxell's baseball career. "I had the doctors check me out. One said that my throwing arm was like a rubber band that had lost its elasticity," he recalls.[8]

Now married to his high school sweetheart, Peggy, Boxell still rejected the notion that his baseball days were over. They moved back to Muncie where he signed with the local semi-pro team for one last chance. But the arm was gone, and so was the promise of bigger money in the big show.

He took a job in the metallurgical lab of a local structural steel plant and he and Peggy bought a house and settled down. Then Boxell turned to his second passion: politics.

At first thought, baseball and politics seem unconnected. But a good pitcher is constantly assessing his situation. He knows the batter's strengths and weaknesses. He tries to stay ahead in the count. He attempts to keep the hitter off balance. He knows what's working that day and what isn't.

A good politician is constantly assessing the situation. He knows the opponent's strengths and weaknesses. He tries to keep his opponent off-balance, and he strives to win. He knows what works and what doesn't.

Larry Allyn Conrad was born in his grandfather's house in Laconia, Indiana, on February 8, 1935.

Larry Conrad, age 2.

Riding Old Blacky in Borden, Indiana: Larry (center), with Larry Lee Johnson (left) and his younger brother, Sidney Johnson.

The 1953 Muncie Central Bearcats.
Larry (front row, left) was the student
manager.

Larry as a Ball State sophomore, age 20,
the year he met Mary Lou Hoover in
English Literature class.

Larry and Mary Lou were married at the
First Presbyterian Church in Fort Wayne
on December 28, 1957.

Larry (center) with Bob Boxell (left) and Senator Birch Bayh, reviewing legislation in Senator Bayh's office, 1963.

Larry meeting President Lyndon Johnson on the occasion of the ratification of the 25th Amendment to the U.S. Constitution, 1967. Larry described Johnson to Mary Lou as "a very big man. Even his ears were huge."

Larry, back home in Indiana, playing with sons Jeb (left) and Andy in the snow at their Daleville house, 1970.

Larry, with his coat over his shoulder and in full stride, campaigning in Madison, Indiana, 1970. This became the signature photo for all of Larry's political campaigns. (Photo by Ray Hafsten.)

Larry's inauguration as secretary of state, 1970. His uncle, George W. Byrum, administered the oath of office, while Mary Lou held the family Bible.

Jane Allen Rooksby (left) and Claudia Prosser talking with Larry during the 1972 campaign.

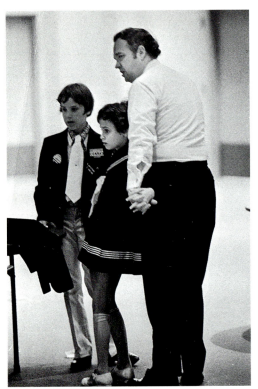

Son Jeb and daughter Amy with their father on the floor of the 1972 Democratic State Convention, following Larry's loss of the gubernatorial nomination.

Cartoon depicting the fight over the Master Plan, which divided the Indiana Democratic party. "Streaking" was a fad during this era. This cartoon was found among Larry's papers; it is not known if it was ever published.

Larry and Mary Lou, with George McGovern and Ruby and Marshall Conrad, 1972.

The debonair and often irascible Robert F. Wagner, Indianapolis attorney and Larry's camapaign manager in 1974 and 1976. (Photo by Sid Rust.)

Larry and Birch Bayh pitching horseshoes at the Conrad Family Picnic, which Larry hosted for his supporters, Zionsville, Indiana, 1975.

A pensive Larry, during the 1976 campaign for governor.

An ebullient Larry, outside Democratic headquarters in Michigan City, Indiana, 1976. (Photo by Jim Messina.)

Larry campaigning in his home county of Harrison with then State Senator Frank O'Bannon, on the courthouse steps in Corydon, 1976. (Photo by Randy West, The Corydon Democrat.)

This unflattering photo of Larry, taken at the Indiana Broadcasters' Association meeting in Vincennes in October 1976, was published on the front page of the Indianapolis News. (Photo by Phil Willis.)

After leaving office in 1978, Larry was much in demand as a public speaker. Here he is as Roastmaster at the 1980 Indianapolis Press Club's Gridiron Dinner. Bottom left: Daughter Amy with Larry at Kappa Kappa Gamma "Dads' Weekend," Indiana University, Bloomington. Bottom right: Larry and Mary Lou "cutting a rug" at one of many civic fund-raisers in Indianapolis.

Larry and his sons. From left, Larry, Jeb, Jody, and Andy.

Larry leading the conga line at the dedication of the refurbished Indiana Roof Ballroom in downtown Indianapolis, 1986. Diane Simon and Mayor Bill Hudnut follow. The person behind Hudnut is unidentified.

Larry and son Jeb getting golfing tips from Larry Bird in French Lick, Indiana. Larry and his sons played the "Conrad Open" every August at French Lick.

Fast friends: the Simons and the Conrads. From left, Herb, Diane, Mary Lou, and Larry, 1987.

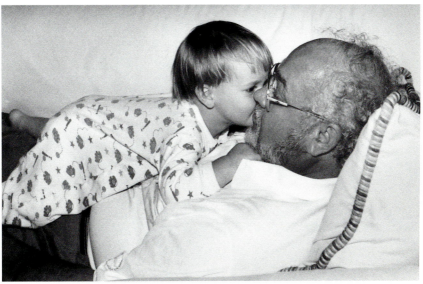

Jeb and Larry with close friend Glenn Howard, Democratic member of the Indianapolis City-County Council and later a state senator from Marion County.

Larry with the only grandchild he knew, Bennett Allyn Conrad, son of Jeb and his wife.

Larry with architectural model of Circle Centre, 1987. (Photo by Robin Jerstad, Indianapolis Business Journal.) Bottom: Frank O'Bannon, flanked by his wife on the left and Larry on the right, in Corydon during his first bid for the governorship in 1987. (Photo by Randy West.)

Four Indiana secretaries of state: From left, Larry, Joe Hogsett, Evan Bayh, and Ed Simcox. This photo was taken at the Indiana Society of Chicago meeting in 1988, shortly after Bayh's election as governor. Bayh was leaving the secretaryship at mid-term, and Joe Hogsett was to be appointed to the position. Bottom left: Larry, during his traveling days, on safari in Africa, 1988. Bottom right: Two Hoosier Democrats in a huddle: Governor Evan Bayh and Larry Conrad in August 1989.

Larry and Mary Lou, the night before he was stricken, in France.

The Conrad bench at Larry's gravesite, Crown Hill Cemetery, Indianapolis. The symbols on the back depict significant parts of his life. The state of Indiana is outlined, showing his birthplace, Laconia. The state flag symbolizes his tenure as secretary of state, and the human silhouettes represent the Conrad family. The scroll symbolizes the 25th Amendment to the U.S. Constitution, and the Indianapolis skyline represents Larry's contributions to that city. State Senator Glenn Howard is one of many who regularly visit the gravesite, sit on the bench, and "talk with Larry" about the issues of the day.

Indeed, looking back, it was no surprise that Bob Boxell was going to be very good at Indiana politics.

"Now as popular as we all know basketball is here in Indiana, God's favorite sport is baseball, not basketball," Larry Conrad would contend in his speeches. "It's right there in the Bible, in Genesis, where God says, 'In the Big Inning.'"

Larry Conrad's beginning in Indiana politics was with Boxell. After assuming the presidency of the Indiana Young Democrats, Boxell appointed Conrad "Executive Director." The two started introducing themselves to the state Democratic leaders. And they got to know Birch Bayh well.

Two weeks after taking the bar exam, Conrad was notified that he had passed. And, this time around, so had Birch Bayh.

The young Conrad was proud to be an attorney. Writing to his oldest friend, Larry Lee, he said he had become "a member of one of the oldest professions, and I am very proud of that fact and I feel that you, with so many others, have indirectly helped me reach the goal to which I so diligently aspired."[9]

Just days after receiving the good news on the bar exam—on Saturday, April 29—Mary Lou entered Ball Memorial Hospital in Muncie and gave birth to their second child, a five-pound baby girl: Amy Lou Conrad. A few months before, the Conrads had sold their house trailer in Indianapolis and bought a small house at 315 Willow Road in Muncie. Larry was practicing law with the firm of Benadum, Cecil and McClellan in downtown Muncie. He also was practicing politics.

Birch Bayh was campaigning hard for the U.S. Senate seat, but he faced opposition within his own party. The mayor of Indianapolis, Charlie Boswell, also wanted the Democratic nomination, and several of Governor Welsh's top advisors favored him. Two other locally elected officials also were making noises about running.[10]

Bayh relied heavily on volunteers to help drive both him and Marvella to the endless city and county meetings throughout the state. He could not count on help from the governor's office because Welsh's closest advisors were convinced that the Democrats could win control of the state legislature only with Boswell leading the ticket for U.S. senator.[11]

Increasingly, Bayh began relying on three key people for campaign planning and scheduling: Conrad, Boxell, and Robert Hinshaw. Hinshaw knew Conrad and Boxell through the Young Democrats; he was the president of the 6th district YD's. "I went to Muncie and met with Larry and Bob and we all agreed to work for Bayh—for free—for as long as we could," Hinshaw recalls. "I lived close to Terre Haute, and was available to drive. Boxell was more politically experienced and he was out making political contacts. Larry, with his law degree, was more of the manager and the organization man."[12]

Hinshaw had volunteered first, Bayh recalls. "Hinshaw was a student at Rose Polytechnic Institute in Terre Haute and in August of 1961 he approached me and volunteered as a driver. At that time our campaign headquarters were in a garage in Terre Haute where we had a mimeograph machine and were mailing letters to state convention delegates."[13]

Bayh recalls meeting with Boxell and Conrad at the Claypool Hotel in Indianapolis where they told him they wanted to help him. "Along with Hinshaw, they were the three musketeers of the campaign," Bayh says.[14]

Conrad was young, full of energy and political interest, and not tied to any faction of the party. "For the campaign manager Birch wanted somebody close to him," Boxell recalls. "He couldn't take anybody off Governor Welsh's staff because nobody knew which way Matt Welsh was going: with Boswell or Bayh. Like all candidates, Birch was going to rely on somebody he was totally comfortable with."[15] That man was twenty-six-year-old Larry Conrad. Conrad was already functioning as *de facto* campaign manager; Bayh officially named him such after the state convention.[16]

When you are at the epicenter of a statewide, high-level campaign in Indiana, you are in a surreal experience which will last for more than a year. Nothing totally prepares you for it. Experience helps, but each campaign is unique. It is defined and driven by personalities and external events over which no single person has control. Dozens of operations must be melded to provide a coherent message to the voters. The candidate and the family must have airplanes and automobiles; they must have speeches to deliver; they must have literature to distribute, and news releases for local reporters. The "road show" must be scheduled, the media must be informed in advance, motel rooms have to be reserved, automobiles serviced, and future events planned. Radio and television advertising must be scripted and produced, and media time must be reserved. All this takes money—enormous amounts of money. The candidate and the campaign manager are constantly pressured and cross-pressured, not only by deadlines, but by contributors and supporters, lobbyists, opponents, relatives, reporters, and staff members.

Conrad thrived in this environment. Working out of a two-room suite at the Claypool Hotel, which he, Boxell, and another Delaware County Young Democrat, Charlie Anderson, had spent two days furnishing with old tables and used furniture, he put in sixteen to eighteen hours a day—and his personal energy was hardly tapped. He was the one who was always available. Sometimes he stayed all night, catching naps on the only couch. At one or two in the morning, when the volunteer who was driving Bayh back to Indianapolis would report in from a pay phone in Paoli or Peru, it was Conrad who would pick up the receiver. During the day, sitting behind a long table, he would puff on cigarettes as he reviewed brochure layouts and speech drafts, scrawling marginal notes in his flowing handwriting. His folksy humor worked on the hundreds of people he met and talked with each week. His organization skills were put to their greatest test yet, and he merged and blended the various campaign operations into the larger picture that he saw in his mind's eye. In those days before computers and photocopiers, he kept track of the details by writing notes to himself and others on 3x5 index cards. They were everywhere in the headquarters, scattered all over his desk and in piles for the other volunteers. Each card contained instructions: "Send brochures to . . . " or "Contact . . . for help on issues." As he would later say about others, his mind, by now, was "double-triggered lightning," and he relished working close to deadline when all others also were focused on the one task before them.

The U.S. Senate nomination was to be decided at the Democratic State Convention on June 22, 1962.[17] But everybody knew that Governor Welsh would make the decision. In a strong party organization state, where loyalists were glued together by patronage provided by the governor's office, Welsh's endorsement assured the nomination for the anointed candidate. But Matt Welsh was a master at knowing when to move and when to stand pat. While his advisors were saying good things about Boswell, the governor himself was noncommittal. The Bayh campaign continued to pressure him. Conrad remembered that "things looked bad for us, so we just kept going to the people twenty-four hours a day, making speeches and going up and down the highways and byways and telling everyone to write the governor a letter. And the mail continued to come in."[18]

The Bayh road show was unrelenting. The governor's office was kept advised of the progress of the campaign, and Boswell and the other potential Democratic candidates were not mentioned in Bayh's speeches. "Our campaign was pretty much geared against Capehart the entire time. . . . [W]e did not make charges . . . against any Democrat, even in the preconvention state," Conrad said.[19]

Bayh's convention nomination was assured on May 10, 1962—two days after the primary—when Welsh called a news conference and endorsed him for the U.S. Senate. Later, Conrad was told that Welsh's endorsement came because there were so many young people involved in Bayh's campaign, and the governor feared losing those young people forever to the party.[20] Indeed, Welsh knew that Birch Bayh had a natural appeal, not only to young people, but to women. A few weeks before the May primary the governor remarked to one of his aides: "You know, it would be a big disappointment to the younger voters and women if we don't take Birch." When the aide, Jack New, relayed this comment to Clint Green, the governor's administrative assistant, Green was disbelieving.[21]

But Matt Welsh was undoubtedly impressed with Bayh for another reason. He saw the way Bayh was campaigning, and Welsh believed in taking a campaign to the people. His own campaigns were testimony. By the time he officially announced his candidacy for his second try for governor, in November of 1959, Welsh had already worn out three engines in his campaign car.[22] But the fundamental factor in Welsh's decision was that Bayh was going to win the nomination anyway. All day Wednesday, May 9, the governor's men, including a young intern, David Allen, were calling the counties and determining the outcome of the delegate races. According to one of Welsh's aides, by late afternoon it was clear that Bayh's delegates substantially outnumbered Boswell's. Bayh had the delegates. Welsh decided to endorse him.[23]

When he learned about the endorsement, Mayor Boswell was irate. He complained to reporters about the "palace guard" around the governor. "Boswell said he was staying in the race, and up to the convention he was very difficult to deal with," Allen remembers. The week after the May 10 endorsement, in Governor Welsh's regular news conference, a reporter asked whether or not the governor and mayor would be on speaking terms during the "month of May" when the festivities for the race were peaking. Welsh replied: "I will attend his breakfast and he will attend my balls." Of course, in his statesmanlike manner, the governor later denied to reporters and his staff that there was any salacious connotation in his answer.[24]

Boswell went so far as to try to drag U.S. Senator Vance Hartke to an endorsement to counteract the governor's endorsement of Bayh. But his rear-guard attack failed miserably.[25]

On June 22, 1962, the delegates to the Democratic State Convention voted a first ballot nomination for Birch Evans Bayh, Jr. for the U.S. Senate.

Immediately after the convention the Bayhs left for a brief vacation. Conrad, taking no time off, began planning the general election campaign.

The poor Indiana equivalent to Camp David is the Aynes House, the governor's cabin in Brown County State Park. It is maintained by the Department of Natural Resources and the governor has access at any time. It was at the Aynes House that the 1962 general election campaign was planned. Several of Welsh's aides drove down to meet with Conrad, Boxell, and Hinshaw. J. Manfred Core, the Democratic State chairman, Clint Green, and John Hurt, a close advisor to the governor, attended. In the space of about three days these men plotted the campaign.[26]

The Bayh people and the Welsh people did not relate well to one another. Jack New, one of Welsh's aides, was not at the meeting, but received reports afterwards. "The reaction was not good to Conrad," he says. Another Welsh aide described his reaction: "This Coooonrod—that's how he pronounced his name—this Coooonrod sat around chewing gum and blowing bubbles throughout the meeting." Clint Green was so distressed that he sent a message to Governor Welsh that he wanted to take control of Bayh's campaign. He believed that the young staff members, such as Conrad, had no statewide experience and were bound to foul it up. Welsh told Green no. "We have too much work here," he said.[27]

A Biography

Conrad never commented on the personalities of the men at the Aynes House. But he clearly remembered the results of the meetings: "[W]e completely laid out the entire campaign personnel-wise, what we were going to do—the strategy, the 'playbook' as they call it now in professional sports, or the game plan—where we were going to try to concentrate, where we had the greatest chance of winning and picking up votes, and generally what we were going to try to talk about. We were not so much on the issues. It seemed to us that Senator Capehart had probably done a fairly good job of covering his flanks. . . ."[28]

Even with the recent decline in Republican party fortunes, Conrad knew that it was extremely difficult for a Democrat to win in Indiana. Mistakes had to be avoided, and the Bayh campaign had to take full advantage of the resources coming from the governor's office through the Democratic State Central Committee. The final campaign plan centered on integrating the Bayh campaign with the committee. Everything was fused for the purpose of maximizing both money and manpower. "What we did was just integrate," Conrad explained.[29]

The Democratic State Central Committee provided the funding. The budget for all Democrats was $500,000, with the majority of this going to the Bayh campaign. The money was raised in three ways. About $290,000 was spent from the 2-percent patronage money accumulated from the control of the governor's office; another $100,000 was raised from individual contributors and about $125,000 was obtained through assessments on the county organizations by collecting $100 for each delegate to the 1962 state convention. While the Bayh campaign received the bulk of the funds, $5,000 was reserved for each of the Democratic congressional candidates, and all Democratic candidates for the state legislature were furnished campaign literature and speech material.[30]

Conrad was blessed by being able to send the campaign bills to J. Manfred Core at the State Central Committee, where they would be promptly paid. But the major strength of the campaign, and Conrad knew it, was the personalities of the two candidates. Months before, Conrad had sensed that Birch Bayh was a new face in Indiana politics. His amiable and open manner appealed to everyone who met him. He was genuine. His speeches seemed to come from the heart without any political stridency or enmity. Compared to Homer Capehart, Conrad knew that this young man represented a fundamental change in Indiana politics.

Capehart's biographer describes the contrast between Bayh and Capehart:

> Capehart was the caricature of an old-fashioned senator: overweight, bespectacled, cigar-smoking, sparse hairline above his large round face, and double chin. The senator's speeches seemed to reflect his appearance and played into the hands of his opponent. Making a fist with one hand

and then the other during speeches, he would pound his right fist into his left, then open both hands and spread his arms. He would act coy: "I don't intend to, but I might get a little politics into this speech." He believed in "good common horse sense." Bayh made an excellent platform appearance. Before a speech he would move through the audience to shake hands. He opened his speeches with a flurry of jokes and anecdotes.[31]

However, this vivid contrast could not hide Bayh's major political problem: voters did not know how to pronounce his name. Was it Bay? Was it Baa? Was it Buy? Conrad tried everything to solve the problem. On the front page of one color brochure, in parentheses, was: "(BAYH PRONOUNCED BY)." On another brochure was the statement: "(BAYH RHYMES WITH GUY)." But the problem would not go away. Brochures were not the answer.

The problem finally was solved in a way that Hoosiers still remember. They remember a song. And they can still sing it:

> Hey look him over
> He's your kind of guy.
> His first name is Birch;
> His last name is Bayh.
> Candidate for Senator from our Hoosier state,
> For Indiana he will do more
> Than anyone has done before, so
> Hey look him over
> He's your kind of guy.
> Send him to Washington; on Bayh you can rely;
> In November remember him at the polls.
> His name you can't pass by,
> Indiana's own Birch Bayh.

The campaign jingle was not discussed in the campaign planning session in Brown County. It was Bob Hinshaw's inspiration.

"Bob Hinshaw was with Birch constantly. They were on the road one night and they heard a song on the radio: 'Hey Look Me Over,' a song from the Broadway show *Wildcat*. Hinshaw wrote the first verse of the jingle, in his mind. He discussed his idea with Conrad and me," Boxell recalls, "and we went for it immediately. We liked it."[32]

According to Hinshaw: "As I was driving, I was thinking of a jingle. It had occurred to me that when Bayh attended meetings he always won people over, but he was able to see so few people. I thought if we could just get him in front of the millions, and have them get to know him, he would win them over. The car radio was on and 'Hey Look Me Over' came on the air. I knew that was exactly what we needed. We had just put out a labor brochure, and the front of it had a picture of guy in a hard hat and the

A Biography

caption said 'Birch Bayh is my kind of guy.' With the tune and the caption, it came to me quickly."[33]

Bayh remembers Hinshaw driving him from Evansville to South Bend late one night when the Broadway song came on the radio. "Hinshaw immediately said, 'This is what we ought to do' and he played with a couple of rhymes. Then he told me that he thought George Romney had used the tune in his race in Michigan. I said, 'Well, if Romney used it, we can't.' And I went to sleep."[34]

About a week later Hinshaw and Bayh were on the road again. By now, Hinshaw had the lyrics to the first verse. Bayh told him to check out the rights to it and find out if Romney had used it.[35]

That was all Hinshaw needed. He conferred with Conrad and Boxell, and they were immediately convinced. Conrad took the idea and Hinshaw's opening words to Mary Lou and asked her to write the rest of the lyrics. Mary Lou was home, pregnant with their third child, and anxious to do something for the campaign. When she finished the lyrics, Mary Lou sat down at the piano and made a tape recording of the song. A few days later—about the third week in September—Conrad, Boxell, Hinshaw, Bayh and two members of the Indianapolis media firm that was working with the campaign—Bob Long and Bill Colbert—met in a hotel room and listened to the tape. "We were all kind of hot on 'Hey Look Me Over,'" says Hinshaw, "but with Bob Long, it did not strike his fancy."[36]

Bayh remembers the meeting well. "They had this big, heavy tape recorder and told me they wanted me to hear this tune. We played it a couple of times. They were convinced it would work."[37]

But Bayh—along with Long—was unsure. "Birch didn't seem to like it," Boxell remembers. "But we contended it was a 'grabber,' and that it would solve the problem of people not knowing how to pronounce his name." After a long discussion, Bayh called Marvella and played the jingle to her over the phone. "She said it was great," he recalls. Finally, he relented. "Let's go for it," he said.[38]

The meeting broke up because Bayh was scheduled for an interview at a local television station. Hinshaw remembers the drive to the television studio: "Bob Long drove us up Meridian Street and he started humming 'Hey Look Me Over.' I turned to Boxell and said: "Perfect advertising is what a person hears once and it sticks in his mind. Now Long has heard this only twice, and he's humming it. How much more perfect do you want?"[39]

Long was convinced. He contacted the Broadway producer, who released the rights gratis for political advertising. Bill Colbert drove Mary Lou's tape to Chicago where a recording company hired professional talent and produced the final version. "We didn't have much money," says Colbert, "and the studio time and talent was costing $2,500 an hour, so we made sure we produced it in 55 minutes. Jamie Silvia, who was a blues-cabaret singer, did the singing and the male voice-over was the man who did Standard Oil commercials."[40]

Conrad immediately pulled all the radio ads from the stations and substituted the jingle.[41] Colbert remembers the jingle played about 6,000 times in the next two weeks.[42]

The response was immediate. "When we heard the Republicans commenting about it, we knew it was hurting them," Boxell recalls.[43]

It was catchy. School children would sing along when they heard it on the radio. Hinshaw remembers driving Bayh to Muncie in late September. In between meetings, they stopped by a Dairy Queen—Bayh could not resist a Dairy Queen—and when they got out of their car, which was festooned with Birch Bayh signs, one youngster with a group of friends in the parking lot pointed at Bayh and asked his friends: "Do you know who that is? That's the guy on the radio who says 'Hey Look Him Over.'"[44] Disk jockeys at the leading radio station in Indianapolis contended it was a "Top Ten" hit and played it again and again.[45] To this day, middle-aged Hoosiers can still sing the first stanza.

As the campaign jingle played across the state, Conrad and Boxell attended a political meeting in Indianapolis. Ralph Tucker, the mayor of Terre Haute, was there. Boxell recalls Tucker referring to Bayh's state legislative campaigns and saying: "I've tried to beat Birch Bayh twice, and couldn't get it done." Boxell replied: "Well, why don't you help us ship him to Washington and you'll have the best of both worlds." Tucker was silent for a moment. "What do you want?" he asked. "Money," Boxell replied. "I'll put together ten thousand for you," Tucker promised. A few days later, the Bayh campaign received the contribution.[46]

After the meeting, Conrad and Boxell returned to the Claypool. Conrad had told the hotel desk where he was and asked to be notified immediately if Mary Lou or Ball Memorial Hospital called. Mary Lou was due to give birth any day. The hotel clerk told Conrad that, while he was gone, Ball Memorial Hospital had called and Mary Lou had been admitted. But the clerk had not called Conrad. "You knew where I was," Conrad said, with a rare hint of irritation in his voice. He and Boxell ran to the car and drove the sixty miles to Muncie in record time, arriving just before Mary Lou delivered their third child: Andrew Birch Conrad. Later that evening, Birch Bayh came by the hospital. The next day in the local morning newspaper there was a front-page photo of Mary Lou in her hospital bed and Larry and Birch standing next to her. The paper credited Mary Lou with writing "Hey Look Him Over."[47]

If Hoosiers remember the campaign jingle from that race, historians and political scientists remember something else: Cuba. For two years Senator Capehart had been calling for an invasion of Cuba to depose Fidel Castro.

On October 22, 1962—only fifteen days before the election—President Kennedy announced a "naval quarantine" of the island. Capehart realized his view was vindicated. And he said so. Conrad remembered the next two days: "Well, immediately, Homer's reaction was, you know, he was not only a prophet but the son of a prophet."[48]

Kennedy's quarantine put the Bayh campaign into a tailspin. This was the first time, but not the last, that Castro would complicate Conrad's life. Twenty-two years later, the two men would meet face to face, and agree on something.

"[Our campaign staff] scrambled very badly for twenty-four or forty-eight hours," Conrad said later. "We were incommunicado. We just didn't know how to react [to the quarantine]." Acknowledging that the young and inexperienced campaign team was paralyzed, Conrad said he finally came to the realization that they were at "home plate" on Cuba. They started trumpeting Bayh's support of the president. Conrad pulled the jingle from the radio waves and substituted a new ad: "Vote Democratic. Back the President for his stand in Cuba. Vote for Birch Bayh." Pictures of President Kennedy were ordered, carrying the tagline: "Back the President in Cuba: Vote for Bayh."[49]

Coupled with the jingle, the "home plate strategy" on Cuba catapulted Birch Bayh into the public's mind. On election night, November 6, 1962, after more than 1,800,000 Hoosiers had gone to the polls, Birch Bayh was declared the winner by 10,944 votes, about one vote per precinct. The closeness of the election kept Capehart from conceding until the next day. When he finally made the statement in a news conference, he hedged, saying he conceded defeat "with reservations," claiming there were still nine to ten thousand absentee ballots to be counted. He charged that the Democrats had spent more than one million dollars during the campaign, while the Republicans found their coffers empty three weeks before election day. Pointing out that this election was the only one he ever lost, he said that he would never be a candidate for public office again.[50]

Seven years later Conrad was asked about the victory he masterminded: "Did you not have any idea that you were actually going to win . . . ?"

Conrad: "Well, it is really unfair to ask me that, because I knew we were going to win from the very beginning. That may sound bad. People say, 'Oh, you didn't either.' I just never questioned it. I just knew that we were in this thing, and were going to win. We were going to prevail, because everything was just right. Homer was on the wrong side, and we were on the right side. I thought it was going to be a tight squeeze, but I just felt that we were going to make it . . . I had complete confidence."[51]

Senator-elect and Mrs. Bayh flew to Washington five days after the election. They met with President Kennedy and Vice-President Johnson. The Vice-President invited them to dinner at his home and advised Bayh:

"Hire the best staff, the best brains you can possibly find. Your staff can make you—or break you. . . . It is more important that they have good minds and experience than that they come from Indiana."[52]

Bayh had not promised staff positions to Conrad, Boxell, or Hinshaw. Conrad and Boxell presumed they would be asked. The phone call to Boxell came in December, from a phone booth in Pennsylvania, where Bayh had stopped for gas upon returning from another trip to Washington. He asked Boxell to meet with him late that night at an Indianapolis hotel. Shortly after hanging up from Bayh, Boxell received a call from Conrad who asked if he had heard anything. Boxell said he had just got off the phone and was to meet Bayh later. Bayh had not called Conrad.[53]

That night, Bayh offered Boxell a staff position in Washington. He was to maintain the senator's political ties back in Indiana. "I was to do the political work," Boxell recalls. "Back in those days there was no big distinction made about political work being done on the senate payroll. Today, they would call it 'constituency contacts.'" Boxell was to report directly to Bayh.[54]

Bayh and Boxell also discussed Conrad that night. Bayh had already decided that Robert Keefe, an aide to Indiana Congressman J. Edward Roush, would become his administrative assistant. "This was one of the toughest decisions I ever made in my life," Bayh contends. "Larry had been so hardworking and so loyal. If anybody had a right to the post of administrative assistant, it was Larry. But I needed somebody with Washington experience who could help me do the job—to administer the office. Larry was an idea man."[55]

Keefe had worked on Capitol Hill and Conrad had not. When Boxell finally left the meeting with Bayh, he was not sure that Bayh even had a position in mind for Conrad. Hinshaw, upon learning of Keefe's appointment, realized there would not be a position for him on the Washington staff.[56]

The phone call to Conrad came about two days later. Bayh offered Conrad the position of legislative assistant. Conrad accepted.

The Conrads bought a house in College Park, Maryland. The Boxells found a home just five houses away, on the same street. When they were both in town, they carpooled to the Hill. In the spring of 1964, following his graduation from Wabash College, Larry Cummings—who was a student volunteer during the 1962 election—joined Bayh's staff and moved in with Larry and Mary Lou. After Mary Lou gave birth to their fourth child, Jodie McDade Conrad, on May 3, 1965, Cummings slept in Jodie's bedroom and occasionally spelled Larry and Mary Lou on the late night feedings.

But Larry and Mary Lou did not see their "family" as consisting only of their four young children. They had an extended family of friends. Their Maryland home was the place everyone was welcome, and Larry's penchant for a good time set the social scene for many of Bayh's staffers and other Capitol Hill acquaintances. With plenty of beer on hand and Mary Lou at the piano, everybody would stand and sing to the current Broadway tunes and the old classics, with an Irish pub song thrown in. Larry assembled a "hills and hollers" instrument from a large galvanized bucket, a wooden pole, and a strong string, and he would "tub thump" in accompaniment to Mary Lou. At the end of a medley he would shout "Innkeeper, more wine for my friends—and fresh horses for the men!"

Mary Lou remembers those early years in Washington as a time when the capital was filled with high hopes and great expectations. "It was a startling contrast to the previous years of law school and mobile home life," she wrote in her diary.[57] Larry, for the first time in years, was able to maintain a regular schedule. He was home virtually every night for dinner, and during the spring and summer months he and Mary Lou would cook out in the back yard, with the young children playing games—including touch football—and roasting wieners on sticks. Larry and Mary Lou knew they would return to Indiana, but while in Washington, Mary Lou was determined that the children would see, and remember, "the people and the places that generated worldwide interest." She planned weekend visits to the monuments and the museums, and Larry would often drive the children down to the banks of the Potomac where they would run along the riverbank.[58]

But during the day, back at the Old Senate Office Building, Bayh's staff was running into problems. Keefe, the Capitol Hill veteran, was a talented political strategist but was unprepared for the administrative and organizational demands of a Senate office. Since Kennedy's election in 1960, there had been a great surge in mail and telegrams to all U.S. senators. At first, Bayh's staff members were expected to draft an individual answer to each letter and telegram, but the volume of correspondence soon overwhelmed everyone. Thousands of letters went unanswered. As early as February of 1963, when Jerry Udell was interviewed by Keefe for an intern position on staff, there were mail bags stacked "six or seven feet high."[59]

By the summer of 1964, when Birch and Marvella began traveling the country on behalf of the Johnson-Humphrey ticket, the backlog of unanswered mail was clearly too large ever to answer. Marvella discovered the problem when she was informed that "somebody in Birch's office had declined an invitation to a party for us." It was the first time she had heard about the invitation. Upon investigating, she discovered that "one secretary had about a thousand unanswered letters stashed away." This incident resulted "in the biggest fight" Marvella and Birch ever had, and increased her resentment of staff members who did not run "a tighter ship."[60]

The senator listened to his wife. "We were not doing a good job," he admits. "Keefe turned out to be not that good an administrator. He fulfilled the role, but he could not say no."[61]

Unless it involved legislation, answering letters was not Conrad's responsibility. But he was caught in the deluge nonetheless. Since he had served as campaign manager, organization Democrats in Indiana were accustomed to communicating with Conrad, and they always had received swift responses. When their letters and inquiries went unanswered, they started marking their mail to Conrad's attention, or asking only for him when they called. Conrad, without the title, began performing many administrative tasks.[62]

Other members of the staff, many of whom were recommended for hiring by Conrad, thought that Conrad should have had Keefe's position. Keefe got the "big job." He was running Bayh's office while Conrad was relegated to researching legislation for a freshman senator. Many staffers presumed Conrad would be jealous of Keefe. On several occasions these staffers would make a disparaging remark about Keefe in front of Conrad, expecting a positive reaction. But they received no reinforcement from Conrad. If Conrad was irritated with Keefe, he rarely if ever let it be known. Conrad had a job to do, and if Bayh wanted his office to operate as it was, it was the senator's decision. And Conrad had long ago determined that personal remarks of a disparaging nature diminished everyone. People produced best when encouraged, not discouraged.

It eventually became obvious to other staff members that Conrad was not at all interested in "running the office." Keefe could do that. Ongoing administrative details did not interest Conrad. Birch Bayh had been right. Conrad was enthralled by ideas, and it was legislation, not administration, that embodied ideas.

There was no highly structured scale of responsibility under Bayh and Keefe. Stephan Lesher, a newspaper reporter who joined the staff in October of 1963 on a fellowship from the American Political Science Association, remembers it as a "carefree arrangement," where he could walk into Bayh's office at any time and show him the most recent newspaper clippings. "There was a great sense of fun and camaraderie," he recalls.[63]

Lax administration was apparent to everyone, but that seemed to be the way Bayh wanted it. He did not want a highly regimented office, and he and Keefe did little to tighten operations. He wanted discussion. He wanted ideas.

Boxell remembers those early days: "We had full discussion and everybody participated. Sometimes we would even vote, and sometimes the vote would turn out to be eight or nine to one, with Birch being the one. And the one won."[64]

Staff memos to the senator were addressed to B^2—a play on Bayh's initials—and soon other staff members adopted their initials as their appellation, with Conrad addressed as "LAC."

The other staff members gradually came to realize that Conrad had no desire to become a permanent member of the Capitol Hill bureaucracy. Someday he was going to be the candidate for public office.

Bayh, as a freshman senator with a law degree, received an appointment to the Senate Judiciary Committee, chaired by Senator James Eastland of Mississippi, and settled uncomfortably into the freshman's role: keep your mouth shut and learn the rules.

Then fate intervened.

3

U.S. SENATOR ESTES KEFAUVER, whose televised hearings on organized crime in 1952 first exposed Larry Conrad to the workings of the U.S. Senate, suffered a massive heart attack and died on August 10, 1963. A member of the Judiciary Committee, Kefauver had chaired the Subcommittee on Constitutional Amendments. Judiciary Chairman James Eastland had decided to abolish the subcommittee, but Fred Graham, the counsel to the subcommittee, convinced Bayh to talk to Eastland and urge him to reconsider.[1] Bayh did so, and learned that Eastland was indeed planning on closing it down. "Fred Graham—who was on his way to CBS—had pointed out to me that I was the only committee member without a subcommittee. I mentioned this to Eastland and told him I did not need any staff members."[2] Bayh's pleas worked. Two days later Eastland changed his mind and said he approved of Bayh becoming chairman.

Bayh was eager. He wanted specific responsibilities. And Eastland recognized that. Unlike other committee chairmen, Eastland understood that his seniority and conservative southern views did not assure him of legislative success. He won new senators over by giving them responsibility and making them chairmen of subcommittees. This gave the new senators a way to add to their staff and yet owe Eastland. Bayh jumped at Eastland's offer. On September 30, 1963, it was made official: Bayh was the new chairman of the Subcommittee on Constitutional Amendments.

Bayh described his new job:

> I spent the next weeks getting acclimated to the new post. Since Senator Kefauver's death, all of the staff members had, like Fred Graham, scattered with the wind and found new jobs. In addition, the space in the Senate Office Building previously assigned to the subcommittee had been absorbed by other senators. Therefore we would have to operate without staff and without facilities. To meet the temporary emergency, I assigned to Larry Conrad, a member of my legislative staff, the responsibility of establishing the future agenda for the subcommittee. Conrad and the subcommittee would operate from a corner desk of my senatorial office, in Room 1205 of the New Senate Office Building; and because of lack of resources, little business was transacted. . . .[3]

But business was soon to pick up.

On November 22, 1963, President John F. Kennedy was killed in Dallas.

Lyndon Johnson's ascension to the presidency left the country without a vice-president, and the U.S. Constitution was silent about succession to the presidency when there was no vice-president. Congress had filled the constitutional void with a statute, but the many questions raised by Kennedy's assassination refocused attention on who should succeed to the presidency. Moreover, the Constitution was silent on the question of presidential disability, and Lyndon Johnson had a history of heart trouble. Bayh referred to this as "a constitutional gap—a blind spot, if you will."[4]

On December 9, Bayh met with Conrad, now appointed chief counsel to the subcommittee, and Bernard (Bud) Fensterwald, Jr., who had previously served as chief counsel. Fensterwald was slender—almost scrawny—and only about 5 foot 7, but his powerful mind overcame any hint of physical weakness. Stephan Lesher remembers him as making "incisive observations" about the whole range of political problems. "He was a political sage," Lesher contends.[5]

In a wide-ranging discussion, Bayh, Conrad, and Fensterwald agreed that a new Senate Joint Resolution should be written dealing with presidential succession and disability and that Conrad should draft it. Bayh described Conrad's mission:

> [I]n his attempt to cover every possible contingency, his first version . . .
> had stretched to five or six pages. He suddenly felt that Madison and
> Monroe were glaring over his shoulder, for his completed version of the
> succession provision alone was, in first draft, longer than all the other
> constitutional amendments put together! Eventually, however, the lan-
> guage was pared down and distilled to a workable length.[6]

Conrad, working nearly around the clock, finished the draft in two
days. Later, he told Mary Lou that he felt like "Thomas Jefferson from Laconia."[7]

On December 12, Senator Bayh introduced the draft as Senate Joint
Resolution (SJR) 139. It was assigned to the Committee on the Judiciary
and, from there, to the Subcommittee on Constitutional Amendments.
Extensive discussion resulted in revisions in the language, particularly in
sections three and four, dealing with presidential disability. On May 26,
1964, the subcommittee approved the drafting of a report that was to trace
the historical background of the problem, clearly state the issues, and
explain how SJR 139 would address the issues. Conrad was to draft the
report, which was then to be reviewed by the other subcommittee members and prepared for printing before being sent to the full Judiciary Committee.[8] But before the report was printed, misfortune struck.

U.S. Senator Edward (Ted) Kennedy had asked Bayh to keynote the
Massachusetts Democratic State Convention in Springfield on Tuesday,
June 9. Marvella was to accompany him. Taking off late from Washington,
the private plane encountered thunderstorms and fog in southern New
England. Attempting to reach the Springfield airport, the plane, bouncing
and weaving in the windstorm, plummeted to earth. It crashed in an apple
orchard, about two miles short of the runway.

It was several minutes, in that wet blackness of a Massachusetts night,
before Birch and Marvella Bayh regained their orientation in the crumpled
aircraft. Their seat belts had saved them. An emergency light came on and
the smell of gasoline was heavy in the air. It was immediately clear to Birch
that Kennedy was severely injured. In fact, his back was broken. He was
conscious, but in excruciating pain. Bayh grabbed his arms, pulled him
from the aircraft, and laid him on a spot of wet grass, away from the plane.
Marvella grabbed a dress she was planning to wear at the state convention,
rolled it into a pillow, and placed it under Kennedy's head. Birch and
Marvella—without shoes—then stumbled through the orchard in search
of help.

Birch had severely bruised and torn muscles in his hip and stomach and
Marvella had suffered hairline fractures in the lower extremity of her
spine. The pilot was dead. Kennedy's aide, Ed Moss, who was sitting in the
co-pilot's seat, died the next day of massive head injuries. Kennedy, who
required three transfusions to restore his pulse, barely escaped death. For
several weeks, it was unclear if he would ever walk again.[9]

That night Conrad, Boxell, Boxell's son, and an old Muncie friend, Kenneth (Irish) Walsh, were in Baltimore watching the Orioles play. After the game, while driving home, they turned on the radio for more baseball scores. There was a news report that Senator Kennedy's plane had crashed that evening. Stopping at a telephone booth, Boxell called a friend in the newsroom at the *Baltimore Sun*. He said the first reports were that the pilot was dead, Senator Kennedy was seriously injured, and there were two unidentified bodies in the wreckage. Walking back to the car in a daze, Boxell relayed the news to Conrad and the others. When they arrived home, Kennedy's office called and reported that the Bayhs were badly injured, but alive.[10]

The next morning Conrad and Boxell caught the first flight from Washington to Hartford, Connecticut. They spoke little. The flight plan took them over Manhattan and Conrad, sitting in the window seat, looked down over the skyscrapers and said: "Boy, that sure is a big town." Boxell laughed and said: "It sure is."[11]

They were met at the Hartford airport by a Massachusetts state trooper who drove them directly to the hospital. When they entered the hospital corridor on the way to the rooms, they saw Robert Kennedy standing in the hallway. "I'll never forget his expression," Boxell recalls; "he looked lost. Desolate."[12]

Conrad and Boxell went immediately to Birch and Marvella's room. Boxell remembers looking at Marvella. She was under heavy medication. The sight of the staffers evoked a reaction in her dazed mind. She looked up at Boxell from her bed and murmured: "You wouldn't be here if Birch were not a U.S. Senator." Boxell leaned down and said, softly: "I'm here because my friends were injured in a plane crash." He patted her hand and left.

They returned to the hospital the next day and Boxell looked through the door at Marvella. She had improved markedly. She wiggled her finger at him, gesturing for him to come in. "She kept indicating to me to lean down, as though she were going to whisper something to me," Boxell recalls. "I leaned over and she kissed me on the cheek and smiled. I smiled back. Then I left. We didn't say a word to one another. We didn't have to."[13]

Stephan Lesher, Bayh's press secretary, also was in Springfield, having arrived on a separate flight. As the Bayhs began recovering, they were moved to a room on the ward. Conrad, Boxell, and Lesher were with them constantly. Lesher began preparing for a news conference that would be held as soon as Bayh was able to stand and walk. At one point, when Bayh had to use the bathroom and no orderlies were available, Conrad and Boxell carried him to the bathroom and Lesher saw the seriousness of his injuries. "He was all green and yellow throughout his midsection," Lesher recalls. "It was where the seat belt had been wrapped, and he was in a lot of pain."[14]

The next day Bayh held a news conference in the hospital. Lesher advised him to "shift his weight" if he became uncomfortable while standing. Bayh replied: "If I move around I will wince." "Exactly," Lesher responded. He remembered the audience and he wanted them to know Bayh was injured. During the news conference Bayh shifted his weight, and he winced.[15]

Conrad and Boxell stayed four days in Springfield, monitoring the medical progress of Marvella and the two senators. When it was clear everyone was on the road to recovery, they flew back to Washington. Now the work of amending the U.S. Constitution fell totally on Conrad's shoulders.

Conrad knew the myriad issues surrounding the question of presidential succession and disability, and, working with other staffers, he proceeded with the report. By now, Conrad was working out of an office in Bayh's suite, which was a converted men's restroom. Jerry Udell, who had joined Bayh's staff the previous year as an intern, also had a desk in the cramped room.

The next week, when Bayh had recovered sufficiently to return to Washington for recuperation, he approved Conrad's plan to print the subcommittee's report and move toward a hearing before the full committee. Along with Lesher, Conrad prepared dozens of pages listing all the possible questions that could be directed against SJR 139. He spent hours briefing Bayh at the senator's home.

Bayh was finally able to attend the meeting of the full committee on August 4, where he defended the resolution. The members finally passed it unanimously. As Conrad and Bayh left the hearing room, Conrad said: "Nice job, Senator, nice job."[16]

For the rest of the year Bayh and Conrad were devoted nearly full-time to the passage of SJR 139. After clearing several more hurdles, the resolution finally passed the Senate and was sent to the House. But when the Eighty-eighth Congress adjourned in early October, the House Judiciary Committee had not acted on it. It was dead for that session.

The final six months of 1964 were a frantic time for Bayh's staff. President Johnson was leaning on Democratic senators to help plan the convention in Atlantic City and later to "hit the road" in support of the Johnson-Humphrey ticket. The president had appointed Bayh chairman of the "Young Citizens for Johnson-Humphrey," and Bayh traveled frequently with Lynda and Luci Johnson to raise money and enthusiasm among young voters.[17] Bayh also relied on his staff members to assist Johnson, and Conrad attended the Democratic National Convention in Atlantic City where he helped organize young delegates for Johnson-Humphrey.[18]

Between the demands of the national convention and election and the Senate struggle on the proposed amendment, Bayh and Conrad abandoned the operations of the Senate office. Over there, Keefe was slowly becoming aware of the internal operational problems, but few steps were taken to solve them. The mail continued to pile up.

Following President Johnson's landslide, Conrad went to work on the Senate Bill Clerk and persuaded him that the proposed amendment should be designated as Senate Joint Resolution 1 in the new Congress.[19] Support in the House was assured when Emmanuel Cellar of New York, the chairman of the House Judiciary Committee, agreed to introduce the same measure as House Joint Resolution 1.

In the U.S. Congress there are many ways to kill a measure, but there is only one route to passage. If a bill or resolution is derailed at any point, such as in subcommittee or the full committee, or on the floor, only a miracle can provide a second chance at passage. Conrad and Bayh knew this. They recognized that 1965 was their year. They needed a two-thirds vote in both chambers. If they stumbled, there would not be another chance.

Bayh's reliance on Conrad was nearly total. "I relied a lot on him," he acknowledges.[20] Conrad determined the subcommittee's agenda, scheduled the witnesses, contacted external groups to persuade them to support the amendment, and kept Bayh informed on the swirl of questions and objections about the wording of the resolution. The Senate scheduled floor debate on the amendment for February 18. The night before, Bayh, Conrad, Lesher, Keefe, Udell, and the new legislative assistant, Clark Norton, worked past midnight drafting responses to every conceivable question that could be asked in the debate. They were working with stacks of papers and books in a nearly vacant office, since Bayh was in the process of moving to more spacious quarters in the Old Senate Office Building. They finally went home about one o'clock in the morning, stacking all the files and books on the one remaining couch.

Conrad was the first to arrive in the morning and, upon entering the office, was astonished when he looked at an empty couch. The original subcommittee copy of the amendment was gone, along with all the files and books. Hoping that the papers had been moved to the new office, Conrad contacted other staff members, only to find out that they had not seen the material. Concluding that the custodians must have cleaned out the office, Conrad traced the missing files to the basement waste area. He quickly summoned Jerry Udell and another intern and told them to start digging through the bales of paper to retrieve the missing records. Conrad compiled a list of the essential papers, and most of them were reassembled, scrap by scrap. "The bales were stuffed into barrels, and there were dozens of them," Udell recalls. "We managed to get through about three barrels and found much of the material."[21] Conrad then learned that several bales had been shipped out early that morning, by train, to Baltimore. He frantically tried to trace those bales, to no avail. Years later, Conrad would remember that morning as "the time the Twenty-fifth Amendment to the U.S. Constitution was lost in the dustbin of the New Senate Office Building."

But Conrad finally recovered the original draft of the amendment as well as most of the briefing notes. They were now ready for the floor debate, which was scheduled to begin at noon.[22] Other business intervened, however, and the resolution was delayed for twenty-four hours. The next day, Conrad had a chair on the Senate floor, from which he would rise and hand documents to Bayh during the debate or confer with him on responses to questions. The Senate finally passed the measure and sent it to the House, where Conrad again attended all the meetings and debates, keeping Bayh informed of events.[23]

The House finally passed the amendment, but in a different version. It was then sent to a conference committee where a compromise was to be reached between the two versions. There were five senators and five representatives on the conference committee. Conrad had the responsibility of scheduling the ten conferees, and finding a meeting time for all of them was a major problem.[24]

When they did meet, the House conferees insisted on a time limitation for congressional action in Section 4 of the amendment, dealing with presidential disability. The senators disagreed, contending that their chamber was "the greatest deliberative body in the world," where no time limitation should ever be placed on debate. After several fruitless meetings, including one in which Bayh angrily stomped out of the conference, a compromise was eventually reached. It required a twenty-one-day limit for congressional action to determine "that the President is unable to discharge the powers and duties of his office. . . ."[25]

On June 30, 1965, the U.S. House of Representatives, by a two-thirds vote, approved the conference report. Six days later, the U.S. Senate, by a vote of 68 to 5, passed the amendment.[26]

Article Five of the Constitution requires that "three-fourths of the several states" ratify proposed amendments. With the amendment clearing the Congress, the battleground now shifted to the fifty state capitals.

While the various state legislatures began scheduling the amendment for ratification, Bayh's subcommittee began planning three other amendments: allowing eighteen-year-olds the right to vote; the Equal Rights Amendment; and electoral college reform. This ambitious agenda was being recognized back in Indiana, with Republicans beginning to refer derisively to Senator Bayh as the "Re-founding Father."

But Conrad's major focus was the ratification of the amendment by the states. For the next sixteen months, as governors or state legislators raised objections to the wording, Conrad and Bayh sent out explanations and rebuttals. Finally, on February 10, 1967, the legislatures of Minnesota and Nevada, respectively, ratified the proposed amendment, making them the thirty-seventh and thirty-eighth states to do so. The Twenty-fifth Amendment was now part of the U.S. Constitution. And Larry Conrad was its father.

Of all that Conrad had achieved and was to achieve, it was of this amendment that he was most proud. For the rest of his life he would refer back to those hours, days, and years in which the amendment was designed, drafted, debated, and enacted. In 1973—as the dimensions of the Watergate crisis were being discovered—Conrad wrote a short paper that was planned as an introduction to his book about the Amendment. In the opening words, he quotes U.S. Representative Clarence J. Brown, Sr. (R-Ohio) in the 1965 debate on the amendment as saying: "Under certain conditions and certain circumstances, a vacancy could exist in the Vice Presidency and a President could name a billy goat as Vice President and some Congresses would approve of that nomination and that selection." Conrad's rejoinder was:

> The 25th Amendment was drafted, passed and ratified at a time of universal good feeling between the President and the Congress, at a time when the majority Congressional party was also the party of the President and at a time when all America was cohered by the recent memory of the loss of a fallen leader. Will those words that held such incontrovertible meaning in 1967 hold the same discipline for us under new circumstances? They do and shall. Primarily because beneath the politics, beneath the historic encounter of executive and legislative branches, and beyond the prejudices of individual personalities, lies a common denominator—preservation of this republic. How that is felt or its degree of feeling may be questioned but that it is felt by those who serve us in constitutional capacities cannot be questioned. While there may be talk of billy goats as Vice Presidents and the temerity of Congresses, the peril of an executive power lapse causes all to hear or sense Sir Thomas Brown's admonitor: "Court not felicity too far and wary not the favorable hand of fortune."[27]

Bayh's success in securing ratification of the Twenty-fifth Amendment was his greatest accomplishment in his first term. But he could not forget that he had been elected in 1962 by only one vote per precinct.[28] Bayh and his staff decided to capitalize on the passage of the amendment by writing the story of its passage, with publication planned for 1968, prior to the November election. Conrad drafted several sections of the manuscript and edited most of the chapters. Boxell suggested the title and in early 1968, *One Heartbeat Away: Presidential Disability and Succession*, was published by Bobbs-Merrill in Indianapolis.

Inexorably the election year approached. For the past five years, sandwiched between his senatorial duties and occasional trips to other states on behalf of other Democrats, Bayh returned again and again to Indiana to keep himself before the Hoosier voters. From 1966 on, Boxell was in Indiana virtually every weekend, maintaining contact with the party organization and Bayh's supporters. It was clear that 1968 was going to be a very difficult election for Democrats. The national issues of civil rights and the Vietnam War were tearing apart the old New Deal Coalition that had defined the national Democratic party for more than a generation. In Indiana, huge fissures in the party organization had opened, with several different factions fighting for control. The 1968 campaign, unlike 1962, was not going to be a coordinated effort with the rest of the Democratic ticket. It was each man for himself.

The pressures of the upcoming campaign were visible early. On January 7, 1967, as Conrad and Bayh were closely monitoring the ratification process for the Twenty-fifth Amendment, President Lyndon Johnson summoned Birch and Marvella to the Oval Office. The president, demonstrating his realization that the Democratic party was facing major problems under his leadership, looked at Marvella and said: "We need to give the Democratic National Committee a new image. We need somebody on the Committee who is Christian, young, sexy, and can talk to the Luci Johnsons of this country." Then he turned to Birch and said: "I want your wife to be vice-chairman of the Democratic National Committee."[29]

The Bayhs were stunned. But Marvella quickly became ecstatic. She finally had the opportunity for a career of her own, and it was on request of the president of the United States.[30]

That evening Bayh summoned Boxell and Keefe to his home in McLean, Virginia, to discuss the president's offer. Marvella, referring to these top aides as "henchmen," listened to their "very clear opinions." They were agreed that if she took the job it would cost Birch votes the next year. With Johnson's growing unpopularity, it was "unwise politics" to be that close to the president.[31]

Twenty-seven years later, Boxell remembered that wretched conversation. "It was one of the most difficult things I ever had to do," Boxell explains. "I knew she wanted the job. I knew she would have been great at it, and here I was urging them to turn down the President of the United States."[32]

Marvella finally capitulated. She said "no" to the president of the United States, explaining that her "first duty was to my husband and marriage."[33]

Bayh's concern with his reelection revolved around his narrow victory in 1962. Now, with the massive problems facing the national Democratic party, Bayh knew the Indiana Republicans would be clearly focused on his race. Bayh was determined to have his campaign organized early.

He named Keefe campaign manager and appointed a young man from East Chicago, David Bochnowski, as his assistant. Conrad, following Bayh's renomination at the Democratic State Convention in June, moved to Muncie where he stayed with his parents. He opened a Bayh campaign office on Main Street and was given the title of Block Program Director.

Working with a secretary and one campaign staffer, Jeff Lewis, Conrad coordinated volunteer efforts in the counties and precincts, particularly with the Young Democrats, and assisted with scheduling.[34] He frequently substituted for Bayh at Jefferson-Jackson Day dinners throughout the state, where, for the first time, thousands of Democrats heard a new young orator speaking of political change, political history, and Birch Bayh:

> Everything in this society is instant. We have instant coffee and instant ice tea. We have instant orange juice and instant ice cream. We've built a highway clear around Indianapolis—fifty-two point seven miles of it—so we can be from Beech Grove to Speedway in an instant. But guvment does not work in an instant. Change takes time. Change takes work. Change takes experience. And Senator Birch Bayh is who spends the time, who does the work, who has the experience.

With each of the Democratic candidates on his own, the Bayh campaign was very sensitive to factional disputes within the party. In the "Campaign 68" manual for Birch Bayh, county coordinators were reminded that "the Senator Bayh for Senator Committee in each county is a Democratic organization working for a Democratic victory in November. . . . As such, it is designed to supplement the activity of the Democratic Party, not to supplant it." The county coordinators were then warned to "maintain harmony with party people," and told that "disputes should be settled promptly with respect for party integrity."[35]

The tumult of that year was never-ending, particularly at the national level. On March 12, a majority of New Hampshire Democratic voters selected President Johnson in their primary, but 42 percent of them voted for Senator Eugene McCarthy. Nineteen days later, on the last day of March, Johnson, with his leadership in even deeper trouble than a year before, announced he would not seek reelection.

Old-time politicians refer to the presidency as "the brass ring." And, among Democrats, there is the saying that a man gets only one real shot at that ring, and when his time has come, he must take it. If he stutters, if he waits, the ring is grasped by another. After McCarthy's surprising finish in the New Hampshire primary, Senator Robert Kennedy's time for the brass ring had arrived. McCarthy had attracted hundreds of thousands of young people to his campaign with his message of ending the Vietnam War. The young men and women, cutting their long hair and dressing in sport coats and skirts in order to "keep clean for Gene," skipped classes and drove from state to state to knock on doors to end the war. These young, idealistic, and worried people were Kennedy's natural supporters. But Kennedy had hesitated, and the students moved to McCarthy.

On March 16, only four days after the New Hampshire primary, and fifteen days before Johnson's withdrawal, Robert Kennedy announced his candidacy.

Kennedy and McCarthy, in most states, were in a head-to-head match-up. But in Indiana, the May 7 presidential primary became a three-way race. Governor Roger Branigin also had entered the presidential race as a "stand-in" for President Johnson. When the president withdrew, the deadline had passed under Indiana law for Branigin to remove his name from the ballot. Hoosier Democrats were going to have a three-way choice.

Four days after President Johnson's withdrawal, in the run-up to the Indiana primary, Robert Kennedy, that afternoon, was speaking to a crowd of over 7,000 in the packed gymnasium on the Ball State University campus in Muncie. As he left the podium and waded through the crushing crowd, nearly one thousand miles away, in Memphis, Tennessee, the Rev. Dr. Martin Luther King had settled into his motel room. Kennedy, stripped of his wristwatch by the grasping students, finally made it to the main exit, where he grabbed the arm of a tall young man—John Irwin—and said: "Hey, big boy, get me to the car." Irwin entwined his arm with Kennedy's and dragged him through the crowd, up the steps, and lifted him on the top of a parked car. Kennedy jumped down to the hood and across to the trunk lid of the car in front—then to the next car, until he leaped to the sidewalk and piled into the unmarked Oldsmobile, driven by James P. Carey, Muncie's Chief of Police. Ethel Kennedy was already in the front seat. Carey sped off, with the Kennedys sitting on top of one another. When Carey dropped them at the Delaware County airport, a police officer told Kennedy that Martin Luther King had been shot while standing outside his motel room in Memphis. "Is he dead?" Kennedy asked. "Yes," responded Officer Bob Reed.[36]

When Kennedy's plane landed in Indianapolis, they drove directly to the site of the inner-city rally at 17th and Broadway. There, as night descended on the Circle City and a misty rain started, Kennedy climbed onto a flatbed truck and spoke extemporaneously to a crowd of over 2,000 people, most of whom were black. And he also spoke to all of America—beseeching everyone to be calm:

> In this difficult day, in this difficult time for the United States, it is perhaps well to ask what kind of a nation we are and what direction we want to move in. For those of you who are black—considering the evidence there evidently is that there were white people who were responsible—you can be filled with bitterness, with hatred, and a desire for revenge. We can move in that direction as a country, in great polarization—black people amongst black, white people amongst white, filled with hatred toward one another.
>
> Or we can make an effort, as Martin Luther King did, to understand and to comprehend, and to replace that violence, that stain of bloodshed that has spread across our land, with an effort to understand with compassion and love.

For those of you who are black and are tempted to be filled with hatred and distrust at the injustice of such an act, against all white people, I can only say that I feel in my own heart the same kind of feeling. I had a member of my family killed, but he was killed by a white man. But we have to make an effort in the United States, we have to make an effort to understand, to go beyond these rather difficult times.

My favorite poet was Aeschylus. He wrote: "In our sleep, pain which cannot forget falls drop by drop upon the heart until, in our own despair, against our will, comes wisdom through the awful grace of God."[37]

While the rest of America's cities exploded in violence that night and for several nights thereafter, Indianapolis was calm.[38]

Thirty-three days later, on Tuesday, May 7, Robert Kennedy easily won the Indiana presidential primary, receiving 42 percent of the vote. Branigin finished a poor second, with 30.7 percent. McCarthy got 27.4 percent.

Less than a month later, Robert F. Kennedy, on the night of his primary victory in California, was gunned down shortly after midnight as he pushed his way through the crowded back kitchen of the Ambassador Hotel in Los Angeles. He died on June 6, 1968.

There is a defining characteristic of those people who seriously reach for the brass ring. They are imbued with some internal energy that is far beyond that possessed by others. They drive themselves, and those around them, at such a quickened pace that other mortals soon fall behind. The nineteenth-century German philosopher Friedrich Nietzsche wrote of "the will to power" as the motive for both individuals and society.[39] Twentieth-century dictators, such as Lenin and Hitler, are sometimes cited as examples of Nietzsche's "will to power." In light of these comparisons, with Kennedy's method of campaigning, it is not surprising that his major critics called him "ruthless." Kennedy's brief presidential campaign was one of the most remarkable campaigns in American history. The likes of it will never be seen again. Theodore H. White, in writing of the 1968 Kennedy campaign, used these phrases to describe Robert Kennedy's energy: "a man whose intensity disturbed their peace; . . . he was the disturber; . . . whirlwind and motion; . . . stretched to the limits of physical and emotional exertion; when he spoke, his hands were always moving, reaching, pleading, begging the people to come with him."[40]

In Indiana, the Kennedy energy attracted a young college woman to his campaign. She was to graduate in June of 1968 from Butler University in Indianapolis with a degree in psychology. Her name was Diane Meyer, and she was from Nappanee, Indiana. Bright, idealistic, and savvy, Diane Meyer heard Robert Kennedy the night of April 4 at 17th and Broadway. "The speech was amazing," she now recalls. "I think that's what turned my life."[41] She immediately signed on with Robert Kennedy's Indiana crusade. When the assassin killed Kennedy, Diane Meyer, now fully committed to political change, moved to Birch Bayh's reelection campaign. She was a receptionist and "gofer." She remembers those days: "Larry Conrad was a name I had heard . . . in the Birch Bayh campaign for weeks—but I had never seen him because he was 'on the road for Birch.' Sometime during my third week, there developed a sense of excitement and festivity in the headquarters—people were animated and buzzing and—as I hung up the phone and turned around—I saw a disheveled cherub with a shoe in one hand and a finger through its sole. When my eyes met the torn elbow of his shirt sleeve, this bag man looked me in the eye and said: 'Hiya Blondie, I'm Larry Conrad. Who are you?'"[42]

That first meeting was an introduction to a lifelong friendship. Like Conrad, Meyer was an only child, and she was struck by his openness and creativity. She came to rely on him for brotherly-type advice, not only on politics, but on personal problems as well. Their friendship was to last a lifetime, and would prevail through a broken marriage and political disillusionments.

As the November election approached, Conrad gradually took over the organizational control of the Bayh campaign, which was suffering from loose scheduling and poor organization. With Keefe having to keep one eye on the Washington office and the other on the campaign, Conrad moved into the void. Working with Boxell, control was reasserted over the schedule and the Bayh organization. "There was big-time slippage in the campaign before Larry stepped in," Udell recalls. "I worked under Boxell, coordinating southern Indiana, and those two guys, Conrad and Boxell, were the best organizers I ever worked with."[43]

The possibility that Bayh could be caught in a looming Nixon landslide provided even greater incentive to Conrad, Boxell, and the other staff members to see to it that Birch Bayh was reelected.

Bayh's Republican opponent was a thirty-five-year-old state senator from Indianapolis, William Ruckelshaus. Remembering the immense impact of "Hey Look Him Over," the Republican State Central Committee was not going to let Bayh use that song again. They purchased the copyright. Fortunately, Bayh had decided several months before not to use the jingle. He never gave a reason. "He just didn't want to use it," Boxell remembers.[44] Actually, Bayh had decided that the timing was all wrong for the jingle. "A lot of people were saying, 'yes, use it,' but I was now a sitting senator. With the Vietnam War raging and with cities on fire, I knew the timing was wrong."[45] Bayh was right.

On election night, November 5, Conrad, Keefe, and Boxell were looking for the early returns from Marion County. This county casts nearly 15 percent of the total votes in the state, and, if a Democrat is going to win, he must hold down the Republican margin in Marion County. It is rare that a Democrat ever carries the county, but if the margin of loss can be held down in Marion, the big Democratic counties up north, such as Lake and

St. Joseph, can offset Marion. The early Marion County returns showed Bayh ahead of his 1962 totals, where he lost Marion County by 18,966 votes. When all the votes were counted, Bayh lost Marion County by only 10,374 votes, and carried the state by 71,885. The rest of the Democratic ticket went down to defeat.

Along with exhilaration, there was a collective sigh of relief from the Bayh staffers. The improved margin of victory was an endorsement of their work accomplishments, both in Washington and on the campaign.

With Bayh reelected, Larry and Mary Lou finally planned a well-deserved vacation. A few days before the election, Alan Rachels, one of Bayh's staff members in Indianapolis, talked with Conrad about "getting away" for a few days. Rachels suggested taking a vacation together, and Conrad replied, "You decide where we'll go, but Mary Lou has always wanted to go to the Caribbean." Rachels booked tickets for Jamaica, and Mary Lou, Larry, Alan Rachels and his wife, and their seven-month-old baby flew out of Indianapolis the Sunday after Thanksgiving. "We really unwound," Rachels remembers. "We had a villa on a cliff overlooking the water. None of us had ever been in such luxury. We were like a bunch of Indiana farmers, living like kings."[46]

But even on vacation, Conrad never really rested. He only relaxed and had fun. He and Rachels raced golf carts around the resort, pretending to be competing for the ultimate race against Ben-Hur. Conrad would disappear and be found talking with waiters and maids, asking them about their families and their lives in Jamaica. "Our valet was named Josh," Rachels remembers, "and Larry said to me, 'We've got to get Josh out of here. He's living on two dollars a day and he's got a wife and kid. All he needs is a job back in the states.'" Rachels dismissed the thought, attributing it to Conrad's natural empathy. But the next day Josh asked Rachels, "Do you think I'd like Indianapolis or Washington better?" Rachels was stunned. "I actually thought that Josh and his family would be with us on the flight back. I didn't know what Larry had promised. I finally told Josh that I was sure he would like Washington better than Indianapolis."[47]

After the vacation, Conrad returned to his Washington duties—without Josh—and found that Bayh's staff was turning over. Diane Meyer came to Washington on the Senate payroll, and Boxell, growing weary of the dozens of nights away from his wife and son, joined an Indianapolis engineering firm and moved back home in March of 1969.

It also was time for Conrad to move. With Bayh reelected, Conrad's "first life" was over. He loved Washington. "People talk about Potomac fever—well, I had it. Washington is so refreshing; so cosmopolitan—it's the capital of the world, as far as I'm concerned," he related several years later. But "the kids were getting older, and I didn't want to be in an economic trap. I didn't want to spend the rest of my days on the staff of a senator."[48]

He and Mary Lou made plans to return to Indiana and begin Larry's own political career. When he told other staff members of this decision, everyone knew things would never again be the same. Jerry Udell was devastated. "Larry and Mary Lou were the focal point of the social life. He was a teacher. He loved to share with people what he knew and what he thought. He taught me everything he could. Obviously, he was the most popular guy on the staff. I was shocked when Larry finally announced he was leaving. It was like grabbing the heart of the office, cutting it out and throwing it away."[49]

Conrad was not sure what political office he would be seeking back in Indiana. In 1966 he had briefly considered quitting Bayh's staff and making the run for the U.S. House of Representatives from the 10th congressional district, which included Muncie. But other candidates were already on the trail in pursuit of that nomination, and the work of the subcommittee was all-consuming. Now, a little more than two years later, and looking at the 1970 congressional contest, Conrad knew he would have to move early. He and Mary Lou decided to move back to Indiana in October of 1969. He reestablished ties with his old law firm in Muncie and they purchased a house in Daleville, Indiana, a small unincorporated settlement on Interstate 69. When asked why in the world he moved to Daleville, Conrad replied: "I knew I'd be spending as much if not more time in Indianapolis than in Muncie, and I saved twenty minutes drive time by being on the interstate. Besides, 'Daleville Democrat' sounds better than 'Muncie Democrat.'"[50]

Within three months of his return he had changed his sights. Another candidate was already running for the congressional nomination, and the party organization in Conrad's home county of Delaware discouraged his candidacy, claiming he had "not paid his dues" in the local party. Conrad knew he could not win if his home county was not with him.[51] Larry and Mary Lou had discussed his running for congress for months before leaving Washington. On one occasion, Mary Lou told Bayh that Larry was thinking of running for congress and asked him, "What do you think?" Bayh responded: "What does he want to do?" One major factor in his thinking was the demands placed on a senator or congressman in terms of campaigning; he is constantly commuting in order to stay in touch with the home state or district. "He was really glad to be coming back to Indiana," Mary Lou remembers. "He had missed it so much and he didn't like the idea of commuting to campaign."[52]

Relying on his connections from the Bayh campaigns, he discussed his candidacy with many Democrats.[53] As he drove to Democratic meetings throughout the state, people constantly questioned him about his plans. Conrad would respond by saying he was "looking at" different offices, including secretary of state. Everywhere he went, he was encouraged, and more and more Democrats were urging him to make the race.[54] It was

Boxell who provided the final reasoning to forego congress and run for secretary of state. "The starting place is secretary of state," Boxell said, "and I think we'll have the party support and a very good chance to win." Conrad agreed, and never looked back.[55]

Jeff Lewis, the young campaign staffer from the 1968 race, had left Bayh's Washington staff in September of 1969 and moved back to his hometown of Muncie. He continued on the payroll of the subcommittee and was assigned "research projects." His real duty was to drive Conrad from county to county.

In February of 1970, Lewis was driving Conrad to a meeting in northern Indiana. Conrad had not told Lewis of his decision. After Conrad finished reading the afternoon newspapers—and throwing them in the back seat— Lewis asked him what he was going to do, what office he was going to run for. "Stop the car," Conrad replied. "I'm going to drive."

Lewis pulled over and Conrad got behind the wheel. Back on the highway, Conrad told Lewis to grab a pad and pencil: "Write this down," he said. And he started dictating the winning strategy for his campaign for Indiana secretary of state.[56]

4

*I find the great thing in this world is not so much
where we stand, as in the direction we are moving
. . . we must sail sometimes with the wind and
sometimes against it—but we must sail, and not
drift, or lie at anchor.*

—*Oliver Wendell Holmes*

THE GREAT RUSH of the 1960s hit the wall at Kent State University on Monday, May 4, 1970, when four students were shot and killed by the Ohio National Guard.

The next morning, next door in Indiana, it was election day; the polls opened at 6 A.M. Far down the ballot there was an office at stake on that May day, the office of "Precinct Committeeman." This office is the foundation of the political pyramid; the cornerstone of Indiana's two political parties. By the time the polls closed at 6 P.M. that evening, 4,440 precinct committeemen were elected in each party.

Hoosiers salivate for the next election. Conrad frequently commented that "The first complete sentence a young Hoosier says, when asked by their mother, 'What do you want?' is 'I want to be governor.'" For generations this had been true.

The May primary is merely the official opening of the political season in a state long recognized as having one of the strongest political party systems in the country. In 1968, the national chronicler of presidential campaigns, Theodore White, claimed that Indiana's two parties belonged "in a Yellowstone National Park of primeval political fauna," and that the Indiana system, along with the Democratic party of Illinois, "is the sturdiest political anachronism in the Middle West."[1]

Safe and snug in America's heartland, Hoosiers have hardened their political traditions into steel. Political practices endure in Indiana long after they have been discarded by other states, or even ruled unconstitutional by the federal courts.[2] Indiana's political traditions and attendant state laws serve as a sea wall, protecting Hoosiers from the swirling tides of change that periodically buffet America. The bare-knuckled political brawls proceed undisturbed on the dry ground of Indiana's ninety-two counties.

But in the late '60s and early '70s the protective wall was neither high enough nor sturdy enough to make Indiana an island. The wave of political reform was surging through the country. Other states were rushing to change their governments by extending terms of statewide officials, reducing the number of elected statewide offices, and even calling state constitutional conventions to rewrite their basic governing documents.

The 1969 Indiana General Assembly was caught by this wave and forever changed state and local government in Indiana. The legislators created a consolidated city-county form of government by combining the city of Indianapolis with Marion County. Quickly dubbed "Unigov," it remains one of the few consolidated metropolitan governments in the country.[3] The legislature also authorized an important state constitutional amendment for a statewide referendum on the 1970 ballot. It extended the terms from two to four years for the offices of secretary of state, state auditor, and state treasurer. This amendment was approved by the voters in November of 1970.[4]

This wave of reform did not wash over Indiana's political parties, however. The state legislature had retained the procedures by which precinct committeemen, county chairs, district chairs, and state chairs were elected. The legislature also retained the power to nominate the governor in the state conventions of the two parties.

When the gubernatorial nomination is made by convention delegates rather than by voters in a direct primary, party organizations are imbued with one of the most powerful political weapons in a democracy: direct control over access to the general election ballot. When nominations are determined by primary election voters, candidates may appeal directly to the voters through the media, over the heads of the precinct committeemen and county chairmen.

In Indiana, when your party wins the governorship, you've won it all. No wonder young Hoosiers want to be governor. Governmental power is concentrated in the governor's office, with the other statewide elected officials being mere ministers who possess very few policy-making powers. Former governor Matthew Welsh once told a state legislator who came to him for advice on running for secretary of state: "You don't want to be secretary of state. That's like being county clerk."[5]

The governor also controls his political party. He names the state chairman. In 1964, Gordon St. Angelo was both the Dubois County chairman and the 8th district chairman when Roger Branigin named him to be his campaign manager for governor. When Branigin won, he named St. Angelo Democratic state chairman. With Branigin's backing, St. Angelo further centralized power in the office of the Democratic state chairman. He was ruthless in collecting assessments from the county organizations, and from businesses that had contracts with the state. He closely monitored the monies due from the license branches. At the statewide 1965 Jefferson-Jackson Day Dinner in Indianapolis, St. Angelo addressed his remarks to "Honored guests, vendors and would-be vendors, jobholders and would-be jobholders, successful lobbyists and unsuccessful lobbyists, Democratic Party faithful and contributors all."[6]

St. Angelo's installation as party chairman was welcomed by Senator Bayh, Conrad, and the other Senate staff members. He appeared to have the organizing talents needed to continue to increase the strength of the party organization.

But the first election cycle St. Angelo presided over was a disaster for the Democrats. Hoosiers threw the Democrats out. They lost control of the Indiana House and Senate. They lost all the statewide races.[7]

St. Angelo immediately began planning the 1967 mayoralty elections. Using state party money, he distributed thousands of dollars to Democratic challengers and incumbents, most of whom won. He purposely sought to strengthen the role of the mayors in the party.[8] The mayors controlled thousands of local patronage jobs and, with city budgets expanding, they had the ability to raise substantial sums of money from vendors. These mayors, with all their patronage jobs, were to remain forever indebted, and loyal, to Gordon St. Angelo.

"The problem with you god-damn people is you're not mean enough," St. Angelo said several years later when he tried to intercede in the 1980 gubernatorial primary on behalf of John Hillenbrand II. "I know how to be mean." By that time St. Angelo had left the party chairmanship to work for the Lilly Endowment foundation in Indianapolis. In a meeting with Hillenbrand and his top campaign staffers in St. Angelo's living room, he warned them, "Nobody can know about this meeting, because of my job. You've got to fire this fund-raiser you've hired. Hell, he's not even raising his own salary." Everybody adjourned to the dining room for a buffet lunch prepared by Mrs. St. Angelo. One week later, the young man in charge of fund-raising was fired.

Of course, St. Angelo's meanness made enemies. Chief among them were the Democratic members of the congressional delegation, including senators Bayh and Hartke. Under Branigin, St. Angelo virtually ignored the congressional delegation, centering all money, patronage, and power in the office of the state chairman. Staff members of the senators and congressmen criticized St. Angelo's leadership, pointing out that any Democrat could have won the governor's chair in the 1964 landslide. There was no genius involved. "St. Angelo was a master politician with no morals," one veteran political observer notes.

But to established, organizational Democrats, St. Angelo was the apotheosis of a party chairman. Referring to his Italian heritage, the party insiders referred to him as "the Don" or "Saint," an appellation St. Angelo relished.[9]

In 1968, St. Angelo threw the full support of the Democratic organization against Lieutenant Governor Robert (Bob) Rock, who was seeking the gubernatorial nomination. Rock was close to both Bayh and Hartke and enjoyed strong support from organized labor. But St. Angelo was going to show who was boss. With Governor Branigin's blessing, St. Angelo backed State Representative Richard Bodine, a former Speaker of the Indiana House.

The 1968 Democratic State Convention was the closest and perhaps the most vicious in Indiana history. Fistfights broke out on the platform and several arrests were made. When the auditors from the Indiana State Board of Accounts counted and recounted the ballots, Rock had won the nomination by two votes: 953 to 951.

Rock's razor-thin victory over St. Angelo's forces was achieved by combining the support of the old Matt Welsh supporters with those of Senator Birch Bayh. "It was payback time," Alan Rachels recalls.[10]

Immediately after the delegates renominated Bayh by acclamation, Conrad, Boxell, Keefe, Rachels, and the other Bayh staff members turned and joined with Jack New and J. Manfred Core to defeat St. Angelo's man, Bodine. "We joined forces with the Rock supporters. We used every trick we could think of to pull it off," Rachels says. He remembers talking with three Bodine delegates on the convention floor and convincing them that Bodine had it won. He then remarked that Senator Bayh had some out-of-town friends at the convention who would like to have passes to get on the floor, and persuaded the Bodine delegates to give up their credentials and leave for home in order to accommodate Bayh's "out-of-town" friends.[11]

Conrad and Boxell, being so closely identified with Bayh, did not work the floor on Rock's behalf. They stayed in their office, insulating Bayh from the fracas. But all the while they were saying good things about Bob Rock.[12]

After his two-vote victory, Bob Rock approached the podium for his acceptance speech. Senator Vance Hartke was standing on the platform and as Rock neared the podium Hartke whispered in his ear, "Now's the time to tell them you want to get rid of St. Angelo."[13]

Obviously, Rock wanted to be rid of St. Angelo. "I would have done anything to get rid of him. He gave me fits," Rock admits. But he did not take Hartke's advice. He knew that fight would bring another bloodbath. Branigin was still governor and still supported St. Angelo. Bob Rock looks back and contends that "Branigin wasn't any good for the Democrat party. Part of a governor's job is to build your party for the future. And Gordon St. Angelo? No. He tended to cause divisiveness, which Democrats couldn't afford in Indiana."[14] Jack New agrees: "Branigin was in over his head."[15] But, at that time, the vital organs of the Democratic party were already hemorrhaging, not only because of the state convention fights, but also because of the national turmoil caused by Vietnam and the civil rights movement. If Rock won in November he could force St. Angelo's removal then. But that was not to be. Rock lost in November and the rest of the state ticket went down as well, with only U.S. Senator Birch Bayh surviving.

The national Democratic ticket also lost. Vice-President Hubert Humphrey was narrowly defeated by Richard Nixon, and the national Democratic party organization, following the riot-rocked Chicago convention and the electoral loss, was in shambles. Less than three months after the election, Lawrence F. O'Brien resigned as national chairman and U.S. Senator Fred R. Harris of Oklahoma, with Humphrey's support, took over. Harris lasted thirteen months. In late February of 1970, the national chairmanship was again up for grabs.

This time Gordon St. Angelo reached. Even with a pitiful record in winning statewide races in Indiana, he wanted to run the national Democratic party. St. Angelo moved the moment he heard Harris was quitting. Using the staff and facilities of the Indiana Democratic party, he called other state chairmen and national committee members to convince them to support him for national chairman. He scheduled visits and drove and flew to thirty-seven states to meet with other party officials.[16]

Senator Bayh received reports on St. Angelo's campaign, but not from St. Angelo. He heard from state chairmen and party leaders in the states St. Angelo visited, and St. Angelo was saying negative things about Bayh and his presidential ambitions.[17] On Thursday, March 5, 1970, St. Angelo withdrew from the contest for national chairman. He did not have the votes. The executive committee of the Democratic National Committee had persuaded Lawrence O'Brien to take the job again.[18]

St. Angelo's badmouthing of Bayh throughout the country convinced the senator that St. Angelo had to go. Although Bayh respected St. Angelo's organizational abilities, it was now clear that he could not be trusted. "It was his own lust for power that caused him to do what he did," Bayh believes.[19] For several years the bitterness had grown between the two men. St. Angelo ignored even minor requests from the congressional delegation. Bayh believed himself to be a major part of the Indiana Democratic party, but St. Angelo paid no homage.[20]

On the other hand, St. Angelo fervently believed that Bayh was steering his own ship and was working against the state organization. He was convinced Bayh had worked for Robert Kennedy in the 1968 Indiana primary when Branigin was on the ballot as a favorite son.[21]

The differences between Bayh and St. Angelo were to persist for decades thereafter. Some of Bayh's backers understood the senator's impatience with St. Angelo, but they did not support Bayh's attempt to oust him in the reorganization of 1970. Boxell, in particular, could not understand Bayh's motives. Even if St. Angelo were removed, Boxell reasoned, the Republicans still had the governorship, and it took that office to raise money and enforce party discipline. Conrad agreed with Boxell. But Bayh, regardless of the advice from his former staffers, had bigger plans. He was not to be dissuaded.[22]

Bayh's supporters believed that St. Angelo sabotaged Bob Rock in 1968 because it was in his own best interest for Rock to lose. That loss allowed St. Angelo to retain the chairmanship and "the action would come on the other end," i.e., through deals with the Republicans.[23] Moreover, Bayh's run for the White House in 1972 would require the complete, total, and undying loyalty of the Indiana Democratic organization, particularly the state chairman.[24]

St. Angelo knew Bayh was not happy with him. "He did not think I communicated well with him," St. Angelo acknowledges. "I tried to keep the congressional delegation informed, but apparently, by his standard, I didn't. But I didn't know about the intensity of his presidential campaign, so he didn't keep me altogether informed either."[25] Actually, it would have been impossible to miss the cues coming from Bayh concerning his 1972 presidential ambitions. At the 1968 Democratic convention in Chicago, Bayh had floated a trial balloon for the vice-presidential nomination, clearly signaling his national ambitions.[26] Moreover, Bayh had received national news coverage the previous November when he led the Senate fight to reject Clement Haynsworth's nomination to the U.S. Supreme Court.[27]

But there was a deeper reason for St. Angelo's antipathy toward Bayh. He did not respect him. "A lot of us had difficulty imagining him as president," St. Angelo says. "We knew the caliber of men like Truman, Kennedy, Johnson, and Humphrey."[28]

For Bayh to oust St. Angelo, he needed help. He did not have enough clout in Indiana to do it alone. He needed Vance Hartke.

The two senators were not friends, nor had they been close political allies. Their estrangement was exacerbated by their staff members, who barely spoke to one another in the corridors of the capitol. One of Hartke's key aides, former Valparaiso University government professor Victor Hoffmann, readily explained to visitors that Hartke worked closer with Republicans from other states than with Birch Bayh because "Bayh has no interest in what other people want, he only cares for himself." On the other hand, Hartke was earning a reputation as being under the influence of large monied interests. As the authors of a leading political almanac commented in 1977: "the state had two senators—Bayh and Bought."[29]

But Bayh knew they had to be together now. He informed Hartke that his forces would lead the fight to remove St. Angelo and Hartke could stay clear of the dispute. Hartke was up for reelection in 1970 and there was no reason for him to be politically damaged in an organizational fight. Robert F. Wagner, Hartke's campaign manager, told Bayh's representative that there was no reason for "a fight right now," and contended that Hartke believed the state chairman was a matter to be decided by the governor and the state committee, not other elected officials. Bayh, however, thought he had Hartke's agreement to stay out of the fracas. He proceeded with his program.[30]

To keep St. Angelo off balance, Bayh sent conflicting signals through the party. He led St. Angelo's admirers to believe that there was to be no challenge. But St. Angelo knew better. He had been tipped by a friend and supporter of Matt Welsh that a challenge was coming.[31] He just didn't know who the challenger was. But neither did Birch Bayh.[32]

Bayh dangled the post in the faces of several men, all of whom declined. The senator tried to persuade likely candidates by saying that Larry O'Brien wanted St. Angelo out because of the fracas he caused in Washington when he ran for national chairman. But party veterans who had the contacts and the prestige were not persuaded, and some of the logical potential candidates were already committed to St. Angelo.

On Friday, May 8, 1970, Bayh finally succeeded in recruiting Ken Cragen, a twenty-six-year-old Whiteland, Indiana, school teacher who had just been reelected Democratic county chairman in Morgan County. "I was assured they would do everything and I only had to do what they told me," Cragen recalls, "and I didn't do much. I met with Bill Wolfe and Jeanette Myers, my district chairman and vice-chairman, and told them I was running. Birch did everything else."[33]

The moment Cragen announced that he was running, St. Angelo knew he was "Bayh's guy."

Larry Cummings, still on Bayh's staff, began making phone calls to county chairs for Cragen. The Bayh forces had to move swiftly because the congressional district officers were to be elected the next Wednesday and they would constitute the new state committee.

That morning, Bayh attended the district reorganization meeting in his home district, the 7th. He spoke against the incumbent district chairman—who was pledged to St. Angelo. But Bayh's candidate lost. At the meeting, Bayh was told that Hartke and his administrative assistant, Jacque LeRoy, had made phone calls into the district in support of St. Angelo. Bayh saw the double-cross. And he was livid.

When Bayh arrived back in Indianapolis late Wednesday afternoon, he marched through the outer area of his U.S. Senate office in the federal building, shouting to his key aides, including Alan Rachels, "Come in here!" He turned to a Larry Conrad volunteer, Claudia Prosser, pointed at her, and said, "You come in here too; it's time you see how this is done."

Bayh's eyes were flashing with anger as he sat down at his desk and called Hartke. "Vance, you screwed me. We're both big boys, and big boys tell the truth. You lied to me. You told me Cragen was acceptable and then you and your staff made calls for Gordon. You screwed me." And Bayh slammed the receiver down.[34]

When asked later what Hartke said during the conversation, Bayh related that Hartke replied, "So, I've lied."[35]

Now Bayh and Cragen knew they were beat. The state committee was in place and St. Angelo had the votes. They reversed their engines and retreated back to Washington and Morgan County. Bayh marched Bob Keefe out on the plank that evening to explain the retreat. Keefe claimed they were much stronger than St. Angelo gave them credit for, but because of defeats in the 5th and 7th districts they were abandoning ship "at this time." Claiming that Hartke did not want a change and that "he's up for reelection," Keefe declared that it would be up to others to take out St. Angelo at the state reorganization meeting.[36]

On Saturday, back in Indianapolis, St. Angelo was reelected without opposition for another two-year term, and announced he would support Birch Bayh for president. Bayh's representative at the state meeting "said all the right things."[37]

Senator Bayh then began telling party Democrats that he and St. Angelo had made up and would work together. Senator Hartke continued to plot his course to renomination, confident that he would be unopposed.

Left alone to sail in the wake of all these heavy cruisers and battleships was one man who had managed to avoid the crosscurrents and whirlpools: Larry A. Conrad.

Conrad knew there were treacherous waters in the Democratic party, but his experience provided what appeared to be a safe passage: stay out of the fight between Bayh and St. Angelo; stay busy on the road meeting with Democrats; and stress the importance of winning the office of secretary of state. There was no sound political reason to get involved in Bayh's fight with St. Angelo, and Bayh understood.[38]

Conrad was already living the philosophy that he had found in the writings of Oliver Wendell Holmes. At the podium, he would tell the Democrats that he had read history and philosophy and government, and nowhere else did he find a personal statement that so succinctly described his view of politics and human nature: "we must sail sometimes with the wind and sometimes against it—but we *must* sail, and not drift, or lie at anchor."

But this philosophy did not provide protection from the political elements. St. Angelo's fight with Bayh also had made him suspicious of Conrad. Conrad was Bayh's ex-staffer—which meant he was with Bayh. Ed Tracey, St. Angelo's administrative assistant, threatened Conrad's workers that Conrad would have an opponent for the secretary of state nomination if Conrad were found working against St. Angelo.[39]

Conrad was the only Democrat traveling the state at that time. Everywhere he stopped, Democrats asked him about the fight between Bayh and St. Angelo. Conrad's standard reply was that he was not involved; he had no preference. St. Angelo and Tracey could never find evidence to the contrary.

On March 26, twenty-one days after St. Angelo withdrew from the national chairmanship race—and as Bayh was calculating his plans to remove St. Angelo as state chairman—Conrad formally announced his candidacy for secretary of state. He did not mention the internal Democratic strife. Instead, he excoriated Governor Edgar Whitcomb's Republican administration, declaring, "I do not believe that the people of Indiana look forward to beginning these crucial years with the education of their young people, the collection and expenditure of their tax money, and the integrity of their laws and courts in the hands of the Whitcomb Administration. Indiana lacks leadership at a time when it needs it most." He accused the Whitcomb administration of "indifference and ineptness" and said that "the people of Indiana deserve better."[40]

Conrad constantly urged the Democrats to concentrate on the Republicans—they were the ones to beat.

And the Indiana Republicans were not without their problems. There was a civil war taking place in the Indiana Republican party. It was waged without real cannons, but, like the real war, it divided north and south. It was every bit as intense as the internecine Democratic fights.

The leader of the southern forces was the governor of Indiana, Edgar Whitcomb. Having beaten Bob Rock in 1968, Whitcomb believed in the conservative credo as espoused by U.S. Senator Barry Goldwater. John Snyder, the state treasurer, was another ally. Their partisans were concentrated in the smaller rural counties.

The northern forces were actually concentrated in Marion County and other urban areas. Several men in their twenties and thirties, including L. Keith Bulen and Richard G. Lugar, had decided that Republicans could win and win regularly in Indiana if they were pragmatic rather than ideological and if they could continue to organize and control Marion County, where Lugar served as mayor of Indianapolis. It was organization, the "nuts and bolts" of politics, that won elections, not ideologies. And Bulen was recognized by both Democrats and Republicans as an organizational wizard.[41]

A chain-smoking, hard-driving Indiana politician, seemingly fueled by a reactor core somewhere deep inside, Bulen believed politics was like any other business; a person would get ahead if he worked hard and out-thought and outmaneuvered the competitors. He demanded absolute loyalty and obedience from his underlings. By 1975 he had been married four times.

The GOP leaders had seen a resurgent Democratic party win both U.S. Senate seats and capitalize on the ideological wars among Republicans. Allied with the Marion County Republican captains were the current secretary of state, William Salin, from Fort Wayne, and an array of younger county office holders, state legislators, and county chairmen, mostly from the larger counties in the northern tier and central Indiana. There was also some support from the urban south. Bulen had supported Whitcomb in 1968 and concentrated resources on the governor's race in order to regain state patronage and power. But it wasn't long before Bulen saw that Whitcomb was not pragmatic. Bulen, with Unigov, had cemented a Republican political foundation in Marion County that could support the entire state. He decided to take control of the Republican State Central Committee when it reorganized on May 13, 1970.

But the governor gets his chairman, and Ed Whitcomb won the reorganization battles. He installed Snyder as the new Republican state chairman. The small county forces won that battle, but they were to lose the war. Whitcomb was a lame duck, and a split soon developed between Whitcomb and Snyder. Moreover, 1970 was an off-year election with a Republican in the White House. That signaled that the out-of-power party, the Democrats, were likely to do well.

But the immediate task in the spring of 1970 was for each party to nominate its candidates, adopt a platform, and prepare for that "peaceful war" that defines a democracy: the general election campaign.

The 2,130 Democratic delegates to the state convention poured into Indianapolis on Tuesday, June 16. All of these delegates had received several letters from Larry Conrad, asking for their vote for the secretary of state nomination. The letters were written and stuffed in envelopes by volunteers at the Conrad house in Daleville. One volunteer, Claudia Prosser, drove from Bloomington to Daleville on several occasions with her friend and IU Young Democrats president, Mary Scifres. Other volunteers, including Nancy Papas, who had worked for Bayh in Washington, also were there, addressing and stuffing envelopes. "Envelopes were piled everywhere in the house," Prosser recalls, "even in the bathtub. After we had them all stuffed, sealed and sorted, we would all go to the backyard and play touch football."[42]

All those mailings and all of Conrad's trips had paid off. St. Angelo's men left him alone. He was unopposed.

The Democratic delegates met in district caucuses in the early evening of June 16 and the candidates for the various nominations moved from caucus to caucus speaking of their qualifications and why they were running. Conrad provided a short "stem-winder" to each group. Following the caucuses Conrad invited the delegates to his hospitality suite at the convention hotel, the Indianapolis Hilton-on-the-Circle. The suite was on the ninth floor and was connected to the outside patio and swimming pool deck.

It was a beautiful evening in Indianapolis and the crowd spilled outside onto the deck where there were hats and balloons, a free bar staffed by Conrad volunteers, and a band playing bluegrass music. William (Bill) Gigerich met Larry Conrad for the first time that night. Gigerich was working for a local radio station and had been a paid staffer in Robert Kennedy's 1968 national campaign. He introduced himself to Conrad and started talking about himself. Conrad pulled a 3x5 card from his side pocket and wrote down Gigerich's name and address. When others interrupted, Gigerich made his way through the crowd and past the band, where he spotted J. Manfred Core, the former state chairman. Gesturing to the band and the balloons, Gigerich said: "Conrad's sure spending a lot of money for secretary of state." Core looked at Gigerich and replied: "He's not running for secretary of state, he's running for governor." Gigerich made a mental note to get to know the Conrads better.[43]

The next morning the delegates assembled in the Coliseum at the Indiana State Fairgrounds. The gavel fell at precisely 10 A.M., just as St. Angelo had promised, presaging an efficient convention preaching harmony and unity.

To avoid protests about the Vietnam War, which had plagued the 1968 convention, staff members for Indiana's four Democratic congressmen, two U.S. senators, and members of the state central committee met beforehand to draft a resolution calling for a "prompt and orderly disengagement" of U.S. troops from Vietnam. The resolution did not specify a date for troop withdrawal. The convention chairman, Representative John Brademas, read the resolution to the delegates and called for remarks. No delegate requested to speak on the issue and, by voice vote, the resolution was adopted.

Moving to the nominations, Bayh was called upon to introduce his colleague, Vance Hartke. In his remarks, Bayh obliquely referred to his abortive attempt to oust St. Angelo: he said he was dismayed by rumors that he was not supporting Hartke. Hartke, with no opposition, was renominated by acclamation. Conrad and Mary Aikens Currie, the candidate for state auditor, were also unopposed, but there was a contest for state treasurer. Jack New from Greenfield, a former staff member for Governor Matt Welsh, easily turned back a challenge from John Chittenden of Indianapolis. For superintendent of public instruction, John Loughlin of South Bend had four opponents and was able to defeat fellow state representative Paul Hric of Hammond on the second ballot, 1,371 to 700.[44]

With the Democratic ticket set, Gordon St. Angelo declared that the campaign theme would be "Unity 70" and that all activities would be co-ordinated by the State Central Committee. It would be a unified campaign, similar to the 1962 effort.

As the Democrats left town, the Republican delegates began arriving for what was to become one of the most bizarre Republican conventions of modern history, perhaps superseded only by the 1992 gathering.[45]

The Bulen-Whitcomb civil war came down to two battles: the nomination for the U.S. Senate, where Bulen backed U.S. Representative Richard Roudebush and the governor wanted John Snyder; and the nomination for state treasurer, where Bulen supported John Mutz and Whitcomb backed State Representative Calvert Brand.[46] William Salin, a Bulen ally, easily won renomination to oppose Larry Conrad for secretary of state. In the two big battles, with huge delegate support from the big counties, both Roudebush and Mutz won. For the first time it became clear that the Indiana Republican party was in the hands of a new general: L. Keith Bulen. Governor Whitcomb's effectiveness as Republican party leader was gone forever.

Like two great, fully manned battleships, the two Hoosier political parties finally swung around to face one another.

Senator Hartke was at the top of the Democratic ticket, and at the controls of the senator's campaign was Robert F. Wagner. Born in Connecticut just nineteen days after Larry Conrad was born in Laconia, Wagner graduated from the state university, completed some graduate courses, and finally took a position with Aetna Insurance. "Every time I was promoted I was transferred," Wagner recalls. During a three-year stint in Tulsa, Oklahoma, he enrolled in law school, thinking a law degree would help his insurance career. With only one semester left, he was promoted again and transferred to Indiana. He was the youngest supervisor at Aetna. Because he needed different courses, he had to repeat the entire third year at Indiana University law school at Indianapolis. He finally received his law degree in 1967.[47]

Wagner was on the fast track at Aetna, but he and his wife, Patricia, had grown tired of the constant transfers. They were raising two children and they decided to settle into Indiana and introduce stability in their lives. After all, it was the late 1960s, Bob had his law degree, and an excellent job.

And then Wagner met Vance Hartke.

There are certain people who get involved in politics who seem to hear sounds others cannot. They have this range of "hearing" that is out beyond normal. They sense what is in the political atmosphere. They know the source of the vibration and they can detect the amplitude and the duration. Robert F. Wagner has that political ear.

Slightly over six feet, broad at the shoulders and with narrow hips,

Wagner sported a reddish brown beard. His wispy hair offset piercing eyes which he would trigger as he cocked his head, opened his lids, and thrust his finger in your face. "There's no guarantees in this god-damn life," he would shout at a campaign aide who would ask about a job after the campaign. Intense, profane, and at times ribald, Wagner struck fear in many and admiration in most. Swaggering into the campaign offices in his tailored shirts and suits and sporting a white hat, he would shout, "What the hell are you demons doing today!" But as much as he was going to change Indiana politics, politics also changed Bob Wagner:

"I was a staid business person, and then I got involved in Vance's campaign in 1970. It changed me. I had been a precinct committeeman, but never involved in managing or running a campaign. I had my eyes opened as to what was happening in our party and in our country. These things were never focused on in business. There were thousands of young people speaking out on the issues of the war and civil rights, and there were all the dramatic events of 1968."[48]

Like Saul on the road to Damascus, Wagner was converted. His conversion was by the white light of politics. When Hartke hired him to manage his campaign, Ed Lewis, an Indianapolis attorney and Hartke supporter, wrote a letter to the senator berating him for being antiwar and warned him about jeopardizing his reelection chances, particularly by hiring some insurance agent to run the campaign. But Wagner, even better than Ed Lewis, heard the political vibrations. He organized a campaign that eventually reelected Vance Hartke by one of the narrowest margins in modern history, 4,283 votes. Now, even Ed Lewis was a believer.

But not Gordon St. Angelo.

St. Angelo recognized that the advantage for the Democrats was in the election cycle. A Republican was in the White House, and the off-year election always gives an edge to the out-of-power party. The Democrats could seize this advantage only by being well-financed and unified. St. Angelo coined the slogan "Unity 70." As in 1962, the State Central Committee would provide overall coordination for the campaign, and a new gimmick would be used to raise money, demonstrate unity, and attract attention to the Democratic ticket: all the nominees would walk Indiana, from the river to the lake.[49]

"If there's one election where sweat equity amounted to something, it was the 1970 general election," Ed Tracey declares. Tracey was coordinating the "Unity 70" meetings for St. Angelo. Rallies were held in all the congressional districts and in every large city. The entire ticket was required to be there, and Conrad emerged as the star speaker at every meeting. "We had a strong ticket and Conrad attracted a lot of attention with his speaking ability," Tracey recalls. One night, while he was driving St. Angelo back from a "Unity 70" rally in Terre Haute, Tracey and St. Angelo discussed

Conrad. St. Angelo revealed his suspicion of Conrad, saying he was a person "hard to get close to."[50]

Wagner agrees that "sweat equity" counted for a lot in 1970, but he extends far less credit to St. Angelo's planning. "Tension was always high between the candidates and St. Angelo. He was critical of my management of the Hartke campaign. He was particularly angry about my insisting that Hartke debate Roudebush."[51]

The debate, however, became a turning point in the campaign. The Republicans had obtained a photograph of Hartke at a black church, giving the "black power" salute while surrounded by blacks. The Republicans duplicated 480,000 copies of this photo for distribution.

"This photo had a demoralizing influence on the Hartke campaign," Wagner recalls, pointing out that polls showed Hartke down by 27 points at the beginning of the race, then pulling even just before the photo came out. "That's when I insisted on the debate."[52]

But the debate would not solve the problem of the photograph. "We were informed that the photos were at an Indianapolis printing firm. I sent some of our guys over there, and they said they were from the Republican campaign. They picked up nearly all the photographs," Wagner recalls, and adds with a smile, "I heard a rumor that a lot of them were later found in the White River. But a few of them were still there and the Republicans picked them up, planning on distributing them in the white areas of Lake County. The Lake County sheriff was informed, and as the car entered the county it was pulled over for a faulty tail-light. The car—and its contents— were impounded."[53]

According to Wagner, this campaign was the last of the "real dirty" campaigns in Indiana. Senator Hartke describes it as follows:

> The campaign, unfortunately, was marred by some antics that came out of the White House which Chuck Colson has admitted were definite attempts to destroy me, and they had some effect. There's just no question about that. But all those tactics which were used by the Nixonites . . . were a part of their whole campaign planning. Their intent was to destroy a candidate, not by direct assault, but by rumor and innuendo, even to the extent where Colson went on television with me and said, "I told lies about Senator Hartke and I admit it. It did have a bad effect upon him in the campaign of 1970." He apologized for it but once the libel was made, you couldn't retract it.[54]

There is plenty of evidence that the "dirty tricks" that were to become the hallmark of the Nixon White House had infected the Hoosier Republican party. An electronic listening device, surreptitiously placed in a potted plant in a meeting room in the ISTA building across from the Statehouse where Hartke's financial committee met, transmitted conversations to the Republican state headquarters. Two blocks east, on the eighth floor of the Illinois Building, where Jacque LeRoy maintained an office next to Wagner, a "bug" was placed under LeRoy's desk. The battery-operated device transmitted signals on FM radio bands at special frequencies. An unidentified source told reporters at the *Indianapolis Star* that a "high Republican official" had ordered the "bugs" because donors who "normally gave to the GOP were contributing to Hartke instead." The *Star* reporters claimed that Edgar L. (Nick) Longworth, a campaign coordinator for Richard Roudebush and former special assistant to Marion County Chairman L. Keith Bulen, attempted to tape-record conversations from the transmitter in the ISTA building in his office at the Republican state committee. It was reported that the "bugs" were placed by employees of International Investigators Inc., a private detective agency operated by a former Republican precinct committeeman, C. Tim Wilcox.[55]

There appeared to be no limit to the dirty tricks. The listening devices were not limited to meeting rooms and campaign headquarters. The private law offices of Ed Lewis, Hartke's close advisor, also were bugged. When a brown leather armchair was sent out for reupholstering, the firm called back and said that a listening device was found attached to the bottom. The bug transmitted for four to five days before the batteries supposedly lost power. Apparently there was monitoring of the device from a car parked nearby, and a tape recording was made of some conversations. Lewis neither confirmed nor denied the existence of the bug, but he did say that in the fall of 1970 canceled checks covering a three-year period were discovered missing from his desk drawer. Lewis had no evidence of forced entry to his law firm, but reporters contended there was "reliable information" that a lock was picked to gain entry. Longworth, one of the alleged GOP masterminds, predictably denied any involvement with the "buggings," saying, "The stories are not true."[56]

Wilcox, however, remembers that both Senator Hartke and Ed Lewis were "targets" of a private investigation and that "a couple of large boxes of information were taken to the U.S. Justice Department, and we were hoping they would open an investigation."[57]

The Hartke campaign eventually filed a civil suit which was settled out of court. Hartke described the settlement:

> Of course, we did recover a cash settlement of almost a quarter of million dollars for the tapping of our phones from 1965 to 1973, the breaking into my headquarters in Indianapolis, and the actual placing of bugs in the office of one of my supporters. The bugs were found some seven years later and the Justice Department had to admit that even they were involved, which was sort of a sad fact—the Justice Department was involved against its own legislative people. It was too bad. But those things you can't change. That was part of the period of our history which ended in the Watergate episode.[58]

The clandestine tricks were aimed at Hartke's campaign, but the unified effort of all the Democratic candidates made the entire ticket vulnerable to the Republican tactics. While Conrad was not the target of the surveillance, Wilcox was aware that Conrad frequently consulted with Ed Lewis. "I know Lewis was huddled with Conrad," Wilcox says. "We had a source inside the Democrat party and he had been there a long time. They had a good ear to the top people. We got some really good information."[59]

Conrad frequently met with both Lewis and Wagner, but he relied on Jeff Lewis to coordinate his campaign operations. Bob Boxell served as an unofficial advisor. After the nomination, Lewis moved into the coordinated campaign headquarters provided by the State Central Committee on the eighth floor of the Illinois Building in downtown Indianapolis. Steve Powell, Lewis's friend from their undergraduate days at Ball State, signed on as Conrad's driver. Powell's younger sister served as the receptionist and typist. "She could type about 35 words a year," Lewis remembers.[60] Conrad's cousin, Robert (Bob) Rooksby, the son of Ruby's brother, joined the campaign and assisted in scheduling and literature distribution. Diane Meyer, now married to N. Stuart Grauel and working out of Senator Bayh's Indianapolis office, volunteered at the Conrad headquarters in the evenings. She was Conrad's scheduler, and laughingly responded when called by the nickname he gave her: Banana.

This first Conrad campaign was the harbinger of all the others. Everyone was in constant motion. Staff members and volunteers were running and walking through the offices and milling in the corridors. With so many volunteers, getting a whiff of marijuana smoke in the hallways, particularly at night, was not uncommon. The crowded offices and corridors gave off the impression of a well-financed, deeply staffed operation. "Actually, we didn't have much money," Lewis remembers, "but we did everything to give the impression that we had money."[61]

Conrad himself was far from wealthy. In late July he issued a news release detailing his personal worth and called on the state legislature to enact a law "requiring all candidates for state, executive, legislative, and judicial office to disclose their personal finances." He reported total assets of $53,017, with the majority of that ($30,000) in home equity in their house on High School Street in Daleville. He and Mary Lou had $5,000 in their checking account, another $4,500 in U.S. Savings Bonds, and two cars, a 1969 Ford station wagon and a 1964 Volkswagen, which was paid off. Their liabilities amounted to $23,300, with $20,000 of that being their home mortgage. They owed $3,100 on the station wagon and had a thirty-day loan for $200. Their net worth was $29,717.[62]

Obviously, Conrad the candidate was in no position to fund his own campaign.

All of the Conrad campaigns would be short of money. In 1970, the competition for funds was fierce. The Democratic State Central Committee was extracting dollars from the county organizations, and Senator Hartke was into every county raising dollars. As Conrad put it, "We were out there in 1970, traveling the highways and byways, going into every little town on the map, trying to turn over rocks and raise ten or twenty bucks here or there. Every time we'd stop, one of the good Democrats would say: 'We're all tapped out. Vance was just in two days ago for a fund raiser and he took it all.' Hartke's people would descend on these little towns like a swarm of locusts, picking out anything green. By the time they left there wasn't a green leaf left on any tree."[63]

The UAW had set aside $15,000 for printing for the Conrad campaign. Using this fund, Lewis ordered 250,000 copies of a photograph of Conrad in full stride, sleeves rolled up, coat flung over one shoulder, and one hand extended, waving to the crowd watching the parade. The photo had been taken by a campaign volunteer, Ray Hafsten, in Madison, Indiana, and Larry and Mary Lou liked it very much. "When the flash went off, I knew it was a good one," Conrad later said. "I told Hafsten, 'that's a keeper.'"[64]

The one-page sheets with the photo were stacked to the ceiling in an empty room. They were referred to as the "Conrad one-sheets." Lewis and Rooksby wrote issue messages which were mimeographed on the back of the paper. The messages were often targeted to specific cities or counties. Once done, the sheets would be bundled and taken down the block to the bus station and shipped to the counties where the local coordinator would pick them up the next day and distribute them at meetings and rallies. "They were a lot cheaper than brochures," Lewis declares.[65]

Their imagination was unbounded. They used all the techniques and tricks they had learned from Bayh's 1968 campaign—and they improved on them. John C. Nichols was retained as the media consultant. Every Sunday morning he would haul in a camera and Conrad would tape a statement. There were fifteen television stations in Indiana outside of the Indianapolis market, and Conrad would have to deliver the same statement fifteen times. Nichols would place the unprocessed tapes in a can and ship them to the stations. The smaller stations, hungry for video on Sunday nights and Mondays, would play them on their news shows. "This drove Salin nuts," Lewis remembers. "He did not know how we could be in so many places at the same time."[66]

But it wasn't only the television tapes that made Conrad appear to be two places at once. Like his grandfather Rooksby, who peddled his wares on the red clay roads of Harrison and Clark counties, Conrad was constantly on the road, frequently making four or five stops in one day. "Walking the state was a nightmare," Diane recalls. "Because of the time changes, particularly in southern Indiana, the schedule was very intricate. I had to design a week-long schedule for walking, with precise directions as to how to get to one person's house and then, down the highway, to another house or some bean supper." One night, when Conrad was walking down along the river, he called into headquarters for Diane. "It was late, and when I picked up the phone he said, 'Banana, do you have a road map handy?' He knew I had a large road map pinned to the wall, and I stood and looked at it. 'Look at this highway down here and tell me what color it is.' I told him it was blue. 'Now move your finger down to the legend, and tell me what a blue highway is.' I moved my finger down the map and found the color code. Next to the color blue was the word, 'Proposed.' Interstate 64 in southern Indiana was not yet built, but I had scheduled him all week along I–64." Diane stayed up all night redoing the walking schedule in southern Indiana.[67]

Mary Lou and the four children also made appearances. On July 4, they appeared in four different parades and in each town the children threw candy from the car as Mary Lou waved at the crowds.

Steve Powell, Larry's main driver, estimates that Conrad was home only six nights in over six months of campaigning. Powell and another young staffer, Billy Rothbard, did most of the driving. One night Rothbard ran into a road grader in Hancock County. The windshield was smashed, and the blade barely missed Conrad's head. Within seconds of the accident, Conrad staggered out of the car, straightened himself, and ran up to the road grader. Extending his hand to the driver, he said, "Hi, I'm Larry Conrad, running for secretary of state."[68] From then on, Powell did all the driving.[69]

Conrad always sat in the front passenger seat and perfected a posture that allowed him to fall asleep, yet awaken in a flash. He had traveled Indiana enough to know all the places to stop for a restroom, grab a sandwich, or, most important, buy ice cream.

Larry's diet was one of Mary Lou's biggest worries. He tended to put on weight easily, and god, did he love to eat. His edacity was the one thing they would argue about. "I would really scold him about his weight," Mary Lou recalls. "He had so much self-discipline on everything except his eating."[70]

Knowing that he would not have regular meals on the road, Mary Lou instructed Boxell to make sure he stayed away from desserts and especially ice cream. Steve Powell remembers it well: "I had strict orders from Boxell to eliminate Dairy Queens from our stops. One night, we were driving to northern Indiana and Larry was asleep. In the distance, off to the right, I saw a Dairy Queen sign. Knowing he was asleep, I thought I could slip on by. Suddenly, Conrad's hands come up and he forms a radar screen with his thumbs and fingers and, with his eyes still shut and without moving his head, he starts beeping, like a radar detector. As I get closer to the Dairy Queen, the beeping gets faster and faster. I speed on by, and the beeping slows down. About two miles beyond, the beeping stops, the radar screen goes down, and he was back to sleep."[71]

Conrad was indefatigable. Months later, after the election, he returned three days early from a family vacation to Florida in order to speak before the Indiana Association of County and District Fairs. He told them:

> I know your fairs. I made them all last summer and I thank you for your courtesy to a young candidate you didn't know. The hot dogs were best at Corydon and the peanuts were best at Goshen and it rained the hardest at the Washington County Fair at Salem. I was there. Sometimes you didn't even know it, but I was there, shaking hands with your people.[72]

In his campaign speeches to Democrats he used the dozens of stories he had committed to memory. When he was at the podium his mind would pull them forward while he was finishing a line from a previous anecdote. In southern Indiana, down in the "red clay country," he would speak of Kentucky, telling the crowd about one of the most famous issues in American politics: whiskey.

> One congressman from Kentucky, who was facing an important primary election, received a postcard from a voter and all that was scrawled on it was:
>
> "Dear Congressman, how do you stand on whiskey?"
>
> The congressman didn't know if he had gotten ahold of an anti-whiskey man or a pro-whiskey man. And he wanted to make the answer the best he could.
>
> So, in one of the most famous replies in the history of congress, he wrote to his constituent:
>
> "My dear friend, I had not intended to discuss this controversial subject at this particular time. However I want you to know that I do not shun a controversy. On the contrary, I will take a stand on any issue at any time regardless of how fraught with controversy it may be. Now you've asked me how I feel about whiskey and here's how I stand on this question:
>
> "If when you say whiskey you mean the devil's brew, the poison scourge, the bloody monster that defiles innocence and dethrones reason, destroys the home, creates misery and poverty—yes, that literally takes bread from the mouths of little children; do you mean the evil drink that topples the Christian man and woman from the pinnacle of righteous and gracious living into the bottomless pit of degradation . . . then certainly I am against it with all my power!
>
> "But—if when you say whiskey you mean the oil of conversation, the philosophic wine, the ale that is consumed when good fellows get together, that puts a song in hearts and laughter on the lips and the warm glow of contentment in their eyes; do you mean Christmas cheer; do you mean the stimulating drink that puts a spring in an old gentlemen's step

on a frosty morning; do you mean the drink that enables a man to mag-
nify his joy and happiness and to forget, if only for a little while, life's
great tragedies, heartaches and sorrows; do you mean that drink, the sale
of which pours into our treasury untold millions of dollars which are
used for the tender care of our little children or blind or deaf or dumb or
aged or infirm, builds highways, hospitals and schools . . . then certainly
I am in favor of it!

"This is my stand and I will not compromise!"

When the applause and laughter faded, Conrad gave them more. He
talked about patronage politics and a former Republican U.S. senator from
Kentucky, John Sherman Cooper:

Senator Cooper once got a letter that said:

"Dear Senator, we have been Republicans all our life and ever since
you've been in politics we've been for you. Whether it was in the spring
or the fall we always fit on your side. We never fit agin' you. Our family
always lined up on your side because we thought you were good for our
family and for Kentucky. And in those forty years I have been a precinct
committeeman I never needed anything, never wanted anything and I've
never asked for anything. But the time is here, it has come. It has arrived.
I need a job. And there's a job open and I'm qualified for it. Eisenhower
is the president and he appoints the job. You say he's a friend of yours and
you say he's a Republican, and now you can get it for me—and I want it.
I want to be Ambassador to the Court of St. James in London, England.

"Signed: Sam Johnson, Punkin Holler, Kentucky."

John Sherman Cooper wrote back and said:

"I'm sure glad to get your letter. Everything you said in there was true.
Your family has been on my side every time I have ever run for office, and
I would not have won if it hadn't been for you. You did everything you
could and I'm appreciative and beholden to you. And I want you to know
right now that I'm ready to respond to your request. The job is open.
Eisenhower is the president, he's a Republican, and I'm a Republican.
He's a friend of mine. He takes my recommendation. I can get the job for
you, and get you appointed Ambassador to the Court of St. James, if
that's what you want.

"But before you decide I want you to get Mary and boys in the living
room and sit and talk this thing over. Because if you become Ambassador
to the Court of St. James in London, the first thing that is going to happen
is that Mary is going to have to get her hair done about three times a week
and it is costly over there in London. And you know how she hates to
wear that corset? Well, she is going to have to wear it about every day.

And she is going to have to have a new dress about every Saturday night to go to one of those state dinners and they are going to cost you five or six hundred dollars. And when you go to those dinners you are going to sit next to kings, maharajahs and consorts. You are going to have to be a master of the King's English. And they are going to set you down at a place where they have fourteen or fifteen utensils and you are going to have to know what one to use every particular time. And they are going to serve you several courses of wine and, boy, it makes you feel bad the next morning.

"And as far as the boys are concerned, they cannot spit in the chancellery, there's no place to fish, and they are going to have to wear their shoes all the time. They can't pick their toes.

"If that's what you want—if you want to be Ambassador to the Court of St. James—you let me know and you've got the job."

About ten days later a letter came back in from Punkin Holler:

"Senator, I knew you wouldn't let us down. We've talked to everybody on the east side of Kentucky that you have offered us this job. And we want you to know we are beholden to you. Like you said, I got Mary and boys in the living room and we thought this thing over. And we reached a conclusion. If you just appoint me Postmaster of Punkin Holler, we'll call this thing closed."

The Democrats would roar with laughter, but Conrad wasn't through. He had to draw the moral, and let the voters know something about him: "Now there's a couple of things to know about this story from Punkin Holler. First, you don't want to set your sights too low, but you want to have something in mind that you're going to get. And secondly, you've got to do some straight talking."

And the Democrats loved his stories and his "straight talking." His lucid mind and his command of language allowed him to shift accents. In southern Indiana he could go back to his earliest roots and speak with that Hoosier version of a southern drawl. In central Indiana he would pull from his Muncie days and speak in the flat-toned voice that TV and radio announcers are expected to have—where every syllable is enunciated and all lilt leaves the language. In the northern tier counties of north central and northwest Indiana, when speaking to Polish groups, he would recite a few lines—in Polish—from the Polish national anthem. Behind the podium in Gary, he would spread his arms, stomp one foot, and the political stories pouring from his lips could have been delivered by any of the black preachers in the audience. And he would tell this story about Martin Luther King:

Reverend King had a good friend who was the Baptist preacher far out in the back woods of Alabama. Once, when he was driving back to Montgomery, he took a detour to the back country to talk with his friend. When he pulled up to the house, the preacher was sitting in his chair out on the front lawn. The Reverend King walked up and greeted him and asked, "How's our people doing here?" And the old black preacher looked up, shaded his eyes from the hot sun and said, "Well Martin, we're not where we ought to be. And we're not where we want to be. But we're all sure glad we're not where we used to be."

Conrad's quotes and stories quickened every crowd. He loved being on the road because he loved people. He had a childlike belief in the goodness of mankind. One of his favorite quotes was an adulterated Shakespearean line about what a waste of time it was to speak ill of others. And Conrad never did. When staff members would grouse about a politician who would not commit, Conrad would remain silent until the topic changed.

While Conrad remained on the road, the "Unity 70" theme began working. By mid-September all the campaigns were coordinated and there were regular staff meetings of the various managers to ensure maximum exposure for the entire ticket.

Conrad's age and experience with the Young Democrats made college campuses a natural campaign stop. On a September trip to Monroe County, he stopped by the Indiana University campus in Bloomington, where he met Claudia Prosser and other members of the College Young Democrats. They accompanied him to the new College Mall in Bloomington, where Conrad was to shake hands and Prosser and the other students were to distribute leaflets. "We just entered the mall and started campaigning when a security officer came up and told us that the owners of the mall, Melvin Simon and Associates, did not allow campaigning in their malls. Our first experience with the Simons was being kicked out of one of their malls," Prosser fondly recalls.[73]

As election day approaches the politicians say, "We're only ten days out and the votes are coming in bucketfuls." In the modern era, "tracking polls" are in the field every night, providing a "rolling average" as to which direction the "undecideds" are breaking. The media specialists are on call twenty-four hours a day to ensure rapid response to the latest attacks from the opponent. The weekend before the election the Indiana politicians are consumed with "getting out the vote" and providing materials to poll workers. The candidates are scheduled as fully and as tightly as possible, trying to reach the greatest numbers of people. On election day itself, the candidate's schedule is built around when he or she will vote. Then there is time for a plant gate, or, perhaps, a "fly-around," where a driver will meet the plane and take the candidate to a large precinct to shake hands or to a phone bank to make calls. Then there is time in mid-afternoon for another plant gate, and another stop in another city before the polls close at 6 P.M. Then it is back to the plane and back to Indianapolis.

On election night, November 3, 1970, the Conrad family and staff members gathered at the offices of an engineering firm in Indianapolis to listen to the returns. Sipping beer and eating hors d'oeuvres, Larry and Mary Lou paced the floor, keeping their ears cocked to the radio. In the early evening, Lou Palmer on WIBC said the secretary of state race was "too close to call." Jeff Lewis, however, had targeted seven counties, and as he received reports from some of these, he was confident of a victory. He told Conrad he expected to win by about 11,000 votes, but Conrad's confidence was not improved. "He was nervous," Lewis recalls. A little after 11 P.M. the radio station declared that Salin was the winner and Conrad turned to Lewis: "Get on that phone and call Lou Palmer and find out what's going on!" When Lewis finally reached Palmer, he asked where in the hell he was getting his returns and Palmer replied: "From the Republicans." Lewis explained that his numbers showed Conrad was going to win. A few minutes later, Palmer was back on the air announcing that the race was still undecided.[74]

Election nights expose the nerves of even the most thick-skinned politician. Before the networks and newspapers formed election night "pools" to collect returns from around the state, campaign staffers and candidates relied on bits and fragments of information to determine what the final totals would be. Until the mid-1970s about half of Indiana's ninety-two counties used the large, cumbersome voting machines and throughout the day there would be reports of a "machine breakdown" where the election judges would have to open the back of the machine and read the totals before a new machine could be installed at the polling place. These breakdowns provided the first clues of a voting trend. And as "breakdowns" were phoned into campaign headquarters, other staffers were calling county chairs and clinging to every parcel of information: "Are the farmers voting?" "What's the turnout in the doughnut?"[75]

Clearly, the 1970 Indiana election was going to be a photo finish. It was nearly 1 A.M. on November 4 and still no winner had been declared for either the U.S. Senate or the secretary of state. The Conrads finally left to drive back to Daleville, listening to the returns as they drove. It was past 3 A.M. when they arrived home and Larry collapsed on the bed, fully clothed. Mary Lou noticed his face was beet red—he had hives, caused by stress.[76]

Lewis also had left, returning to campaign headquarters in the Illinois Building. He lay down on a cot for a nap. He got up every two hours to check more returns, and was gaining more and more confidence as the morning wore on.

By 10 A.M., eighty-four of the ninety-two counties had reported and Lewis was sure of Conrad's victory. Conrad returned to headquarters about noon and asked Lewis: "How does it look?"

"It looks good, Larry," Lewis responded. "There's not enough votes left in the remaining counties for Salin to catch us."

Slowly, a big, wide grin came over Conrad's face. A great smile of satisfaction.[77]

After making some phone calls, Conrad drove back to Daleville. It was not until late afternoon that the news reports finally declared Conrad a certain winner. But the Hartke race was still too close to call, and would not be settled for many days.

The final vote totals showed Conrad the winner by 26,143 votes out of 1,693,177 votes cast. Conrad carried exactly one-half of the ninety-two counties, with Salin having a majority in the other forty-six. The victory formula was the traditional Indiana formula for a Democratic win. The Democrats held down the Republican margin in Marion County, with Salin winning by only 6,035 votes. Likewise, although Conrad lost six of the seven doughnut counties, Salin's majority in the doughnut was only 19,695. Lake County, however, came roaring in for the Democrats and Conrad, producing a majority of 34,706 votes. The other large counties, with the exception of Allen, also produced for the Democrats. Conrad carried St. Joseph by 15,967, Vigo by 7,769, and his home county of Delaware by 4,308.[78]

The Democrats swept all the statewide races, losing only one of the four judges on the appellate court. It was a resounding mid-term victory for the Indiana Democratic party.

Larry Conrad was the secretary of state of America's eleventh most populous state. And he was setting his sails for the next campaign, for governor.

5

I do solemnly swear that I will support the Constitution of the United States and the Constitution of the State of Indiana and I will faithfully and impartially discharge the duties of the Secretary of State according to the best of my skill and ability, so help me God.

—Oath of office sworn by Larry A. Conrad,
December 1, 1970

GEORGE W. BYRUM of Laconia, Larry Conrad's uncle—his mother's brother-in-law—and, in Conrad's words, "one of God's noble men," administered the oath of office to Larry Conrad in the rotunda of the Statehouse on Tuesday, December 1, 1970. Conrad's entire family was there, including Mrs. Ida Lou Conrad of Muncie, his eighty-six-year-old grandmother, in a wheel chair.

Conrad spoke of "the dawn of a new time, a new age, and, I would hope, a new sense of and about politics in Indiana." In a brief speech, which he had written himself, he sought to inspire and uplift. He quoted Thoreau:

"I learned this at least, by my experiment, that if one advances confidently in the direction of his dreams, and endeavors to live the life which he has imagined, he will meet with a success unexpected in common hours. In proportion as he simplifies his life, the laws of the universe will appear less complex, and solitude will not be solitude, nor poverty, nor weakness. If you have built castles in the air, your work need not be lost; that is where they should be. Now put the foundations under them."

He then proclaimed his intention, as secretary of state, "to go to work to put, by executive deed and legislative act, foundations under our castles."[1]

He was now secretary of state, but he was not certain of the length of his term. Aside from electing Democrats, the voters also had approved the state constitutional amendment lengthening the term of the secretary of state from two to four years. However, it was not clear if the amendment applied to Larry Conrad, who was elected in the same election. It would be more than a year before the Indiana Supreme Court decided the matter.

When Conrad entered his new office on the main floor office of the Statehouse he did not have all of the fifty-two staff positions filled. Just days before, he had settled the most important appointment, the office of deputy secretary of state. This person was the chief administrative officer of all the divisions of the office, including the corporate and the securities divisions. Jeff Lewis, Conrad's campaign manager, obviously expected a job, as did most of the other campaign staffers, including Steve Powell.[2]

Lewis contends that Conrad offered him the position of deputy secretary of state, but he turned it down. "The deputy, or Larry himself, always had to be in the office, and I didn't want that," Lewis says.[3] Conrad gave him the title of administrative assistant and, a few days before taking the oath of office, Conrad called N. Stuart Grauel. Grauel was not entirely sure he should take the position of deputy secretary of state. "Actually, I considered myself to be a Republican until I met Bayh and Conrad. Moreover, I didn't know anything about government. I was in banking," Grauel recalls. But he decided to take the position. His wife of fifteen months, Diane Meyer, was still working in Bayh's Indianapolis office and was by now firmly committed to Conrad. Since 1968, her personal attachment to Conrad and his family had deepened.[4]

Others were joining the staff, reporting to either Grauel or Lewis. Terrence Straub, a losing congressional candidate in 1970, was hired to be the liaison with the state legislature. William (Bill) McCarty, another defeated congressional candidate, came on board. Steve Sutherlin was appointed as the securities commissioner, an important division that regulated all securities issued in the state. Steve Powell became his deputy. Bill Bannon, a former campaign staffer for Hartke who maintained excellent contacts with organized labor, was named director of the corporations division. Ezra Friedlander, who had practiced law in Lake County, took the part-time position as corporate counsel. Bob Rooksby also was on board, reporting to Lewis.

It was a young staff. Conrad was thirty-five; Sutherlin was thirty-three; Grauel and Lewis were both twenty-five. "It was a stellar gathering of young minds," claims Vicki Weger, Conrad's secretary, who was twenty.[5]

"We were mighty impressed with what we'd done," Lewis remembers. "We had beaten the Republicans twice in a row, first with Birch in 1968, and then with Larry. We thought we could beat anybody. We were true believers—bona fide zealots. We knew all the answers."[6]

Grauel agrees: "We were all young and naive, and all of us were in a hurry. We had no respect for time in the trenches or the established pecking order."[7]

The established political pecking order in a strong two-party state is the party organization. But Conrad had not come up through the party organization. His sponsor was Birch Bayh. In fact, in the secretary of state's office, Conrad himself was the only bridge to the old organizational people—those men and women he had worked so closely with in 1962 and 1968. Many of those people were now on the sidelines, having been replaced during the Branigin years under the authority of St. Angelo.

Conrad's secretary of state's office was wide open and carefree, with staff members reporting to work when they wished and working as late as they wished. There was a strong resemblance to the "fun and camaraderie" of Birch Bayh's Senate office in 1963 and 1964. The youthful enthusiasm and the imaginative programs that had been so successful during the campaign continued. Grauel attempted to introduce some administrative procedures, but many of the staff members ignored them. The relaxed atmosphere continued unabated.

Visitors were always welcome. Vicki Weger—Conrad always called her "Miss Vicki"—would lead the tours of dozens of school children into his office where Conrad would tell them his duty was to make sure "nobody steals the state seal." Other staffers would interrupt whatever they were doing to talk with Conrad and the visitors—to tell jokes and stories. David Letterman, a friend of Lewis's from Ball State University days, was a weatherman for an Indianapolis television station and would occasionally walk in unannounced to swap stories with Lewis and Conrad. During one visit, Letterman said to Conrad: "I want a job for about $15,000 a year. I'll just hang around here and tell jokes." Conrad replied: "I've got that job."[8]

There was arrogance and brashness—and some jealousy—among the various staff members. But they all presumed one thing: Larry Conrad was going to run for governor in 1972 and it was their jobs to get him the brass ring. They knew they could do it. They already had come this far. They couldn't be denied.

They geared up quickly. Seven weeks after the inauguration, on January 21, 1971, Lewis wrote an internal memo to Conrad which detailed the "political battle plan for the next six months—February through August." He pointed out that the most "important image we have to maintain . . . is one of cooperation with the entire party throughout the state," and the "underlying theme always should be electing Democrats to office" in the municipal elections in November of 1971. He suggested that Conrad spend "two days a week on the road," with the first priority being Lake County. He proposed a dinner in Conrad's honor to be held in Lake County "shortly after the filing for office closes in February," thereby assuring that "everyone would come to this . . . if for no other reason than to see who is there."

Lewis sketched out a tentative schedule, week by week, which would ensure Conrad's presence in every part of the state. He then proposed that various staff members be held responsible for certain sections of the state. Rooksby was to be assigned the 8th district, in southwestern Indiana—an area Rooksby referred to as "lapland" because it "overlapped" Kentucky. Bill McCarty would handle the 10th district in east central Indiana, Terry Straub the 11th and 6th districts in Marion County and the doughnut, and Page Gifford was assigned the 4th district.[9]

By February 19, Lewis had appointed other "coordinators" for specific counties and informed several "girls" in the office that they were assigned to a specific coordinator. Referring to a meeting with the coordinators, Lewis memoed Conrad: "We discussed satisfactorily, I think, the correct responses to the stock questions as to your potential candidacy for the office down the hall." He then proceeded to tell Conrad one of their assignments: "In your travels, those coordinators will accompany you to their respective areas, whereupon you shall wow, marvel, dazzle, gather, pluck, shine and subsequently amaze them."[10]

The coordinators would routinely travel the state and meet with Democratic leaders and public officials. Reports on these meetings would then be written in memo form back to Conrad, Lewis, Straub, or Grauel. The coordinator was instructed to keep one copy in his files. Conrad kept a three-ring binder in the center drawer of his desk where he would file the memos, by author, in chronological sequence.

On Saturday, February 27, 1971, Bill Bannon traveled the 7th district, meeting with six different officials in five different counties. He was probing for possible support for Conrad in the 1972 governor's race and asked about other likely candidates, such as Matthew Welsh, John Dillon (a former attorney general), and Robert V. Welch (an Indianapolis businessman).

In a memo to Lewis, Bannon wrote that one county chairman "spent the whole time raving about what a great guy R. V. Welch is," and noted that another chairman "offered to let Larry use his cottage and pontoon boat anytime he would like to get away for a rest."[11]

Similar staff memos poured in. On the same day Bannon was in the 7th district, Rooksby was in the 9th, where he had four meetings in three counties in three hours. The next weekend Straub swung through the 4th district where he visited nine counties in two days. The written memos characterized each of the meetings in personal terms. Regarding one mayor in the 4th district, Straub wrote: "He seems to be in good shape, very well organized and there isn't much we can do for him." Straub described one woman vice-chairman as "an energetic 70-year-old type who thinks very highly of Matt." From another county chair, Straub heard a disturbing complaint about patronage in the secretary of state's office, and he detected the first stirrings of St. Angelo's opposition. The county chairman "grumbled about our not having all our employees cleared. He showed me a letter from the State Committee saying we still had a number of employees to clear. I assured him that is no longer the case." St. Angelo had wasted no time in placing pressure on Conrad, a man St. Angelo found it hard to get close to. Straub finally dismissed the complaint of the county chair by commenting that "he is your basic organizational Democrat."[12]

But the Conrad program was not limited to gathering political intelligence. There was an aggressive communications program. Vicki Weger maintained two shoeboxes full of 3x5 cards at her desk containing names, addresses, and phone numbers of "everybody from precinct committeemen to Robert Redford." When Conrad saw a newspaper clipping or had an idea for someone, he would give it to Vicki who would send it out the same day. "He was a communicator," she says. "He never let the other person have the last written word. If he sent something out and received a thank-you note back, he would send another note thanking the person for the thank-you."[13]

Lewis saw to it that the other mailing lists were continually updated and properly filed. In early February, a mailer was put together for Valentine's Day. Every woman on the mailing list was to receive a valentine card from Larry Conrad. John C. Nichols, still a consultant to Conrad, arranged to have the cards printed. Thousands of cards were mailed to assure they arrived on the appointed day. There was a notation made on every 3x5 card that the woman had received the valentine. The 3x5 cards were filed in alphabetical order by county. Eventually, this program was expanded and became known as the BAID program: Births, Anniversaries, Injuries, and Deaths. The cards were constantly updated. The coordinators clipped newspapers from their respective counties. They made sure pertinent information was entered on the cards. Whenever a staff member was notified that somebody was sick or had died, a card, signed by Conrad, was mailed. By July, this massive mailing campaign was costing a great deal of money. One staffer wrote a memo to Conrad, Lewis, and Boxell, informing them that "we have a large number of mailings going out and we have a great need for stamps."[14]

While the young staff members were maintaining, in Lewis's phrase, "as fast a pace as possible," Conrad himself was not yet committed to the 1972 gubernatorial race. He realized, and staff reports confirmed, that former governor Matt Welsh had great support in the party. As Boxell now says: "Matt Welsh was a very popular former governor who a lot of people owed."[15] Moreover, Conrad personally respected Welsh and viewed many of his decisions as governor—such as the endorsement of Birch Bayh and his fight for the sales tax—as acts of courage.

But in early 1971 it appeared that the Democrats had a genuine shot at winning the 1972 elections. Richard Nixon's Republican administration was stumbling. In late November of 1970 a daring raid by the U.S. military to rescue American troops in North Vietnam had failed. By early February of 1971 the South Vietnamese army, with heavy air support from the U.S., invaded Laos. These and other events kept the Vietnam War on the front pages. Antiwar activists set their plans for a massive demonstration in Washington on April 24.

The domestic economy also was in trouble. Inflation was increasing. The Nixon administration began planning a ninety-day freeze on wages, prices, and rents, which would be announced on August 15, 1971. By the end of the year, Nixon devalued the dollar by 8.57 percent.

Moveover, the Indiana Republican party was still engaged in its civil war. Clearly, Ed Whitcomb was a weakened party leader, but he still held the high office. Indiana Democrats had swept the 1970 races, held both U.S. Senate seats, and enjoyed at least a public persona of being united.

Indeed, 1972 held potential for the Democrats. Conrad and Boxell understood that everything possible had to be done to politically prepare Conrad to be on the Democratic ticket.

In mid-May Boxell opened a "political section" and established a $250 checking account at a local bank to purchase supplies and pay travel expenses. Boxell and Grauel were authorized to cosign the checks. Twenty-five percent of the "2-percent" money that was being paid by office employees was diverted into the checking account, with the remaining 75 percent remitted to the Democratic State Committee. This diversion of 2-percent money clearly signaled that Conrad had his own political agenda. And it did not necessarily coincide with St. Angelo's.[16]

Within two weeks Boxell was receiving the first of several "layout sheets" listing all the delegates to the 1970 state convention and had made assignments to "seven girls" to call every delegate in the evening hours.[17] At a coordinator's meeting on June 1, Boxell informed the staff members that they "should get letters out to people met or seen on field trips immediately after the trip" and that "LAC should do the same and whoever travels with him should get names *and addresses* . . . so that a letter can go out from LAC." Finally, Boxell stressed the importance of phone calls: "We have a WATS line to the whole state. Use it. We should take advantage of our phone system and keep in touch with people on a weekly basis."[18] At the time, the WATS line was unlimited and unmeasured. Later, the state switched most lines to measured service.

On June 14, Lewis wrote a progress report to Conrad and Boxell on the political program. It stated that the "data gathering information of delegates started slowly, but is moving very well now." Lewis "had a meeting with all personnel regarding the project and explained to them . . . what we are attempting to accomplish." He emphasized that their participation would continue to be expected, and "by that I did not mean that they do this or lose their job, but I did stress very strongly that LAC's political success is directly connected to their employment, and that if he is not successful in two years, they will have to look for another job. I also said

that of all the people they could work for politically, no one is more deserving than the Secretary and if they had any problems with commitment
then they should reconsider their being here. They understood very well.
There has been a marked improvement in their attitude regarding the
particular project."[19]

While the political preparations continued, Conrad was weighing his
options. One of them—running for lieutenant governor on a ticket with
Matthew Welsh—seemed particularly attractive. At the time, it was unclear that the state constitution would be amended to allow the governor
to succeed himself and serve "eight years in any period of twelve years."[20]
Hence, as the sitting lieutenant governor, Conrad would be favored to run
for governor in 1976. Moreover, given Welsh's recent health problems, it
was likely he would only serve one term even if the amendment passed.[21]

Conrad did not discuss his thoughts about the lieutenant governorship
with his staff, knowing that they were hell bent for the governorship, but
he did mention them to Mary Lou, and he discussed the pluses and mi-
nuses with Bob Boxell.

Mary Lou thought that a run for governor in 1972 was premature. She
expressed her opinion not only to Larry but Jeff Lewis as well. Boxell
recalls that the staff was in no mood to listen to anything about any other
office. "He was under a lot of pressure from his staff to run for governor,"
Boxell says. "They were going to steamroll the thing. They didn't realize
what was involved in running against a popular former governor like
Matt Welsh."[22] Vicki Weger agrees: "From the moment we walked into the
Statehouse in December of 1970 we all knew we were going for governor."
And Lewis remembers it clearly: "We heard rumblings that Matt Welsh
was thinking of running for governor. I thought, 'Fuck Matt—we're full
speed ahead.' Now I know how you can get that way. It's the intoxication
of power."[23]

Political advice was pouring in to Conrad from friends and acquaintances. David Bochnowski, who was on Senator Bayh's Washington staff and
had worked with Conrad in Bayh's 1968 reelection campaign, wrote to
Conrad about his staff:

> Like it or not, *you must face* the fact that you have a young staff and they
> have offended many of the old guard. I am not trying to say that this has
> been the fault in all cases of your staff. The old guard may naturally
> resent the youth movement. But *you do have to recognize* that the problem
> does exist. Ignore it, and you will in all probability lose.[24]

In the same memo, Bochnowski offered his advice on making the race:

> There are many good reasons why not to run—you will not have the
> money; you cannot attract the right staff; the burden would be too great
> on your family; or other personal considerations. A reason not to run,

however, predicated on the fact that you might lose, cannot stand. If you believe you can make a difference, that you can provide leadership and purpose, then you must have the guts to do what you believe is right. "Sometimes we must sail with the wind and sometimes against it, but we must sail."[25]

It was clear in the late spring of 1971 that Matt Welsh was running. Conrad's coordinators and other volunteers were now being called "Conrad Crazies" by Welsh supporters. Welsh's people were trying to secure endorsements. He was accepting invitations to speak at county Jefferson-Jackson Day dinners. He was attending meetings of precinct committeemen, particularly in the larger counties.

On July 20, 1971, in a news conference in the Hilton Hotel in downtown Indianapolis, Matthew Welsh made it official. He was running. He announced that he had received numerous requests to run from "others interested in the political scene." And he made sure these "requests" resulted in endorsements. That evening, at a dinner in his honor in Martinsville, five of the six counties from the 6th district endorsed Welsh for governor.[26]

Boxell's reaction was immediate. In a July 24 memo to Conrad, he wrote:

> Matt's announcement has, in my judgment, created a situation which requires a slight change in our planning and procedure.
>
> Survival is the first instinct among organization politicians especially in a patronage minded state such as Indiana and I am concerned that too many people, who are inclined to be for you, are becoming more uncertain of your plans as a result of either not promoting [yourself] or are giving serious consideration to going with Matt. The reasons are numerous, but I will cite just three:
>
> 1. Many are genuinely convinced that Matt has the nomination assured.
>
> 2. Some feel they could hold with you until the last moment and then you would decide not to make the race.
>
> 3. Many are convinced that you have already reached an agreement with Matt. The latest example of this is a brief conversation I recently had [where I was told], without any hesitation, that he had on good authority that you had agreed to run for Lieutenant Governor with Matt. This, in my judgment, is the most potentially dangerous situation which now confronts us. Unless we soon confide in a few people we are faced with the distinct possibility of losing them and should you decide to run for Lieutenant Governor, we face the certainty of some people being convinced in their own minds that such an arrangement was made long ago and that they were being used.

Boxell recommended that a "list of people" be compiled "that we should talk to" at the annual Indiana Democrat Editorial Association (IDEA) meeting at French Lick in late August.[27] The discussions with key people would allow an assessment to be made of the "intra-party reaction, the Republican reaction, and the reaction, if any, of the general public." It also was important, Boxell warned, to stress that no agreement had been made to run for lieutenant governor and that Conrad would not make any announcement until after the city elections in November.[28]

With Conrad's approval, the staff immediately began implementing Boxell's recommendations. By August 13, each of the coordinators had submitted a list of Conrad supporters to Rooksby. These supporters were to be "contacted immediately and urged to attend the IDEA convention," where they would work the crowd for Conrad.[29]

Help also came from other quarters. In an obvious attempt to hold off party endorsements for Welsh, the treasurer of the Lake County Democratic Central Committee, Nick Angel, sent a letter on August 13 to all the "District and County Chairmen and their Committees in the State of Indiana" saying that "the Democratic Party of Indiana doesn't have to dig up an ex-Governor from the Sixties to run in the Seventies." Without mentioning Conrad by name, Angel asserted that "our Party has generated many new and outstanding candidates that can be democratically nominated and elected, who would make a major contribution to the advancement of Indiana at a time in History when proper action must be immediately initiated."[30]

By all accounts, Conrad's IDEA program was a rousing success. Flanked by his staff members, Conrad staged several events, including a breakfast for all those attending. Late on Saturday night, the popular "Conrad Sing-along" was held in an upper room, with Mary Lou at the piano. All the guests joined in singing the songs of Indiana. It was a revival of the many parties Larry and Mary Lou had hosted since they were married. About 2 A.M. Sunday morning Conrad's staff members and volunteers pushed his literature under each hotel room door, ensuring that every Democrat saw Conrad's name the first thing in the morning.

The Conrad program was working. On September 7, 1971, Boxell reported to Conrad, by memo, that French Lick "was a huge success," and that each person specially invited was being asked to provide "a brief memo regarding the general impression they received and . . . examples as to how they arrived at their impressions."[31]

Several Conrad supporters wrote of their impressions of French Lick. One attorney from northwest Indiana wrote:

> With few exceptions, people feel that Matt Welsh is the Democratic candidate for governor and will be after the convention next year. When asked why, there were no real valid reasons other than the fact that he has

overwhelmed a number of people with the supposed support he has. I found out that if your candidacy was declared, and it appeared that there was a reasonable base for support, that these very people I talked to would love to turn around and jump on the bandwagon.

lis attorney expressed the opinion that Conrad's "individual showing at e convention versus that of Matt Welsh was most impressive, and in me instances, overwhelming. I feel certain that this could possibly have direct relation on delegate votes from persons who were at the IDEA nvention."[32]

After IDEA, Conrad's political coordinators again hit the road. They ld Democratic officials that Larry "probably would" run for governor, ut wanted to make sure Democrats won the municipal elections first.[33] A pecial eight-page brochure was prepared for mailing, with Conrad's rofile on the front and the tag line "Larry Conrad: Your Secretary of tate." Interspersed with pictures of Larry and Mary Lou, the text read: 'Larry Conrad was elected Secretary of State. Now he wants to return the support you gave him. He wants to help elect Democrats to office this fall. Larry believes the 1971 elections will determine much of our success in the 1970's. He wants to help—he knows it takes a team to win!"[34]

Additional help for the mayors was forthcoming from Conrad. Lewis left the secretary of state payroll and moved back to his hometown of Muncie, where he coordinated Paul Cooley's reelection campaign for mayor. During September and October, Conrad was again on the road—relentlessly—making appearances on behalf of the local Democrats.

Boxell, meanwhile, was choreographing a two-stage approach to land Conrad in the governor's chair. First, a message had to be sent to Welsh asking whether or not he would select Conrad for the second spot on the ticket. Second, if Welsh rejected Conrad, it was necessary to persuade the political leaders in the largest counties that Matthew Welsh could not win; only Conrad was capable of winning the governorship.

To get the message to Welsh about Conrad's interest in being lieutenant governor, Boxell talked to the mayor of East Chicago, Robert (Bob) Pastrick, who was leaning toward supporting Welsh. Pastrick, who also knew Conrad well and respected him, agreed to ask Welsh his choice for lieutenant governor. Welsh would be in Lake County in late September, where Pastrick would pop the question. As soon as possible after talking with Welsh, Pastrick was to call Jim Capehart, an Indianapolis attorney and longstanding Bayh supporter who was committed to Welsh. Boxell and Capehart were old friends, and they had agreed that Boxell should be at Capehart's home when Pastrick called.

Boxell was convinced that a Welsh-Conrad ticket was the best match. But he knew a major impediment to such a ticket was the Democratic State Central Committee. "There were some members of the State Committee who did not want Conrad's political career to prosper," Boxell says, "and it was clear that Welsh wanted the support of the State Committee and would not jeopardize it over the nomination for lieutenant governor."[35]

Capehart invited Boxell to his home. J. Manfred Core and another close advisor to Welsh also were to be in attendance. When Boxell arrived that evening, Capehart informed him that the other two could not attend. Boxell immediately suspected the worst. He asked Capehart: "Did you hear from Pastrick?" Capehart said "Yes." Boxell pushed: "Well, what did he say?" Capehart answered: "Well, he had no objections to either Bodine or Conrad, but he knew Bodine better."

There was a long silence in the Capehart house. Boxell finally asked: "Who do you think will win the World Series this year?" The rest of the evening was devoted to baseball.[36]

The next morning, Boxell reported the conversation to Conrad. Clearly, Conrad was surprised and disappointed. "He was prepared to run for lieutenant governor," Boxell recalls. Both of them understood Welsh's political position, where he wanted the full support of St. Angelo and the State Committee. Finally, Boxell asked him if he intended to go ahead with running for governor. Conrad replied: "What do you think?" Boxell answered: "If you're going, let's go."[37]

This was a major turning point in Conrad's career, and, looking back, Boxell regrets the reliance he placed on the Pastrick-Welsh conversation. "It was constructed by third parties," Boxell says, "and it may have been just a question of semantics. So many times, a lack of communication can change a lot of things."[38]

St. Angelo concurs: "By 1972 we had shifted the power from the county chairs to the mayors. I raised a lot of money for the mayors in 1967, and they were of the opinion Matt had the best chance in 1972 and Larry should wait for 1976. And a pact could have been made on that."[39]

But the pact was not made. It was now time to move on to the second stage of Boxell's program. One of the first political leaders approached was the mayor of Fort Wayne, Ivan Lebamoff. Boxell, Lewis, and Conrad drove to Fort Wayne and made their pitch. Boxell remembers asking the mayor: "If we bring you a legitimate poll showing Larry to be the strongest candidate, will you support us?" The mayor started talking and said a lot of nice things about Larry. "He said everything but yes," Boxell recalls. And Boxell's experience with heavy hitters told him never to assume anything. Afterwards, as they were talking in the parking lot, Boxell remarked to Conrad: "Don't count on him. We're just wasting our time." Conrad replied, "I didn't get that out of what he said." Boxell shook his head and thought to himself, "Here is the most trusting politician I ever saw."[40]

November 2 was election day. That evening Conrad spent several hours at his desk making congratulatory phone calls to mayors and city council winners. The major Democratic loss that night was in Evansville, where Russell Lloyd won the mayor's chair for the Republicans for the first time in sixteen years.

The local elections were now over. Conrad had to decide.

The reports from the "Conrad Crazies" provided the political information needed to identify his strengths and weaknesses in each of the ninety-two counties. As the December memos poured in, recommendations were made as to where delegates would have to be recruited and "slated" for Conrad.

Conrad's final decision was discussed only with Mary Lou. "We did most of our talking in the morning, before work," Mary Lou remembers. "At first I didn't think we should go. I thought we should wait until 1976. But we kept discussing it and I started realizing that the race in 1972 would bring name recognition and more people to us, even if we lost."

Finally, one morning in early December, while Larry and Mary Lou were in the bathroom getting ready for work, Larry said, "I've got to decide on this. What do you think?" Mary Lou said that she thought the race would give good exposure. "I knew he really wanted to run, he was already there," Mary Lou recalls. Then Larry said he was going to do it. "It was just a statement," Mary Lou says.[41]

Clearly, he wanted to be governor. He had harbored that ambition from his earliest days in Muncie. His experience told him that timing was everything, but he also had a fatalism about politics. He knew when your turn came, you had to take it, even if the timing was wrong. To hesitate was to make yourself a victim of the pressures and events created by others. Years later, after leaving public office, Conrad would say in his speeches: "I've got a checklist in life, and one of the items on that checklist was to run for the highest office in Indiana—the Office of Governor." In that bathroom in their new house on North Meridian Street, in early December of 1971, he checked that item off his list.

As the new year began, Boxell wrote a memo to Conrad providing a general assessment "of the political situation in Indiana as it pertains to you." He described Welsh's position as being "obvious—it is now or never." Concerning Robert V. (Bob) Welch, he wrote: "Bob will enter the race only if you do. His only hope is that you and Matt collide head-on and thus force a blood letting and prolonged balloting from which he could emerge as a compromise. [Bob] feels he has been led down the primrose path by St. Angelo and, to a lesser degree, by Matt."

Referring to Bodine, Boxell observed that "his hand has been forced. He must win the nomination for Lieutenant Governor or face political oblivion. He tried on two occasions to get Matt's endorsement for his present candidacy. He failed."

In his summary to Conrad, he stated: "The primary elements exist for an accord with Dick and/or Bob. I think they are worthy of your consideration. Unlike the others, you have not exhausted your options and this time around is not your last hope. I think Matt is ahead at the present time, but consider his strength soft. I feel a decision and an announcement must be made in the near future, but feel you have played your options very well."[42]

The Conrad "political section" was now in full swing. The fly-around announcement was tentatively scheduled for Monday, January 31, a date Lewis called "particularly good because the legislature will not be in session." Lewis also set forth a series of assignments for various staff members, assuring that all aspects of the announcement were covered. Powell was responsible for the media, including the press kits. Aboard the forty-passenger chartered aircraft, he was to "make sure that the press leaves the plane and gets directly to the news conference, where space will be provided for them, and then make sure of their return to the plane on time." Rooksby was the advance man, "in charge of coordinating with the various local people," and at each airport "we have designated a crowd chairman and sign chairman. The crowd chairman will get 8 to 10 people whose responsibility is to get 8 to 10 recruiters who get 8 to 10 people to the airport." Rooksby was to be in the advance plane, "which will arrive 20 to 30 minutes ahead of the big plane to ensure things are in order."[43]

While Lewis provided the logistics, Straub provided advice on Conrad's message. The problem, as Straub defined it, was to "so structure LAC's announcement of candidacy as to set him apart. . . ." To accomplish this, Straub suggested a comprehensive message tied to a call for a Constitutional Convention in Indiana to rewrite the 1851 constitution. Such a convention, Straub maintained, would be able to address such issues as "property taxes as a financial base for our schools; revenue raising at the local level; reapportionment; human rights; and reorganization of the executive branch of government, i.e., a cabinet style approach."[44]

The plans were to change, however. The January 31 announcement was too soon. All the logistics for the fly-around could not be accomplished in such a short period. The announcement was moved to Friday, February 4. Conrad scrapped Straub's idea to make a state constitutional convention the umbrella issue of the campaign. It was not something to propose in the announcement. Conrad had experience in constitution writing, and he knew the work that had to go into it. Before embarking on such a mission, the people had to be persuaded of the need. Conrad was convinced the voters were moved by more immediate and tangible issues. He decided to zero in on the bread and butter issue of the economy, and he pulled together the statistics to show that Indiana was lagging.

His announcement speech was only one and one-half pages, double-spaced. He was talking to Democrats—Democratic delegates, to be precise:

> Many in our party have been saying for months that the nomination is "locked up." This is strange coming from Democrats who have always taken great pride and derived great strength from the fact that our party [is based] on broad participation from all segments of society. We hear a great deal about citizen participation in the nominating process. The opportunity has now come to translate words and theory into direct and specific action.

> I direct this appeal to all and especially to those Democrats who have labored so long and so faithfully, who have rejoiced at our successes, who have grieved at our losses, but most importantly, who have remained faithful to the principles and traditions of the Democratic party. You, above all, have earned the right to be heard. You, above all, should demand exercise of that right. And you, above all, should be instrumental in the final decision.

> I do not believe that the working Democrats of Indiana are content to be told: run for delegate; spend your money; take time away from your work; come to Indianapolis in June; but don't worry about nominating anyone because that decision was made for you a year ago.

He then made mentioned his "late" entry into the race, and he took a new angle. The reason he waited was not because of the municipal elections. Instead: "I have waited to see how others who seek or propose to seek the Democratic nomination for Governor intend to confront the complex and contradictory issues of the 1970's. I have not heard thoughtful and considered proposals. I have heard only negative and outmoded attacks on the other party and other individuals. For these and other reasons, I am announcing today that I am a candidate for the Democratic nomination for Governor of Indiana."

He concluded by talking about his campaign: "I will campaign for that office in the only way I know. I will travel more miles, see more people, discuss the issues in greater depth, ask more questions, listen more intently than any other candidate for this office, be he Democrat or Republican."[45]

He repeated these words in eight cities in one day—from Indianapolis to Fort Wayne to South Bend to Gary to Terre Haute to Evansville to Clarksville and, finally, back "home" in Muncie. When reporters at each stop asked about the issues in the campaign, Conrad was ready:

"Indiana is not where it ought to be—and there are no signs it is going anywhere." Then, the litany began:

> Indiana is 50th among the states in the amount of money it contributes to the blind, alternating from month to month with Mississippi for this low spot on the totem pole.

Indiana is 50th in the amount of money it contributes to people who are mentally ill.

Indiana is 45th in the amount it spends on vocational rehabilitation, behind Guam, Puerto Rico and the Virgin Islands.

Indiana is 33rd in the amount spent on police protection.

Indiana is 40th in the way the legislature handles its legislative business.

Indiana is 45th in the per capita expenditure for education.

The list went on and on. He ranked Indiana on environmental protection. He criticized the lack of home rule in the cities. He swiped at Governor Whitcomb's program for worker safety: "Indiana makes a greater effort to insure the safety of animals than to provide for the safety of its working men and women."

"Indiana is in the middle of the pond and not going anywhere. Well, we're going to move to the river and drink some new water," Conrad declared.

His litany got him through announcement day, where the large crowds at each stop applauded every line. There was an estimated 750 people to hear his announcement in Clarksville, and even more showed at the Hotel Roberts in downtown Muncie. Mary Lou was at his side at every stop. The Conrad style and the Conrad organization were working.

For the rest of February and all of March, the Conrad political section stepped on the accelerator. Boxell had acquired a storefront near downtown Indianapolis, at 622 East Market Street, to serve as campaign headquarters. Boxell moved into a back office and took over the management of the campaign. Grauel, who remained on the state payroll, was there every lunch hour and every evening when he was not traveling. Lewis, Powell, Rooksby, Straub, and the other coordinators had desks at headquarters, but they were on the road nearly five days a week, checking out their counties and identifying delegates. Claudia Prosser joined the campaign staff and watched the Conrad children when Mary Lou was on the road. Volunteers in Marion County staffed the phones and prepared the mailings. And Conrad was on the road. By mid-May, he personally had visited more than seventy-five of the ninety-two counties—most of them at least twice—and the remarkable pace that he set in 1970 was exceeded.

The hectic schedules of the candidate and staff members no longer permitted time for lengthy memos on the political situation in the various sections of the state. Reports were now made verbally, although David Bochnowski, who had joined the campaign staff, kept meticulous records on the most important people: the likely delegates to the convention.

Party leaders who endorsed Conrad were listed in the second news-print brochure issued by the campaign. And it was apparent that Conrad had problems. Only ten mayors had endorsed him, and the largest city on the list was Muncie—only the seventh largest city in the state. Only ten of the ninety-two county chairmen and eight county vice-chairmen were on board. Of the thirteen city and county elected officials listed, eleven were from Delaware County and Muncie. The largest counties were holding back. Of the ten most populous counties, only Delaware and Elkhart were represented. There were no endorsements from Allen, Lake, Marion, St. Joseph, Tippecanoe, Vanderburgh, or Vigo. Madison County was repre-sented, but only because State Senator Tom Teague, from Anderson, was with Conrad—and state senators had no patronage with which to control delegates.[46]

With the leaders of the party organization in the large counties holding back, it was imperative that Conrad "delegate slates" would have to be filed in several of the large counties. The staff members would have to identify and recruit people to file for the office of "Delegate to the State Convention," and the word would have to go out to primary voters to elect the Conrad slate. In effect, this tactic was declaring war in the large coun-ties against the established party organization. If the county chairmen and mayors were not committed to him, Conrad was going to bypass them.

This was a revolutionary tactic in Indiana politics for a state convention nomination. Previous campaigns for the gubernatorial nomination zeroed in on the delegates. Candidates would host elaborate "delegate dinners" throughout the state where they and their advisors would "work the tables" and attempt to get commitments one on one. News releases were issued only to display campaign activity—hoping that the delegates would be impressed. In effect, the existing party organization was the "kingmaker," and any grassroots effort around the party leaders was guaranteed to invite organizational retribution. Candidates were expected to cater to the county chairmen and reach out directly only to the likely delegates. The traditional approach made sense because the county chair-men had one huge advantage in controlling their convention delegation: they could appoint any "vacancies." Under state law, if nobody filed for convention delegate, the county chairman had the power to appoint some-one to represent that delegate district. Obviously, when there was to be a contest for a nomination and the county chairman favored one candidate, he or she would appoint a delegate only if the person vowed to vote the chairman's preference. In this way, the organization, as Birch Bayh discov-ered in his 1970 attempt to oust St. Angelo, was built layer by layer. And, of course, the man at the apex of the pyramid was Gordon St. Angelo.

The Conrad campaign tracked St. Angelo. The same brochure that listed the early endorsements carried a headline: "State Chairman Comments on Governor's Race." The story read:

> State Chairman Gordon St. Angelo two weeks ago in New Albany told the news media that he would stay neutral in the Governor's race. Larry Conrad commends the State Chairman for his action. It insures a unified party behind the Democratic nominee for Governor.

But St. Angelo was not neutral. He was with Matthew Welsh.

To elect their delegates, not only did Conrad's organization have to identify supporters who would file for the office of delegate, but Conrad himself had to directly communicate with the Democratic primary voters to persuade them to vote for his slate. Conrad's campaign was the first modern convention nomination campaign that made a major thrust directly to the voters. And it was also to be the last, for in 1976 the nomination would be decided by all the Democratic voters in a direct primary.

Twenty-three billboards were ordered, primarily for Lake County. Mass mailings were programmed and television spots were planned and budgeted in all the television markets, except Chicago and Louisville.[47] Boxell and Conrad adopted a two-pronged approach. First, the message was that Conrad was the new, issue-oriented candidate for change in the party. Second, the campaign emphasized that Conrad was the one who could win in November. A late campaign brochure contained a quote attributed to Conrad:

> Candidates and political parties can no longer avoid, evade, or ignore the critical issues confronting our state. The people demand to know what candidates believe, what they propose to do and why. We cannot win by any other means. I know this, the people of Indiana know it, and the delegates to the Democratic State Convention had better know it now, or we will all find out the hard way in November.[48]

The Conrad campaign viewed issues as the road to winning. This philosophy was repugnant to most party organization leaders, who thought issues only got in the way of voters. It wasn't issues that mattered, it was patronage jobs.[49] If a patronage worker owed his job to the organization, he would vote the way the organization told him to vote. And most of the leaders and patronage workers remembered Matthew Welsh. He had provided the state patronage when he was governor—and Secretary of State Larry Conrad had only fifty-two jobs.

Mayor Pastrick, who was the emerging leader of Lake County Democrats, remembers the situation: "I wasn't with Larry in 1972. I talked with all the party people and the elected officials in Lake County and they all remembered Matt Welsh and what he had done for them. They liked Larry, but they thought they owed Matt."[50]

In many respects the Conrad campaign was the Hoosier version of the hundreds of campaigns being waged throughout the nation in that same year. They were campaigns that quickened the new generation of voters— that leading edge of baby boomers. Nationally, George McGovern pro- vided the expression. Issues did matter. The war mattered. The Equal Rights Amendment mattered. Civil rights mattered. The environment— and "Earth Day"—mattered. The most highly educated generation of Americans was paying close attention to issues because there was a stark realization, brought home by that one war that America was destined to lose: what government did made a difference in America's living rooms.

And getting government to change American policy on Vietnam was also changing American views of their own government. The great institu- tions of America, including the national government, were witnessing the erosion of that cultural undergirding that authorized them to decide fun- damental questions. Now it was clear that the answers to those questions could mean life or death in an increasingly unpopular faraway war. Au- thority was being drained away from the centralized institutions and into the hands of new groups and individuals.

This drainage of authority also was overtaking the most powerful democratic institutions America had created: political parties. In the sum- mer of 1972, in Miami, the McGovern campaign had enough votes on the floor of the Democratic National Convention to refuse to seat the Illinois delegation headed by Chicago mayor Richard J. Daley. In Daley's place, the McGovernites seated an insurgent delegation headed by William Singer, an amateur Democrat who served as alderman of a near north side ward in Chicago and who was to lose, resoundingly, to Mayor Daley in the next mayoral primary. Daley, the man perceived as "the Boss" of the Democratic party, was ignominiously handed his walking papers by the national convention.

Larry Conrad was not the William Singer of Indiana. He had too pro- found a respect—even admiration—for Indiana's strong traditions and unique practices. But Conrad did know that a new political day was dawning in Indiana, and the light was to illuminate dark corners of Indi- ana party politics and show people things that were not easy on their eyes. He innately saw the big picture. For Indiana to change—and to keep pace—Hoosiers would have to see themselves clearly and confront the problems "right down the gunsights."

The first issue Conrad addressed was one that would dominate Indiana politics for the next ten years: property taxes. Hoosiers had seen their property bills skyrocket in recent years, fueled primarily by the increasing costs of education. The baby-boom generation was "packed together like no other generation in history. Not only were more children enrolled than ever before, there was also a teacher shortage."[51] In Indiana, as in other states, school construction and the hiring boom lagged behind the population explosion. In the 1950s, the Indiana legislature required school districts to merge through a process called "school consolidation." But the local school districts had dragged their feet. Citizens in small, rural towns were outraged that they would lose their local high school and their local basketball team. The delays associated with school consolidation worsened the problem of school finance, because the demand for new schools was pent up. By the late 1960s, as more and more districts consolidated, new high schools finally were built on the Indiana landscape—many in cornfields several miles from the small towns. And the new buildings and the new teachers required to staff them meant higher property taxes.

"Hoosier property tax payments have increased by over 100 percent in the last ten years," Conrad explained in his speeches and brochures. "Between this tax and growing inflation, people can no longer afford to own and improve their family homes. Rented homes are deteriorating, farmers are being forced to sell their land, and business is encouraged to leave Indiana."

The other candidates running for governor, in both parties, had to acknowledge the issue of property taxes. But they were vague. They only talked about controlling such taxes. Matt Welsh, trying to avoid the epithet of "high tax Welsh" because of his support of the sales tax back in 1963, spoke only in generalities about the need for property tax reform. Welsh did not even offer suggestions to the State Democratic Platform Committee, which was charged with drafting a plank on state taxes.

The candidates for the Republican gubernatorial nomination were deeply divided on the tax issue. The Speaker of the House, Otis R. Bowen, who had announced for the Republican nomination in November of 1971, was the most specific of the Republicans. He had reason to be. He had supported a bill in the 1971 legislature to place controls on property taxes and raise other tax rates to provide additional revenue. Governor Edgar Whitcomb vehemently opposed the bill, which failed in the waning days of the session. But by the spring of 1972 even Bowen had backed off the specifics of a "tax re-structuring," saying only that "visible and lasting" property tax relief had to be forthcoming and that additional revenue could be secured through increases in either the sales tax or the income tax."[52]

The tax issue was rapidly becoming the symbol of the factionalism in the Republican party. By early June, Bowen's four opponents for the nomination were all taking shots at Bowen and his tax stand. But most of these candidates, including Owen County Circuit Court Judge William Sharp, had no tax program of their own. They merely pledged, as did GOP gubernatorial candidate Edgar Whitcomb in 1968, not to raise taxes.

Among the candidates in both parties, Larry Conrad was different. He not only described the problem, he had a solution: "Indiana needs a broad-based, graduated, personal income tax now. One that taxes people according to their ability to pay, not because they own a home or want to improve their land."

For many Hoosiers, a graduated income tax was political heresy. There was palpable resentment in Indiana toward the federal graduated income tax. The 1851 Indiana constitution did not authorize an income tax, and when the voters in 1932 finally authorized the General Assembly "to levy and collect a tax upon income, from whatever source derived, as such rates, in such manner, and with such exemptions as may be prescribed by law," there were many legal challenges to the amendment. It was not until after World War II, in 1948, that these legal challenges were finally resolved, and the amendment stood.[53]

In his speeches, Conrad explained his tax stand both in theory and in detail. He pointed out that the property tax was imposed in the last century "to pay for improvements that would increase the value of land. Things like roads and streets and drainage pipes. But now we pay for schools, and these schools are miles away from homeowners. These schools do not directly add to the value of land. School bills should be borne by all the people, through a graduated income tax, based on the ability to pay."

Several groups, particularly business groups, as expected, opposed the income tax. The Indiana State Chamber of Commerce had several "tax experts" review Conrad's tax program and they produced a "blistering critique" that made "previous critiques look mild."[54]

But one group applauded Conrad's gutsy stand—organized labor. Labor leaders had tangled in public with recent Democratic governors. The United Auto Workers (UAW), in particular, had led the fight against Welsh's sales tax proposal in 1963. Dallas Sells, the popular president of Region 3 of the UAW, once contended that his biggest disappointment in his long service to the UAW was losing the fight to keep the sales tax out of Indiana. Sells knew the sales tax would hit poorer people the hardest, even with some exemptions provided. He favored a graduated income tax, where the amount of a person's salary would determine his or her tax bracket. And that's what Conrad supported, without reservation.

Conrad's days with Senator Bayh had placed him on solid personal terms with many labor leaders, particularly those from the UAW. He had carefully nurtured those contacts and took every opportunity to build his own support among UAW members. Now, in his run for governor, local labor leaders began endorsing him. They remembered Welsh's sales tax. Now there was a new force in Democratic gubernatorial politics who agreed with them on taxes. His name was Larry Conrad.

In hearings before the State Democratic Platform Committee on taxation, which was chaired by State Representative Michael K. Phillips of Boonville, St. Angelo's former administrative assistant, Conrad's aides presented detailed programs for a graduated hike in income taxes and a control of property taxes. Phillips, in attempting to sidestep the issue, said the party would likely be more interested in "the philosophy of tax reform" than in any details of a tax package.[55] But the taxation plank was not as "philosophical" as Phillips hoped. As passed by the committee, it contained three Conrad-like statements:

1. Reduction of property taxes through statewide tax increases;

2. Increases in statewide taxes based on "ability to pay";

3. State financing of a "substantial" part of public school costs.[56]

Clearly, in the run-up to the state conventions, the only two gubernatorial candidates discussing the major issue of the day—state taxes—were Conrad and Bowen. Their nominations would assure that the November election would be defined by a debate over the future taxing and spending plans of state government. Such a debate, however, was not to happen in Indiana in 1972.

Conrad did not confine himself to the tax issue. He saw a growing concern about crime in Indiana. He pledged to spend more on state and local police "training and compensation." He stressed rehabilitation of criminals by criticizing the Indiana Department of Corrections, claiming that "Indiana's prisons do not correct, they only serve to corrupt." He pledged a vocational education program in the prisons and promised to upgrade prison facilities: "If we do not clean up our prisons, the social costs of crime will mount and society will continue to squander its precious human resources."

He tied drugs to the rising crime rate, pointing out that "drugs are the greatest single cause of violent crime in our cities." But he saw that the spirit of the law was to reform, calling out "to treat and cure those sickened and harmed by drug addiction and abuse," by providing for a "full-time, fully funded state agency to control this epidemic problem."

He talked about Indiana's cities being under siege and "forgotten by state government." He called for a new Department of Community Affairs which would "represent the long forgotten case of our cities" and help attract federal assistance to Indiana's urban areas, where three out of five Hoosiers lived.

He saw issues intertwined. Primary and secondary education were connected to civil rights and they, in turn, were tied to economic impoverishment. He pointed out that "when people in poor, rural areas or within our center cities cannot find the same quality education that is available to students in wealthy districts, all society suffers."

Conrad painted the big picture. He insisted that his news releases and speech drafts connect all the lines of the picture. Government was a system in which all the issues and all the problems were interrelated. What we did in education affected what we did in economic development. What we did in our cities had a direct impact on our rural areas. What we did with property taxes was going to affect our schools—and our income taxes. Like any system—even a sewer system, or a stereo system—all the parts of the political system were interconnected. A problem was not an isolated element to be solved with a one-shot program. What happened in Fort Wayne affected Evansville, and what happened in Lafayette would ripple clear to Rising Sun.

His incessant harping on the issues caused consternation in Welsh's campaign. But still Welsh refused to be specific. In a radio interview in New Castle in early June, Welsh said he "was confident property tax relief will be the paramount issue of the 1973 session" and that he favored "a tax restructuring." But he provided no details.[57] When Welsh responded to reporters' questions in such vague generalities, Conrad shot back: "[The people of our state] will not tolerate government by deal or campaigns of evasion. In 1972 Democrats will not be satisfied with candidates who have the answers to everything and the solutions to nothing."[58]

Conrad did not attack Welsh personally. In fact, he never mentioned his name. The former governor was not personally to blame. It was the system that had grown old and, like an octogenarian, was suffering from hardening of the arteries. Of course, giving that impression was unavoidable: Welsh was fifty-nine years old; Conrad was thirty-seven. Conrad remarked to delegates from Posey County, "This election has to be a break with the past. It's got to be a new spirit. I'd like to have Indiana the kind of state that would have others looking to us for a change." To Muncie Democrats he repeated the theme: "[The people] want someone who has confidence in himself and who is bold enough to strike out at what he wants. They do not want someone who is looking for political security."[59]

One man put in the middle of the Conrad-Welsh race was U.S. Senator Birch Bayh. Bayh was on excellent terms with Welsh. He had supported Welsh in 1960, and he knew that his ascension to the U.S. Senate in 1962 was in large part attributable to Welsh's endorsement. On the other hand, Conrad had been his campaign manager and his top aide in the U.S. Senate. Bayh waited and waited. But Bayh's staff would not let the pressure recede. They knew Larry well. They had worked with him and for him. Some adored him. They wanted, and expected, Bayh to endorse Conrad.

Bayh thought the way out was to have Conrad run for lieutenant governor. He saw the advantage to both Welsh and Conrad of such a ticket. If the ticket won, Conrad would be Welsh's successor. If the ticket lost, Conrad would still be the favorite for the nomination in 1976. But Conrad had rejected the option. Bayh was trapped.

He finally decided to do nothing. In a meeting with Conrad, Boxell, and Alan Rachels in Bayh's office in the federal building in Indianapolis, Bayh indicated that if he were pushed, he would be with Welsh, but he intended to stay out of the fight. Conrad did not respond. Rachels was greatly relieved. He had already pledged his support to Welsh.[60]

"I was concerned Larry would alienate a lot of Welsh supporters, and I was concerned about Larry's future," Bayh contends. "I told him he should bide his time and not alienate the old-timers. We didn't need a contest. The timing was wrong."

That candid conversation soured relations between Bayh and Conrad for some time. "We had a very candid relationship, and the fact that I dared to speak out and tell Larry what I thought documents that. But my assessment shook our relationship for a little while," Bayh admits.[61]

Bayh was able to avoid an endorsement of Welsh prior to the convention. But Conrad was on his own. He was not going to get any help from his old boss.

Conrad's convention delegate slates enjoyed only mixed success on primary election day, May 2. Boxell and the coordinators were very successful in recruiting candidates for the 2,152 delegate positions, particularly in the larger counties such as Marion, Vanderburgh, and Vigo. But in Marion County, the Conrad slate was crushed. In the westside 19th Ward in Indianapolis, the regular organization, which was pledged to Welsh, filed eight candidates. Conrad's campaign filed another eight people, and three other unpledged delegates entered the race. The regular organization slate referred to the Conrad Crazies as "the Christamore Bunch" because many of them lived in the Christamore housing settlement. All eight Conrad delegates were defeated.

In the 20th Ward, on the near north side, only four Conrad delegates won out of eleven slots. In the suburban areas of Marion County—in Perry and Warren townships—the Conrad slate won only six of thirty-two delegates. The Marion County drubbing was so extensive that Boxell took action to challenge the election of delegates pledged to Welsh. Contending that the regular organization's slate of delegates violated both the new reform rules of the national Democratic party and Indiana law, he charged that candidates for delegate to the state convention "had to sign a pledge to support Welsh as a condition of being slated." This challenge was presented to the State Central Committee. The new Marion County chairman, William M. (Bill) Schreiber, disavowed any knowledge of such tactics and contended that the results were mixed as to which slate won.[62]

The only "dirty trick" in the preconvention Conrad-Welsh battle occurred in the second week in June when state convention delegates received a mailing signed by a Kokomo attorney who was largely unknown in the Democratic party. His letter included copies of articles from a Dayton, Ohio, newspaper and contained unflattering references to Welsh that accused him of being involved, years ago, in a securities scandal. Conrad immediately disavowed any connection with the mailing, saying "that neither I nor anyone associated with me had any knowledge of this. I do not condone it and I have not and will not at any time question the integrity of Matt Welsh." Conrad said he understood this to be "a bitter personal dispute . . . which is totally and absolutely removed from this campaign."[63] Nothing more was said.

By late May and early June it was clear that Welsh had the lead in delegates. More than forty mayors had endorsed him. On Friday, June 9, East Chicago mayor Robert E. Pastrick made it official: he was for Welsh. From the newly elected chairman of Lake County, the endorsement was a hammer blow that threatened wholesale movement of the 217 Lake County delegates to Welsh. Boxell responded that "we did not expect to win the battle of endorsements" and that Pastrick's move "will have some effect, but not much." But Boxell had to admit that if the endorsement were to move the Lake County delegates to Welsh, "then the whole tenor of our campaign has been wrong. Conrad has been campaigning on the basis the delegates will make up their own minds."[64] Just a week before the convention was to open, the 3rd district Democratic organization provided written pledges of support for Welsh.[65] It appeared the whole northern tier was collapsing around Conrad.

Conrad tried another tactic. He released his financial statements and called on Welsh to do the same. Conrad had first released his finances during the 1970 campaign for secretary of state. Now, nearly two years later, his net worth had grown by about $3,000, to $32,750. He still was paying on his home mortgage and stated that his annual salary of $23,500 as secretary of state was his sole income. He challenged Matt Welsh to release his financial statements, but the Welsh campaign put it off, saying Welsh "has not decided whether to make such a personal disclosure."[66] Welsh never did decide.

The Welsh campaign was confident, but his staff continued to work. Their "run-down sheets" of delegates in seven counties in East Central Indiana showed him with a commanding 4 to 1 lead. The only soft spot was Wayne County where the mayor of Richmond, Byron Klute, was a Conrad supporter, and Klute expected eight or nine of the eleven Wayne County votes to hold for Conrad.[67]

In the last ten days before the convention, the Conrad headquarters on East Market Street was once again controlled chaos. A new delegate mailing was sent each day. Nichols, the media coordinator, arranged to have several hundred 45-rpm records made. They were entitled "Larry Conrad on the Issues," and they were mailed to all uncommitted delegates. In the final mailing to delegates, Conrad was pleading for the delegates to support him. His brochure stated: "BEHIND THE CURTAINS OF THE VOT-ING MACHINE, YOU, AND YOU ALONE, ARE THE BOSS." On the back, in blue letters on white background, were the words:

> After 12 centuries on this planet still only half the people have the right to vote. The right to determine one's political destiny is the wellspring from which all rights emanate.
>
> It is that right, and the historic tradition that comes with it, which will be presented to you on June 20 at the Democratic State Convention, when you walk into the voting machine, pull the red lever that faces you and face the voting machine alone.
>
> At that moment, you, and you alone, are the boss.
>
> It is there that you finally use your God given faculties to make the determination that is so necessary to the workings of the Democratic process.
>
> Larry Conrad will stake his political life on his belief that representatives elected by the people in the true Democratic fashion will exercise that right, without intimidation, fear, or threats and with the responsibility of a one hundred and eighty year tradition.
>
> Given those circumstances, he's prepared for the consequences in the words of the scriptures to let the yea's be yea's and the nay's be nay's.[68]

While the mailings poured out of headquarters, Conrad was on the road, personally calling on delegates. On one occasion he arrived before daybreak at a delegate's home. He rested in the car until the houselights went on. Then he jumped out, knocked on the front door, greeted the just-awakened delegate, and asked him if he could cook breakfast. By noon Conrad was back in headquarters where the telephone was "like a part of his body, a life-sustaining link to those voices and thoughts of those delegates out there. . . ."[69]

Conrad's calling list was derived from a three-ring binder where the names, addresses, and phone numbers of each of the 2,152 convention delegates were contained on sheets, filed by county. Similar to Welsh's "run-down sheets," this binder contained the latest information on each delegate, whether he or she was with Conrad or Welsh or still undecided. "This is the doomsday book," Conrad told a reporter.[70] Other campaign staffers referred to it as the "D-Day Book" or the "Delegate Bible."[71]

The Conrad campaign received a very minor boost on Saturday, June 17, two days before the convention, when Abe Dilbeck, a businessman from Haubstadt in Gibson County, endorsed Conrad. He had announced for the Democratic gubernatorial nomination the previous December and had made a few campaign appearances. But Dilbeck was politically powerless; he had no delegate support.

There was immense pressure building on the Democratic State Central Committee. Also at stake in the state convention were seventy-six Democratic National Convention delegates. Hubert Humphrey, Edmund Muskie, and Mrs. George Wallace were all scheduled to appear as part of a united effort to deny George McGovern any Indiana delegates. Humphrey had won the Indiana primary in May. He was assured of 55 delegates on the first ballot, with Wallace receiving the other 21. McGovern had not been on the May ballot in Indiana. He was fighting for delegates who would provide second-ballot support if McGovern lacked a majority on the first ballot.[72]

With national media attention assured, St. Angelo promised that the convention was to be tightly controlled. On Monday, June 19, the delegates arrived for the first political convention to be held in the new convention center in downtown Indianapolis.[73]

That evening the district caucuses met and selected members for three key convention committees: rules, resolutions, and credentials. The Conrad campaign conceded the committee positions and Welsh supporters won virtually every one. Welsh's supporters proclaimed that Conrad's failure to mount challenges for the committee assignments meant he had virtually conceded the gubernatorial nomination. The Conrad campaign, however, responded by saying that the Democratic State Central Committee already "had guaranteed Welsh forces control" of the committees.[74]

Both camps were predicting victory. J. Manfred Core, who was again advising Welsh, estimated Welsh's strength at 1,450 delegates, declaring that "it might even go higher." Boxell predicted that Conrad would win by between 200 and 300 votes. "The Conrad people are beginning to emerge and show their colors. We are going to have an electrifying finish. I feel it, Larry feels it, and so do his people," Boxell declared. Then he ducked: "If I am wrong, it won't be the first time."[75]

At the convention center, St. Angelo's iron fist was very much in evidence from the beginning. Since 1970 he had known how to keep control of a state convention. He ordered each district chairman not to allow his or her caucus to endorse any candidate. Contestants for the nominations were not permitted to speak to the caucuses—an unprecedented prohibition that the Conrad supporters viewed as a direct slap in the face, knowing that Conrad's speaking abilities far surpassed Welsh's. St. Angelo was keeping the delegates corralled; they were not going to be stampeded by Larry's oratory.

Everywhere they turned the Conrad supporters ran into St. Angelo's iron fist. Welsh's campaign was allowed to operate out of a room on the first level, close to the convention hall. Conrad's room was upstairs, away from the delegate traffic. There were only four telephone hookups on the convention floor, and St. Angelo allotted two for Welsh and two for the State Central Committee; Conrad was not going to be able to communicate from the floor. When a radio reporter was tipped off about the telephone hookups, he mentioned it on the air. St. Angelo finally backed down and provided telephone jacks for the Conrad campaign staff.[76]

St. Angelo called the convention to order at 10 A.M. on Tuesday, June 20. Security was tight, with about sixty police officers positioned around the hall. There were even four fully armed police officers from Fort Wayne standing next to the Allen County delegation. When Lewis asked a state committee staff member why armed police officers were on the convention floor, he was ignored. Lewis saw their presence as a visual display of intimidation.[77]

About two weeks before the convention, St. Angelo had summoned the Conrad and Welsh advisors to a meeting to explain convention procedures. David Bochnowski, Stu Grauel, Terry Straub, and Greg Schenkel, who had just joined the campaign staff from the secretary of state's office, listened to St. Angelo explaining that everything was going to be kept on schedule and run in a businesslike fashion. All floor demonstrations were to be tightly controlled and limited to only a couple of minutes. "Everything was to be fair and controlled," Schenkel remembers him saying.[78]

Conrad was to be nominated first, then Welsh. East Chicago City Judge Frank Callahan was selected to give Conrad's nominating speech. When he took the podium and began speaking, the public address system faded and most of the delegates could not hear his remarks. When he finished, there was a brief floor demonstration, lasting about three minutes, with Conrad supporters standing and waving signs. When South Bend mayor Jerry Miller took the podium to nominate Welsh, the microphone had been miraculously repaired, and his booming voice filled the hall. As he concluded by nominating "the next governor of Indiana," all the lights went out. In the hushed darkness of that huge hall, slide projectors suddenly displayed pictures of Matt Welsh on the side walls. Then some side doors flew open and the Ben Davis High School Marching Band entered the arena playing "Happy Days Are Here Again."

Conrad was in the middle of a television interview on the convention floor when the lights were cut. That was the end of the interview. As the lights slowly came up, the Welsh supporters jumped from their seats and followed the band through the room, cheering and waving placards. There was no attempt to gavel the demonstration to order. For nearly ten minutes the Welsh supporters had command of the Democratic State Convention. When asked about the Welsh demonstration over twenty years later, St. Angelo said: "Concerning the Ben Davis Marching Band for Matt, if the band was there, it was a helluva good idea."[79]

After all the speeches and the talk and the demonstrations, the delegates lined up at the voting machines to cast their vote for the gubernatorial nomination. Of the 2,152 possible delegates, only 13 failed to show. When the machines were closed and the tallies recorded, Matthew Welsh was the clear winner: 1,318 to 821.

With the rest of the state ticket nominated, Welsh and Conrad entered the convention hall, arm in arm, waving to the raucous crowd. Conrad took the microphone first. He parodied a then-popular television wristwatch commercial when he said: "I found out that I can take a licking and keep on ticking." Mary Lou was on the platform next to him when he declared that the two of them would work to "support this fine state ticket." He predicted a Democratic victory in the fall. Then he introduced Matt Welsh.[80]

Conrad's remarks drew praise from all quarters. Here was a man who had gone after the nomination as though, in his phrase, he was "killing snakes," and when he lost he pledged to fight on for the winner.

One of the Conrad delegates on the floor that day was John Livengood, an easy-going and unassuming man whose inner compass is guided by some magnetic force that seems as natural and as unobtrusive as the North Pole. Nobody can dislike John Livengood, but many people made the mistake of underestimating him. He had just turned twenty-five, and hearing Conrad's concession speech was a defining moment in his life.

Born and raised in Richmond, Indiana, Livengood had been around local politics all his life. His father, a lawyer, firmly believed in the principles of the Democratic party, and John inherited a deep-seated commitment to that organization. He had taken off during his senior year at Wabash College to be a VISTA volunteer, which delayed his graduation until 1971, after which he returned to Richmond to prepare for a career in politics and public service. While working part-time at a local school-bus manufacturing plant, Livengood filed for the nomination for Wayne County treasurer. His father also talked him into running for delegate to the State Convention, as a candidate pledged to Larry A. Conrad. "I beat a veteran Democrat who had been the superintendent of the state highway garage and he was pledged to Matt Welsh," Livengood recalls.[81]

That concession speech in 1972 totally won Livengood over: "What sealed my commitment to Larry was how he handled his defeat. He took the podium right away and pledged his support to the party. He had a strong belief in the party, the party as an institution."[82]

Livengood lost the Wayne County treasurer's race that November, but six months later, in May 1973, he received a call from Conrad. Conrad had an opening on his staff for a speechwriter, and he remembered the loyal support John and his father had given him. John had indicated he would like to work in the secretary of state's office, and Conrad offered him the job. He accepted, and stayed on the secretary of state's staff until Conrad left office in 1978.

Nobody on that convention floor in 1972 could have suspected that the next time Indiana would elect a Democratic governor, the chairman of the Democratic State Central Committee—the leader of the party in Indiana—would be John Livengood. No chairman since J. Manfred Core could boast of such an achievement.[83]

In the post-convention stories, the political reporter for the *Indianapolis Star* commented that "Conrad was credited with putting on a fine campaign and his 821-vote total was more than some veteran observers had foreseen for him in preconvention estimates."[84] But a look at the voting patterns reveals that Conrad's 38.38 percent of the total vote was confined to his home base. He carried only two of the eleven congressional districts: his home district, the 10th, and the adjacent 5th district. He was clobbered in northern Indiana, with the 3rd district (LaPorte, St. Joseph, and Elkhart counties) giving him only 28.85 percent. Surprisingly, however, the 1st district, totally within Lake County, voted 45.58 percent for Conrad in spite of Pastrick's endorsement of Welsh. But Marion County, the 11th district, buried him. Conrad received only 25.42 percent of the votes from Marion County.

Following his acceptance speech, Matt Welsh walked up to the second floor and entered Conrad's convention center headquarters, where he shook hands with Conrad's staff members and, in a subdued manner, asked for their support and congratulated them on the campaign.

Conrad's workers were still in shock. They listened politely. But underneath there was a seething resentment created by the way the convention had been manipulated. To a person, the Conrad workers thought St. Angelo had lied. "We thought we had a shot, but we never really did," says Greg Schenkel. "We underestimated how good and strong the other side was—and we were young enough and dumb enough to believe some of the things they told us."[85]

Terry Straub agrees. "I learned a lot from that convention," he says. "The biggest thing I learned was don't ever take anything at face value, and expect the worst."[86]

Claudia Prosser puts it differently: "The forces of evil came flat-up against the forces of good."[87] And in the minds of the Conrad supporters, evil won.

The young Conrad workers were devastated. "My heart just shut down," Vicki Weger says with sadness. "When I left the convention center I spotted Bill Brighton's car. He was the mayor of my hometown of Terre Haute and was also on St. Angelo's payroll. I had recruited delegates from Vigo County and most of them won. In fact, we carried Vigo County by one vote. But Brighton was St. Angelo's person on the credentials committee and he was sending notes to the watchers, written on the back of matchbooks and napkins, saying 'Let this person vote in your delegation.' We couldn't stop that. Well, when I saw his car in the parking lot, I put a note on it: 'Wait until next time.'"[88]

A Biography

While the weary Democrats wandered home that night, Matthew E. Welsh conducted a lengthy news conference in which he proclaimed he would not announce any "precise" tax proposals during the general election campaign, explaining that he wanted to see the composition of the next legislature before developing a program. He confessed that he had not read the Democratic platform that had been adopted by the convention, saying he had been too busy "talking to the delegates." He claimed he would win in November by using the same tactic he used in 1960: "campaigning, campaigning, campaigning."[89]

There were four others nominated for the state ticket. Richard Bodine was the candidate for lieutenant governor; Theodore D. (Ted) Wilson—the first African American ever nominated by either of the two parties—was running for attorney general; John Loughlin was again the nominee for superintendent of public instruction; and Jeanne Trixler, with Conrad's support, was the nominee for reporter of Supreme and Appellate Courts.

The custodians in the downtown convention center only had one day to clean up, because there was to be another political brawl that week in that hall; the Republicans were coming to town.

The 1972 Republican state convention was the line of demarcation for the Hoosier GOP. The battle for the gubernatorial nomination split the Republicans into four camps, with three of the forces agreed upon only one thing: stop Otis R. Bowen.

Governor Whitcomb had made public his disagreement with Bowen, particularly over the tax issue. The governor thought he had struck an alliance with L. Keith Bulen, the "boss" of the Marion County GOP. They endorsed Owen County Circuit Court Judge William T. Sharp, who had previously served as a municipal judge in Marion County. Sharp announced for governor only twenty days before the start of the convention. The leader of the Republicans in the State Senate, Phillip E. Gutman from Fort Wayne, also was in the race, along with the former chairman of the Public Service Commission, W. W. Hill, Jr., of Indianapolis—who had publicly broken with Governor Whitcomb.

Bowen was clearly the front-runner. He had lost the Republican nomination to Whitcomb in the 1968 convention and had patiently pursued the 1972 nomination from his podium as Speaker of the House. The fractious GOP could not put the program together to derail Bowen, but it was not for lack of trying. A few days before the state convention, Governor Whitcomb announced that it would be "very difficult" for him to support Bowen, and sent signals he preferred Judge Sharp. When the Republican delegates met in their district caucuses on the evening of June 22, the 11th district caucus was presided over by L. Keith Bulen. He had Indianapolis mayor Richard Lugar deliver the word to the delegates that they were expected to support Sharp.[90]

This last-ditch effort was to fall far short. Sharp had not laid the groundwork that Bowen had, and once again Vanderburgh County was going to be the key. According to one of Bowen's men, Lieutenant Governor Richard E. Folz—who was from Evansville and had won a place on the 1968 ticket with the argument that geographical balance was important—played a key role. Now, four years later, Folz had decided to leave politics and had broken with Whitcomb. But before he left, Folz was going to protect the interests of Evansville and the 8th district. In overtures to Bowen, he agreed to swing the 8th district votes to the Speaker in exchange for another lieutenant governor nomination from Vanderburgh County. He wanted State Senator Robert D. Orr on the ticket with Bowen. When Bowen agreed to the deal there was nothing Bulen and Whitcomb could do to stop a first-ballot victory for the physician from Bremen.[91]

Bulen, however, sees that convention differently: "Folz was a blip in that convention. Bowen and his men did not understand our organization. My coalition was Marion, Allen, and Vanderburgh counties, and I dealt with Don Cox and Mayor Russell Lloyd in Vanderburgh." Bulen contends he asked Bowen how many votes he needed out of Marion County. "I gave Bowen 50 delegates out of Marion County, exactly what he said he needed. In order to get the 50 delegates to vote for Bowen I gave out straws and numbers and picked them. I don't think Bowen ever understood what was happening in that convention, nor, at the time, did Orr."[92]

Bulen recognized that Whitcomb had to be placated. "Governor Whitcomb and Bowen did not get along and I knew it would not take much for Whitcomb to cut off our 2 percent money and move on the license branches. If that happened, the party wouldn't have any money in the fall. We couldn't afford to alienate the governor. I could still talk to him and keep him on the line. Bowen never understood that. Bowen considered it an affront that I did not deliver more votes [from Marion County]. He thought he knew everybody at the convention. He viewed me as stopping him. He thought he knew everybody in town, but he didn't know everybody in the Marion County party just because he had been in the legislature for years."[93]

When the first ballot votes were counted, Bowen won easily, receiving 1,243 votes to 364 for Sharp, 354 for Gutman, and 108 for Hill. It took three ballots to deliver Robert Orr, however. State Representative John C. Hart of Indianapolis had entered the race for lieutenant governor, purportedly with Bowen's backing, but when the Bowen-Orr deal was arranged, Hart had to be elbowed aside.

With the two state tickets determined, the political advisors and party regulars began planning the November campaign. In late June it appeared that the Democratic ticket was well positioned. A Republican poll in January revealed that Welsh had a 31-point lead over Bowen, largely on the basis of name recognition.[94] Moreover, the state Democratic party appeared to be more united than the Republicans.[95]

Larry Conrad kept his word to the convention; he campaigned for the Democratic ticket whenever he was called upon to do so. Moreover, he and Boxell made available whatever information they had. A week after the convention, Boxell wrote a memo to "Governor Welsh" in which he discussed the talents of the various Conrad staff members and volunteers for the purpose of suggesting how they could be of use in Welsh's campaign.

He described Terry Straub as a person who will "argue a point, but once a decision is reached will work with effectiveness to implement the decision," and pointed out that he "has an excellent relationship with the McGovern forces." Rooksby "did very well in [his] area of responsibility" and was a "very good day-to-day 'nuts and bolts' political operative." He said that Jeff Lewis "needs occasional prodding," but did "extremely well in Allen County despite the obvious obstacles." Stuart Grauel was an "excellent organizer" who "raised a surprisingly large amount of money." He wrote that David Bochnowski was "excellent in organizing and implementing specific projects," noting that he was in charge of convention arrangements and "everything was detailed in writing to an infinite degree and implemented exactly according to schedule." Noting that Bochnowski was "not a political strategist or tactician," he would nonetheless be "invaluable in organizing a series of fundraising affairs, scheduling, etc." John Nichols was "the best time-buyer I have ever been associated with." Boxell then listed a dozen names of individuals throughout the state who "worked hard and produced with a minimum amount of friction." He suggested that they could play a role in Welsh's field organization.

Boxell revealed that "we raised hardly any money through the traditional sources," and provided Welsh with a list of six men who "should be helpful now since all campaigns are constantly seeking new sources of financing."

Finally, Boxell provided his own suggestions for Welsh's campaign:

> We are all aware that 1972 presents problems similar to or perhaps in excess of 1960 and 1968. However, a McGovern candidacy does not present a totally bleak prospect if rational McGovern people are integrated into the campaign. Your campaign has some built-in advantages which I am certain you have considered. For example: identity is not a problem and thousands of dollars which might be spent to identify the candidate could possibly be used to finance a massive registration effort. I mention this because I believe that the best chance of winning this election lies with the basics of good political organization: polling, registration and get out the vote.[96]

For Conrad, the summer and fall schedule was almost relaxed compared to the convention campaign. For the first time since the summer of 1967, Larry and Mary Lou could look forward to spending time at home with the children and with members of their "extended family." Virtually every weekend when Larry was not on the road campaigning for the ticket, there was a party at their home on North Meridian Street. Larry perfected a special recipe for fruit-juice drinks which he dubbed "Bahama Mamas." The young staffers and friends would drop by to eat, drink, tell stories, and sing, while Mary Lou played the piano. Jeff Lewis and David Letterman developed a comedy routine, with Jeff as the "straight man," letting Letterman get the laughs. Stu and Diane Grauel were always there. Jane Pauley, who was working as St. Angelo's secretary at the State Central Committee, frequently came by the house. She was soon to announce that a local television station had offered her an on-camera job. It was her first step on the way to New York and the "Today Show."

When the Democrats met in Miami on July 10 to nominate George McGovern, Conrad brought the television sets out into the back yard where, every night, all week long, the party would continue. Everybody cheered and jeered the speeches.

On Sunday, July 22, Larry and Mary Lou hosted the only event of the year to show appreciation to his supporters and volunteers, the first annual "Conrad Family Picnic," at a farm outside Zionsville. A statewide mailing was sent and on a Sunday afternoon over 400 people joined the Conrads for hot dogs, hamburgers, and merriment.[97]

But the good times could not relieve the personal emptiness many felt. Slowly but surely staff members made plans to leave the office and pursue careers elsewhere. The magical mystery tour was over.

Jeff Lewis announced his resignation. He was returning to Muncie to go into business. Straub announced he was leaving, and Rooksby began looking. Vicki Weger was tired of the everyday commute from Terre Haute and decided she would quit at the end of the year. The bright young staff members had lost their innocence on that convention floor on June 20.

They could detect it even in Conrad. One summer day in July, Larry invited several staff members to come with him to the tavern across the street from the Statehouse where he would buy sandwiches and soft drinks. They would then sit on the Statehouse lawn in the shade of a buckeye tree and have a picnic lunch. "None of us had been talking about the loss," Weger recalls, "and when we all sat down in the shade and unwrapped our sandwiches, a security guard walked over and told us we had to move—we couldn't sit on the grass. We started packing up and as we walked up the steps to the office Larry said: 'When you're down they really kick you.'"[98]

Democrats everywhere that year were getting kicked. The McGovern campaign went into a tailspin, beginning with the Miami convention. It crash-landed when Thomas Eagleton was removed from the ticket on August 1. McGovern attempted to get airborne again with a series of policy proposals which promised to spend, spend, spend. McGovern's national campaign headquarters in Washington "dripped gossip and steamed with dissent, like a boiler leaking at every joint."[99] Everywhere, state and local Democratic nominees were running away from the wreckage of the national ticket. When the Welsh campaign called on Conrad to speak throughout the state, Conrad quickly discovered that he was the only person defending George McGovern.

The Indiana polls showed the free-fall of the Democratic ticket and the surge for the Republicans. In July, a Republican poll showed Welsh at 43 percent; Bowen had 34. The Republican campaign began harping on Welsh to either endorse or repudiate McGovern. He did neither. By October, the Bowen ticket was ahead by one point: 44 to 43 percent. The Republican poll showed Nixon at 65 percent, with 26 percent for McGovern. Welsh knew he was in trouble, but he did not know what to do. He could not overcome that huge margin.[100]

The Bowen campaigners knew they were gaining fast. Bulen then devised the knockout punch. He remembers it well: "The last five days is what I called the 'crisscross.' We formed eight different teams of candidates, from the state ticket down to state legislative candidates. We had nearly 100 advance men for the teams. We rented planes and flew them all over the state, preaching the message against Welsh. When we started it, the Welsh campaign would try to respond to the first charge, then there would be another charge coming from another section of the state, then a third charge. We just hit him with a deluge. We had so many people moving around that we were able to drive out five or ten miles from the media city and walk in on a low watt radio station with local candidates for live interviews. I think the Welsh campaign just quit . . . we overwhelmed them."[101]

Welsh's promise to win the race by "campaigning, campaigning, campaigning" could not be kept.

One of the issues the Republicans were using was taxes. It was the issue Welsh refused to discuss except in generalities. Reminding Hoosiers that Welsh had imposed the sales tax without any commensurate tax relief, Bowen continued to harp on a "tax restructuring" that would provide "visible and lasting" property tax relief. For the first time, the October poll showed that Welsh was starting to lose the tax argument, with 23 percent of Hoosiers viewing him negatively on taxes, while 22 percent viewed him favorably. In a post-election poll, the two reasons Hoosiers cited most frequently for voting for Bowen were a new tax structure (14%) and property tax relief (10%).[102]

On November 7, 1972, Nixon carried Indiana nearly two to one over McGovern. That was enough for Otis R. Bowen, M.D. He beat Welsh by 303,000. The entire Republican state ticket was elected.

The Democratic debacle was accompanied by a fundamental change in Indiana election rules. The voters also approved the constitutional amendment permitting the governor to succeed himself—to serve "eight years in any period of twelve years." Otis R. Bowen was now in a position to run in 1976 for reelection—and serve for eight years.

In the early spring of the year the Indiana Supreme Court also had ruled that the 1970 amendment that changed the terms of the state administrative offices, including the secretary of state, applied to the incumbents, thereby setting the expiration of Conrad's term in 1974. He could seek reelection that year and, if successful, was the odds-on favorite to be the Democratic nominee for governor in 1976. He had taken his shot in 1972. He had lost graciously. He had campaigned hard for the ticket and was the bright spot in the state of all those Democrats who were trying to fire up the troops. Indeed, as Larry and Mary Lou took a vacation trip to Florida in December of 1972, it appeared that 1973 would be a good year, full of family, fun, and preparations for 1974.

*This paper was prepared by the six "boiler room"
staff members and others to further the political
career of Larry Conrad. It was basically designed
to be used as our principal reference as Larry
moves thru [sic] the process of being elected Gov. of
Indiana and beyond. We will review this document
almost daily but will only rewrite and up date [sic]
on a quarterly basis. The "facts," as we report
them here, were apparent in May, June, and early
July of 1973. Only seven copies of this material has
[sic] been produced as to ensure complete security
of this information. It would be a serious advantage loss to share this material with people too lazy
to compile it for their own use.*

—from the "Foreward" [sic] to the Master Plan

IN THE CHILDREN'S book *The Three Billy Goats Gruff* the hungry billy goats
wanted to cross the bridge and go to the hillside where there was a fine
meadow full of grass "where they could eat and eat and eat, and get fat."
But under the bridge lived a troll "who was as mean as he was ugly," and
he planned on stopping the billy goats. And he planned on eating them.[1]

To Indiana politicians over nearly four decades, Ed Ziegner was the
troll. But of the hundreds of politicians who tried to cross the bridge to the
hillside, Larry Conrad was the one that Ziegner really got his teeth into.

If there were a journalism school at one of our universities with a mission of training the next generation of Ed Ziegners, the classes would be held in gravel pits, and everyone's hair would be as closely cropped as a steel wire brush.

Edward H. Ziegner was of average build and height. He roamed through the Statehouse corridors with a slight stoop, as though he was always staring at the marble floor, figuring out the movements of political man. His black and gray hair was crew-cut. He never smiled. When he spoke he brought his head up fast. His voice was deep and rough. He looked and sounded like a drill sergeant.

A World War II veteran, Ziegner patiently awaited his arrival as Dean of the Indiana press corps. By 1973 he had already spent more than twenty years covering state politics and government for the *Indianapolis News*. His newspaper was vastly smaller in circulation than the morning *Star*, where Robert (Bob) Mooney served as the chief political reporter, and rumors frequently flew through the city that the Pulliam family, which controlled both papers, was pulling the plug on the *News* because of huge financial losses. But the rumors were wrong; Ed Ziegner's byline appeared day after day, and his political column appeared every Saturday.

With far fewer readers than Mooney, Ziegner attempted to make up for it by serving as the statewide stringer for other newspapers, such as the *News-Sentinel* in Fort Wayne. But his real attempt to compensate for his smaller readership was by getting the big stories first and earning the reputation of always having the inside scoop. He cultivated his sources, and frequently served as an unofficial advisor to candidates and political leaders. In 1969, when Indianapolis mayor Richard Lugar attempted to pressure House Speaker Otis Bowen to pass the Unigov legislation by releasing Bowen's personal phone number and asking citizens to call him, it was Ziegner who tipped off the Marion County Republican chairman, L. Keith Bulen, who was in Washington, D.C., at the time. When Bulen answered the phone in his hotel room he heard Ziegner's voice: "Your young mayor sure fucked up today." Bulen had to take the next flight to Indianapolis and smooth the ruffled feathers of Speaker Bowen.[2] A year later, when Gordon St. Angelo was making his reach for the chairmanship of the Democratic National Committee, he frequently called Ziegner from around the country to inform him on the progress of his campaign and ask his advice.[3]

Ziegner prided himself on knowing the inside story. When something occurred that he had no foreknowledge of, he would explode with indignation. In 1968, when J. Manfred Core and Jack New held a news conference to announce that they were running Bob Rock's campaign for the gubernatorial nomination, Ziegner jumped to his feet yelling, "What do you mean doing that!" New was surprised, but then realized that they had just announced something of which Ziegner did not have advance knowledge. It was not part of Ziegner's plan.[4]

A Biography

When the Indiana General Assembly was in session, and during election campaigns, Ziegner supplemented his reporter's salary by publishing a newsletter filled with his ruminations on Indiana politics. Many a public official was pulled into Ziegner's "shack" at the Statehouse and interviewed while Ziegner pounded the typewriter keys.

If you were a campaign staffer, and offended Ziegner by refusing to release to him first, he would rant and scream at you louder than any other reporter you'd ever met. If he disliked you, he would use every tactic, some cheap and trivial, others dramatic, to hurt you. And if Ziegner liked you, he did you favors. If he favored you for governor, he allowed you to write a guest column, which would appear on the Saturday of a normal weekend. If he opposed you for governor, your guest column would run on the weekend of the Fourth of July, or the Saturday before Labor Day, when readers were on holiday. If you questioned him about it he would reply: "It's my column, if you don't want to submit something, don't."

During the first few months of 1973 the national headlines were still given over to Vietnam. The previous August the last units of U.S. ground troops were withdrawn, but in December President Nixon ordered the resumption of bombings over North Vietnam. However, other events started finding their way into the newspapers. On January 22, 1973, the U.S. Supreme Court released the *Roe v. Wade* decision, and state laws prohibiting voluntary abortions before the third month were declared unconstitutional. On February 7, the U.S. Senate established a Select Committee on Presidential Campaign Activities, to be chaired by Senator Sam Ervin, specifically charged with investigating the Watergate conspiracy.

The political headlines in Indiana during this time were dominated by the new governor, Otis R. Bowen, and his "tax package." He delivered on his 1972 campaign promises by persuading the legislature to pass a property tax control package, which froze both the total amount of money local governments could raise through property taxes and the property tax rates for public schools. Another bill doubled the state sales tax, to a total of 4 percent, with the extra sales tax revenue dedicated to a "Property Tax Replacement Fund" which would be used to cut all property tax bills in Indiana by 20 percent. This is what Governor Bowen called "visible and lasting property tax relief."

The coverage of issues and events, like everything human, has a life cycle. When issues are first spawned they either die quickly or attract the attention of others. When those "others" are reporters, a "feeding frenzy" sometimes results, in which reporters and broadcasters all seek any piece of information related to the story. Rumors are frequently printed and broadcast without verification, because the pressure to "get it first" in a building story always outweighs the journalistic judgment to "get it right." Even the most experienced reporters and columnists fall victim. The previous July, many of the national reporters and columnists had such a feeding frenzy. Following George McGovern's selection of Missouri Senator Tom Eagleton as his vice-presidential nominee, rumors began flying that Eagleton suffered from depression and mental strain. *Time* magazine reported the allegations, as did most of the newspapers throughout the country. In the midst of this building story on Eagleton's mental health, syndicated columnist Jack Anderson reported on his radio show that he had "proof that Eagleton had an arrest record of half a dozen charges of drunken and reckless driving." The charge was false. Jack Anderson had no proof.[5]

If members of the national media fall victim to such errors and pressures, members of the statewide media also are susceptible. But the arena is different, and the motivations are much less diverse. While hundreds of outlets cover the national stories, only a handful are devoted to the happenings in most of our state capitals. The two Indianapolis papers were the newspapers devoted to the continuing coverage of Indiana state government. The major Indianapolis television stations tolerated a regular turnover in broadcast reporters; the men and women who staffed the TV newsrooms were more akin to the "news readers" of Great Britain than to professional journalists purportedly trained in American universities.

The small Indianapolis press corps, overwhelmingly dominated by white males, was vulnerable to the biases, motivations, and conclusions of only one of its members, whether he be a reporter or an editor. The personal relationships among the reporters are the major check on this vulnerability. As in any craft, news writers assess their colleagues. They learn the lessons from the others and they draw conclusions as to the quality of their colleagues' work. They know the good ones from the bad ones.

It was not easy to determine if Ed Ziegner was a good one or a bad one. His competitive nature and persistence often resulted in his getting the story first. He had developed a solid network of political sources that newer members of the press corps could not match. His long experience in Indiana had earned him the respect, if not the admiration, of lobbyists and academics. He would often criticize news releases and speeches from candidates and public officials as lacking in substance and having no data. Yet he often observed that the greatest speech he ever heard was Governor Adlai Stevenson's acceptance of the presidential nomination at the 1952 Democratic National Convention, and, great though that speech may have been, nowhere in it was there a statistic. Ziegner often filled his regular Saturday column with silliness, tossing out personal observations on the political future, pretending to be a computer called "Uniquack," and including fawning observations about state legislators and party leaders.

One person Ziegner never fawned over was Larry Conrad. He seemed revolted by Conrad's lucidity and quickness of mind and tongue. Ziegner was convinced that Conrad possessed some psychological gift, as yet undiscovered, of mesmerizing people into a blind trance. "A person would go into Conrad's office and leave thirty minutes later thinking Conrad was a god," Ziegner contended. "Well, there are no gods in Indiana politics."[6]

While Nixon, Watergate, Bowen, and the Indiana General Assembly were getting the headlines, personnel changes were taking place in the Indiana secretary of state's office. Conrad had been shaken in the late summer of 1972 when money came up missing in the Corporations Division of the office. "We suspected something," Deputy Secretary of State Stu Grauel remembers, "and we called in the State Board of Accounts and the State Police."[7] Grauel fired two employees and the blanket bond for the office reimbursed the state for the missing amount.[8] "Larry was very hurt by this," Mary Lou recalls. "He couldn't believe anybody would be dishonest. He thought if somebody on staff needed money, they should come to him. They were like members of our family."[9]

There is a qualitative difference between organizing and administering. Conrad could organize. He clearly saw objectives and goals, and he could plan the activities to reach them. From his earliest days in Laconia, he was the organizer. But he did not enjoy day-to-day administration. He recognized that truth when he worked for Bayh in Washington, where Bob Keefe was the office administrator and Conrad worked on constitutional amendments. But now, as the elected official, he regretted he was not a tighter administrator. In fact it was Grauel, with his banking background, who was responsible for providing administrative control over the office, but the furious political pace of the previous eighteen months—and the arrogance and brashness of the political operatives—made it impossible to impose tight administrative controls. Moreover, Grauel's time and attention had been diverted into political fund-raising. Now with many staff members leaving and political fund-raising unnecessary, Grauel expected to run a tighter ship.

The political section had been shut down following the 1972 defeat. Jeff Lewis was gone; so were Terry Straub and Vicki Weger. Grauel, of course, was still serving as deputy secretary of state. John Livengood had come on board in May, to help with speechwriting and election administration. And Conrad had a new secretary, replacing Vicki Weger: Claudia Prosser.

Claudia Prosser first met Larry Conrad in October 1969, when she was a sophomore at IU-Bloomington. She had become active in the College Young Democrats and decided to run for recording secretary of the statewide Young Democrats. The state meeting was in Fort Wayne, and Claudia and Mary Scifres, another college YD, drove up together. At the Saturday night banquet Larry Conrad was the featured speaker. He was introduced as a former executive director of the Indiana Young Democrats and a campaign manager and legislative assistant for U.S. Senator Birch Bayh.

"He gave the most incredible speech I had ever heard. I bought it hook, line and sinker, and did from then until the day he died," Claudia said later. In that speech Conrad mentioned the red clay country of southern Indiana and the "hollers" of Borden, Indiana. Claudia Prosser was probably the only other person in the room who knew anything about Borden, Indiana. Her grandparents are buried there.

Claudia won the job of recording secretary, but her mind was now on Larry Conrad. She contacted him and volunteered to help him in the secretary of state's race.

That spring, as school was winding down, Claudia and Mary would drive to the Conrad home in Daleville to help prepare the bulk mailings to be sent to the delegates to the state convention persuading them to vote for Conrad for secretary of state.

Throughout the 1970 campaign Prosser would catch the bus from Bloomington to Indianapolis and perform volunteer duties for the Conrad campaign. She stayed in touch with Conrad after his election as secretary of state, and was an enthusiastic worker for him in the 1972 run for the gubernatorial nomination. After his announcement in February of 1972, she dropped out of college and moved to Indianapolis, where she stayed at the Conrads' house on Meridian Street to tend to the children while Mary Lou campaigned. She was paid $50 per week out of the campaign committee and frequently worked nights at the headquarters on Market Street.

On the Tuesday before Thanksgiving in 1973, Claudia Prosser was at her desk, just outside Conrad's door in the secretary of state's office. It was an overcast day. The temperature was fifty degrees at ten-thirty in the morning when Ed Ziegner walked down the stairs of the Statehouse to the main floor.

If there was one thing Ziegner understood, it was timing. That November day in 1973 was "organization day" of the 1974 Indiana General Assembly. All 150 state legislators were in Indianapolis to elect their legislative leaders and introduce the first bills of the session. Accompanying the legislators were all the lobbyists and political reporters. Whatever was published in the Indianapolis newspapers that day was assured to have maximum impact.

When Ziegner shuffled into the reception area of the secretary of state's office, he peered over his glasses and, in his gravelly voice, announced to Claudia Prosser: "I'm here for my appointment."

Conrad had arrived at his office just minutes before Ziegner entered. He had begun his day in the dentist's chair. The angst, the anger, the fear, the pain, and the disgust which began that morning would plague Larry Conrad for years. The cause? Not the dentist, but the Master Plan.

Anyone asked to list the most significant events in Hoosier politics in the twentieth century would be forced to name the takeover of the Republican party by the Ku Klux Klan in the 1920s, which led to the resignation

A Biography

and imprisonment of Governor Warren T. McCray and the near resignation of Governor Ed Jackson,[10] and perhaps Governor Paul V. McNutt's stunning reform agenda in the 1930s. They would have to include Homer Capehart's Cornfield Conference in August of 1938, which began the rebuilding of the Republican party, and the attempt by the Republican general assembly in 1941 to strip executive power from Democratic governor Henry Schricker by passing "ripper" bills, which eventually were declared unconstitutional. They would list the stunning defeat of Republican Senator Capehart in 1962 by Birch E. Bayh, Jr.; Governor Matthew Welsh's proposal of the 2-percent sales tax in the famous 1963 special legislative session; and possibly the highway scandals under Republican Governor George Craig. They might mention the passage of Unigov in the 1969 Indiana General Assembly, and the vice-presidencies of Thomas R. Marshall, Charles W. Fairbanks, and J. Danforth Quayle. And somewhere on that list, perhaps not in the top five, but certainly in the top ten or fifteen, would be the Master Plan.[11]

Twelve sections, not counting the Foreword; one hundred and ninety-seven pages on legal-size paper; the document is nearly an inch and a quarter thick.[12] More than twenty years later, dozens of people still have their copies. Former governor Otis Bowen thinks his copy is in his attic. The mayor of East Chicago, Robert Pastrick, has at least two copies buried in his files. Russell (Bun) Gallahan, a Democratic leader in Miami County, has a copy. Indianapolis attorney Robert F. Wagner has a copy. But Gordon St. Angelo says he does not have a copy, contending he "sent it to somebody up north and never got it back."[13]

When Conrad greeted Ziegner in his office, they shook hands and Ziegner sat in the chair in front of Conrad's desk. He came right to the point. A copyrighted story in the home edition of the *Indianapolis News* that afternoon would have a front-page article revealing the existence of a "Master Plan" which set forth a program for Larry Conrad to take over the Indiana Democratic party which would lead to his election as governor. Ziegner told him that the story would summarize the plan. He then asked for Conrad's response.

Conrad was stunned. He denied knowing of such a plan. He said he had never seen such a document and "doubted that such a document existed." Ziegner informed him that he had a complete copy and Conrad replied that he "would certainly like to see it." Conrad admitted that it was "conceivable" that some of the people who worked for him had put such a document together, but they were certainly "not authorized to do so." Ziegner then zeroed in on St. Angelo, telling Conrad that the plan contained references to replacing St. Angelo as state chairman. Conrad said that he had discussed with people in his office various changes in the political organization that might be beneficial, "but not necessarily for me," and he denied there had been any discussions about replacing St. Angelo. Ziegner scribbled in his notebook, thanked him for his time, and left.[14]

Within a few minutes, a phone call came in for Conrad. It was from St. Angelo. Stu Grauel answered first and told St. Angelo that Ziegner had a document called the Master Plan. When Conrad clicked on, St. Angelo told him that he had just received a copy in the mail. Conrad said that he did not have the document, and St. Angelo replied that his was available to photocopy. Conrad dispatched Claudia Prosser to St. Angelo's downtown office to bring back the document.

Prosser remembers the day well. The events have been branded on her brain: "I went to St. Angelo's office. When I entered I remember it was very dark. He had dark paneling, no windows, and the lights were low. He was sitting behind his big desk in the dark. He said to me 'This is awful—just when things were going so good.' And then he cried."

St. Angelo handed Prosser the copy, but kept the envelope in which it was mailed. "He said something about how he wanted to check it for fingerprints," Prosser later recalled. She went back to the secretary of state's office, photocopied the document, and returned the original to St. Angelo's office. He was gone. Prosser left the document with the secretary.[15]

St. Angelo remembers the events somewhat differently. He says the document was returned to his office by two guys "who went to a hotel room" to read it.[16]

Ziegner's story was headlined "Conrad for Governor 'Master Plan' Bared." Ziegner wrote that he was "convinced of its authenticity."[17] The next day the Fort Wayne *News-Sentinel* featured the story on page one, headlined: "Conrad Denies Governorship Master Plan."

There was something in the Master Plan to offend everyone, except Gordon St. Angelo. He readily admits: "Whoever did write it treated me pretty well in it."[18] But if you were a farmer, you were a complainer and "would never be an asset to the Democrats." If you were a member of a union, you "care more for your camper than your country." If you were just a voter you were "too dumb to understand what Nixon is up to." If you were Governor Otis R. Bowen, M.D., you were called a "friendly quack," and a "do-nothing Governor" like Roger Branigin. If you were a young person you could be "turned on" by a "few words from Bobby, John and Martin," and afterwards you "can't be reasoned with. . . ." If you were a black legislator you were "inept."

As the slurs continued, section after section, strange attitudes were attributed to Conrad: "As *Larry* has frequently pointed out, a college man is far superior to one without a degree."[19] Also: "Larry, and we all agree, feels we should disband the [Young Democrats] organization after he becomes Governor and let them join the Jesus Freaks which will then, inturn [*sic*], kill that movement."

Conrad was shocked. He had never said such things. He never looked down on any person, regardless of their formal education, and referred to his own uncle, George W. Byrum, the man who had sworn him in as secretary of state, as "one of God's noble men" precisely because he was self-educated; Byrum had never gone to college. And disband the Young Democrats? Conrad had served as the executive director of the Young Democrats. That organization gave him his political start. The previous year he had fought to provide a seat on the Democratic State Central Committee for the president of the Young Democrats.

In comments to reporters later that afternoon, Conrad said: "I consider it to be the most slanderous, libelous, concocted instrument with crass and insensitive disregard for personalities and ultimate effects which I have ever seen." He reported that he was "collecting affidavits from my staff who have all indicated they have nothing to do with the composition of the so-called Conrad 'Master Plan.'"[20] He also said that he was "investigating which state and federal agencies would have jurisdiction over the distribution of such material" in an attempt to "help reveal who is responsible. It seems as though we have our own department of dirty tricks right here in Indiana." Jane Allen, Conrad's news secretary, in commenting on who may have written it, said: "They may have been formerly involved in Democratic politics. They know what they are talking about, but the jargon they use is not ours and some of it is out of date."[21]

Conrad knew immediately that the document was intended to destroy him politically. He began placing calls to several people, asking them to come by to discuss the Master Plan. He called Bill Schreiber, the Marion County (Indianapolis) chairman. "After I looked at it, I told Larry to move swiftly and surely on it, or it would nibble him to death."[22] He summoned Jim Kelley, who was planning to run for Marion County prosecutor in 1974. Kelley came to the office that afternoon and, behind closed doors, discussed the political fallout with Conrad. "Obviously, Larry was calling political people for their advice," Livengood later concluded.[23]

One call went to Bill Gigerich. Gigerich was in Florida on a Thanksgiving vacation when the phone rang. "Bill, I've got a problem," Larry said. He asked Gigerich to come back early from his vacation to meet with him, and he briefly described what was in Ziegner's article. Gigerich caught a flight back and on Friday met with Larry in the secretary of state's office. Gigerich remembers that Grauel and Rooksby were there, along with Dallas Sells and Don Yeagley from the UAW. In a conference room, Gigerich "glanced through" the document. "I never read it all the way through," he recalls. "As I thumbed through it, I felt afraid. You see that somebody's out there who will go out of their way to destroy you—and you are helpless. You do not know where it came from, but it was coming right at you, nobody else."[24]

On Friday, Conrad placed another call to an old friend in Washington, D.C.—a former chief counsel to the Senate Subcommittee on Constitutional Amendments—Bernard (Bud) Fensterwald, Jr. Conrad and Fensterwald had maintained contact since Larry left Washington, and Conrad had immense respect for his "incisive observations," in Stephan Lesher's phrase. Fensterwald made plans to fly to Indianapolis as soon as possible, and told Conrad he would assist him and retain a private investigator from Washington, D.C., Ken Smith. Fensterwald and Smith arrived on Saturday morning, taking rooms at the Howard Johnson's Motel on West Washington Street. Fensterwald's first question to Conrad was: "Do you have any reason to think that Donald Segretti has been in the state?"[25]

The horrors of Watergate were now suspected of being visited upon Indiana—and upon Larry Conrad. The Saturday after Thanksgiving, Ed Ziegner's subject for his weekly column was Watergate.

Larry called Mary Lou that Tuesday afternoon. She was working as a part-time secretary in Indianapolis. "He told me that the evening paper was going to release a story and he wanted me to meet him at home as soon as possible," Mary Lou recalls. "His voice was lifeless, unfamiliar," she wrote in her diary.[26] She read Ziegner's story on the way home and could only ask, "Who, who could have done this? The 'Why' was obvious: he was too popular in our party." At home on Meridian Street, they talked into the night, continuing to ask one another, "Who, who?"[27]

Larry and Mary Lou could find no answers.

Phone calls were pouring into Conrad's office and home from Democratic officials throughout the state who had received copies of the Master Plan in the mail, with no return address. Mayor Bob Pastrick in East Chicago received one. So did Marion County Democratic chairman Bill Schreiber and John Dillon, the former state attorney general. Acting on Fensterwald's suggestion, Conrad asked several staff members to report to work on the Friday after Thanksgiving—a state holiday—to volunteer in getting letters out to every person mentioned in the document. In the letter he wrote: "I am sorry that my interest and position in Indiana politics may in any way cause you embarrassment," and he promised that he would "talk to you directly about this matter" in the next several days.[28]

After Fensterwald and Smith arrived, they called together some of Conrad's closest political advisors for a meeting at his house. Several of those attending agreed to help meet any legal and investigative costs, and then Fensterwald and Smith announced that certain actions had to be taken immediately. Their strategy—much like Bill Schreiber's recommendation—was based on moving swiftly and "getting on top of the situation." Waiting would only ensure more bombardment by those responsible for disseminating the plan. Conrad had already informed the press that he was seeking affidavits from his staff members that they had no knowledge of or involvement with the plan. Smith recommended that this be enlarged, and that past and present staff members be requested to take a lie detector test. They also described procedures they were going to take to trace the envelopes in which copies of the documents had been mailed, and recommended that Conrad request technical assistance in fingerprinting and typewriter comparisons from the Indiana State Police, the U.S. Postal Service, and the FBI. They also recommended that the secretary of state's office in the Statehouse be "swept" to determine if any electronic listening devices were planted.

The magnitude of the problem settled around Conrad's mind like a thick, poisonous cloud. He felt a brutal betrayal. "In a very real way, he died that day in November of 1973," Mary Lou relates. "From then on his full faith in people was gone. Gone forever. He still could place some trust in others, but he lost his glitter and his sparkle."[29] Larry could not or would not eat. He started losing weight. He couldn't sleep at night. "The house became a silent fortress," Mary Lou wrote. "We virtually withdrew from the outside world. We went through the motions of living, for the sake of the children. But we were heartbroken."[30]

Fensterwald and Smith moved swiftly. The office was swept for listening devices, but none was found.[31] Smith gathered the main office staff members together and demonstrated how they could hit their telephone sets with a pencil, while talking, to interfere with any listening device that might be planted in the phone.

They also investigated the manila envelopes in which the document had been mailed. While preparing a formal request to the Indiana State Police for technical assistance with fingerprinting, they began tracking the source of the envelopes by contacting stationery stores in Indianapolis. Bill Gigerich recalls that one clerk in a downtown stationery store recognized the odd-sized envelope, and reported that the Democratic State Central Committee, which maintained an account at the store, had recently requested a supply of those envelopes. The clerk remembered the order because the store had an insufficient number in stock and had to special-order more.[32]

Clearly, the Democratic State Central Committee disseminated the document widely. One county chairman received a copy in a manila envelope with no return address. But the mailing label misspelled his street, and in a mailing from the Democratic State Central Committee a few days later, he recognized that same misspelling.

Gordon St. Angelo admits that he distributed the document. Indeed, he provided a copy to Conrad. He remembers mailing the document to others. At the time, St. Angelo thought Conrad was vastly overreacting, and he claims he told him so: "I met with Larry and Stu Grauel and one other person at the old Sheraton Hotel on North Meridian. Conrad was almost a 'basket-case' and Stu wasn't much better. I told them they were blowing it out of proportion and I said they should invite everybody mentioned in it and have a sort of reverse gridiron meeting to handle it humorously. It was a joke. They didn't listen to me."[33]

Jack New, then the state treasurer, also thought Conrad overreacted. "I know it shook up the office," New says, "but I don't think it amounted to a cup of hot spit."[34]

But New and St. Angelo are alone in contending that Conrad was over-reacting. When asked to reflect back twenty years to those days, Conrad loyalist Bill Gigerich says: "There was no overreaction to it. How could you overreact to it? You have to defend yourself. You couldn't joke about something like that. The people behind it thought Larry would fold the tent. When it hit Larry, it knocked him back on his heels. If he would not have reacted to defend himself, he would have been destroyed and his reputation would have been gone forever. They were attempting to destroy his credibility and his character. The Plan used language and said things that Larry would never have said."[35]

Another Conrad staffer, John Livengood, agrees. "I don't think Larry overreacted. He was looking at possible indictments. A promising political career was being destroyed before his eyes. The Master Plan was purposely put together to destroy him."[36]

A more objective observer also agrees there was no overreaction. Gordon Englehart, the Indiana political reporter for the *Louisville Courier-Journal*, remembers those days. "Clearly, if you are sitting on the sidelines, sure, you can say there was overreaction. But if you are Larry Conrad, planning for bigger things, then he was not really overreacting. Politics gets to be intramural, like it is within the Beltway in Washington, D.C. Outside of the party regulars, nobody was really paying attention. But Larry had to be worried about the party regulars."[37]

As copies of the Master Plan arrived in the mailboxes of the county chairmen and Democratic elected officials, there was an immediate reaction. Mayor Pastrick admits his feelings were badly hurt. "I couldn't believe that anybody would actually write that kind of stuff. A lot of people knew that I was a strong supporter of Birch Bayh and I liked Larry Conrad, and some of them tried to tell me that these people—my good friends—were engaged in cellblock plotting. And I really didn't know," Pastrick recalls. Conrad called Pastrick and denied any involvement. "He said it was a plot against him. I always knew him to be a man of his word, and I accepted his word."[38]

Marion County chairman Bill Schreiber also saw his concern mounting. "Conrad was unable to deal with the problem," Schreiber said, "and there was a growing fear, particularly in Marion County, that the Master Plan was going to negate the effects of Watergate on the Democratic ticket."[39]

Ziegner called early the next week, requesting an interview with Conrad on Friday morning. Conrad agreed. On Friday evening, November 30, in the home edition of the *News*, Ziegner's front-page article was head-lined: "'Doomsday Book' Was Kept On Delegates, Conrad Says." The lead was: "Secretary of State Larry Conrad today confirmed the existence of a 'doomsday book' kept on delegates to the 1972 state convention in which he lost the nomination for governor to former Gov. Matthew Welsh, but said it was merely a record of pro-Conrad, pro-Welsh and uncommitted delegates and contained no derogatory information or remarks." Ziegner also wrote that Conrad "said he personally did not call it the 'doomsday book' but 'there were some people who did call it that.'"

As we have already seen, Conrad's staff did keep such a book, some-times referring to it as the D-Day Book or the Delegate Bible. In June of 1972, Paul M. Doherty, a reporter for the *Indianapolis Star*, in a feature on Conrad and his gubernatorial campaign, quoted Conrad as saying, "This is the doomsday book."[40] Every candidate for a state convention nomina-tion kept similar records. Matthew Welsh's campaign referred to his records as "run-down sheets." Otis Bowen also maintained such a cata-logue of delegates.[41]

So the existence of the doomsday book was no revelation; the article was merely a pretext to bring up the Master Plan once again. Ziegner noted that Conrad continued to deny personal knowledge of the plan. Then he peppered Conrad with questions about the document: Did Vicki Weger and Claudia Prosser work less than forty hours a week on their state jobs? Conrad said no. Ziegner followed up: There are rumors Prosser worked in the Conrad home and stayed with the Conrad children on state time. Conrad replied, "I don't think so," but acknowledged that Prosser lived at his home for many months after the 1972 state convention until moving out "two or three months ago." What about Weger? Conrad admitted that Weger worked Vigo County for him in 1972 and "she may have been there during normal business hours," but "she more than put in a full week for the state by working nights and at other times." He conceded that Weger "didn't always make it here on time," but explained that she was driving to Indianapolis from Terre Haute.

Ziegner's questions kept coming: Did a vice-president of a southern Indiana bank pay a portion of personal expenses incurred at the 1973 convention of the Indiana Democratic Editorial Association (IDEA) at French Lick? Conrad confirmed that he paid "maybe $300." Ziegner's next question: "Is it a remarkable coincidence that the Master Plan called for Conrad and a group of young people to play a touch football game in front of the French Lick hotel during the IDEA meeting—and, indeed, such a game was played?" Conrad responded: "I don't know. I don't remember that situation. I don't recall that, to be honest with you." Ziegner claimed that another reporter, not from the *News*, had been approached by a Conrad staffer in the hotel who informed him that the football game was under way and suggested that the reporter go out and watch. According to Ziegner, "the reporter, on deadline, did not do so."[42]

Following this story, Conrad's depression deepened. The feeding frenzy became even more ferocious. A radio reporter contended that Conrad and Prosser were romantically involved, and mentioned that Prosser lived with the Conrads. Conrad called the reporter. All he could do was deny it.

A few days later, on December 10, Conrad's request to the Indiana State Police Board for technical assistance in determining who may have prepared the Master Plan was tabled by the board members, claiming that they had no evidence that criminal activity was involved. Governor Bowen's assistant, William Lloyd, attended the meeting. He said that he believed that political, rather than governmental, involvement was present, and urged the board to defer action.[43]

The next day, Ziegner struck again, on page 1:

> The office of Secretary of State Larry Conrad has sent out requests for purely political information not connected with state business and has used state stationery.
>
> In addition, state WATS telephone lines may have been used by the Conrad office to obtain political information from various counties in the state. . . .[44]

Ziegner reported that "The *News* has obtained possession of a set of political documents, all originating in Conrad's office, that ask detailed political information from Conrad 'county secretaries' in the counties involved."

Once again, Ziegner had Conrad on the ropes. All Conrad could do was deny. Concerning state employees doing political business on state time and using state stationery, Ziegner quoted Conrad: "No, no. Well, I don't know about state stationery. From time to time the county secretaries that we try to establish out in the state try to get us any sort of information relating to the office, as well as political activities. We did put together a packet at one time, asking them to send us newspaper clippings and material that would be helpful to us knowing what was going on in various places throughout the state."

Ziegner then quoted from one "document" from the purported "set." It was addressed "Dear County Secretary" and signed by one of Conrad's aides, Bob Rooksby. It said: "If you have any questions or need to contact the Indianapolis office at any time, please call 317–633–6531 collect, person-to-person for Bob Rooksby. The receptionist will answer and say that he is out of the office. She will then get your number and we will return the call as soon as possible." Conrad acknowledged that there were no privately paid-for telephone lines in the office and Grauel told Ziegner that the use of state stationery for political purposes was "not a standard practice."

In the fifteenth paragraph of Ziegner's story, he revealed the existence of the "BAID" program—births, anniversaries, injuries, and deaths. This program had been instituted by Jeff Lewis in 1971 and continued after Lewis left Conrad's office. Two paragraphs later, in a revealing sentence, Ziegner wrote: "His extensive program for political activity in the state, Conrad said, is not designed to bypass the regular Democratic county organizations." Obviously, Conrad's denial of bypassing the party organization, which is not bracketed by quotation marks, was in response to a question from Ziegner, who must have been curious about Conrad's position relative to the Democratic party organization, which was led by Ziegner's friend, Gordon St. Angelo.

Finally, in the last three paragraphs, Ziegner returned to the question of "ghost employment" and the use of state stationery and telephone lines. Concerning the 1972 "Ghost Employee" law, Conrad admitted: "I haven't read that law, so I can't comment directly on that, but I'm sure that was the purpose of it, to make sure that state got everything it was entitled to get from people who are working. I believe that is the case, so far as we are concerned." Conrad also said he would "find out" how state stationery came to be used and commented, on the use of WATS lines, that "It may have been, but as far as I'm concerned it hasn't been."

Six days later, on Monday, December 17, 1993, the *News* once again featured Conrad: "State Police Say 'Nay' To Conrad." The State Police Board voted unanimously that morning to deny any technical or laboratory assistance to Conrad. The article mentioned that the department, by law, "operates on a nonpolitical basis."[45]

From his law office on the south side of Indianapolis, Robert (Bob) Wagner was reading Ziegner's stories. He thought: "This Larry Conrad needs some real help."

After managing Senator Hartke's 1970 victorious campaign, Wagner had been offered a position with Ed Lewis's law firm. He had decided to leave Aetna Insurance, "much to my wife's chagrin," he remembers. But he turned Lewis down. He wanted his own law firm; he wanted to make it on his own. With three other partners, one of whom was black, Wagner opened a law office at 120 East Market Street downtown. "I made my desk out of two sawhorses and a door," he recalls, "but I think we had the first integrated law firm in Indianapolis."[46]

Relying on some business from organized labor resulting from contacts Wagner had maintained since the Hartke campaign, and having left Aetna on good terms, he began building his practice. During Conrad's 1972 campaign for governor, Wagner helped raise some money but was otherwise not involved. "I went over to the Statehouse and people were doing all the political work in the basement of the secretary of state's office. Rooksby was the ramrod, and Boxell would come by. They pretty much relegated me to mailing envelopes and I decided it was pretty much a waste of time. I decided I wasn't going to get involved. They had an inner

124

circle and you couldn't penetrate it. There was an arrogance in that staff. They were smug. And at that time I did not have a close relationship with Larry."[47]

In mid-1972, Ed Lewis again approached Bob Wagner about joining his law firm. "Ed had steered a case or two my way and we had stayed in touch. He said I was the only person he had ever asked twice to join him. The second time, I accepted." Wagner left his partners and moved to the South Madison Avenue offices of the new firm, Lewis, Bowman, St. Clair and Wagner.

"When the Master Plan hit I thought they were beating on Conrad good," Wagner remembers. "I had mutual friends call me and ask me to help Larry out because he was getting hurt." That's when Wagner called Conrad. From that day forward, Wagner was in charge of Conrad's political life.

Few Indiana politicians base their decisions on ideas and values. Most view politics as a game played by individuals who seek money and power. This approach stresses personalities and motives, not ideas or values. But even in Indiana there are two levels of politicians. On the lower level are those who see politics as a game like Monopoly. On the higher level are those who realize that gaining power brings with it the responsibility of promoting certain values and realizing certain ideas. This higher order of politicians realizes that there is a deep and abiding difference between the two political parties in America, and the difference is in political philosophy.

Bob Wagner is one of those higher order politicians. And Conrad's troubles troubled Wagner.

Larry still could not sleep at night. He started smoking again, after successfully quitting for nearly a year. Mary Lou ordered some sleeping pills, hoping that they would help him rest. He had difficulty going to work, and when he did arrive he would only read some newspapers. He barely glanced at the mail. He took few calls. Livengood, who sent memos to Conrad on nearly a daily basis, saw him deteriorate. "He wouldn't talk about it. I would send memos in to him and they would come back marked 'O.K.' Before he would have torn them apart. He always made extensive comments all over them. Instead of teasing me . . . or urging me to look at something else . . . or complaining in his teasing way . . . he just started going through the motions."[48]

For the first time, at age thirty-eight, Conrad's life was beyond his control. The unceasing thoughts about political betrayal and his own limitations as an administrator were like hammer blows on his brain. For the first time, he considered getting out of politics and public life. He thought about resigning his office.

He barely spoke to anyone. "He isolated himself in the basement," Mary Lou says, "and about all he would do is watch TV and play with the race-cars on the floor with the boys. I thought all along that they didn't want to hurt us physically, but they wanted to kill him mentally and politically."[49]

About every other day Wagner would come by the house in the morning, on his way to the law office. "This was a very bad time for Larry," Wagner recalls. He would find Conrad in the basement, often sitting in his recliner, wrapped in a blanket. Wagner would ask questions and often Conrad would not respond.

These two adults, Mary Lou Conrad and Robert F. Wagner, provided the inner strength and support for the man who had moved to his basement with his shattered faith and fortunes. Mary Lou was to provide the personal energy and support. Bob Wagner was going to take care of the politics. At first, Mary Lou also was reeling. "I could not handle the stories," Mary Lou remembers, "and I still can't. This was not journalism. It was anonymous attacks." She wrote a letter to Ziegner, a passionate letter describing the devastation his stories were causing, and pointing out the stories were based on anonymous sources. Larry's mother, Ruby, also was alarmed about Larry and wrote to Ziegner. Ziegner replied to neither.[50] Mary Lou finally closed the curtain in her mind. She could not control what the newspapers were printing about her husband. But she could control her home. She could control her family.

"Mary Lou was at her best at this time," Prosser remembers. "She was protecting her home and her family. She was holding them tight. She was a pillar of strength for all of us."[51]

Fensterwald and Smith had urged Conrad to request that current and former staff members take lie detector tests to determine if they had any role in preparing or distributing the Master Plan. All of the current employees volunteered immediately, but several ex–staff members balked. Wagner and Conrad waited to see what the results of the tests would show.

Everyone agreed on the course of action, but the looming question in everybody's mind was: Who wrote it?

If Democrats and Republicans agree on anything in Indiana political history, it is that the Master Plan was written to severely embarrass Conrad and ruin his political career. Clearly, the document was not written solely for Conrad. It was not addressed to him in any way that anybody— including Conrad—would recognize. The cover sheet reads as follows:

T. M. P.

FOR

LARRY

The initials "T.M.P." obviously stand for "The Master Plan," but those three words do not appear anywhere in the document. They are inferred from the initials. But "T.M.P." was addressed to "Larry." There is an inherent difficulty in determining why it was addressed in this manner. If it were designed as an internal "paper" for Conrad's eyes, in all probability it would have been addressed to "LAC." By late 1971, all staff members were addressing memos to Conrad with one of two appellations: "Larry A. Conrad" or "LAC" (without periods between the letters). "LAC" was clearly the preferred mode, with Boxell, Bochnowski, Friedlander, Lewis, Powell, Rooksby, Straub, and Weger all using the three initials. Yet nowhere in the 197 pages is "LAC" used. When there is an equivalency for Conrad in the Master Plan, it is "L.C." In the first chapter, L.C. is used six times, and there are ten references to "Larry." If Conrad were to see the initials "L.C." he would not immediately recognize them as his; he was LAC, and had been since his early days on Bayh's staff. On the other hand, the writer knew how to refer to Birch Bayh. Eight of the twelve sections refer to the senator as "B^2." The Master Plan was intended for reading by people other than Conrad. There are no references to "you" in the written word, which is the style in any correspondence intended to provide advice to a specific reader. For example, a sentence in Section III reads: "We are trying here to list those 'over the hill' members that could be of great financial aid to Larry's campaign." It does not say: " . . . to your campaign"; or " . . . to our campaign." It refers to the campaign of a third party, somebody named "Larry."

This "person" problem runs throughout the document. At one point, in describing a potential financial contributor, the report says: "He is not one to invite to sit in Larry's box at Inauguaral [sic] Ball. . . ." Such a sentence, if intended for Conrad's eyes, would have been written: "He is not one to invite to sit in your box at the Inaugural Ball."

Section XI of the document constantly refers to Conrad in the third person and contains many statements which are intended to be read by somebody else. For example, in the conclusion to the section, the writer states:

> Larry will be going almost full time as we move through the vital schedule of events. The back up which the staff must furnish will be complete. Whatever he wants, he will get. His moods are horrendous and must be anticipated. The schedule will take his weight down which will be helpfu [sic]. He may want Jane to travel with him or perhaps someone else. We must keep him happy, relaxed and objective throughout the entire schedule of events. This will require a great, great amount of attention on our part.

> The family must adjust to this program. We won't have any complaints reach Larry from the kids as this upsets him. He will not change his schedule but his mood will become negative which will be damaging.

The Master Plan was not written for Conrad's consumption. It was written for public consumption. And it was Ed Ziegner who made it public.

Ziegner, apparently convinced that the document was authentic, none-theless could only conjecture about who wrote it. "If I had two guesses, it was Larry who wrote it or somebody in his office under his direction."[52]

When Ziegner reached a conclusion, for whatever reason, the matter was closed. L. Keith Bulen recalls: "Ziegner was very hard to convince when he made up his mind. He would stick to his conclusion even though he was wrong. But he had the sources, and your sources made you."[53]

The Master Plan was written to ensure anonymity for the author or authors. Of the twelve sections, or chapters, four of them have notations on the first page stating: "Compiled by . . . ," followed by one or more numbers. For example, Section II was "Compiled by 115"; and Section III was "Compiled by 115, 116 & 111." Nowhere in the text is any "compiler" identified.

Such anonymity is not consistent with any of the dozens of political memos that were written by the various staff members in Conrad's office. All of those memos identified the author, either by full name, last name, or initials. The authors never used numbers as codes.

The foreword states that the document, written in early July of 1973, "was prepared by the six 'boiler room' staff members." But only five numbers are mentioned as "compilers." And there was no "boiler room" operation in the secretary of state's office. The phrase "boiler room" was popularized in the political campaigns of Robert Kennedy, where a small group of staff members would receive all incoming information, such as mail and phone calls, and route them to the appropriate persons. Such an operation demanded experienced people who could make quick judg-ments to decide questions at the moment, rather than route calls to other, more senior, campaign officials. The Kennedy "boiler room" also served as a backup phone bank where, when incoming calls were light, the staff members would call voters on the candidate's behalf. Mary Jo Kopechne, who drowned in 1969 on Chappaquiddick Island when Senator Edward Kennedy's car went off the bridge, had been one of Robert Kennedy's "boiler room" staffers.

In July of 1973 Larry Conrad did not have a "boiler room." He no longer had a political section. He did not even have a campaign headquarters.

But why would Ziegner take the lead on the Master Plan when he could not ascertain the author or authors? Ziegner's answer was in the form of another question: "Larry had a large part in it. Who else could it have been?"[54]

There were always more questions than answers about the author. Gordon St. Angelo agrees with Ziegner: "In my opinion it was internal [to the secretary of state's office] by somebody who thought he was doing Conrad a big favor."[55] On further reflection, St. Angelo added to his theory: "I never heard and I never thought that Larry himself had any hand in writing it. In an office like that, a lot of people are competing with one another to get close to the man and this may have been one of those situations where somebody wrote this to get his attention, if it would get to him, and those things sometimes backfire. This may have been such a case."[56]

In nearly every case, Conrad's former staff members theorize that St. Angelo had a hand in either preparing or widely disseminating the Master Plan. As one former staff member asks: "Who stood to profit from the Master Plan?" And the speculative answers come pouring forth from dozens of people: (1) St. Angelo stood to profit because he was not close to Conrad and suspected Conrad would remove him as state chairman if Conrad were the 1976 nominee; (2) St. Angelo had a motive to retaliate against Birch Bayh because of Bayh's attempt to oust him in 1970, and Conrad was Bayh's protege. Such retaliation would likely result in Conrad's defeat, thereby damaging Bayh; (3) by toppling Conrad, St. Angelo was assured of getting his man, Jack New, the gubernatorial nomination in 1976 and, win or lose with New, St. Angelo's position was secure because of the understandings he had with the Republicans.

Former Conrad staffers also cite the favorable treatment St. Angelo receives in the Master Plan. Almost alone in receiving such treatment, St. Angelo acknowledges he was "treated well." Indeed, the document even refers to St. Angelo by his favorite nickname: "the Saint."[57]

What was eminently clear in 1973 was that the men in charge of the Indiana Democratic party had no candidate who could defeat Larry Conrad for the gubernatorial nomination. Matthew Welsh's political career was over, and nobody else had a statewide following that could even come close to matching Conrad's appeal. If the established powers were to keep control, Conrad had to be stopped. But that could not happen through the ballot box. He had to be brought down by scandal.

But Conrad's staff members also acknowledge their naivete in attempting to navigate the swirling waters of Hoosier politics. Remembering the iron-fisted control that St. Angelo exercised over the 1972 Democratic State Convention, they had forewarnings that the power of the established organization was immense, both over nominations and the careers of officeholders. The staff members made mistakes. Big ones. "I can see now why St. Angelo saw us as an easy target," Claudia Prosser says.[58]

John Livengood, who joined Conrad's staff only six months before Ziegner released the Master Plan, thinks the document, or large portions of it, could have originated in Conrad's office: "It could have been a product of what was written by staff members in the office. But it would not have been done under Larry's direction." When Livengood read the document he remembered that a political planning session held in Brown County in the spring of 1973 covered certain topics that later appeared in the Master Plan.[59]

Conrad acknowledged the possibility that some information in the

Master Plan was taken from files in his office, but he insisted that neither he nor anyone currently working in the office had anything to do with its preparation or distribution.[60]

During the first two weeks of December, Ken Smith continued his contacts with Conrad's employees and ex–staff members, requesting them to take the polygraph exams. The pressure brought down on current and former staffers strained and sometimes snapped relationships. "It was like the last scene in an Agatha Christie mystery, when the inspector has everyone sitting in a circle staring at one another and everyone is wondering who in that room did it."[61]

Three individuals—John Nichols, Jeff Lewis, and Steve Powell—became the focus of attention. Nichols had formed a political consulting firm called Media, Inc. in November of 1973. Jeff Lewis joined the firm as vice-president and Steve Powell was also offered a position. Powell had served as state president of the Young Democrats in 1973 and, upon his election, Gordon St. Angelo provided him a desk at the Democratic State Central Committee.

Powell was bitter about the way Conrad had treated him after he left the secretary of state's office in May of 1972. Finding himself again in need of a job, he had approached Conrad for help, and Conrad referred him to the state auditor, Mary Aikens Currie. She hired Powell, but he was resentful that he could not rejoin Conrad's staff. He viewed the newer Conrad staffers as neophytes. "They did not know what they were doing," he contends.[62]

The media firm was blessed with a $5,000 contract, arranged by St. Angelo, to provide consulting services to the two Democratic caucuses in the Indiana General Assembly. "We were looking for money," Powell states, "and we had been lured and wooed effectively by Gordon St. Angelo."[63]

Powell claims he first saw the Master Plan in John Nichols's office at Media, Inc. Bill Schreiber had brought a copy of the document over to the office and Nichols, Lewis, Schreiber, and an attorney for Media, Inc., were reading it when Powell entered the room. He recalls that they were discussing the document and laughing about some of the characterizations. They all agreed that it was a "disaster for Larry."[64]

When Nichols, Lewis, and Powell were asked to take the lie detector tests, they panicked. Powell sought advice from St. Angelo and recalls that he was advised not to take the polygraph because there were possible indictments forthcoming against Conrad and other staffers for violating the ghost employment statute. Powell remembers St. Angelo indicating that Powell could perhaps be granted immunity, but it would never get to that point if Conrad did not run for reelection.

Conrad had personally telephoned Powell and asked him to take the lie detector test. Powell's uncertainty grew. He did not know what to do. He respected Larry Conrad, although he was angry about the new staff members Conrad had hired. He knew of St. Angelo's dislike of Conrad, and his promise of being in the political consulting business meant he had to stay on good terms with St. Angelo.

Powell did not want to take the polygraph. And he had a reason to be frightened. A few days before, at Gordon St. Angelo's suggestion, he and John Nichols had met with Ed Ziegner at Ziegner's house. St. Angelo acknowledges that he might have urged Powell and Nichols to talk to Ziegner. "That sounds possible," he says. "If they had more to add or deny, I would tell them to go to Ziegner. That happened a number of times on other things."[65] At the time, however, St. Angelo vehemently denied that he asked Powell to meet with Ziegner. He told a reporter from The Associated Press that the meeting was Powell's idea.[66]

Powell and Nichols agreed that Nichols would do most of the talking. When they arrived at Ziegner's house, Ziegner immediately started the questioning, zeroing in on charges of ghost employment in the secretary of state's office. He mentioned the names of several employees and asked what duties they performed. He inquired as to whether or not Nichols and Powell had knowledge of political duties being performed on state time. Ziegner also asked if either of them knew who had written the Master Plan. Powell was surprised at the question. He thought Ziegner surely would have known, having been the one who broke the story and wrote that he was convinced of its authenticity.[67]

Following the meeting with Ziegner, Powell finally decided to take the polygraph. He felt he had no choice. During the first session—after about six attempts—the results were inconclusive. He was asked to come back the next evening. When he arrived, and before he was strapped to the machine, he finally admitted to the polygrapher that he had talked to Ziegner the previous week. The test then showed him to be telling the truth. But even having passed the test "with flying colors," Powell did not have a sense of relief. After the polygraph test, he walked back to the office of Media, Inc., passing by the Circle. It was snowing. A choir was on the steps of the Soldiers and Sailors Monument, singing Christmas carols. Powell stopped and listened to the carolers. It was then he decided he had to leave Indiana.

He walked back to the office, just a block away in the Illinois Building. Nichols was there. Powell told him that if he could pay off his debts he would like to get out of the whole mess—leave Indiana, and maybe try to finish his education in Arizona. Powell remembers Nichols asking him if he was serious, and when Powell said he was, Nichols told him he would help arrange something. They discussed how much money Powell would need and then Nichols drafted a statement which he asked Powell to sign. It stated that certain persons were engaged in political activity while employed in the secretary of state's office. Powell remembers Nichols writing several names on the sheet. Powell signed it. He recalls that he was assured no one would ever see it.[68]

The deal was finalized. Powell was to receive a check for $2,400, a one-way plane ticket to Arizona, and a job at a travel agency, Apache Travel, in which Gordon St. Angelo at one time had had an interest. Powell then drove to his parents' house in Salem, Indiana, and waited to hear from Nichols concerning when he would receive the money.[69]

Jeff Lewis was the last person to take the polygraph, on Friday, December 14, 1973.[70] The following Monday St. Angelo convened an executive session of the Democratic State Central Committee. During their discussion of the Master Plan, a phone call was placed to Conrad asking him to meet with the State Committee on December 26 "to discuss an independent investigation." Conrad agreed. Then the seventeen members present unanimously passed a resolution that they had "a political and moral obligation to protect the party and political system."[71]

The lie detector tests were completed. But the Democratic State Central Committee had just begun its test of Conrad.

On Wednesday, December 19, at a news conference in his office, Conrad reported that he and seventeen of his fifty-seven current employees had taken and passed the lie detector tests, as well as eight of an estimated twenty-five to thirty former employees. Among them were Jeff Lewis, John Nichols, Steve Powell, Vicki Weger, Claudia Prosser, Bob Boxell, Bob Rooksby, John Livengood, and Stu Grauel.

Michael E. Beaver, the polygraph examiner, reported to Conrad that "The subjects told the truth during their examinations. It is the opinion of this examiner that the above subjects did not wittingly participate in the preparation and distribution of the Master Plan."[72]

Conrad's release of the lie detector results quickened the pace of the State Committee's response. The day after Christmas, nineteen of the twenty-two members met with Conrad and informed him they were planning on establishing a "Special Committee for the purpose of resolving questions concerning the authorship and distribution of the alleged plan and the accuracy of the contents."[73] Wagner was there. He did the talking for Conrad. He told the committee that the approach of the Democratic party—"investigating themselves"—was foolish. A dangerous precedent would be established forever, and others would have to be investigated in the future. They would, in effect, be putting Conrad "on trial," and it would have no credibility with the media or the general public. He strongly urged the members "not to do this—we are doing it to our own kind," and emphasized that great damage could be done to the party. One member of the committee, Wagner recalls, replied by saying it was their job to "cleanse the Democratic party." The motion passed authorizing the formation of the special committee. Conrad and Wagner left the meeting without further comment.[74]

Wagner was convinced that St. Angelo was orchestrating events. Indeed, St. Angelo was "prompted" to have a state committee investigation because Conrad had brought in a private investigator and conducted polygraph examinations. Attempting to remain at arms' length from the decision, he contended it was a state committee decision, not his alone, for the party to investigate.[75]

Wagner had no choice but to go along. If Conrad refused to cooperate with the special committee it would have the appearance of "stonewalling" an authorized investigation by the party. St. Angelo and the state committee had Conrad cornered.

The formation of the special committee nearly broke Conrad. Now, in his mind, the matter was going to drag on and on. There would never be any relief. He had wide emotional swings, sometimes trying to laugh at his situation by calling it "small stuff," while, the next moment, his eyes would be moist and he could not speak. Grauel, Fensterwald, and Wagner tried to prop him up emotionally. Grauel remembers Fensterwald encouraging him to run for reelection in 1974, arguing that he could win.[76]

On Friday, Conrad and Wagner pledged full cooperation with the special committee. They reiterated their position that no public statements should be made by the "offices of the State Committee, the Secretary of State or the Special Committee until the independent inquiry is completed."[77]

The special committee was authorized to investigate the incident and report its findings only to the Democratic State Central Committee and the secretary of state. Members of the State Committee were asked to recommend people for the committee, and Conrad also submitted names. From a list of forty, St. Angelo selected four: Paul G. Jasper, a former Indiana Supreme Court Justice and ex-president of the State Police Board; Elton H. Geshwiler, the mayor of Beech Grove; Jackie L. Shropshire, an attorney from Gary and former law partner to Gary mayor Richard G. Hatcher; and Willis N. Zagrovich, president of the state AFL-CIO. Two of these members, Geshwiler and Zagrovich, were mentioned in the Master Plan. Geshwiler was described as being "on good terms" with Gordon St. Angelo. Zagrovich was described as an "ineffective leader of the AFL-CIO," and an ethnic slur was used in referring to Mrs. Zagrovich. Shropshire was not mentioned in the Master Plan, but his former law partner, Mayor Hatcher, was a long-time ally of St. Angelo. Jasper was not mentioned in the Master Plan either, but he was well aware of the heat it was generating. Before he accepted St. Angelo's appointment, he remembers calling Senator Birch Bayh and checking to see if he should serve on the committee. He remembers Bayh saying, "Go ahead, Paul, if Gordon has asked you to do it."[78]

Although there was an explicit understanding that no public comments would emanate from Conrad, the State Central Committee, or the special committee, Ziegner got the story. And he did not get it from Conrad or Wagner. Once again, timing the story for maximum impact, Ziegner waited until the 150 members of the Indiana General Assembly convened on Monday, January 7, 1974. On the front page of the *Indianapolis News*, next to a story headlined "Bowen Opens Short Session," was the headline: "State Demos Begin 'Conrad Plan' Probe." Ziegner wrote that St. Angelo confirmed there would be an investigation conducted by a small group of prominent Democrats chosen from a list "nominated" by both St. Angelo and Conrad.

The special committee held its first meeting on Friday, January 18, 1974. The members selected Jasper as the chairman. They also "employed" Michael K. Phillips from Boonville to serve as the legal counsel to the committee. Phillips was St. Angelo's former administrative assistant.

At the first meeting, Wagner requested that the proceedings be recorded. The members denied the request, saying there would be no transcript or recordings made of the proceedings. They scheduled additional meetings and instructed Phillips to contact potential witnesses.

Wagner's decision to cooperate, at least initially, led him to provide information in his possession. He agreed to submit to the committee the questions asked by the polygrapher. He agreed that Conrad would submit any relevant documents or materials that would come under the purview of the committee. But Wagner had many concerns. It was not clear when the special committee's functions would cease. With two attorneys on the committee and Mike Phillips also present, there were still no clear answers about the rules and procedures it would follow. It was undecided if Conrad had the right to cross-examine any witness. Finally, there was no clear understanding of what role Gordon St. Angelo and Mike Phillips would play.[79]

"I knew the committee was handpicked," Wagner says, "but I did know Mayor Geshwiler to be a decent man."[80]

Wagner's legal acumen led him to understand the real significance of the hearings. They were looking for ghost employment. Paying people state wages for political work was a crime. If evidence was developed, and if the Republican prosecutor of Marion County, Noble Pearcy, decided to seek indictments, more than Conrad's political career would be destroyed. Conrad was at risk of being placed on trial and being convicted of a felony.

The worst thing a political leader can do is be unsure of himself. That uncertainty radiates to all those around, burning up confidence in and respect for the leader. Conrad was uncertain. He was stumbling. Now, with Wagner's worry about a runaway special committee that could turn into a lynch mob, Conrad had had enough. He wanted to quit. A few days before, he had invited some of his closest supporters to his house. They gathered in the living room. Mary Lou remembers he had an "anguished and defeated expression on his face" as he "quietly and simply said that he could not run again." He explained he did not think it was worth it. A "deathly pall settled over the room," in Mary Lou's words. When the friends left, Mary Lou thought it was "the final poignant moment of Larry's political career."[81]

The day after the special committee met, Wagner, Ed Lewis, and Conrad got together in Wagner's law office. When Wagner again explained his concerns, Conrad replied that he was giving up. He wanted out of politics. His only concern was his campaign debt of about $20,000 that was left over from the unsuccessful 1972 campaign.

Wagner had called St. Angelo the previous day and a deal was outlined that the Democratic State Central Committee would pay off Conrad's debt if he resigned. After some discussion, an agreement was reached, and Conrad and Wagner went downtown to meet with St. Angelo. When they walked in, St. Angelo greeted them and Wagner saw Mike Phillips. He asked St. Angelo what he was doing there, and St. Angelo replied that Phillips was helping him. Wagner said, "Get him out of here." Phillips left.

Conrad sat on a couch and said nothing. Wagner told St. Angelo that Conrad was willing to resign. "You've got your way," Wagner said, "but the only thing I'm asking is for you to pay the campaign debt." St. Angelo said he understood, and agreed.

Wagner pressed. "You have to pay the debt off first, then he'll resign."

"I won't do that," St. Angelo said. "You know I'll do what I say."

Wagner responded: "I know I'm honest," and left the sentence unfinished.

St. Angelo said that could not be the deal. Conrad had to resign first. "I've got all the cards," he said.

"We're going to do everything to preserve Larry's reputation," Wagner replied, then he motioned to Conrad and said, "Let's get out of here."

They left. Conrad had not said a word.

"You're not resigning," Wagner told him in the car. "They have thrown down the gauntlet. I'm not convinced your debt would ever be paid." Conrad was silent.[82]

With the deal off, the special committee was to continue meeting. Since it had been previously agreed that no public statements would come from Conrad or the special committee, there was suddenly an eerie silence in the media about Conrad and the Master Plan. The *Indianapolis News* did not run an article about Conrad between January 7 and March 4, 1974. This nearly two-month gap was to be the longest pause in coverage in the *News* in the eleven months of the controversy. When the Conrad stories resumed in the *News*, very few were written by Ziegner. Two younger reporters, Art Harris and Skip Hess, took over the assignment.

The "Report of the Special Committee" was given to Larry Conrad and Gordon St. Angelo on February 20, 1974. Among its "findings" were the following:

That the post mark contained on the envelopes in which the master plan was mailed to the original receipients [sic] and received on or about November 20, 1973, indicates that the distribution originated from Indianapolis. That the identity of the person or persons responsible for the distribution of the "Conrad Master Plan" is unknown. However, the Committee has determined from the member of the news media who received a hand delivered copy that the person presenting the copy was a [sic] "honorable person of high integrity."

That the envelope and tape binding the envelope were the type among others purchased and used by the various departments of the State of Indiana.

High echelon employees within the Secretary of State's Office assisted in the gathering and compiling of sensitive information which parallels some of the substance of the "Conrad Master Plan."

Programs exist in the Conrad Campaign Organization and Structure including the County Secretary's Plan, the BAID Program, the Labor Program, and the Township Trustee Candidates Program, which are very similar to the substance of the alleged "Conrad Master Plan."

The atmosphere in the Secretary of State's Office coupled with the politically talented staff of the Secretary of State suggests that persons employed in the Secretary of State's Office may have had knowledge of or assisted in the preparation of material that became the "Conrad Master Plan."

Finally, the report concluded that "there is a strong indication that the Conrad Master Plan was a product of persons having close knowledge of the operation and functioning of the Office of the Secretary of State. For these reasons, there is strong indication that the Secretary of State should have known about the Conrad Master Plan." Furthermore, the committee contended that the content of the document "is scurrilous and without factual foundation and is the absurd conclusions of the writer or writers," and that Larry Conrad "should have more closely supervised and been aware of the activities of his employees."

The report recommended that the Democratic State Committee "divorce itself from such person or persons" who had written the Master Plan "at such time as the person or persons become known." The committee then recommended that "all candidates for public office pledge and obligate themselves to administer and manage their offices to provide the utmost in service that time, money, and equipment of said offices will allow."[83]

Wagner viewed the report as "innocuous."[84] For all their trials and tribulations, the special committee had found nothing. But the State Central Committee, which was to receive the report on February 23, was not through. At that meeting, all of Wagner's fears were to come true. One of the members of the State Central Committee said that it "was a good report, but it did not cover the whole thing." He claimed that he asked the question: "Did they find any evidence of ghost employees?" and the special committee members admitted that the whole second floor was nothing but political.[85]

Wagner thought the report was the final report—and it was titled as such—but the State Committee voted to "direct the committee to submit its findings concerning the political involvement of employees of the Office of Secretary of State during state working hours."[86] The February 20 report was to be considered only an interim report—there was to be a final report and the State Central Committee wanted evidence on ghost employment. They were looking for evidence of a crime.

Wagner was now firmly convinced that the special committee was a setup, designed not to get at the facts but to ruin Conrad. Wagner knew of only four witnesses who had appeared before the committee: Conrad, Rooksby, Grauel, and Lewis.[87] Wagner contended the first report was "billed as a final report, but [the state committee] recessed for lunch and then decided it was an interim report."[88]

This programmed effort by the state party organization to dump Conrad from the ticket was the wrong tactic. When the State Central Committee decided to come after him on the basis of having committed a crime, fury started stirring in Conrad. His worry and his shame slowly turned to anger. The last week of February, he and Mary Lou went to Washington, D.C., where he spoke at length with Fensterwald and other friends about the situation. He received encouragement from everyone to announce for reelection. However, he did not discuss the matter with Senator Bayh.

As though the heat released from Conrad's purported boiler room was not enough to raise the discomfort level in the Democratic party, St. Angelo once again turned up the burners. When Conrad returned home, he learned that on March 3, 1974, the 9th district Democratic Committee, under the chairmanship of Bill Trisler, who also served as St. Angelo's executive assistant, had released a statement claiming that Conrad would be "a great liability" to the 1974 state ticket. Trisler urged Conrad to bow out of the secretary of state's race. He contended that the concern over the Master Plan threatened to jeopardize Birch Bayh's reelection.

Trisler's statement came on the heels of two statements issued the previous week by district chairs who felt that Conrad's "presence on the state ticket might hurt the party's chances in the general election."[89] Here was a perfect political wedge: claiming that Bayh's survival depended on killing Conrad.

But it wasn't just Trisler and the Democratic State Central Committee against Conrad. Now the Republicans decided to become involved in the "Dump Conrad Movement." The chairman of the Republican State Central Committee, Thomas S. Milligan, said that "Conrad and the Master Plan won't be much of a campaign issue if Conrad decides to step out of the political picture and not seek renomination."[90]

But Conrad had supporters—very important supporters—and they finally started coming forward. On Friday evening, March 8, as Larry was in the basement, watching television, the doorbell rang. Mary Lou opened the door and standing on the front steps were several people. Claudia Prosser's parents were there. Her mother was vice-chairman of the Barthlomew County Democratic party and had issued a public statement the previous Tuesday urging Conrad to run again.[91] Don Yeagley from the UAW was there. So was Bob Pastrick. Bun Gallahan, the 5th district chairman, was there. Gallahan also had released a statement earlier in the week saying the movement to dump Conrad was led by people whose "heads would roll if he became governor," and contended that the members of the State Central Committee might be against him, but the vast majority of county chairmen were with him.[92]

Mary Lou invited everyone in. She then ushered Larry upstairs. They all sat around the dining room table. The guests were angry. "You've got to defend yourself," Mary Lou remembers one of them saying. "We're with you, but we can't do it without you."

That's what Conrad needed to hear. He had felt alone, isolated. He had seen his career ruined, and saw nothing in the future except legal challenges and shame. Now there were people refusing to give up. They were refusing to wither. He got mad.

On Saturday, he was silent most of the day. On Sunday, Larry leaned over to Mary Lou and said, "I've decided to run again." Mary Lou heard him say it in a different voice than she had been hearing for the past three months. "It was the most positive statement he had made in months. I knew it was the right decision for all of us," she wrote in her diary.

Later that evening, Claudia Prosser was sitting on the floor of her apartment in Indianapolis, watching television, when the phone rang. It was Larry. "There are two people you never want to see mad," Conrad told her. "The first one is Boxell, and the second one is me. We're going to go."[93]

Prosser was surprised. She knew the last few months had been the worst days in Conrad's life. She knew he had been reevaluating his life and his career. He had mentioned to her the horror of Watergate and what it was doing to the national government. "This was a very bad time," Claudia recalled. "He was very disheartened until he finally got mad."[94]

Conrad's anger had been fueled earlier that day when he received his copy of the final report of the special committee. Signed by the four members, it reported the following "findings":

The facts show strong evidence of major political activities and resulting irregularities on the part of some employees of the Secretary of State during working hours and at the taxpayers expense.

We recommend very strongly that the Secretary of State reduce his staff to those persons needed to conduct statutory requirements of the office.

All supplies, equipment, automobiles, stamps, and phones of the Secretary of State's office should be used solely for the benefit of the State and its citizens and if used for other activities, should be replaced or repaid to the state.[95]

Conrad understood the implications of the report. His anger overcame his fear. He was convinced he had to fight.

Nobody was more pleased with Conrad's decision than Robert Wagner. He was infuriated by the press reports concerning the findings of the interim report of the special committee. Wagner now could go on the offensive.

Wagner called a news conference for 2:30 P.M., Tuesday, March 12, at which Conrad announced that he would seek a second term regardless of what conclusions were in the reports of the special committee. Conrad pointed out that the special committee, in its initial report, found no proof that he had any knowledge of the Master Plan and, taking a swipe at St. Angelo and the State Central Committee, he emphasized that the "perpetrators of this farce [are] Democrats." He said he would not be driven from office by "a few character assassins or a small group of fanatical people." Finally, he pointed out that there was an agreement that no public comments would be made on the interim report of the special committee until the committee had completed its work—and that agreement had been broken.

In fact, there had been an agreement that no "public comments" concerning the work of the special committee would be made "by the offices of the State Committee, the Secretary of State, or the Special Committee until the independent inquiry is completed." St. Angelo, however, claimed that the "agreement was a personal one between Conrad and himself, not binding on anyone else."[96] That, of course, was a tortured interpretation of the agreement of understanding between Conrad and the Democratic State Central Committee.

Stu Grauel was at Conrad's news conference. "We had him all pumped up," Grauel says. But realizing that his swings of emotion were wide, Wagner, Grauel, and Mary Lou had decided that he would leave town following the announcement. "We made arrangements for him and Mary Lou to go to Washington to visit old friends and we booked them on Amtrak. That night I drove them to the station to catch the 11 P.M. train, but it was six hours late. We just waited around the old decrepit Union Station until about 5 A.M., and I loaded them on the train to Washington."[97]

The same day Conrad announced his candidacy, another anonymous document stirred the waters of the Democratic party. This time, the target was Gordon St. Angelo. The letter was dated March 7, 1974, and was signed, "An Individual with a Guilty Conscience." The writer claimed to be "involved with the office of Gordon St. Angelo" and to "have been a party to a 'Dirty Tactics Plan'" that St. Angelo "uses when he has a personal grievance against someone who he feels is getting too politically powerful." Contending that the Master Plan "was conceived and prepared by Gordon St. Angelo and Bill Trisler," the writer claimed to have been "one of a party to printing this plan, and it was printed from material written by Gordon and Bill." The writer alleged that St. Angelo had used similar tactics against John Bottorff, a former secretary of state, and claimed that St. Angelo was planning to go after Senator Bayh in the near future.

The author indicated the letter had been mailed to the managing editor of the *Indianapolis Star*, John Bottorff, Larry Conrad, and Birch Bayh.[98]

Robert Mooney, the chief political reporter for the *Star*, made the letter the main topic of his Sunday column on March 17. Mooney claimed the "spurious letter possibly aimed at starting an ouster movement against . . . St. Angelo appears to have fizzled before it sizzled." Mooney stated that Senators Bayh and Hartke both said they would not participate in any such move, and that Conrad had indicated that he "has enough troubles of his own at this time without becoming involved in any ouster attempt."

The letter caught the attention of the reporters when one of Bayh's Washington staffers talked with Bob Rutherford of the Indiana Broadcasters Association and asked if Rutherford or other reporters had seen the letter. Rutherford had not seen it, but he used the story on the air and it was fed to several radio stations. Apparently the letter had been mailed to Bayh's Indianapolis office, but the senator and the staff in Washington had not read it.

Mooney showed a copy of the letter to St. Angelo on Friday, March 15, and St. Angelo's reaction was immediate:

> This is the kind of dirt I have been expecting ever since the Conrad Master Plan became public. People who are capable of writing documents as insensitive and cheap as the Master Plan would deviously write such an anonymous letter concerning myself and Bill Trisler. Perhaps this is what we who have served for a long time find so discouraging about the "New Politics" as the honor and integrity of the politician are destroyed by radical zealots. I again denounce this trend which threatens to destroy what little honor is left for the well-intended politician. I again deny any involvement in the Conrad Master Plan.[99]

The day Mooney's column appeared, Bob Wagner was in Phoenix, Arizona. While Larry and Mary Lou were headed to Washington on Amtrak, Wagner had received a very important phone call. It was from Steve Powell in Arizona.

Two months before, in early January, as we have seen, Powell had flown to Arizona and had obtained a job as a tour guide for Apache Travel, a travel agency in which St. Angelo previously had an ownership interest. St. Angelo does not remember assisting Powell in getting this job, but he does recall that Powell knew he "had interests in travel agencies."[100]

In his call to Wagner, Powell said he was still extremely upset over the Master Plan. His conscience was bothering him. He was having trouble sleeping at night. Wagner immediately made arrangements to fly to Phoenix and talk to Powell.

In the early afternoon of March 17, 1974, James Stephen Powell made a sworn statement to Robert Wagner in the presence of a court reporter. Powell testified to his duties in the secretary of state's office and his leaving Conrad's employ. He talked about his job with Mary Aikens Currie in the state auditor's office, and his brief tenure as president of the Young Democrats. He also told of his relationship with Media, Inc., and disclosed that St. Angelo had told him on two occasions that he could receive immunity from prosecution. He said that he was distressed over the Master Plan. Then he revealed the following:

> On or about January 2nd, 1974, I was given two checks by Media Incorporated. The one to pay off my debts was for $2,300 gross, less $621.30 in federal taxes, $134.55 for Social Security taxes, and $46 in state taxes. The actual amount I received was $1,498.15.
>
> The other check was for $215.23, for a TWA flight to Phoenix, Arizona, on January 2nd, 1974, being Flight 181, plus $100 expense money.
>
> I attempted to cash both checks at Indiana National Bank at the corner of Capitol and Market Street in Indianapolis that same day. They would only cash the smaller of the two checks because of insufficient funds in Media Incorporated's account.
>
> I spoke to either John Nichols or Jeff Lewis about the deficiency, and was told that a deposit had been made, and that the check was good.
>
> I then returned to the bank branch and made further inquiry about the account. I was shown a check for approximately $2,400 (the amount was the amount of my debts, plus the cost of the plane ticket) made payable to either John Nichols or Media Incorporated. The check was drawn on the First National Bank of Arizona, and was signed by Gordon St. Angelo.[101]

Wagner now had the evidence. And he decided it was time to use it.

The next day Wagner was back in Indianapolis. He made arrangements to meet with Paul Doherty of the *Indianapolis Star* in a hotel room on Thursday. He presented Steve Powell's deposition and explained, in detail, the history of the special committee and how the February 20 report was changed to an "interim report." He reported that the second report was delivered to Conrad on March 9, but was never made public. There was reason to believe that it was being returned to the special committee for a third report. Wagner made it clear that he thought St. Angelo was orchestrating the entire affair in an effort to ruin Conrad. Then Wagner left the hotel room—leaving Doherty with copies of the materials.

The next day Wagner was scheduled to fly to Washington with Charles Deppert of the AFL-CIO. Deppert remembers the flight well: "When we got airborne Wagner said to me 'While we are flying to Washington that goddamn St. Angelo is going to resign. I've got him by the throat and I'm not going to let go.' When we landed in Washington, Wagner went to the telephone and called Indianapolis. He was informed St. Angelo had quit. Wagner was very happy."[102]

On Sunday, March 24, on page one of section two of the *Indianapolis Star*, Robert P. Mooney reported that St. Angelo was resigning effective April 6 to take a position with Lilly Endowment effective April 15. St. Angelo had hinted at quitting the previous Friday, when he spoke to a group of Democrats in South Bend. Mooney quoted St. Angelo as saying: "My adversaries will be glad to see me go and my friends think it's too good of an opportunity for me to pass up. Under these circumstances, everyone will be happy."[103]

On Monday, at a news conference at state headquarters, St. Angelo confirmed that he was quitting. He said, "The field I am going into will preclude my active political participation," but added that he was merely going "to change my arena, but not the purpose." He refused to confirm that he would be moving to Lilly Endowment, saying, "That will be announced later." He said that negotiations with his new employer had begun in late August or early September of 1973 and "finally last week we came to a definite conclusion and commitment."[104]

St. Angelo's nine-year, three-month rule over the Indiana Democratic party was over.

Did the Master Plan force St. Angelo to quit? Not according to St. Angelo. "[The Master Plan] was the last thing I wanted to happen. I made up my mind in 1972 at the national convention that I was getting out. I was at my peak. I was chair of our national delegation. But we had no patronage [in Indiana], and after an all-night session at the convention, I went back to the hotel room at 6 A.M. and told my wife I was getting out. I was so disgusted with the party. I was afraid the damn Master Plan would affect my move [to Lilly Endowment] and I had spent eight to ten months discussing this move. It was not what it was doing to Conrad. It was what it might do to me. The best thing to happen to me would be a tranquil move to Lilly Endowment."[105]

St. Angelo says he purposely tried to stay away from the controversy. He tried desperately not to comment on the events because he was in the job transition. His resolve to quit the chairmanship was strengthened after the disastrous Democratic defeat in November of 1972. "I wanted to walk out, not be carried out," he declares.[106]

His close friend, Ed Ziegner, confirmed that St. Angelo's move to Lilly Endowment had been in the works for some time. In his weekly column following St. Angelo's resignation, Ziegner wrote that "weeks ago St. Angelo pledged an old friend to secrecy, told him of the possibility of the offer, and sought his opinion. 'You're a damn fool if you don't take it,' he was told, if the offer came. 'You can't be state chairman forever.'" Obviously, the way Ziegner punctuated his story, the "old friend" pledged to secrecy was Ziegner himself.[107] Years later, Ziegner shed more light on St. Angelo's resignation: "He didn't think so at the time, but the luckiest thing that ever happened to Gordon was going to Lilly Endowment. He has a good paying job without people picking at him."[108]

With St. Angelo gone, Conrad and Wagner were now on the offensive. Wagner made plans to open a campaign office in the Illinois Building. Friends and supporters came rushing to Conrad's side. The day after St. Angelo announced his resignation, Democratic officials throughout the state received a letter from Democratic State Representative Leo A. Voisard. In it Voisard defended Conrad, claiming that some "Powers That Be" were seeking to "bring down a bright young leader." He urged all who received his letter to contact Conrad and pledge support to him, saying "We will not sell the 1976 governorship to the Republicans for 30 pieces of doubt by crucifying an innocent man."[109]

St. Angelo's resignation created an immediate stir in the party. Who would replace him? Bill Trisler began calling members of the State Central Committee to inform them of his availability. Fred Garver, a lawyer and lobbyist from Boggstown and a former staff member in the Welsh and Branigin administrations, also began to express his interest in the post. Former Speaker Richard Bodine of St. Joseph County said he was interested. There was also a move to get former Governor Matthew Welsh to agree to take the job, at least on an interim basis, but he declined. Other names were floated in the media, including Vigo County chairman Ed Stapleton, a Conrad backer, and Ken Cragen, Bayh's candidate against St. Angelo in 1970.[110]

The State Central Committee was scheduled to meet on Saturday, March 31, in Batesville. Four days before the meeting, Judy Burton, vice-chairman of the committee, raised objections to having the Batesville meeting serve as a reorganization meeting at which an interim chairman would be elected. She cited party rules, which specified that when the chairmanship becomes vacant, the vice-chairman takes the job and schedules the reorganization meeting, and pointed out that "party leaders hardly can expect county officers and those below to follow the rules, as they have been urged to do, if the rules are not followed at the top."[111]

What was going to happen in Batesville was once again in the hands of the two Democratic U.S. senators from Indiana: Hartke and Bayh. And once again they were not together.

Bayh, of course, was up for reelection in 1974. Hartke declared that if Bayh wanted to intervene to elect his choice, he was free to do so. Hartke was staying out of it.

Bayh was obviously relieved that St. Angelo had quit. For several years he had viewed him as a "Machiavelli."[112] But Bayh was very reluctant to get involved in another reorganization fight. He remembered well his defeat in 1970. Moreover, Bayh's personal life had undergone a major change since 1970. In October of 1971, Marvella Bayh had undergone surgery for breast cancer and had undertaken an eighteen-month regimen of chemotherapy. Bayh had withdrawn from the 1972 presidential race, saying "I want to be at her side—not in Miami, Milwaukee, or Los Angeles."[113]

Bayh's sole goal in 1974 was to win reelection. He briefly considered backing one of his staff members, Larry Cummings, for the chairmanship. Cummings was well liked by the members of the State Central Committee and was the son-in-law of Judy Burton, the committee's vice-chairman. But St. Angelo enjoyed the strong support of at least fifteen of the twenty-two committee members, and St. Angelo was for Trisler. For Cummings to make it, Bayh once again would have to personally intercede, and this time the fight would occur in his reelection year. Moreover, even with his personal intervention, he was likely to come up short once again. "We just didn't have enough support," Bayh says.[114] Bayh ducked. On Thursday evening, March 28, the senator met with Trisler. After a long discussion, Bayh pressed his view that the party organization had to be opened to more people and he expected Trisler to work closely with Bayh and the rest of the Indiana congressional delegation. When Trisler gave assurances to Bayh that he would do so, the senator decided to endorse him. "I wasn't really looking for somebody to be mine," Bayh contends. "I wanted somebody who could be trusted, and Bill said all the right things."[115] The next day, Ziegner had the story: "Sen. Bayh Backs Trisler For State Party Chairman."[116]

When the Democratic State Central Committee met on Saturday, Trisler was elected by unanimous vote. Three committee members abstained: Bun Gallahan, the 5th district chairman; Henri Gibson, the 11th district vice-chairman; and Alan Stephen of Rochester, who was voting Judy Burton's proxy. Gallahan said he was not opposed to Trisler, but objected to the violation of party rules that had been pointed out by Burton.[117]

The long-awaited "Final Report" of the special committee was not presented to the State Committee in Batesville. Trisler, who had called on Conrad to step aside just four weeks earlier, suddenly changed direction. Now, as state chairman, he was singing a new tune. "This is a new day," Trisler said. "We will allow all Democrats to run . . . and I am in favor of Conrad running. He has every right to run the same as everyone else." Trisler said the final report did not come before the State Committee because "nobody showed up to answer our questions." He proclaimed that the pledge to release the final report on the Master Plan was made "under a different chairman."[118]

The agenda for the State Committee meeting in Batesville did include an item on the report of the special committee. Paul Jasper, however, said that he did not attend the meeting because St. Angelo had called him the night before and asked him not to come.[119] In all likelihood, the report was shelved as a show of good faith on Trisler's behalf.

But the Master Plan had severely damaged Conrad's political reputation. One opponent, Robert McCallen of Wabash, had already announced his candidacy for the nomination for secretary of state. He was immediately endorsed by the 4th district chairman, Jerry Lantz of Fremont, and the 2nd district chairman, Maurice Mason of Hebron. Others besides McCallen were also rumored to be interested in the race because of Conrad's troubles. The primary election, which would select delegates to the state convention, was only five weeks away. With the pall of the Master Plan hanging over the entire party organization, Wagner knew he had to move swiftly.

Indianapolis Star reporter Paul M. Doherty had not yet written an article connecting St. Angelo's resignation and Powell's affidavit. Finally, on April 5, his story appeared: "A key element in the dramatic events . . . appears to be what could be called the Case of the Missing Young Democrat." Doherty reported on Powell's relationship with Conrad and St. Angelo, including St. Angelo's help in securing him a job in Arizona. He then wrote:

> But one reliable and well informed Democrat says he learned before St. Angelo announced his resignation . . . that persons acting in Conrad's behalf were pressing St. Angelo to get out, using information furnished by Powell.
>
> Another reliable source in the party had told a reporter two days before St. Angelo bowed out that the chairman was on the defensive on the issue of Conrad's renomination, because of allegedly damaging information which had come into the hands of the Conrad forces.[120]

The response to Doherty's story was immediate—and, as usual, it came from anonymous sources. The final report of the special committee was leaked to the press. Once again, the story was on the front page. Ziegner claimed that the release of the final report was "authorized" by the Democratic State Central Committee at its Batesville meeting. He summarized the conclusion that Conrad should reduce the number of staff members in his office and pointed out that all four members of the special committee had signed the report. Ziegner was unable to locate Conrad for his response, because Conrad was home, sick, but Ziegner did talk with Wagner. "The report deals in innuendo, as did the first report," Wagner told the reporter. "I don't find it satisfactory, and I don't feel it deals in the truth." Bill Trisler, the new state chairman, stayed out of the line of fire by saying he had "no comment at all." Ziegner's story then mentions St. Angelo, claiming that his resignation was "in no way connected with the master plan controversy."[121]

With Ziegner again writing about the controversy, Wagner knew he had to move quickly. Doherty's story on April 5 was the first positive story on Conrad in nearly four and one-half months. But St. Angelo and the state party—having anticipated the Doherty story—had their counterattack ready. Wagner knew Conrad had to stay on the offensive. He immediately scheduled a news conference for April 10. In statements made to a reporter from The Associated Press, Wagner said Conrad in his news conference would "disprove charges of political work on state time by his staff" and would include names of party officials who "tried to railroad Larry Conrad out of office." He revealed that Conrad's statement would not name the author of the Master Plan, but "will show exactly what has been going on since then." The AP reporter, Darrell Christian, had talked by telephone to Steve Powell the previous evening, who had told him that "former Democratic State Chairman Gordon St. Angelo [was] an active figure . . . in disseminating derogatory information about Conrad's staff." Christian also contacted St. Angelo for his response, and characterized St. Angelo's position as charging that "the Powell statement was an indication Conrad was seeking a way out of the furor by using St. Angelo because he no longer is state chairman."[122]

On April 10, Conrad came out swinging. Pounding the conference table in his Statehouse office, he said he was committed "to build a new responsive state party." He declared that a number of people on the Democratic State Committee were "honestly and genuinely concerned about the party," but that others "have been taken in" and that if those individuals do not adjust, they "present a problem." Conrad accused St. Angelo of having been among those who tried to capitalize on the Master Plan and force him from office. He attacked the special committee: "I suggest that the special committee operated in a completely closed atmosphere, getting only information controlled by persons interested in my political assassination." He said that he had never favored the creation of the committee and contended that when the State Committee went ahead he specifically requested that persons named in the Master Plan not be included on the committee. When asked if he would support Trisler as chairman, Conrad replied: "I am not in a position to support him at this time," but he also said his position on Trisler was "not irrevocable."[123] Conrad and Wagner had put Trisler on notice.

Conrad's "tell-all" news conference was designed to solidify support among his loyalists and illuminate the changes now possible in the party with St. Angelo's departure. What Conrad and Wagner did not anticipate was the ferocity with which St. Angelo and his loyalists would counterattack.

The *Indianapolis News*, on the same day as Conrad's news conference, ran a story headlined: "Political Aids [*sic*] on Conrad Payroll." Art Harris and Skip Hess reported that "at least nine persons . . . in Conrad's office this year were hired to perform political functions while on the state payroll," based on "evidence and testimony presented to the Special Committee." Reporting that they possessed "copies of documents, one marked 'personal and confidential,'" Harris and Hess claimed the information pointed to ghost employees and political activity, including the use of state facilities and supplies and expenditure of state monies for political or personal purposes. They then listed eleven specific "never-made-public findings" of the special committee, including:

> At least nine employees in the secretary of state's office, according to a January, 1974, personnel manning table, were political employees;
>
> A number of people [were] hired and placed into job classifications for which they are not qualified in order to provide for additional income for those individuals;
>
> One employee, classified as an attorney, is not admitted to practice law in the state;
>
> One employee on the state payroll served as Conrad's chief speech writer;
>
> Employees served as baby sitters or assisted the Conrads personally during state time at their residence. . . . [124]

Just as Conrad's staff members were regaining their confidence and seeing a reinvigorated Conrad on the attack, they were pinpointed as the culprits. Livengood, of course, was the "chief speech writer"; Prosser was the one charged with being a "baby sitter" on state time. But they could not even catch their breath, because, the very next day, Ziegner came at them again.

In a front-page "commentary," Ziegner, mixing his metaphors, contended that Conrad's "'tell all' news conference, promoted as possibly 'earthshaking,' turned out to be a heavily mildewed, very wet ladyfinger." Ziegner eviscerated Conrad, saying that "he still doesn't know who [wrote] the master plan"; and that Conrad admitted he "made no public protest over the membership of the [special] committee." He said that Conrad had no plans to downsize his staff and that he "declined to name any names" of people who "were trying to drive him out of politics."

But on Powell's testimony, Ziegner had a fact wrong, which led him to write a very revealing paragraph:

> Earlier this week, Powell, a onetime Conrad staff member, gave Conrad an affidavit stating that Powell had given Gordon St. Angelo . . . a list of persons possibly involved in "ghost employe" [sic] work in Conrad's office, although he had no actual knowledge of this.

Powell's affidavit, which was based on his sworn statement to Wagner, specifically said that John Nichols had drafted the statement and listed the names of the staff members doing political work. Powell said in the affidavit: "I signed the document because I wanted out. John Nichols told me that the document would be kept in a safe and used as 'insurance.'"

There was no way Ziegner could have known from the affidavit, or from Conrad's news conference, that St. Angelo physically possessed the "list of persons" with Powell's signature on it. The list, as far as Powell and Conrad knew, was still in Nichols's safe. Ziegner would have known St. Angelo had it only because Nichols or St. Angelo allowed him to know. One or both informed Ziegner. Indeed, the "insurance" demanded of Powell had not worked, but it was used anyway.[125]

Despite Ziegner's revealing slip-up, he plowed ahead, doing everything to protect St. Angelo. In the same article he made sure St. Angelo had his say: "St. Angelo, in rebuttal to Conrad's affidavit from Powell, said Conrad is trying to make St. Angelo a scapegoat and added: 'A blind jackass will kick a dead lion.'"[126]

The breach between Conrad and St. Angelo was total. More than two decades later, St. Angelo agrees. "We were always estranged. The division came when Birch Bayh came after me [in 1970]. We never got together." This "division" came about even though Conrad was not involved in Bayh's attempted ouster of St. Angelo. And St. Angelo admits he had no evidence of Conrad's involvement with Bayh: "If Conrad was part of Bayh's effort to remove me, it wasn't apparent. Plus, he drew from the same sources as Bayh, so it wouldn't have made any difference if he were involved."[127]

Bayh did not trust St. Angelo, and the feeling was mutual. And St. Angelo did not trust Conrad because of his association with Bayh. "The reason I wanted to get rid of Gordon St. Angelo was the same reason he wanted to get Larry. St. Angelo couldn't be trusted," Bayh says.[128]

There was to be no respite. The day after Ziegner rushed to St. Angelo's defense, Art Harris and Skip Hess were back on the front page of the *News* with a story contending that five persons on Conrad's payroll in October of 1973 "were assigned to receive written and telephone information for Conrad's reelection campaign." The story was largely a rewrite of Ziegner's article of December 11, 1973, in which the BAID (Births, Anniversaries, Injuries, and Deaths) and county secretaries programs were revealed, only now the reporters were naming names: Robert Rooksby and Jane Allen, who had recently married and moved to Atlanta, Georgia; Pamela Modrowski; Claudia Prosser; and Bruce Simon. All five were quoted in the article, and each of them stated that they performed political work only on their own time. Prosser said, "We had areas of responsibility, and we did them on our own time. I won't deny I worked on political matters, but I took care of it after hours." Bob Rooksby claimed that he worked 60 hours a week and denied that he ever did political work on state time. He did acknowledge that he asked "county secretaries" to call him collect and promised to return the call on the WATS line, and said, "I'm very sorry I put that together. I probably shouldn't have done it. I didn't see anything wrong with it. I probably shouldn't have done it." He also admitted that using state stationery for the county secretaries program was a "mistake."

The reporters then dropped the bombshell: "The records indicating office personnel and their assignments on the county secretaries program has [*sic*] been turned over to Marion County Prosecutor Noble R. Pearcy, who said he would determine whether to present it to the grand jury for examination."[129] The two reporters for the *News* had, at their own instigation, voluntarily turned over their materials—from unrevealed sources—to the prosecutor. There had been no threat of a subpoena. Not content to merely write the news, they were going to make the news. They had taken the step Wagner had anticipated—and feared. Now Conrad needed more than just political advice, he needed legal counsel.

From the beginning Wagner thought that the Master Plan controversy would likely end up in court. He couldn't have anticipated, of course, that one of the state's leading newspapers would instigate the action. In December 1973, when the State Committee formed the special committee, Conrad and Grauel had retained Wagner as their legal counsel. Grauel remembers writing a check to Wagner for either $200 or $250, and asking him to "hold" the check until Friday because he had insufficient funds in his account. "I think he had to hold Larry's check, as well. That's how broke we were," Grauel recalls.[130]

The Saturday and Sunday following the revelation that the prosecutor had the reporters' records, Wagner devised Conrad's next step. Once again, he was to go on the offensive.

First, Wagner had to neutralize the Democratic State Central Committee. And he saw how to do it. If they had investigated Conrad before, would they be willing to investigate the latest allegations? If so, they would have to inquire as to how the *Indianapolis News* received anonymous materials which were provided only to the special committee. Wagner fired off a letter to Bill Trisler:

> The Special Committee investigating the Master Plan, and their attorney, stated that no notes were taken during the course of the proceeding; no documents were received into evidence; and all information received would be kept confidential and only reported to the Democratic State Committee.
>
> Nonetheless, an unknown person recently submitted many documents to the *Indianapolis News* in an obvious attempt to further embarrass my client. It seems highly probable that only one of five persons could have done this.
>
> I am particularly interested in whether another Committee will be appointed to investigate and offer findings on these most damning activities that were recently brought to light. In view of the precedent established in the Conrad case, I would hate to believe that the Conrad investigation was pushed by a few opportunists. Hopefully, it was an investigation many agreed with and certainly the improprieties recently disclosed should be handled in the same judicious manner.[131]

Trisler did not want to touch it. He wanted nothing more to do with special investigations. He assured Wagner there was no plan to launch another special committee. Finally, Wagner had neutralized the investigatory power of the Democratic State Central Committee.

Second, Wagner realized they had to go on the offensive with the prosecutor. On Monday, April 15, Conrad wrote a letter to the Republican Marion County Prosecutor, Noble Pearcy, in which he stated:

> The Grand Jury under our system of Government is the only true extension of the will of the people. I ask your assistance in arriving at the truth in all of the following:
>
> A. The origin and distribution of the so-called "Master Plan."
>
> B. The activities concerning the selection and conclusions of the "special committee."
>
> C. The source and credibility of unsigned materials circulated by unidentified persons.

D. Any and all activities of myself and my staff relating to all phases of my office.

Conrad assured Pearcy that he would have the "complete cooperation of my office." He also pointed out that after the issuance of the final report of the special committee, the *Indianapolis News* referred to "more unsigned reports and documents which had come from an unidentified source." Then Conrad drew his conclusion: "Evidence has now been disclosed which reveals that the special committee was spoon-fed information in an atmosphere designed not to reveal, but rather to conceal the truth. An example of the chicanery is found in the attached 'Affidavit' from Steve Powell, who was coerced into issuing a false statement and then paid to leave the state to insure his silence."[132] Conrad released a copy of his letter to Pearcy to the media.

Pearcy replied to Conrad's letter by making clear the grand jury was not "going to investigate a political squabble. But there may be questions of violations of the 'ghost' statute and of use of state materials for political purposes."[133] Pearcy also revealed that he was seeking information from the State Board of Accounts on the number of full-time employees in the secretary of state's office.[134]

That same day a public statement was finally issued by John C. Nichols of Media, Inc. He said Conrad was "one of the most dedicated and progressive Democrats in the state of Indiana" and that he considered Conrad and his family to be "my dearest and closest of personal friends." When Nichols was asked about Powell's affidavit, Nichols replied: "I am not in the affidavit business. I am in the advertising business. The smear campaign now being conducted by some people serves one purpose: the detriment of the Democratic party."[135] This statement by a self-described "dear and close personal friend" was soon to be withdrawn. When it would be withdrawn was just a question of timing.[136]

On Saturday evening, April 20, the Democratic State Central Committee put on their biggest fund-raising gala of the year, the annual Jefferson-Jackson Day Dinner. Ziegner's column that day focused on the J-J Dinner and laid bare his biases. Claiming that many Democrats were overoptimistic about winning in 1974, Ziegner said that "more experienced and wiser heads" in the party, "such as State Treasurer Jack New and Senate Minority Leader Bob Fair, two of the articulate and thoughtful party leaders" were warning against complacency. After this fawning statement, Ziegner again pinned Conrad to the wall:

The Democrats . . . have a state problem with . . . Larry Conrad, his "master plan," various investigations by Conrad and others of who did what to whom and when. . . .

Conrad is running for renomination, "toughing it out," although four district chairmen asked him not to run and many in the party are uneasy about how much of a target he will be for the Republicans.

Right now the GOP appears to need targets. If Conrad is there, they will shoot at him, again and again and again.

Then Ziegner let his readers know what he expected the dinner speakers to do:

Gordon St. Angelo ... who led the party for nine years and three months, a record, will be honored at tonight's dinner in the Civic Center. He should be; in his tenure he did quite a job for his party and, as far as that goes, for the whole cause of better government and politics.[137]

The column belonged to Ed Ziegner. But the Jefferson-Jackson Day Dinner belonged to the Indiana Democratic party. And the dinner speakers did not devote their remarks to paeans of praise for St. Angelo.

Six days after the dinner the *News* carried a small item in its "City Desk Memos" column, where "darts and flowers" for the week were awarded to certain people and organizations. The leading item under "Darts" was: "Democratic State Chairman William Trisler, U.S. Senators Birch Bayh and Vance Hartke and all the other Democrats who spoke at Saturday's Jefferson-Jackson Day dinner, for failing to thank or praise former State Chairman Gordon St. Angelo."[138]

The May 7 primary election was now less than two weeks away. Pearcy's investigation placed a leash on Conrad. He had to be in Indianapolis. His speaking engagements were confined to Marion County and the doughnut. He was a candidate for renomination but he could not campaign—certainly not in the way that he had always campaigned.

And the leash kept getting shorter. On April 25 and 26, the two reporters from the *News* had Conrad back on the front pages. This time it was over political phone calls.[139] Harris and Hess had obtained computer printouts of all the long-distance phone calls made from Conrad's office for one month in 1972, nine months in 1973, and one month in 1974. They claimed that "hundreds" of these were "political and personal" and included several thousands of dollars' worth of calls to places such as California, Florida, Washington, D.C., New York City, and the Bahamas. The calls were "charged to telephone credit cards issued to Conrad's office or dialed direct from the state phones." They reported that seventeen telephone credit cards had been issued to Conrad's office and "the major portion of the calls placed to Washington were made to Sen. Birch Bayh's office and to his aids [*sic*]."

They cited several specifics. Three calls had been placed to George Washington University Hospital in Washington where Stephan Lesher was recuperating from a heart attack from August 28 until September 21 in

1973. Conrad admitted that he had made the calls, and, when asked if they were state business, Conrad replied: "Well, ah, yeah. I thought so. He's a correspondent for the *Times, Time,* or *Newsweek,* or one of those."

Those calls to Stephan Lesher did not directly involve state business. They involved something much more significant: the impending resignation of Vice-President Spiro Agnew. Lesher, after leaving Bayh's staff, had gone to work for *Newsweek* magazine. When Conrad reached Lesher, he had only recently been released from intensive care. After chatting about his condition, Conrad suggested that *Newsweek* should consider an article on how the Twenty-fifth Amendment would be used in the event of Agnew's resignation. At one point, Lesher recalls, Conrad wondered if "we might get together a 'My Turn' piece," if nothing else. Lesher was very interested, because he was one of nine reporters who had been subpoenaed to testify about Agnew. After Lesher's release from the hospital, he took a recuperative vacation on the beach. It was from there that he called his editor and suggested an article on how the Twenty-fifth Amendment would apply to a vacancy in the vice-presidency. "My editor asked: 'What are you doing worrying about articles?'" Lesher recalled, "implying that I should be resting. We did not write a column, but I am sure Larry was contacted by *Newsweek* as a source for an article in the magazine."[140] Indeed, the constitutional amendment Conrad had written was going to be put to use for the first time.[141]

The *Indianapolis News* also quizzed Conrad about two telephone calls made to "the office of a Washington attorney, who represented one of the convicted Watergate burglars." These calls had been placed by Conrad to Bud Fensterwald in the days following Ziegner's release of the Master Plan.

> Q: Can you tell us anything about a call to Bernard Fensterwald in November?
>
> Conrad: Yes, I talked to Bernard Fensterwald.
>
> Q: State business?
>
> Conrad: Well, I considered it to be such.
>
> Q: Was it about the Conrad master plan?
>
> Conrad: Well, that was part of it.

Now the Master Plan was turning in on itself. Calls that Conrad had made immediately after Ziegner broke the story were now being used as examples of political use of the office. Having been pushed into a massive tar pit, whenever Conrad tried to move, he was sucked further and further into the goo.

Wagner obtained the printouts of the telephone calls from the Department of Administration and the State Board of Accounts. Livengood was assigned the task of determining which calls were "personal" and which involved state business, and recalls:

> I spent night after night poring over the telephone printouts. The state had switched from unlimited and unmeasured WATS to measured WATS lines, and I think our office just continued to operate as though they were unlimited and unmeasured lines.

> I made many calls trying to verify whether or not the number was valid and the call concerned state business. I remember talking to a guy in South Bend and I identified myself as being from the secretary of state's office. He said to me "are you calling to see if the phone calls were legitimate?" And I said, "yes." He said, "I have the same problem in my company. I have people who make calls from the elevator phone . . . and I had to put that phone in because of OSHA regulations."[142]

Art Harris and Skip Hess were also poring over the computer printouts. On Monday, April 29, they wrote another front-page story for the *News* headlined, "36 Tell City Calls On State Bill." They reported that the calls were made chiefly to the Tell City mayor's office or to the mayor's home. The mayor of Tell City was Walter Hagedorn, and he was the father of Michael Hagedorn, who served as the new corporation counsel in the secretary of state's office.

When contacted about the calls, Michael Hagedorn revealed his frustration about Conrad's uncertainty and vacillation: "If you're trying to ruin my career you've got another think coming. I'm not going to lay down like Larry Conrad. If you fight me, you'll know you've been in a fight." He also asked if the reporters would "be interested in running a constructive story on all the things we've done in this office."

Stu Grauel revealed that the office was checking all the phone billings from 1971 to the present.[143]

The next day the two reporters wrote that the State Board of Accounts was "conducting an audit" into the long-distance calls charged to Conrad's phones and credit cards. Harris and Hess, however, had been totaling the costs of all 1,636 long-distance calls for the eleven months for which they had printouts. The total spent on the calls was $3,118.88. They compared this figure with long-distance charges for the governor's office ($6,628.37), the attorney general ($5,746.03), the state treasurer ($28.19), and the state auditor ($567.55).

Many of Conrad's calls were to Senator Bayh's office in Washington. When asked about them, Bayh responded: "When was it a crime for one politician to call another politician?"[144]

The telephone bill revelations spurred other Democrats to seek the secretary of state nomination. Robert McCallen had already announced, and Bill Schreiber, the Marion County chairman, started contacting party leaders to tell them he was considering becoming a candidate. Schreiber was very concerned that "Conrad's problem with the Master Plan would create major problems for the Democratic party, particularly in Marion County, where the media were playing the story. Conrad was unable to deal with the problem and I thought he should be replaced on the ticket." Schreiber said that he initially supported Fred Garver, but when Garver decided against running, Schreiber began making his plans. "I sensed a need to replace [Conrad], and I had good prospects."[145]

Others were rumored to be interested in running, including Indiana House Minority Leader Phillip E. Bainbridge. State Representative B. Patrick Bauer of South Bend began making phone calls to test the water for his candidacy.[146] Bauer thought he was well positioned to make the run. He saw the party being split between the party organization and the Bayh supporters, including Conrad. He was not a member of either faction, and thought his legislative experience gave him an edge over Schreiber.[147]

As more and more opponents were surfacing, Conrad, on May 3, held another news conference. This time he released Powell's sworn affidavit, which directly implicated Nichols and St. Angelo in the Master Plan. He also said that he was continuing to "get to the bottom" of alleged abuses of long-distance telephone calls and pledged that if any of the calls were unauthorized he would "personally pay for them." He revealed that the only "concrete evidence" he currently had about unauthorized credit card calls indicates they were made by John C. Nichols, "who has never been a state employe [sic]." He then described Nichols as "the same person that reportedly paid off Steve Powell to leave the state and issue a false statement regarding my office." Then Conrad took on the *Indianapolis News*. "During the past six months I have vigorously defended a series of front-page charges that originated in the *Indianapolis News*, involving a so-called Master Plan. I did so because I was right. These sensational articles appearing in this paper involve more than honest reporting of the news. It is an obvious attempt to do what certain persons were unable to do before, and that is remove me from the political arena."[148]

Nichols, in responding to Conrad's attack, said he was discussing the matter with his attorney.[149]

Election day is one of those times when one can obtain maximum impact for a story dealing with politics. And John C. Nichols and his attorney decided that was the day to play the news of a $500,000 libel suit against Larry Conrad and Robert Wagner. Nichols's attorney, William B. Olsen, filed the suit the day before the election. Claiming that Conrad's and Wagner's comments at the Friday news conference and in interviews reflected "derogatorily on the plaintiff's professional honesty and integrity," Olsen asked for $250,000 "in special damages," another $250,000 "in exemplary damages, and all other relief just and proper in the premises."[150]

Olsen said in a news conference that Nichols had been a victim of private accusations and harassment since the Master Plan was disclosed, and that such abuse had reached "an intolerable level." He cited one example of such harassment. He claimed Nichols had received a bill recently for printing invitations to a "Good Friday" cocktail party for Conrad's reelection. He said that a Conrad employee whose name he did not know, "representing himself as an employe[*sic*] of Media Inc. ordered the printing work and the bill submitted to Mr. Nichols."[151]

The only other time Conrad's "Good Friday" cocktail party was mentioned in the press was in Ed Ziegner's "commentary" on April 11. The last paragraph said: "Conrad confirmed he is holding a $50 a person fundraising cocktail party Friday at the Marott Hotel. Asked if it wasn't unusual to hold such an event on Good Friday, he answered, 'Well, we had to have one, and that was the only day available.'" One can only speculate as to why Ziegner asked Conrad about the Good Friday fund-raiser in early April, only to find out on May 7 that it was to be cited in the lawsuit brought against Conrad.

Wagner was ready with a reply to the lawsuit. "Truth is the defense," Wagner said. "As Mr. Nichols well knows, in any suit brought, he must make a full disclosure. Based on the information we have received, Mr. Nichols has already indicated he did use the secretary of state's credit card number and had offered reimbursement, which would suggest that there was, in fact, impropriety." Responding to the allegation that someone in Conrad's office had charged the printing for the Good Friday cocktail party to Nichols, Wagner replied that the firm hired to print the invitations "was directed to send the bill for printing to the [Conrad] campaign office on the 5th floor of the Illinois Building."[152]

As the news of the lawsuit landed in the morning papers on May 7, Hoosiers were going to the polls. Conrad visited a few polling places in Marion County during the day and, that evening, made congratulatory phone calls to Democratic nominees throughout the state.[153] Now, with precinct committeemen and delegates to the state convention elected, his campaign for renomination shifted into high gear.

Wagner and Conrad focused on the party reorganization meetings. County chairmen would be elected on Saturday, district chairmen the following Wednesday. They were compelled to try and oust some of the county chairmen and district chairmen who had led the fight to dump Conrad. If they could not demonstrate some organizational strength, the new Democratic State Central Committee could be lured into another open break with Conrad.

But the "old regulars" were ready. The day after the primary, one member of the Democratic State Central Committee, Jerry Lantz, the 4th district chairman, mailed a packet of newspaper clippings to several precinct committeemen and elected officials in counties where the current Democratic county chairman was a Conrad supporter. The objective was to persuade those committeemen to remove the Conrad supporters from their party posts in the upcoming county reorganizations. In his cover letter, Lantz wrote: "The enclosed articles will show you the irregularities which do exist and are not being found by the proper authorities. Your county chairman has been supporting this candidate and I feel you and the delegates [to the state convention] should evaluate the situation for yourselves. If this continues, the end result on November 7th could be a loss for the entire Democrat Ticket."[154]

One of the recipients of Lantz's letter and packet was the mayor of Rensselaer, Emmett W. Eger. He immediately sent Lantz's letter and the copies of the newspaper articles to Larry Conrad, with a cover letter: "I do not know a Mr. Jerry Lantz, in fact I never heard of him. I am too busy to be bothered with this kind of 'Junk Mail,' and if Mr. Lantz paid attention to his own business he would not have time for this type of operation. Come see us."[155]

Indeed, Conrad had many friends out in the districts. But a hard count of the players did not demonstrate that Conrad could succeed.

The only solid district for Conrad was the 5th, where Bun Gallahan was assured of reelection as district chairman. There was a possible opening in the 1st district, where Bob Pastrick and Richard G. Hatcher had opposing slates in the Lake County primary. Pastrick's slate won, and with Pastrick being county chairman, he could remove Hatcher as district chairman. Another Conrad victory was possible in the 2nd district, where the district chairman, Maurice Mason of Hebron, had been an outspoken opponent of Conrad. He had already endorsed McCallen. Two loyal Conrad supporters in the 2nd district, Don Michael and Stan Nice, were placed in charge of removing Mason. In the 3rd district, Freda Noble wanted to be reelected, but there were strong St. Angelo supporters waiting in the wings. Jerry Lantz—the author of the anti-Conrad missive—was stepping down as the 4th district chairman, but Conrad's support among likely county chairmen in that district did not bode well. In the 6th district, John Anderson, the district chairman, could not be defeated. In the 7th, Charles Shuee was to have opposition, but it was unlikely he would be defeated. Down along the river, in the 8th district, the district chairman was retiring, but Michael Phillips, the attorney for the special committee, was favored to replace him. Over in the 9th district, Trisler had decided to seek another term as district chairman, in hopes of being reelected state chairman. Conrad had an active supporter in the 9th, Warren Rucker, the mayor of Madison, but it was a long shot to remove Trisler as district chairman. In the 10th, Charles Howell of Richmond had not played an active role in dumping Conrad, but William Wolf of Greenfield, the former district chair, was interested in taking his old job back and had Conrad's support. Bill Schreiber, of course, was guaranteed control of the 11th district chairman by virtue of his position as county chairman.

The old regulars appeared to have plenty of strength, and in case their power was ebbing the *Indianapolis News* was standing by to shore them up. The Friday after the primary—and the day before the county reorganization meetings—Art Harris and Skip Hess took another page-one bite out of Conrad. The topic again was phone calls. "More than 200 calls made to and from Muncie, hometown of Larry Conrad, have been traced by the News to relatives, friends, and political associates of Conrad and his aids. The calls were paid for by Indiana taxpayers." In tracing long-distance calls in December of 1972 and the first eight months of 1973, the reporters revealed that ten calls went to the home of Marshall and Ruby Conrad on Rex Street. When asked to explain the calls, Marshall Conrad said, "I'm his Dad." Another twenty-one calls were to the home of Jeff Lewis and his parents. Several of these calls were charged on state credit cards after Conrad had claimed the cards were invalidated. But in checking with Indiana Bell, Harris and Hess reported that "none of the seventeen credit cards issued to Conrad's office in 1973 and 1974 has been invalidated."[156]

The next day, the Democratic precinct committeemen and vice-committeemen in the ninety-two counties elected their new county chairmen. Schreiber was easily reelected for Marion County, and Bob Pastrick was retained as Lake County chairman. Jeanne Trixler, the Huntington County chairman, did not seek reelection. She was now serving as the secretary in Larry Conrad's campaign office in the Illinois Building. Overall, Conrad picked up some county chairmen, but it was clear there was insufficient support for a majority on the state central committee.

On Friday, May 17, Art Harris and Skip Hess concluded their inquiry into Conrad's phone bills. The headline was above the masthead and read: "Conrad Phone Bill $67,236 In 39 Months."[157] The dollar amount reported in the headline was the total cost for phones for all the months Conrad had been secretary of state. Of that amount, $23,500.78 was in long-distance charges. The reporters were unable to report on how much of that figure was personal or political calls. They merely reported the previously published figure of $3,118 over an eleven-month period. Stu Grauel did admit that calls made from Grayling, Michigan, to Indianapolis in the summer of 1972 were made by him, when he was at summer camp with the Indiana National Guard. Otherwise, Grauel said, he could not single out persons he believes may have made unauthorized calls because of Nichols's libel suit against Conrad and Wagner. Grauel also indicated he was still awaiting an official finding from the State Board of Accounts as to the cost of any personal or political calls. The article concluded by pointing out that there had been no "restitution made to the state for the calls."

All Conrad and Grauel could do was cooperate with the State Board of Accounts. Grauel spent many hours with Livengood and the examiners from the state board trying to determine the nature of each phone call. The intention was to determine precisely the cost of inappropriate calls and reimburse the state. But the investigation was taking time, and the *News* kept reminding its readers that no reimbursement was forthcoming.

Then another salvo hit Conrad. On Tuesday, May 21, Harris and Hess had another page-one story: "Conrad Gas Billings High For Single Car."[158] In all his months in office, Conrad had spent $4,674 for "parts, lubrication, fuel, oil, wash, wax and labor," on state oil company credit cards. Singling out one month, March 1973, the article reveals the "a total of 309.6 gallons of fuel" were charged in such cities as Evansville, Michigan City, Clarksville, East Gary, Cloverdale, and Rensselaer.

The gasoline credit cards provided a tracking of Conrad's relentless travel. But that wasn't all. In addition to Conrad and Grauel, ten other staff members had signed the credit card receipts, including Dan Davis, Vicki Weger, Jeff Lewis, Steve Powell, and Bob Rooksby. Indeed, the four gasoline credit cards issued to the office had been used by many staff members. What Harris and Hess implied was that the amount of purchases could not have been all related to state business, since staff members were supposed to use state vehicles from the motor pool. If their personal vehicle was driven, they were to purchase fuel themselves and submit forms for reimbursement.

Here was another charge of misuse and abuse of public office. Finally, with this story out, Governor Otis Bowen made a public statement. Conrad had previously called for an investigation into the other elective offices and their telephone calls. In a taping of a television program entitled "Report from the Statehouse," the governor said that Conrad's problems with credit cards "have been a good warning to all of our people to be careful, and if there's any question, don't do it." He said that "whenever you have gasoline credit cards and telephone credit cards out, you always run into that danger. We have attempted to reduce all of these areas where we would have some misuse. We have had cards turned in. We've kept credit card issuances down to as few as possible."[159]

Bowen's carefully worded statement appeared to defuse the question of gasoline credit card purchases. Indeed, he implied that misuse of credit cards could perhaps be found in other state government offices. Once Bowen spoke, the issue of gasoline credit cards was never again prominently mentioned in the press.

Conrad could only await the results of the investigation into the telephone calls. There was nothing he could personally do until the final total of unauthorized calls was determined. In the meantime, he had to stay focused. The state convention—and his renomination fight—were less than four weeks away.

The 2,152 delegates to the state convention were to meet in district caucuses on Monday evening, June 17. With Schreiber entering the race—and having command, as county chairman, over 299 delegates—it was mandatory that Conrad take command of the 217 delegates from Lake County.

Lake County—frequently called the "State of Lake" because of its proximity to Chicago—had been rent with factionalism. The racial animosities in Lake County boiled over into the political arena in 1967, when Hatcher won the mayor's job in Gary against the opposition of the county organization, chaired by John Krupa. When Hatcher prevailed, Pastrick was convinced that Krupa had to step down. In 1972, he did, taking a job in the city water department of East Chicago. Pastrick became county chairman as well as mayor. He remembers those days well: "[Krupa] had to do business as he saw fit when he was county chairman, but I thought we needed all segments together. Our power was lessened without that. I knew we had to get along with Richard Gordon Hatcher, so I made him district chair and allowed him to represent the party downstate, on the State Central Committee. I like to believe that I was trying to get the county to take a certain path and hate would go the other way. We were trying to heal wounds and fully bring blacks into office and various appointed positions, such as the election board. I hoped they would feel that they had some control over the electoral process."[160]

But Pastrick and Hatcher could not come together in the 1974 primary. They backed rival candidates, and Pastrick's people won. Both men had been on good terms with Gordon St. Angelo. Indeed, as state chairman, St. Angelo had provided both of them financial support in their runs for mayor. But Pastrick's ties to Conrad went much further back. "I became close to Larry in the 1962 Bayh campaign. By then I was regional director of the Young Democrats of America and I had campaigned for secretary of state in 1960. J. Manfred Core and Clint Green asked me to come down and work in the Bayh campaign and Larry was the campaign manager," Pastrick recalls.[161] This long relationship with Conrad did not automatically translate into political support, however. Pastrick's first duty as party chairman was to the Lake County organization. In 1972, he wanted to be with Conrad against Welsh, but the former governor had deeper support in Lake than Conrad. He had asked Welsh if he would prefer Conrad or Bodine for lieutenant governor. He had hoped Welsh would have named Conrad.

Now, though, he could be with Conrad. He had won the fight with Hatcher and replaced him as district chairman with the Calumet Township trustee, Dozier Allen. About ten days before the convention, Pastrick called a "delegate caucus" in Lake County, to which he invited all the potential candidates for secretary of state. Bauer and Schreiber were there, along with Conrad. More than three hundred people were sitting in metal chairs in the meeting hall. Pastrick introduced the local candidates and then called on Pat Bauer for remarks. Bauer alluded to Conrad's problems, but stressed that he was not aligned with any statewide faction within the party. He laid claim to understanding Lake County because he was from "next door," in South Bend. The applause was polite.

Next came Bill Schreiber. He talked about his ability to win the office, emphasizing that there could not be a weak link on the ticket. Playing to Bauer's theme, he stated he understood the urban areas of the state, and that a partnership could be forged between the two largest counties. The applause was polite.

Then Larry Conrad was introduced. Screams and yells erupted from the crowd. Larry strolled to the podium. He had no notes. Then he began: "I'm back in my hometown!"

Everybody roared. Their cheers went on and on. Conrad was laughing and pointing at people in the audience, calling them by their first names. When the din finally quit, he said:

> You know my personal philosophy of politics and life. You have heard me say it again and again and again.

> The great thing in this world is not so much where we stand, as in what direction we're moving. Sometimes we must sail with the wind. Sometimes we must sail against the wind.

Then he paused. You could hear people whispering the next line, waiting for his delivery. One man roared, "But you *must* sail!" Everybody cheered.

Conrad threw his head back and laughed. Then he started shaking his head: no, no, no.

> Sometimes you can't sail! Sometimes you have to do what John Krupa does . . . and, baby, that's ROW, ROW, ROW!

That was it. The men and the women and the children were now standing on their metal chairs screaming "LARRY . . . LARRY . . . LARRY! ROW . . . ROW . . . ROW!"

In the tumult, Schreiber, who was sitting on the stage to the right of the podium, motioned to Pastrick. Pastrick leaned over and Schreiber—having to yell over the noise—said: "I hope this won't influence how you're going to vote." Pastrick looked into his eyes and said: "Bill, these *are* the voters."

The Lake County delegation was going for Conrad.

But there were problems elsewhere. It was clear the race was coming down to Conrad and Schreiber. Aside from early endorsements when the "dump Conrad" movement was underway, Robert McCallen had received no support. He withdrew. Pat Bauer, though, had not given up. He continued to make appearances and started calling on Conrad to answer the charges against him, claiming that Conrad and his aides "have admitted using the office for political purposes."

But Bauer was beginning to realize that he was far behind Conrad and Schreiber, a very distant third. He remembers his assessment: "Larry came out swinging, and once he did, I knew the whole matter was less a problem than it had been portrayed."[162]

Schreiber, however, forged ahead. Unlike Bauer, Schreiber made very few references to Conrad and the problems with the Master Plan. Instead, he attempted to convince delegates that he was the better nominee for secretary of state because he could help the ticket—and Birch Bayh—because he was from Marion County, Richard Lugar's base. His attacks were on Lugar and the Republicans, not Conrad, not the Democrats.

Conrad was assured of solid support from Lake County and his home district, the 10th. With help from Michael, Nice, and Gallahan, he would have some solid support in the 2nd and 5th districts, even though Maurice Mason, who had been reelected as the 2nd district chair, was for Schreiber. But there were problems elsewhere. Jerry Miller, the new chairman of the 3rd district, was for Schreiber. The 6th district chair, John Anderson, lined up the same way. In fact, Conrad's attempt to topple some of the district chairmen fell far short of the mark. His renomination would depend on the hundreds of direct contacts he had made with delegates. He would not be getting much help from the members on the State Central Committee.[163]

Conrad's solid support in the UAW began filling the void. Dallas Sells and Don Yeagley started working those UAW members who were delegates to the state convention. These two managed to forge an agreement with other labor leaders to form a "Labor for Larry Conrad Committee." The head of the UAW, Dallas Sells, pulled no punches. He announced that if Schreiber defeated Conrad, the UAW would not put any resources into the Democratic state ticket. Instead, they would campaign only for Birch Bayh and the congressional nominees. Don Yeagley recalls that "we owed it to Larry Conrad. There has never been a candidate who connected with our members better than Larry. In fact, we couldn't do anything else. Our members would have come out against us. It was like Larry was a member of the UAW."[164]

Coming on board with the UAW were Henry (Babe) Lopez, the president of Local 1010 of the Steelworkers, and Robert Brown of the International Association of Machinists and Aerospace Workers. The announcement of the committee was delayed until the day before the convention was to convene. But the groundwork was laid, and the labor leaders predicted that nearly 500 delegates would be union members.[165]

To counter Conrad's labor support, Willis Zagrovich stepped forward. Although the board of directors of the AFL-CIO had voted not to endorse any candidates prior to the state conventions, Zagrovich—the president of the AFL-CIO, and member of the special committee—on Saturday, June 15, endorsed Schreiber. He claimed it was a "personal endorsement" only. Zagrovich did not go as far as Sells, however. He pledged he would support the Democratic state ticket, even if Conrad were the nominee.[166]

Birch Bayh, who was scheduled to be renominated on the same day as the state ticket, was again feeling the pressure of the political vise. The old organization was pushing from one direction—led by Marion County— and the Conrad supporters were pressuring from the other. Bayh, protecting himself, stayed neutral. He could not risk losing any of the Democratic base vote in Marion County because his likely opponent, Mayor Richard G. Lugar, had the organization and the recognition to beat him handily in the state's largest county. With Schreiber as Marion County chairman, Bayh needed his full assistance. In fact, Bayh had attended the Democratic slating convention in Marion County prior to the primary and stayed all day, shaking hands with the precinct committeemen and shoring up his support.

The day before the convention convened in district caucuses, Bauer pulled out. The next evening, when the caucuses met, Bayh made it clear he was staying out of the Conrad-Schreiber fight. "I have felt that if we are going to have a Democratic convention that operates under Democratic principles, where delegates are elected to do a job, then they ought to do that job," Bayh told reporters. "There would not be any use to have a convention if I or somebody else would dictate to them, and that is what has got us into some of the problems we have now. I have certainly never practiced that and don't intend to start now." For the second time in two years Bayh's ex-staffer, Larry A. Conrad, was in a convention battle. And for the second time, Bayh was neutral.[167]

Conrad required 1,077 votes to win. Wagner was confident of victory. He calculated that they had nearly 1,400. But the Schreiber supporters were not finished. In the various downtown hotels posters were taped to walls proclaiming that Conrad would soon be indicted. Following the district caucuses, Wagner was informed of the posters and he immediately headed to the Hilton Hotel. Searching the various floors, he finally found the man he was looking for, Jim Kelley—the nominee for Marion County prosecutor and a Schreiber supporter. Confronting Kelley in a hallway, Wagner accused him of circulating the posters, and demanded that they be torn down. Kelley denied it, and threatened Wagner by saying, "You better hope I'm never elected prosecutor." That was enough for Wagner. While other delegates gathered round, Wagner stared directly in his face and yelled, "Let's go outside to the alley—just the two of us—and we'll settle this once and for all."

Kelley began looking around frantically and yelled, "Get Bob Mooney. Get Mooney, quick." But nobody moved, and Mooney wasn't there. Kelley backed off. Wagner swung on his heels and marched down the corridor to the elevator. Kelley was not heard from again.[168]

The next day, while senior senator Vance Hartke delivered the keynote address, Conrad was busy on the convention floor, shaking hands with everyone. Mary Lou and the four children established a "Conrad Box" in the gallery seating where delegates and guests stopped by to pick up buttons and talk. Mayor Pastrick delivered the nominating speech for Conrad, saying he was "a man who never has told me anything less than the truth, and whose loyalty to our party is unquestioned." He then directly addressed the Master Plan and the subsequent allegations:

> There has been talk of political activity in Larry's office. *We* are the people who encouraged these things. We called for Larry to attend our bean dinners. We called for Larry to speak for us. We called for Larry to help us with our problems. We called for Larry to help with our campaigns. *And Larry Conrad always helped.* And now, *I am ashamed to say,* there are some among us who would chastise Larry Conrad for doing the things *we* asked him to do![169]

He thundered that "the improvements he has made in the secretary of state's office are too numerous to read."[170] When his words ended, the convention floor erupted. The demonstration was planned, but the enthusiasm was spontaneous. "The Conrad forces were back," Mary Lou recalls, "and they were stronger than ever."[171]

Richard B. Stoner of Columbus, the Democratic national committeeman, nominated Schreiber. Jerry Miller, the mayor of South Bend, gave one of Schreiber's seconding speeches.

When the voting machines were opened and the delegates began lining up to cast their ballots, several disputes broke out over alternate delegates. Wagner had feared that the change in party rules governing proxy votes would work to Conrad's disadvantage, particularly in Marion County. The new national party rules prohibited elected delegates from naming their own proxies. Instead, a "pool" of alternate delegates had to be selected from each county and, in the event an elected delegate failed to attend, the county chairman would select the alternate delegate from the pool. When Conrad paid his filing fee for the state convention on June 5, Wagner and Conrad met with Trisler and agreed on a compromise. The county chairmen would retain the right to name the alternate delegate, but Trisler had agreed to send a letter to all county chairmen urging them to allow the regular delegate to select the substitute from the pool, with the county chairman rubber-stamping the selection. Obviously, Trisler's message to the county chairmen was not transmitted to all the delegates, because about thirty delegates or alternates appealed to the credentials committee for a ruling as to who was eligible to vote. These appeals delayed the final tabulation of the results, but they could not change the outcome.[172]

Conrad won easily, receiving 1,332 votes to Schreiber's 784. The vote total was only 68 votes off from Wagner's count of 1,400, and constituted a 62.9 percent victory.

The seemingly interminable hours spent calling and visiting Democrats throughout the state had yielded results. No other person had spent so much time in the trenches, one-on-one with party activists. When the full weight of the Democratic State Committee and the Indianapolis newspapers was thrown on Conrad, the delegates came to his rescue.

Conrad's acceptance speech to the convention was brief. Mary Lou and the children were at the podium with him, and Mary Lou remembers her eyes "brimming with tears." Then, to her surprise, Larry turned to her and asked her to speak to the delegates. She had not prepared any remarks. As she adjusted the microphone, she remembered all the past conventions. She thanked the delegates, then said:

> In 1972 I was hurt to see Larry's campaign brochures being stepped on here on the convention floor. In 1973 our hearts were stepped on. But we're back again. We're ready to help. We're coming to your counties, and we're going to win in 1974."[173]

And she lit up the convention stage with her patented wide smile.

In his concession speech, Schreiber congratulated Conrad "not only for his victory but for his gentlemanly behavior," and urged all the delegates to remove their "Conrad and Schreiber buttons" and leave the convention center in unity to work for the ticket in November.

Schreiber had surmised for several days that he would lose the nomination. "My campaign was predicated on Ziegner writing more articles, and the statewide press playing them," Schreiber said. "But the moment I announced—from there to the state convention—the articles stopped. I think the Indianapolis papers saw Larry to be the least attractive Democrat candidate. They made a decision to stay silent because they desired to infect the entire Democratic ticket going into November."[174]

After the rest of the state ticket was nominated by acclamation, the winners held a news conference on the second floor of the convention center.[175] Senator Bayh spoke first. He was asked immediately if Conrad's presence on the ticket would hurt the party. He answered quickly: "No. We don't have to be on the defensive, as you look at the problems that confront our country and confront every home in America today as a result of the inability of the President and this administration to solve the problems that confront us."

Then it was Conrad's turn. As he took the podium, he visibly winced as he shook the hand of a supporter. His right hand, raw and red, was swollen to half again its size. Earlier, as he had been working the convention floor, he soaked his hand in ice water whenever he had the chance. Conrad openly admitted that he had come very close to leaving politics altogether. "It got to the point where things piled up and I just could not get myself going," he said. "I don't think I've ever been so depressed as I was about two months ago. I had got to the point where I thought, 'who needs this grief?'" He then credited Mary Lou with getting him out of his depression and geared up for the convention fight.[176]

He responded directly to his problems with the Master Plan. He said he "made an effort to set forth the facts." Observing that "life is too short to be bitter," he stated that he hoped his impressive victory would quiet the critics in the party. "I think we've put it to rest."

Conrad may have thought the Master Plan was put to rest. But he still did not know who wrote it.

In fact, the Master Plan had not one author, but at least three. A word-by-word computer analysis of the entire document reveals several spelling and word-usage patterns that verify that it had multiple authors. For example, a common abbreviation of the word "through" is "thru." The author of sections I, IV and VII used this abbreviation. Where the word is used elsewhere in the document, it is spelled "through." A second writer composed sections III and XII. In these chapters, the word "politicos," meaning veteran politicians, is properly used. But someone who has never seen the word spelled—has only heard someone else say it—may mistake it for "politicals." In Section II, this mistake occurs, indicating that it was written by a third author. It is clear that the second writer, the author of sections III and XII, also wrote sections VIII and IX. In all four chapters, the word "commitment" is misspelled "committment." Whenever "commitment" appears elsewhere in the document, it is properly spelled. The third writer—the author of section II—in all likelihood also was responsible for sections V, VI, X, and XI.

The entire document could have been as much "compiled" as written. Certain paragraphs appear to be inserted in some sections that bear little relevance to the topic under discussion. Moreover, the compilation was extremely hasty. For example, the outline for Section V, which appears on the cover sheet for the chapter, is not followed in the text. In Section II, two different pages are numbered "31," and in a profile of Democratic leaders in Indiana's counties, only eighty-eight of the ninety-two counties are mentioned; Harrison, Hendricks, Henry, and Howard counties are omitted. Three of these four counties would have been very important to Conrad's political future. One, Harrison, was his native county. Henry is next door to Delaware County and would be part of his east central Indiana base. Howard County has large labor union locals, particularly UAW, which would provide a core of support for Conrad.

Indeed, whoever wrote Section II was neither intimately familiar with Conrad's political support nor fully informed about the nature of Indiana's counties. Could any of Conrad's current or past staff members have collaborated to produce such a document? If they did, they made many, many errors. The most glaring error was the frequent references to "tapes," purportedly containing audio conversations or dictation recordings referring to political leaders and reporters. Tapes were referenced in discussing seven different individuals, including Robert Fair, Richard Bodine, Robert Pastrick, and Gordon Englehart, with such statements as "interesting tapes" and "We have 3 great tapes."

But there were no tapes. Stu Grauel states: "We never had audio tapes or dictation tapes. The Master Plan refers to tapes, but the only tapes of any kind we ever had were the old tickertape typewriting tapes that allowed us to replicate letters. This was primitive equipment compared to today's technology."[177]

The frequent references to tapes only added to the mystery of the Master Plan. The existence of a voice-activated taping system in President Nixon's Oval Office had been revealed to the nation on July 16, 1973, a time that coincided with the writing of the Master Plan.[178]

The document indeed contained bits of information that must have come from Conrad's internal files. But there were many carbon copies of memos that had been kept by various staff members. As staff members left, there was no systematic procedure to see what documents they were taking from their desks. But much of the information in the Master Plan was fictitious, such as the references to the existence of audio tapes. If a key staffer to Conrad had been involved in the collaboration to assemble the document, such fiction is unlikely to have been included.

With all the sloppiness in the Master Plan, how could Ed Ziegner have been "convinced of its authenticity"? Certainly, none of the other leading reporters based in Indianapolis were as convinced. Gordon Englehart did not think "there was any substance to it. It was interesting only in that it spawned thousands of hours of comments, but in terms of anything substantial, it was nothing."[179]

Ziegner's conviction was tied to the person who gave him the document. A careful reading of Ziegner's stories reveals that the document was hand-delivered to him; it was not mailed. Ziegner acknowledged this before the Special Committee. The first report of the Special Committee states: "[T]he Committee has determined from the member of the news media who received a hand-delivered copy that the person presenting the copy was a [sic] 'honorable person of high integrity.'"[180]

Nearly two decades later, Ed Ziegner was asked: "Who hand-delivered a copy of the Master Plan to you?" He answered: "A copy came into my hands. It must have been hand-delivered, but I can't remember who would have given it to me. It could've been any of three or so people. I just can't remember." At the time, Ziegner was critically ill and confined to his bed. When asked again for names, he replied, "It could have been Gordon St.

Angelo or Jack New. I don't remember."[181] Both St. Angelo and New vehemently deny giving the document to Ziegner. St. Angelo says bluntly: "I didn't write it and I had nothing to do with it going to the paper."[182] When asked if he either paid or ordered someone else to write it, he responded: "That's probably as ridiculous as saying I wrote it."[183]

Indeed, Gordon St. Angelo did not write the Master Plan. From an examination of several documents that were written by St. Angelo, one concludes that his writing style and his word usage are not the same as those in any of the sections of the Master Plan.

Jack New also denies having anything to do with leaking the document to the press. He claims Stu Grauel gave him a copy, and that he also received one in the mail. He claims he had no advance knowledge of it, although Steve Powell contended that St. Angelo told him, some three weeks before the story broke, that New had a document that was damaging to Conrad.

New acknowledges that he received some of the blame. "I know some people blamed me and they also blamed Gordon." But New is convinced the document "came out of Larry's office."[184]

Many Conrad supporters name the triumvirate of Media, Inc.—John C. Nichols, Jeff Lewis, and Steve Powell. Lewis and Powell deny having had any hand in it. A close search of the dozens of memos written by these two individuals while they were employed either on campaign staff or in the secretary of state's office bears this out. The abbreviations and common phrases each of them used in their memos are not consistent with what appears in the document.

Unfortunately, no memo exists in any of the records and materials from those years that was written by John Nichols.

Conrad had decided that whoever wrote the Master Plan was not important.[185] He knew the purpose for which it was written and distributed. But now, in the late spring of 1974, he was beginning to emerge from that thick poisonous fog that had enveloped him. With his renomination, he had crossed halfway over the bridge. Now he could clearly see the meadow on the other side. And he was in full stride. What remained to be seen was whether or not a troll was poised to pounce again.

As the delegates filed out of the convention center, Pastrick and Jerry Miller, the mayor of South Bend, the new 3rd district chairman and Schreiber supporter, were walking side by side when Ed Ziegner walked up behind them and said: "Jerry, you took a loss today, but in the end you'll be the winner."[186]

7

I do not undertake this campaign expecting it to be easy for me or for the people of this state. We should not be satisfied until people all over America wake up in the morning and wonder what the Hoosiers are doing that day. I want us to begin on this day to prepare for that day. I would like us to look to the future with the same kind of spirit, courage and determination that caused George Rogers Clark to make his trek to Vincennes, LaSalle to sail down the Kankakee, Governor Morton to stand with Lincoln against dissolving the union—and Indiana to beat UCLA. It is that spirit with which I announce this candidacy for governor and solicit your aid, because in the last measure it's not what I promise I will do, it is rather what Hoosiers join us in doing.

—Larry A. Conrad announcement speech for governor, December 14, 1975

LARRY CONRAD'S ASCENT to the governor's chair depended on his 1974 reelection as secretary of state. President Richard Nixon's deepening problems over Watergate forecast a very good Democratic year. But the eyes that watched the Indiana Democratic state ticket saw Conrad as the vulnerable one. If he failed, it would be the Master Plan that caused his demise. And if other Democrats lost with him, he would be to blame.

But Conrad was back in his element. He was campaigning. Claudia Prosser moved to the campaign staff, and Bob Wagner, through the summer and fall, was in control. And Conrad? He was on the road, drawing renewed strength and energy from the people. "I have never worked for a better candidate than Larry Conrad," Wagner asserts. "He always did what we assigned him to do, and he would come back asking for more."[1]

Even with Conrad on the state ticket, there was a semblance of unity among the Democrats. All of the nominees, including Senator Bayh, were incumbents. All of them were veteran campaigners. They knew the state. The Republican ticket, on the other hand, was having problems.

The Republican state convention nominated, as expected, Mayor Richard G. Lugar for the U.S. Senate.[2] But fissures opened in the other races, and it took all of Governor Otis Bowen's political muscle to hold the party together.

Apart from organizational fights leading up to the reorganization of the Republican State Committee, the GOP was being hammered on the anvil of Watergate. About one month before the June convention, Lugar questioned President Nixon's "morality," and he was quickly criticized by other Republicans for speaking out against the Republican president.[3]

Two weeks later, on June 6, the Republicans hosted a $100-a-plate fundraiser in Indianapolis, raising nearly $350,000 for the 1974 campaign. Governor Bowen, in his remarks to the party faithful, bluntly admitted the problems posed by Watergate, saying it was "public confidence unmet, public trust broken and public promise belied."[4]

The only major Republican battle that made it to the convention floor was for the nomination for secretary of state—the man who would run against Conrad. William L. Allen III, city judge from Jeffersonville, was pitted against Michael M. Packard, chief deputy for the Indiana Bureau of Motor Vehicles. Packard's position with the license branch system provided him an automatic access to the ninety-two Republican county chairmen. But even with this advantage, he had a formidable enemy: L. Keith Bulen, who continued his control over the Republican party organization.

To Bulen, the secretary of state's nomination was important only as it affected Richard Lugar. He had worked nearly full time to elect Lugar mayor of Indianapolis, and now, with Unigov accomplished, he wanted him in the U.S. Senate. The Marion County Republican organization was very strong. Even with the *Indianapolis Star* investigating scandals in the Indianapolis police department, Bulen knew that Lugar would run well in Marion County and the doughnut. Where Lugar needed help was in other areas of the state. The other nominees—including secretary of state—should come from outside central Indiana. This is "geographical balance," and Bulen believes in it: "Geographical balance is very important on a state ticket. The people take local pride in one of their own getting on the ticket. It's the local guy that is making good, having somebody succeed. I know some people think it doesn't matter any more, but it does. All you've got to do is talk to the people."[5]

William Allen was from Clark County, on the river. It was a heavily Democratic county, but he had successfully won the city judge's race in Jeffersonville. Bulen reasoned that Allen's candidacy would bring some of those voters to the Republicans.

Bulen applied his standard formula for winning convention races. He teamed his Marion County delegates with those from Vanderburgh County (Evansville). But Packard had sufficient strength in Lake and Allen counties to withstand Bulen's traditional coalition. Bulen moved elsewhere for support, and he found it in the doughnut counties. It was barely enough. When the votes were tallied on the convention floor, Allen beat Packard by only six votes: 1,025 to 1,019.

The other nominations were uncontested, and the nominees came from different sections of the state. Bulen had his geographical balance.[6]

The Democratic ticket was wasting no time in getting organized to do battle with the Republicans. The Democratic State Central Committee rented a spacious office in a former automobile dealership at 10th and Meridian in Indianapolis and immediately began scheduling candidates throughout the state.

Conrad's campaign again was short on money. The debt from the 1972 race against Matthew Welsh had been whittled down to about $6,000 by holding fund-raisers earlier in 1973.[7] Without money for media, Conrad was back to his old tried-and-true method of campaigning: meeting all the people. The Senate race between Bayh and Lugar generated most of the news coverage, but even that race was overshadowed by Watergate. In late July, the U.S. Supreme Court unanimously ruled that President Nixon had to surrender documents and tape recordings to the special prosecutor. On July 27, the House Judiciary Committee approved two articles of impeachment against Nixon. On the last day of July, John Ehrlichman was sentenced to twenty months in prison for authorizing burglaries and perjuring himself before the Watergate grand juries. That same day, the House Judiciary Committee approved a third article of impeachment against Nixon, charging him with unconstitutional defiance of committee subpoenas. On August 5, the White House released transcripts of a conversation between the President and H. R. Haldeman. The transcripts revealed that six days after the Watergate break-in, Nixon had ordered a halt to an FBI investigation into Watergate. That same day, the Gallup Poll released results of a national survey in which 64 percent of the American people said they favored the impeachment of Nixon. Nixon's presidency was over. He resigned by the end of week.

The destruction of Nixon's presidency enervated the Indiana Republican party. Tom Milligan, the state chairman, admitted that "Watergate has inflicted deep wounds on the nation and the Republican Party." Governor

Bowen said that Nixon's admission of an attempted cover-up "is a grave disappointment to me."[8]

While the Republicans were reeling, the Democrats continued campaigning. Conrad was spending at least one day a week in Lake County, trying to guarantee a massive Democratic turnout in November. Wagner accompanied him on one trip to Lake County. Running ahead of schedule, they stopped in a small community just off the interstate. They climbed out of the car and started walking door to door, distributing pamphlets. One woman informed Wagner that she was going to vote Democrat, but that Conrad had a big Republican enemy in town, the owner of the local grain elevator. Wagner found his address for Conrad, who immediately walked to the man's house and knocked on the door. When the man came to the door, Conrad said, "I'm Larry Conrad and I'm running for secretary of state. When I'm elected I'm going to tear down every grain elevator in the state, except yours." The man erupted in laughter. Later, he sent a campaign contribution to Conrad.[9]

For the first and only time in their lives, Birch Bayh and Larry Conrad were on the same ticket. Their shared experiences over the past twelve years had informed them of certain "must" events—dinners and fairs and festivals they genuinely enjoyed. Whenever possible they would try to campaign together at such events. Years later, when the two of them were reminiscing, Conrad remembered one such campaign stop:

> Remember that time, Birch, we were campaigning together—I think we were over in Covington, or Williamsport. It was our last stop of the night, and after the dinner the owner of the restaurant—who has his chef's apron on—grabs us and takes us through the kitchen and out the back door. He reaches over and grabs a jug of homemade brew and says: "Want you two to have a little of this special after-dinner drink." Birch, you grabbed and hoisted the jug and took a big swig. Your face turned red and your eyes started watering. You handed that thing to me, pointing to it and nodding, like it was French champagne. I grabbed it and took a pull. It felt like a hot poker was jammed down my throat. I fell to my knees on the ground, gasping for air. As I was on all fours, shaking my head, trying to breathe, I heard the guy say to you, "pretty good, huh?"[10]

Bayh's U.S. Senate campaign had little difficulty in attracting news coverage, but, as usual, the race for secretary of state was nearly invisible. Finally, on August 20 in Merrillville, Conrad said something that landed him on the front page. He commented that he would not be "morally bothered" by a state lottery in Indiana, and anticipated that the next legislature would consider a state lottery as a means of raising revenue. When queried about public support for a lottery, Conrad, in his ebullient manner, started characterizing Hoosiers: people in southern Indiana were "rednecks"; Hoosiers living between Columbus and Kokomo were "straitlaced Presbyterians"; and residents of Lake County "run around wild." In his rapid-fire delivery, he declared that he was a redneck by virtue of his birth on the river; and, being a Presbyterian, he was straitlaced; and he loved running around wild in Lake County because he considered it his second home. He added that many Hoosiers were buying lottery tickets from neighboring states, and questions about an Indiana state lottery were those most frequently asked him on the campaign trail.[11]

His opponent, William Allen, immediately responded, claiming that he was opposed to all types of gambling, and a lottery was gambling; Conrad's remarks were an "insult"; Conrad's use of the word "straitlaced" was an affront to churchgoers; and his other remarks were "demeaning" to large numbers of Hoosiers.[12]

Conrad fired back. Characterizing Allen's remarks as "negative campaigning," he explained that he was personally opposed to gambling. But that was not the question. "What I discussed is whether or not we should pursue the lottery as a possible means of opening up a new area of revenue to help us with some of the stifling problems we have in this state. Some [revenue] sources have to be opened up. I think we have to pursue all of them, as other states have. We can't just sit here and let the whole thing pass by."[13]

But like the bottle rocket on a Fourth of July night, this bright flash of an issue in the secretary of state's race disappeared quickly in the dark skies of Watergate. On September 3, John W. Dean III began his prison sentence for obstructing justice, and, five days later, President Ford granted Richard Nixon "a free, full and absolute pardon" for any criminal acts during his presidency.[14] The issue of a state lottery in Indiana was not to be reported again.

Two weeks later, however, Conrad was back in the news. Again, it was the Master Plan and the telephone calls. Throughout the summer, the State Board of Accounts had been continuing its investigation into the telephone calls and, at the request of Marion County Prosecutor Noble Pearcy, it was researching the exact times of employment for certain staff members in Conrad's office.

During the week of September 16, Wagner and Grauel met several times with Kenneth R. Beesley, an examiner for the State Board of Accounts. Using Livengood's research, they reached agreement on the numerous phone calls that could not be attributed to state business. These calls totaled $7,284.43. An additional $469.46 was found to be unauthorized expenditures for the office, including $125.00 for honorary secretary of state certificates, $101.80 for Indiana and U.S. flags sent to Indiana servicemen and women serving in Southeast Asia, $78.89 for gasoline purchases by Grauel, and $153.85 for a mobile telephone in Conrad's campaign car. The grand total was $7,753.89. These findings were submitted to Noble Pearcy.

Wagner was convinced when the first allegations were made about unauthorized calls that full pressure had to be kept on the State Board of Accounts to conduct similar audits of the other elected officers in state government, following Governor Bowen's statement in May, in which he alluded to the possibility that other offices could have similar problems. This tactic appeared to be working. In July, Dallas Sells, the head of the UAW, wrote Bowen, asking that he not release any report on Conrad's office until all other state offices were investigated. Bowen rejected the request. He marched an aide forward to say that the "public and certainly the media are entitled" to any audit report of the State Board of Accounts. The aide did not refer to any audit of other offices.[15]

On September 23, Conrad convened a news conference in his office where he announced he was personally reimbursing $7,753.89 to the state treasury. He and Stu Grauel had borrowed the money over their own signatures. Conrad said that his payment was "in no way an admission of wrongdoing on my part, nor does it suggest that I ever authorized persons within my office or outside of my office to use the state telephones for other than business-related matters." But he was frank about his own limitations: "To suggest we never make errors is to suggest we are not human; to profit by our errors makes us better people." Then he concluded: "I feel the payment demonstrates good faith and assures the people, beyond any question, that my office will keep the trust given me when I was elected. Much of what I have paid may never be recovered; much of what I have paid could, in fact, be business related."[16]

Conrad never asked any current or former staff members to reimburse him. This was puzzling to John Livengood, who was willing to help with the reimbursement even though he had not made any of the unauthorized calls. "Larry never asked others on staff to help pay for the phone calls. But he thought of staff members as extended family members and if a staff member made a mistake, it was his mistake. He said in the news conference that he was responsible."[17]

Conrad's news conference brought an immediate response from his opponent. William Allen said, "Conrad and his staff have misused tax dollars in a number of ways. At the very time Mr. Conrad was billing himself as 'Mr. Clean' for revealing his personal finances, he was using taxpayers' money for improper purposes."[18] Conrad and Wagner did not respond.

Two days later, the *Indianapolis Star* finally wrote an editorial about Conrad and his problems. In a tepid statement acknowledging Wagner's contention that other state offices should also be investigated, the *Star* said:

> The sum of $7,753.89 representing state funds allegedly spent for non-state purposes has been restored to Indiana by Secretary of State Larry A. Conrad. The State Board of Accounts also has forwarded to Marion

County Prosecutor Noble R. Pearcy a report on an investigation it has made into purported irregularities in the operation of Conrad's office.

Have there been irregularities in spending in other state offices? The funds handled amount not just to thousands but millions.

Those in charge of keeping accounts on state funds must make certain that irregularities will not occur.[19]

It was the telephone calls—and Conrad's reimbursement—that became the focal point of the State Board of Account's report. But the report also questioned the employment of two persons on Conrad's staff, George Rehm and David Bochnowski, both of whom "were enrolled in colleges at the time of employment [and] there were instances where dates of employment did not coincide with college vacations or seasonal breaks; however, class attendance records were not available."[20] This accusation, however, was to be lost in the conflicting charges and countercharges over the official status of the report and whether or not Pearcy would use the report in grand jury proceedings.

With the State Board of Accounts report in his hands, Pearcy moved quickly. He declared that the report would not be submitted to a grand jury because it was not "certified" by the State Board of Accounts. Beesley, the state examiner, responded that the report "was never intended for the grand jury." It was "informational" only. He also explained that the report was not certified because he would have been exposed to legal liability if it were certified and no criminal intent could be found on Conrad's behalf.[21]

The next day Bowen's aide, William Lloyd, tried to squirm out of the problem by maintaining that the report was not "certified" because such certification was not needed. If the grand jury wanted to see the report, Lloyd said, then all that would be required would be for a subpoena to be issued to the state examiner. Lloyd then declared that the "review indicates that the entire procedure has been conducted in the normal and standard way."[22] The report was not going to be certified and Pearcy was not going to submit it to the grand jury.

With only one month left before the November 5 election, it appeared the matter was dead. But the *Indianapolis News* was still trolling. On Wednesday, October 9, Art Harris and Skip Hess wrote a page-one story entitled "Conrad '72 Campaign Calls Charged To State." Relying on the Board of Accounts audit, the reporters alleged that the state had been billed for 212 long-distance phone calls to a telephone number belonging to the 1972 Conrad for Governor Committee. The first such call was made on February 8, 1972, four days after Conrad had announced for governor. The calls ended three days before the state convention, where Conrad lost to Welsh. Harris and Hess contended that the calls followed a "pattern," in that they were made from cities on dates when Conrad or his aides were campaigning in those areas. For example, John Nichols made $482.23 worth of long-distance calls from Ohio, where he also was serving on the campaign staff of a Democratic candidate for Congress.[23]

On the same day that the *News* reopened the Conrad case, the *Star*'s inquiry into police corruption in the Indianapolis police department finally drew blood. L. Keith Bulen resigned his positions as 11th district Republican chairman and Republican National Committeeman from Indiana, citing "personal reasons." He then contended that "agents of the Indianapolis Newspapers, Inc.," had brought an FBI investigation down on him. Calling the investigation "routine," he claimed the FBI had to respond "to months of incessant personal visits by representatives of the Indianapolis Newspapers, Inc., bearing allegations and rumors in an effort to pull the newspaper's chestnuts out of the fire by trying to discredit and destroy a good police department, the finest city and county administration in our history, and ultimately, the political structure. . . ." Bulen claimed that the two Indianapolis newspapers "issued orders to local officials, and literally ran local government in Marion County." This control, Bulen maintained, ended when he obtained political control of Indianapolis in 1966. The *Indianapolis News* printed Bulen's statement on page one.[24]

Nearly twenty years later, Bulen asserted that his real reason for resigning was politics: some organizational Republicans were alleging that Bulen wanted Richard Lugar to lose the Senate race so he could maintain his position through the Republican National Committee and control all federal patronage in Indiana. But Bulen's highest priority was always the election of Richard Lugar.[25]

The newspaper did not confine its investigation to the patrolmen and administrators of the police department. They also went after the prosecutor, Noble Pearcy. Throughout the spring and summer, newspaper articles criticized Pearcy's decisions. Pearcy retaliated; at one point two reporters of the *Indianapolis Star* were indicted. Now, with Pearcy refusing to take the Conrad report from the Board of Accounts to the grand jury, this decision became an issue in the continuing battle between the prosecutor and the newspapers.

On Friday, October 11, the *News* reported that Pearcy flogged the State Board of Accounts over their uncertified report. He contended in a letter to Beesley that "you did not dig into the facts already uncovered and did not pursue leads already handed to you." He lacerated the board, saying that they "did not do what the statute commands" and that their dereliction of duty left the prosecutor "with an uncertified, unpursued investigation which adds up to nothing." Beesley refused comment, saying only, "We're working toward an answer."[26]

Pearcy's attack on Beesley and the Board of Accounts did not convince

Bob Mooney of the *Star*. From the beginning, Mooney's articles had consistently downplayed the significance of the Master Plan. But now Mooney saw something else. He called Pearcy's blast at Beesley "phony." He pieced together the political reasons for Pearcy's action and revealed that the UAW was lining up support for Pearcy's reelection. The Marion County CAP council of the UAW refused to endorse James F. Kelley, Pearcy's Democratic opponent, and Pearcy had met the previous week with members of the UAW, the Teamsters, and other unions. Quoting an unidentified source from the UAW, Mooney wrote that "Pearcy is going to get [union] support."

Mooney knew a political deal when he saw it. Conrad was the UAW favorite (Mooney referred to Bayh and Conrad as the "Gold Dust twins of the UAW"), and the unions were going to save Conrad by backing Pearcy as long as the prosecutor would not pursue an indictment. Dallas Sells and Buford Holt from the UAW did not deny such a "deal," but Mooney wrote that they "minimized speculation" that such a deal was made.

Even with such a deal, Mooney blamed Pearcy, not Conrad. He characterized Pearcy's criticism of the State Board of Accounts as a "smokescreen to which the public long has been accustomed." But Pearcy's action, Mooney speculated, "probably brought smiles to Conrad and the UAW."[27]

If Mooney was going to let Conrad off the hook, the reporters of the *News* were not so inclined. On Monday, Harris and Hess came after Conrad again, claiming that his preconvention campaign in 1972 had charged 434 political telephone calls to the state. Relying again on the printouts from the Board of Accounts, the story raised questions as to the amount of reimbursement Conrad had made for personal and political phone calls.[28]

The *News* finally finished its assault with a long editorial the Saturday before the election. The newspaper called on citizens to "Vote Conrad Out," claiming he was "unfit for public office" because of the unauthorized telephone calls, questionable employment practices, and huge gasoline expenditures. The editorial gave no reason for electing William Allen. In fact, the editorial did not even mention Allen's name.[29]

Then Ziegner waded in. In his page-one story the day before the election, he predicted that the "controversial Secretary of State . . . may run behind his Democratic ticket mates."[30]

Despite Ziegner, Conrad and the other Democratic candidates were filled with confidence when the polls closed at 6 P.M. on November 5. As the campaign staffers and supporters gathered at the Democratic campaign headquarters at 10th and Meridian, the first returns were coming in from Marion County. They looked good. Lugar was losing his home county, the largest in the state. The Democratic tide kept building. It was clear there was to be an overwhelming Democratic victory. Bulen's geographic balance for the Republican ticket was not working in 1974.

The final tally showed a resounding Democratic victory. All the state-wide candidates carried Marion County, and the farther down the ticket, the greater the Democratic margin. Bayh won his third consecutive election by 75,152 votes, defeating Lugar in Marion County by 6,554. Conrad ran ahead of Bayh statewide, beating Allen by 117,316 votes.

But Conrad's totals revealed some minor damage left from the Master Plan. The stories, of course, had played prominently in Marion County and the doughnut. Conrad won Marion County by only 3,336 votes, the worst showing of any Democrat on the ticket. Conrad lost the seven doughnut counties by 14,929 votes, again trailing Bayh, who lost by 10,167. The rest of the ticket also lost the doughnut, but by substantially reduced margins.[31] Conrad also trailed the state ticket in St. Joseph County, where he garnered 41,056 votes to Bayh's 45,216. Although the entire ticket won comfortably in St. Joseph, Jerry Miller's opposition to Conrad held down his margin of victory.

But where there was no entrenched opposition to Conrad, or where the Master Plan stories did not play prominently, Conrad roared. In Lake County he led the ticket, winning by 46,901. Bayh's margin in Lake was only 31,917. In all, Conrad carried sixty-six of the ninety-two counties. Bayh carried fifty-nine.[32]

Ed Ziegner had problems with the Democratic sweep. In his article the day after the election, Ziegner did not mention Conrad. Incredibly, he attributed Democrats' victory to Gordon St. Angelo, mourning that "one man was missing" from the Democratic celebration, the one deserving "a good deal of the credit." He complained, "No one thanked [St. Angelo] Tuesday night. Someone should have. He had a part in the victory, too."[33]

Conrad's victory was his vindication. He was totally cleared, not only by the offices of government but by the people. His fight, however, had changed him, and it had changed Mary Lou. "Previously, I had not looked at the negative side of life," Mary Lou wrote in her diary. "I was a model for Pollyanna. Now, I was a only a year older, but eons wiser. I certainly was more skeptical. I was much more realistic."[34]

With his impressive reelection, the decision to run for governor in 1976 was preordained. After his second inauguration as secretary of state, the Conrad family left for vacation in Florida. While there, Larry told Mary Lou he thought he had a "good shot at the nomination. I knew he had to do it," Mary Lou declared in her diary.[35]

If Conrad could have chosen the year to run, he would not necessarily have picked 1976. He was fully aware that the Republican party was more united under Governor Otis Bowen than it had been in some time, and Bowen was eligible to run again. Bowen's popularity seemed to be growing, and the Republicans had plenty of money. But the events of recent years left Conrad no choice. After having eluded the web of intrigue that had been thrown over him by the perpetrators of the Master Plan, Conrad's ultimate vindication would be to win the Democratic nomination for governor.

Politically, Conrad could find solace in two facts. First, he knew Hoosier voters periodically chose a new face, or a "new style of politics," to replace the old. This happened in 1962 when Birch Bayh had defeated the stolid and predictable Homer Capehart. Second, presidential politics would play a role in Indiana, and Gerald Ford was not gaining in popularity.[36]

Finally, fate was involved. When it is one's turn to go for the brass ring, one must go. The tides of political fortune are never controlled by one person. The year was 1976, and it was Larry Conrad's time.

Conrad announced for governor, for the second time, in the large ballroom of the Indianapolis Convention Center on December 14, 1975. The main corridor of the building was lined with tables, where placards rested reading "District 1," "District 2," and so on, through "District 11." All Indiana Democrats were invited and about 1,500 attended. They lined up at their respective district tables to obtain name tags. In his post-announcement news conference, Conrad again advocated the adoption of a progressive income tax and pledged that he would continue controls on property taxes. The next day, Conrad flew to Fort Wayne, South Bend, Gary, Terre Haute, Evansville, and Clarksville to repeat his announcement.[37]

For the first time in the modern era, Indiana would nominate the candidates for governor in a direct primary election, the first Tuesday after the first Monday in May. By state law, the delegates to the state convention had lost their power to name their nominee for the highest state office. The bill was supported and signed by Governor Bowen, who declared that the direct primary "is not good for the party system, but it is good for the people."[38]

Switching the nomination to the direct primary did not bother Conrad. In his 1972 race for the nomination he had already broken out of the old ways of campaigning for the nomination by taking his case directly to the people. He contended that the change would not "hurt the parties at all; as a matter of fact, I think it will strengthen the precincts. But you can't wait to start. But then, I go pretty hard all the time anyhow."[39] The change shifted Conrad's campaign tactics only slightly. In those frenetic months of 1971, his staff members had crisscrossed the state visiting county chairmen and likely convention delegates and had written all those lengthy memos about their political "findings." All that was unnecessary now. The task was to communicate with the hundreds of thousands of likely Democratic voters who would make the choice for governor. A clear and convincing message was mandatory, as was the money to deliver the message. The campaign was to be controlled by the message, the money, and the manager.

Robert F. Wagner remained as Conrad's campaign manager. He saw the 1976 primary as a continuation of Conrad's vindication. "We had taken

Larry from the depths of where he was—from all the ridicule—and we won the fight in 1974. We got nominated and elected, receiving more votes than Birch Bayh."[40]

Conrad and Wagner were now close friends—a friendship welded in the white-hot heat of political scandal. Their bond was based on telling the truth—the whole truth. "I told him I didn't think we had a chance of beating Bowen. Otis was popular. His property tax program was popular and he was the first sitting governor eligible for reelection. I met with Larry often and I told him again and again it couldn't be done," Wagner recalls.[41]

But the primary nomination was something different. It fascinated Wagner. He was a man who loved challenges, who thrived on risks. "There were quality opponents in Bob Fair and Jack New," Wagner remembered, relishing the memory of being able to beat the best.

But of even greater import was the continuing struggle to free the Democratic party from the shackles of the old establishment—the conservative, largely white male leadership that had run the organization for so long. Wagner describes it: "The primary was an extension of what we had fought for before in the continuing struggle with the Democrat establishment. The party had to be opened to all the people. It was a matter of principle. The guy in the labor union, the men and women in the street, they were not part of our party. Both Conrad and I had an absolute commitment to that principle. We talked about it all the time. I agreed to run the primary. But I told him I was not committed to the fall campaign. My law business was good. I was real busy, and I didn't think we could win in the fall."[42]

In October of 1975 Wagner opened the second headquarters of the Conrad for Governor Committee in a two-room suite at the Howard Johnson's Motel on West Washington Street in Indianapolis. Claudia Prosser moved from the secretary of state's staff to the campaign staff, where she functioned as receptionist, scheduler, secretary, chief mimeograph operator, and the oil that kept the office operations running smoothly. Conrad and Wagner hired two staff members, Bill Gigerich and Jim Coyle. Gigerich had been working in the Marion County auditor's office when Conrad had called the auditor, Jerome Forestal, and asked him to "spring him loose" for Conrad's campaign. "I was a little surprised that Forestal agreed," remembers Gigerich, "because the Marion County Democratic party was badly split following the 1975 mayor's race, where R. V. Welch defeated Bill Schreiber. I didn't know if he wanted to be that aligned with Conrad. But he agreed, and I made arrangements to join the campaign staff."[43]

Jim Coyle also worked in the Auditor's office, and Gigerich knew his talents well. Coyle was a pasty-faced young Irishman with flaccid cheeks, slanted eyes, and Brillo hair. His voice was hardly coherent as he would stroll around the office mumbling, "We're doing the best we can with what we've got." He slept in the suite, filled every ashtray with his unfiltered Camels, and would repair to the bar at every opportunity. A passionate Democrat who believed that the Irish Republican Army was too conservative, Coyle thought that the best weapon in America was the telephone, and he used it. He compiled lists of committeemen and delegates and county chairmen and he routinely dialed them to talk politics and promote Larry Conrad.

Next came two new "road men"—drivers and advance men: Pat McCarty, a young lawyer, was hired to coordinate northern Indiana; and Richard (Dick) Malcolm left his job with an energy cooperative to join the staff as the southern Indiana coordinator.

The official Conrad for Governor Committee was co-chaired by Lois Lawrence from Elkhart County and the Rev. Landrum Shields, a black minister who was the senior pastor at Witherspoon United Presbyterian Church in Indianapolis. Herbert Simon, the president of Melvin Simon & Associates of Indianapolis, agreed to serve as treasurer.[44]

With the committee formed and the skeleton staff ensconced in the downtown motel, Conrad again hit the road. "When two or three are gathered together, then I want to be there," he preached to his staff.

But the Conrad campaign ran into a perennial problem: money. "Larry was literally living on the road," Wagner says. "We'd get him to one town and we'd have to scrounge to find food and gas money to get him to the next town. When he came in to the campaign headquarters I had him making phone calls for money, something he detested."[45] Wagner squeezed money from every nook and cranny. He even shamed one county chairman into borrowing money in the name of the county committee in order to donate to Conrad.[46] The money problem dominated everything. By the time the primary was over, the Conrad campaign had raised only about $80,000.[47] But Conrad never relented. His only complaint would be that he did not have enough on his schedule. He had to see everybody. He had to be everywhere.

Like a farmer in southern Indiana, Conrad went after the voters as if he were a dowser with a divining rod looking for fresh water. Once, while riding up Broadway to downtown Gary, he yelled to his driver, Pat McCarty, "Pull over!" He jumped out of the car and sprinted up the walk to the front porch of a house where an elderly black man was sitting. After about five minutes of conversation, Conrad returned to the car. "What was that all about?" McCarty asked. Conrad replied, "That guy's been sitting there for a couple of hours, watching the traffic go by. Well, tomorrow he's going to be talking to all his friends saying, 'yesterday this guy named Conrad, who is running for governor, came up to my porch and talked with me.' And all his friends will know that I've been here."[48]

How do you win a gubernatorial race without money in a state that always ranks near the top in the amount of campaign expenditures per vote? Wagner looked at the asset side of the campaign, not the deficit side. He understood that Conrad had an army of devoted followers in the state, the "Conrad Crazies." These individuals had developed a personal relationship with Larry over the last three election cycles, and now, with the governorship again at stake for their man, they were eager to be involved. In this, Conrad's fourth statewide campaign in six years, these people were the key. "What could we do with them?" Wagner asked himself. "We had no money." Sensing those political vibrations on the Hoosier landscape, Wagner devised the solution. It was a program costing no money; it required only volunteers, working in their homes.[49]

He established a "telephone pyramid" with the Conrad Crazies, where, by primary election day, every Democratic household in the state would have received at least three phone calls to vote for Larry. He put Gigerich and Coyle to work on the lists and placed Diane Meyer Grauel and Jane Allen Rooksby at the apex of the pyramid.[50] It would start with Diane and Jane calling ten people per day, who would, in turn, call ten people, who would also call ten people, and on and on. When the phone calls were completed, the volunteers sent the call sheets back to headquarters, where Gigerich and Coyle tabulated the results and prepared new calling sheets. By April 11, less than a month out from the primary, Wagner estimated that over 38,000 people were part of the pyramid, making telephone calls to Democrats.[51]

And organized labor came on board. The UAW and the Machinists endorsed Conrad. Don Yeagley, the director of the UAW's Community Action Program (CAP), installed telephone banks in several CAP offices throughout the state where volunteers called UAW members "to remind them that we've endorsed Hartke and Conrad."[52] Bob Brown of the Machinists provided both dollars and volunteers. The Steelworkers, under the leadership of Don Kearns, did not want to make a formal preprimary endorsement. Instead, they provided additional people for the phone pyramid.

Others started coming in droves, including me. I walked into the Howard Johnson suite in early December and saw Wagner sitting at his desk in front of the window, staring at a news release. He looked up, cocked his head, and said: "What the hell do you want?" I told him Larry had sent me and I was to tell him that I was to be hired. "That fat little guy thinks I've got some money over here to pay you?" he shot back. "Hell, I'm not even getting paid."

"Larry told me I was to be his speechwriter," I replied. "He said he didn't really need one, but every campaign was supposed to have a speechwriter, and that's what I'm to be called."

Wagner laughed.

"Yeah, Larry and I talked," he said, "but there's no goddamn money. If you'll volunteer until after the primary, then I'll be able to pay for some research and writing."

"You've got it," I replied.

Three days a week and every weekend, working around my classes at Ball State University, I drove to the downtown motel and started assembling information for news releases and speeches. John Livengood provided reams of material from the previous speeches he had written for Larry. The two of us quickly agreed—consistent with Conrad's instructions—that John would continue writing all materials for Larry that pertained to the secretary of state's functions and I would handle all the political releases. By mid-January the two motel rooms resembled a paper recycling plant. Newspapers, news releases, lists of names and phone numbers, and reams of copy paper were everywhere. One room contained a small table for "conferences," where visitors would have to shove boxes of paper aside in order to pull out chairs to sit down. Coyle was living in the suite, and one bathroom counter was piled high with his toiletries and dirty shirts. About twice a week Claudia Prosser would come through the connecting door of the two rooms, holding her hands out as they dripped mimeo fluid. "This damn machine is broken again," she would proclaim.

By early March Wagner was seeking larger quarters. After checking several locations, he made arrangements to rent the third floor of the Fair Building, at 311 W. Washington St., just three blocks east of Howard Johnson's and one-half block from the Statehouse. The Democratic State Central Committee was located on the first floor. A small suite of offices on the north side of the third floor was rented by the Hartke reelection campaign. The entire third floor had been most recently used as the Indianapolis Army induction center, where physical exams were given to draftees during the Vietnam War. As you opened the door through the long wooden partition, you could follow the outline of footprints which were glued to the linoleum floor. These footprints had guided the young men to their proper spots where they would strip and cough and prepare to go to war.

Wagner was increasingly confident of a primary victory, and ordered volunteer carpenters into the new headquarters to construct individual offices for staff members. Of course, he still worried about money. But there were two other things on his mind, as well. He was confident that the 1974 election had erased the negatives on Conrad that were a product of the Master Plan. But, like any professional campaign manager, he had his doubts. He also worried about Conrad's name recognition. Although Conrad had been on the state ballot in 1970 and 1974, and had generated much attention in his run for the nomination in 1972, Wagner knew those actions did not automatically translate to the voters.

Wagner had to find some answers. He cut a deal with his former candidate, U.S. Senator Vance Hartke, to "piggy-back" onto a statewide poll of

Democrats. Wagner added to the poll a complete set of questions on the gubernatorial race. The results were mixed.[53]

More than a third (36.3%) of the Democrats had never even heard of Larry Conrad, and another 13.3 percent did not know enough about him to rate him favorably or unfavorably. For all of his campaigning, for all of his publicity, only one-half (50.35%) of the Democrats had heard of the Indiana secretary of state, Larry A. Conrad.

In comparison to Bob Fair and Jack New, however, Larry Conrad was a household name. More than three-fourths (78.4%) of the respondents had never heard of Bob Fair, or did not have enough information to rate him. New's name recognition was somewhat better, but still, 66 percent didn't know him or could not rate him. Wagner knew immediately that he had to increase Conrad's name recognition.

The good news in the poll was that those Democrats who knew enough about Larry Conrad to rate him, liked him. His unfavorability rating, or negative, was only 5.9 percent. This was confirmation that Conrad had overcome the problems with the Master Plan.

The "favorability rating" of a candidate is one of the most important factors in persuading undecided voters. A high "unfavorability" can cripple a candidate. Once a candidate's unfavorability approaches 20 percent, that candidate is in trouble. When one out of five people who recognize you views you unfavorably, that can spread like a virus and infect other voters.[54]

The same poll that showed Conrad with only a 5.9 percent negative, registered a 29.6 percent unfavorable for U.S. Senator R. Vance Hartke. Indeed, Hartke was in trouble, and the Democratic congressman from the 8th district, Phil Hayes, was capitalizing on those negatives to wage a pitched battle for the Senate nomination.[55]

There was very good news for Conrad in the horse race question: "If the primary election were held today, would you vote for Conrad, Fair, or New?" The responses showed Conrad with nearly a two-to-one lead over both opponents. Conrad had 24.96 percent of the vote, with Fair receiving only 4.76 percent and New garnering 9.14 percent, with nearly two-thirds (61.14%) undecided.

The numbers were encouraging, but the remaining one-half of the Democratic electorate had to become acquainted with Conrad. That meant television and radio commercials. Wagner, using the poll numbers to guide him, called in several local advertising people and asked for help in writing media scripts. The focus would be on the high cost of utilities and the "energy crisis." He also collaborated with a Washington, D.C., media consultant, Johnny Alum. Finally, four scripts were agreed upon, and a camera crew was hired to film the television ads. Wagner, who had been sequestering all available dollars for the media buy, started reserving television time backwards from May 4. He also produced 100 radio tapes of the commercials and mailed them to various county chairmen and supporters, asking them to append a local "disclaimer" and buy time for Larry on local radio stations.

With the radio and television commercials produced and slated to run, Wagner's confidence grew. The telephone calls were showing increasing support, not only among the party leaders, but among the voters as well. Gigerich and Coyle conducted a telephone survey of precinct committeemen in Marion County which showed Conrad ahead by more than a two-to-one margin. Several Marion County ward organizations endorsed Conrad, although Schreiber headed off an attempt for a formal endorsement by the county committee. A straw poll at a Democratic dinner in the small county of Martin showed Conrad with 44 votes to 14 for New and only 8 for Fair. The Lake County chairman, Bob Pastrick, climbed on board the first week of April—and his roar was heard throughout the Democratic party. The executive committee of the Lake County Central Committee voted 42 for Conrad, 8 for Fair, and 1 for New. Pastrick then hit the road for Conrad, spending the week of April 12 in Marion County, speaking at ward meetings and union halls. In a news release issued April 14, Wagner reported that over 2,000 phone calls had been completed by the "pyramid" in Warrick County and the vote was 1,760 Conrad, 145 Fair, 28 New, and 460 undecided. In the last week of the campaign, Wagner announced that forty-one of the ninety-two Democratic county chairmen had formally endorsed Conrad and reported that "of the remaining fifty-one county chairmen, approximately 50 percent are helping us personally but remaining neutral in their official capacity in the party." He also said that over 200,000 phone calls had been completed throughout the state and "we hope to top a half million by election day, May 4."[56]

As in 1972, Conrad did not mention his Democratic opponents by name. Bob Fair and Jack New were veterans of political wars, but Fair had never been on the statewide ballot and Jack New, serving as the state treasurer, could not match Conrad's vim-and-vigor approach to politicking. Jack New, a party veteran, was twelve years older than Conrad. Following his graduation from Indiana University in the late 1940s, New was immediately involved in Democratic politics. "In those days it was a lot tougher than today," he maintains. "You had to make a living and provide for your family, but if you were to be devoted to politics it meant you had to make the time; often you had to steal the time from your work and your family."[57] New was a strong supporter of Matthew E. Welsh, and worked for him in the 1956 state convention, where the gubernatorial nomination was won by the mayor of Terre Haute, Ralph Tucker. Welsh came back in 1960 not only to win the nomination, but to become the only Democrat to win in November. New, along with Clinton Green and John Hurt, was in the inner circle. New joined Welsh's staff and in 1964 he began his own political career, winning the nomination and the election for state treasurer on the ticket with Governor Branigin. Serving only a two-year term, he was defeated for reelection in the Republican landslide of 1966. In 1968, teaming up with Welsh's state chairman, J. Manfred Core—and with the help of Bayh's staff members—they stunned Governor Branigin and Gordon St. Angelo by nominating Lieutenant Governor Bob Rock over State Representative Richard Bodine for governor. When Rock lost, New again thought of seeking election as state treasurer. "In 1969 I went to St. Angelo and told him I wanted to run again. I wasn't sure what his reaction would be, given what I had done in 1968. But he was very cooperative. He let me chair several district party meetings around the state," New recalls.[58]

Late in 1969 Larry Conrad visited Jack New in Greenfield. "He came by my house and told me he was running for secretary of state. I said, 'Fine, but if you're planning for governor, I won't be with you.' Larry was not real good at hiding his feelings; he just stared at his shoes. I knew he was really looking at governor down the road, because, like a lot of candidates, when one guy does something that works, everybody tries to copy it. [Republican Ed] Whitcomb had been secretary of state and then ran for governor and made it."[59]

New was not surprised when Conrad challenged Welsh for the Democratic nomination in 1972. His misgivings about Conrad grew while the two of them served as statewide officials. Referring to Conrad's staff, New says: "Larry hired 'funny people.' He hired one fellow who had been arrested for drugs. I asked Larry why in the world he would hire such a person and Larry replied: 'Don't you believe in giving a person a second chance?' And he would hire people and they would be gone in three months. He didn't have any older people on his staff. Stu Grauel, however, managed to get him through all that."[60]

Jack New loved the administrative details of governing. Conrad did not. "This disturbed me about Larry. He loved to campaign, but he did not seem to know the issues. With respect to government, Larry was very much lacking," New contends.[61]

New made the commitment to run for governor early. When he announced his candidacy he had already prepaid some of his expenses. He knew Conrad was the man to beat. He was also aware that Bob Fair wanted to take his turn to grab the brass ring. "Fair very much wanted me to withdraw, and he called Matt Welsh to try to get me out of the race. Matt did not advise me one way or the other. But I knew my votes would not go to Fair. They would go to Conrad. I said no."[62]

Shortly after New announced, he was interviewed by Bob Flynn, one of the Statehouse reporters from Evansville. Flynn asked him why he was running, suggesting that Conrad deserved the nomination. New remembers answering: "Maybe he has the Prince of Wales complex," referring to Conrad as a king-in-waiting. Conrad, of course, read the story. "He came over to my office and talked to me about it. I apologized to him. I was flippant. That was the only time I said something negative about Larry. I was too flippant."[63] From that point on, New concentrated on Bowen's record and criticized Conrad only by referring to the old Master Plan, asserting that Conrad "would have trouble withstanding the scrutiny of statewide news media in the fall."[64]

While Robert Fair, Conrad's other opponent, was liked and respected in the state legislature and by lobbyists and reporters, the rest of the Democratic party hardly knew him at all. He was in his tenth year in the legislature and was the leader of the minority Democratic caucus in the State Senate. Formerly an FBI agent, this attorney from Princeton, in Gibson County, was part of the long line of Democratic leaders coming from southeastern Indiana.

Fair was a distinguished-looking man with thinning gray hair. His mild demeanor was effective in the many legislative negotiations that occur in the hallways of the Statehouse. He took pride in his legislative accomplishments, even though he was in the minority. Nearly every budget passed by the legislature had items in it that were Bob Fair's handiwork.

But his Statehouse reputation did not extend elsewhere. He tended to legislative business, not the Jefferson-Jackson Day banquet circuit or the meetings of the Democratic Women's and Men's clubs. Like many other Hoosiers, however, he wanted to run for governor, and he considered 1976 to be his time.

"I was in the Senate as long as I wanted to be, and I made up my mind to either go up or get out. Some people approached me about the congressional race in my home district, but I wasn't interested in that. I had lived in Washington. The only race I considered was governor," Fair recalls.

Fair did not share New's misgivings about Conrad. If Conrad did not know state policies as well as himself, Fair did not find that disturbing. "Larry was a people person," says Fair. "That was the part of politics that appealed to him, and he was very good at it."[65]

Fair and New were experienced politicians. They both represented the old, regular establishment of the Indiana Democratic party. New, in particular, had been a party insider for over twenty years. Conrad had deep respect for the political traditions of Indiana, but he sensed a new day was coming, and the old establishment was going to be swept away. And he was going to be the agent of that change.

The promise of the Conrad campaign was to overturn the old ways and open the party to new people and new ideas. Conrad's approach to politics and campaigning represented all of this. Wagner adopted two campaign slogans to capture this message. The first slogan was "No Strings Attached," and Wagner printed thousands of press-on lapel tags with Conrad's classic picture—with his coat thrown over his shoulder—that read "No Strings Attached." For Polish neighborhoods in South Bend and

A Biography

Lake County, the phrase was translated into Polish. The second slogan was intended to capture Conrad's populist style: "He's a lot like you."

While Wagner sought to make a subtle distinction between Conrad and the two "party regulars," Conrad ignored Fair and New. True to his previous campaigns as both candidate and campaign manager, Conrad knew the real opponent was the Republican. He concentrated on Bowen, and he honed in on the most salient issue of the time: utility costs. The effects of the five-month Arab oil embargo, which began in October of 1973, were still being felt in 1976. Everywhere Conrad went he spoke of the "energy crisis" in Indiana, pointing out that utility rates for most families had increased by "nearly four hundred dollars." He proposed eliminating the sales tax on utility bills and cutting the state gasoline tax by shifting to an ad valorem tax, maintaining that the same amount of tax revenue would be generated because gasoline prices had nearly doubled. He also called for the state to take the lead in energy conservation, thereby reducing the need for more power plants and oil refineries. He set forth specific changes he intended to make in the Public Service Commission, the appointed board that approved utility rates. He pledged he would shake up the commission, establish a "code of ethics" for the commission members, and make the public counselor's job a full-time position with more staff.[66]

Fair and New could not withstand the Conrad whirlwind. Not only was Conrad seemingly everywhere in Indiana, but the endorsements from labor and county chairmen kept pouring in, and the phone calls kept going out to the voters. "It really wasn't much of an election," New concedes.[67] Fair concurs. "Conrad was so far out in front that we couldn't even see him," he says.[68]

One of Conrad's staff members in the secretary of state's office, Russ Grunden, used his flair for doggerel to summarize the race:

Jack New's got the money,

Bob Fair's got the experience,

But Larry Conrad's got the votes.

On primary election day, Larry and Mary Lou voted early. Since early March, Mary Lou had been on the campaign trail continuously. Kevin Zirkle was her main driver and Mary Finnegan was her traveling companion. When Larry was in southern or central Indiana, Mary Lou was up north. When Larry went to Lake County, Mary Lou was down on the river. While traveling, she worried constantly about the children. Every morning when she got in the car at 5:30 A.M. she would run her mental check list: Did I post the trip schedule so the children will know where I will be? Is there enough milk in the refrigerator? Are there enough clean socks and underwear? By now, of course, the children were political veterans themselves, and Mary Lou knew the family was on remote control. The children always checked in with their mother, but it was almost always Amy—the one daughter in that Conrad brood of four—who made the phone call to report everything was O.K. on Meridian Street.

The worries about the children and the weariness of the long hours were what Mary Lou disliked about campaigning. What compensated for it was not only meeting new people at every stop, but seeing old friends from her fourteen years in politics. Like most people, she was still nervous when making a speech or answering questions from a television reporter. Her first official "political speech" had been in 1970 in Orange County, where she was certain she would be unable to finish the first sentence. By now she was poised and adept at handling questions. And she loved to express herself in her natural ways. If the senior citizens' center she was visiting had a piano, she would immediately sit down and begin playing a medley of "golden oldies," from "You Are My Sunshine" to "Shine On Harvest Moon." The residents were soon singing in a cacophony of voices.

Primary election day was the culmination of all the effort. Larry and Mary Lou went to the polls together, then they parted. Mary Lou was to greet voters at a Marion County polling place while Larry moved from poll to poll throughout the county. She wrote about that day in her diary:

> Today, as I stood in the voting booth, I felt good. I must admit I always run scared, particularly after the past experiences of the razor-thin victory in 1970; the heartbreak of the 1972 convention, and the emotional devastation of the Master Plan in 1973. Real joy and relief are not possible for me until the votes are counted. Well, we'll soon know for sure how this primary race will turn out. I took one more satisfying glance at my husband's name on the voting machine, and pulled the lever. Well, Larry, this one's for you![69]

After the polls closed, the entire Conrad family converged at their house. Marshall and Ruby were there. Ruby had brought a large batch of her fried chicken, plus potatoes, gravy, and brownies. Confusion reigned in the household. Larry and Mary Lou had radios and television sets in virtually every room, and several neighbors were there helping track the returns. Mary Lou remembers one of the boys shouting, "Hey Dad, you just won Clark County," and then Andy yelling, "Hey Mom, do I have to wear a tie to headquarters?"[70]

At the downtown headquarters, Wagner confined the growing crowd to the large front rooms while staff members were in back offices calling counties to obtain the latest returns. Wagner was very confident, but even he was surprised at the early numbers. "Keep 'em coming," he yelled to the staff.

Wagner called Conrad every twenty minutes, informing him of the results. Early in the evening, with about 75 percent of the votes counted, Conrad had a lead of 64 percent, with New at 19 and Fair at 17 percent. Those percentages were to hold.

The final totals showed Conrad with 358,421 votes, New with 105,965, and Fair with 91,606. Conrad roared through Lake County, garnering more than 72 percent of the vote. He lost only three counties: New's home county, Hancock; Fair's home county, Gibson; and Governor Bowen's home county, Marshall.[71]

Less than two hours after the polls closed, Conrad and his family were on their way to headquarters for the victory statement. With Mary Lou at his side, Conrad looked into the television cameras and proclaimed that his victory was due to "people involvement" in his campaign. He credited his county committees and volunteers for getting out the Conrad votes by staffing the telephone banks in eighty-seven of the ninety-two counties. He acknowledged that Otis Bowen would be a difficult opponent, but said: "If I thought he was unbeatable I would not have undertaken the effort. I hope to woo some Republican voters."[72]

With Conrad's lead insurmountable, Wagner had ordered the staff to open the kegs of beer which had been held in reserve for the celebration. Dozens of people were milling around the headquarters, singing victory songs and chanting "Larry! Larry! Larry!" Wagner, who not only partook of the beer, but poured a few drinks from his private whiskey bottle which he kept under lock and key in his desk, swaggered through the crowd, hugging and kissing everybody he encountered. By 11 P.M. he was sitting on the floor in a pool of spilled beer, leaning against the wall. Mary Lou and Larry were leaving and Mary Lou leaned over and kissed Wagner on the forehead and said, "Thank you, Bob." Wagner looked up at her, broke out in a wide grin, shook his head slightly, and said, "Mary Lou, this isn't just a victory, this is a fucking landslide!" Mary Lou and Larry laughed, and left for home. Mary Lou remembers that "we left the headquarters all too soon. We had all worked so hard to reach this plateau and I didn't want it to end." She remembers the drive home. The euphoria of victory. She thought for a moment about "the month of May" and the fact that, for the next few days, at least, the six Conrads would be a "real family again," eating meals together and sleeping under the same roof. Then their car passed the governor's residence, about twenty-five blocks south of Conrad's home. "I know it will take at least another 25,000 miles of campaigning to move those 25 blocks," Mary Lou wrote in her diary.[73]

Back at headquarters, ecstasy reigned. "Primary election night, I was dumbfounded," Wagner recalls. "The results kept coming in and they kept getting better and better. I felt like we were beating the world."[74]

Jack New issued a concession statement in which he credited "Conrad's hard work over a long period of time" as the reason for his victory. He said his own campaign was "a day late and a dollar short." New pledged his support to Conrad and said the three-way primary contest did not endanger Democratic unity.[75]

Bob Fair's campaign manager, Charles (Chic) Svihlik, responded to press inquiries and said that Fair's campaign staff was "completely enthusiastic" about supporting Conrad.[76]

That night was the zenith of Larry Conrad's political career. He was sitting atop the Democratic party of Indiana, catapulted there by two-thirds of the Democratic electorate. But from the mountaintop there was a higher mountain in sight, across the valley: the general electorate. Conrad and his staff and his "Crazies" could see it. To get there they had to descend into the valley and prepare to wage war with one of the strongest political organizations in the country.[77]

The next day Claudia Prosser and I were the first to arrive at the headquarters. Beer cups full of stale brew covered the tables and trash was strewn across the floors. After cleaning up a bit we talked about the central question: "Where do we go from here?" It was the month of May. Conrad was going to the track to watch the Indy cars practice. The Indianapolis Black Expo was scheduled to open in a few days at the convention center. The apparent nominee for lieutenant governor, State Senator Tom Teague, had to be contacted and brought into the campaign structure. The state convention, which was to nominate the candidates for attorney general, superintendent of public instruction, and reporter of the Supreme and Appellate Courts, was only five weeks away. It was time to plan new schedules and new speeches.[78]

Wagner, we were sure, would provide the direction. But Wednesday turned to Thursday, and then to Friday. The week went away, and the staff did not hear from Wagner.

Wagner was working, but not out of campaign headquarters. The biennial reorganization of the Democratic party was beginning, and Wagner wanted one thing. He wanted Bill Trisler out as state chairman. He wanted the Conrad Democrats in control of the party organization.

"After we won the primary I thought we had the power to take on anyone in the party. Bill Trisler was closely associated with St. Angelo and we had to have a new and fresh Democratic party. That's what Larry and I had fought for. I wanted Trisler out. There were some people who had not been enthusiastic about Larry, but they were now all on board. And these were mainstream Democrats who would have followed us," Wagner remembered.[79]

Conrad and Wagner met for two hours on Thursday, May 6, and Wagner pressed hard to remove Trisler. Conrad did not agree, and Wagner was livid. "Larry was unwilling to do this," Wagner recalls. "He didn't feel he had it in him to run for governor and fight the organization battle also. It would have been a war on two fronts." The meeting ended with no final decision. Wagner told Bob Mooney of the *Indianapolis Star* that "Larry has a lot of thinking to do about it."[80]

Wagner kept working. He called Bob Pastrick. He met with Dallas Sells and Don Yeagley of the UAW. He discussed the chairmanship with Don Michael, the Cass County Democratic chairman, and Bun Gallahan, from Miami County. Gallahan and Michael met with Conrad and urged him to make phone calls to the state committee members in support of Michael. "He was reluctant to do that," Michael recalls; "he said that we all had to be careful to keep the party united if we were to have any chance of winning."[81] When Conrad would not move on Michael's behalf, Wagner kept probing. He asked for suggestions on who should replace Trisler. He discussed the matter with Senator Hartke, who had narrowly won renomination over Congressman Phil Hayes. But without Conrad personally willing to get involved in ousting Trisler, Wagner knew there would be no spirit in the fight.

Conrad's reluctance hardened. He did not want turmoil in the party while he was trying to defeat Otis Bowen. Moreover, he thought he could get along with Bill Trisler. Trisler had openly opposed Conrad in 1974, but once he was state chairman he did nothing to derail Conrad's primary election campaign. Wagner acknowledges that "Trisler kept out of our way in the primary. He did not interfere with our campaign."[82]

Conrad actually liked Bill Trisler. He appreciated the southern Indiana style of politics out of which Trisler had emerged, in Jackson County. He thought he could work with Trisler. Moreover, Boxell was advising him to leave the organization alone. The state committee did not have any resources to help, and the turmoil would deflect attention from the general election. Finally, of course, if Conrad were elected, he could remove Trisler at any time. As had been the case with St. Angelo in 1968, Trisler's job was saved by a nominee who wanted to be a governor, not a dictator.

The campaign staff continued to report to work every day. Preparations were made for the Democratic booth at Black Expo, and I began writing the platform to present to the state convention. Conrad was splitting his time between the secretary of state duties and the track, where a fund-raiser was planned for carburetion day at one of the suites on the first turn. Rumors started that Wagner had quit the campaign because Conrad would not appoint him state chairman.

Wagner never seriously considered becoming state chairman. Many others had suggested that he should be, but his law practice was growing, and the chairman's job demanded full-time attention. If he had been tempted at all, it was because of his deep desire to throw open the doors of the Democratic party and welcome all those people who had been excluded by the St. Angelo–Trisler leadership. But he did not have the time to be state chairman.[83]

Wagner's disappointment in not replacing Trisler was in keeping with the old political adage that a winner—particularly a landslide winner—should get something. He conferred with his law partner, Ed Lewis, and a call went to Bill Gigerich, summoning him to the law offices on the south side. When Gigerich arrived, only Lewis and Wagner were there. "We're going to get something out of this," Wagner told Gigerich. "We're going to make you secretary of the State Central Committee. And Trisler is staying." Gigerich agreed.[84] Wagner contacted Conrad and told him of the plan. Conrad agreed. So did Trisler. On Saturday, May 15, the officers were elected for the State Central Committee and Gigerich was unanimously installed as the new secretary.

But the rest of the campaign staff did not hear from Wagner. He had pledged only to run the primary campaign. Now, with no reorganization fight, he informed Conrad he was going back to his law practice.

Conrad could not let that happen. His campaign was already in suspension, just days after a massive victory. He needed Wagner. He had to get the campaign moving.

Wagner began feeling the pressure from the nominee. "A lot of people called me and told me that I had brought Larry this far and I should take the next step. Some even said that Larry was ready to quit and resign from the ticket if this thing didn't get moving," Wagner says. But he remained convinced that Otis Bowen could not be defeated, and he responded to the callers by saying that he had promised Larry that he would manage only the primary, not the general election campaign.[85]

But Wagner was loyal. He expected loyalty from others, and what he expected from others he expected from himself. Conrad knew this, but getting Wagner to acknowledge it was another matter. Conrad took the matter up with the one man to whom Wagner would listen.

Three weeks after the primary, Wagner was in his law office, attending to his business, when the phone rang. It was Ed Lewis. "Ed asked me to come down the hall to his office," Wagner recalls. "I walked in and Larry was sitting there with Ed. He was the last guy I expected to see. Ed looked at me and said, 'You just have to do this.' I told Larry, 'I don't think we can win. I don't think we can win.' Those were the only two people I ever said that to. The rest of the staff and the rest of the people never knew I thought that." The discussion went on and on. Conrad argued that very few people ever had the chance to be in the position they were—to be a nominee for governor—even if there was only an outside chance of winning. He spoke of the obligation to the party. He said that if the campaign shut down, the Republicans and the reporters would have a field day.

Wagner listened. He acknowledged that Jimmy Carter had a realistic chance to win the presidency, and if the Democrats were going to win anything in Indiana, it was going to take Conrad's organization. He recognized that the enormity of Conrad's primary victory assured him of a united party. "I more or less made the decision then that I would return," Wagner says.[86]

Wagner was back on board. He immediately issued a news release claiming that Otis Bowen was "vulnerable," pointing out that Bowen had

A Biography

purchased both radio and television ads immediately after the primary because of Conrad's "genuine grassroots support throughout the state."[87]

Then Wagner's attention shifted to the upcoming Democratic State Convention, to be held on June 14 and 15. The major fight on the convention floor was for the nomination for attorney general.

Virginia Dill McCarty had sought the Democratic nomination for attorney general in 1972, losing to Theodore D. (Ted) Wilson, a black attorney from Indianapolis, who, in turn, lost in November. Wilson was seeking the nomination again. McCarty approached Wagner for his and Conrad's support. Wagner was leery. Jim Kelley, the Marion County prosecutor, was telling people he was going to be McCarty's floor manager, and Wagner wanted nothing to do with Kelley. Wagner remembered Kelley's threats against Conrad in 1974. "I met with McCarty and her supporters and told them I could work it out, but it had to be done my way. We had to get Kelley off the floor."[88]

Shortly before the balloting for attorney general began, Conrad staff members fanned out on the convention floor distributing badges that had a circle design with the capital "C" ringing the names of Carter, Conrad, and McCarty. The word spread fast: Conrad was with McCarty. It took three ballots, but when the final votes were counted, McCarty won easily, 1,150 to 823. She was the first woman ever to win either major party's nomination for attorney general.[89]

The Democratic team was now assembled, but the campaign was in serious trouble. There was no media money. The Democratic State Central Committee was virtually broke, having only a few thousand dollars available for printing. Wagner knew it was an impossible fight, but he again forced his thinking to the asset side of the political equation. Across Indiana's political landscape there were only two visible outcroppings that signaled a way for the Democrats to climb the mountain. First, a statewide voter registration effort had to produce huge numbers of new voters. With the party organization, the Conrad Crazies, and organized labor united, such a registration drive might work. If these new voters could be coupled with the growing popularity of Jimmy Carter, the "help from the top" might translate into a ballooning support for the rest of the Democratic ticket in Indiana. All this was a very long shot, but it was the only shot worth taking.

While Wagner turned his attention to orchestrating the state convention, he instructed Gigerich and the other staff members to design a program for the most massive voter registration drive ever undertaken in Indiana. Gigerich swiftly designed an elaborate field program, complete with printed instructions that would return information on new registrants to the Conrad headquarters in Indianapolis. From there, direct mail was planned for every newly registered voter.

It was decided that Conrad would announce his plans in his speech to the delegates at the state convention. Saying that his campaign would produce a "new order" that would "open Indiana government," he pledged to "personally meet with every Democratic precinct committeeman in the state in the next two weeks." He then revealed the voter registration effort: "From these meetings we will launch a voter registration drive that will touch every neighborhood and street in Indiana. In 1776, voting was a revolutionary idea. It still is!"[90]

It was up to Claudia Prosser to deliver on this promise to "personally meet with every Democratic precinct committeeman." Sandwiching in special requests and issue briefings, Prosser assembled packed schedules for Conrad over the next two weeks. As Conrad crisscrossed the state, starting in the northern tier, county chairmen brought their precinct committeemen together to hear him call for an all-out effort to register voters. For the first time in years, the Democratic gubernatorial nominee was actually going to the base of the party organization, beseeching them to be directly engaged in the "American revolution of 1976." While the "road men" delivered boxes of instructions and registration forms to county chairmen, hundreds of other forms were shipped out of Conrad's Indianapolis headquarters. Gigerich and Coyle pulled in volunteers to work the phones to guarantee that the materials arrived and that the committeemen and volunteers were poised and trained to register new Democrats.

Two days after the Democrats nominated their state ticket, the Republicans assembled in their state convention. All the incumbents were renominated without opposition. The media coverage given the Republicans revealed the massive problem the Conrad campaign would face in getting publicity. The *Indianapolis Star* ran a front-page picture of Bowen entering the GOP state convention, flanked by supporters wearing T-shirts that read, "I Luv the Guv." During the Democratic state convention there was not one photo in the *Star* of Larry Conrad.[91]

Conrad did pick up an early endorsement, however. The Indiana Fraternal Order of Police unanimously endorsed him, citing his commitment to increase state support for funding police and fire pensions. An article about the endorsement ran on page 32 of the *Indianapolis Star*.[92]

Conrad simply could not receive coverage in the *Star*. While the editors buried any of Conrad's endorsements, they managed to scrounge a negative story for the front page. On Tuesday, July 20, 1976, the Viking 1 spacecraft, after a 214-million-mile voyage, landed on Mars. As with all newspapers around the country, it was the lead story in the *Star* the next morning. But immediately underneath the Viking 1 story, in even bigger type, was the headline: "Conrad Manager, Co-op Linked." The "kicker" for the Conrad headline was: "Office Denies Conflict Of Interest." Written by John S. Mason and William M. Shaw, the story reported that Robert F. Wagner "is the attorney for a trucking co-operative which has a crucial legal matter pending in Conrad's office" and that the Indiana Co-operative

Handling Association could "fail financially if Conrad's office issues an unfavorable ruling."

Conrad was attending the annual meeting of the National Association of Secretaries of State in Dover, Delaware, when one of the reporters reached him. Conrad said his involvement in the case was peripheral, adding that the director of the corporations division, Page Gifford, routinely handled such matters. He said he had talked with Wagner about the case and Wagner said he represented one of the parties. "But to tell you the truth, I can't remember which party," Conrad was quoted as saying.

When Gifford was contacted he acknowledged it was taking an inordinately long time to reach a decision on the matter, but he quickly denied that Wagner's involvement played any role. "I don't take my orders from Bob Wagner and neither does Larry Conrad," Gifford said. "And as far as the question of legal ethics, that is a matter for Bob and his law firm to decide."

The booming page-one story that played as prominently as Viking 1 actually involved a standard petition submitted to the corporations division that questioned the not-for-profit status of the trucking co-op. The petition was signed by several independent trucking companies which were for-profit and therefore subject to the regulations of the Indiana Public Service Commission.

The reporters suggested, but offered no proof, that some of the trucking interests opposing the co-op "could be potential contributors to the Conrad campaign." They then reported that the co-op delivered coal to a generating plant that was part of the Indiana Statewide Rural Electric Co-operative (REMC). The coal was from a southern Indiana mine that was represented by Felsom Bowman, one of Wagner's law partners. The story concluded: "Wagner and his firm's senior partner, Edward D. Lewis, both are former campaign managers for United States Senator R. Vance Hartke (D-Ind.), a longtime supporter of rural electrification."[93]

Now the Conrad campaign was in damage control. But compared to what they had been through, this was easy. Later that day, Wagner called a news conference at headquarters, where he explained the administrative process concerning the case, denied that his role as campaign manager had any bearing on the corporations division of the secretary of state's office, pointed out the story was filled with innuendo and hypotheticals, and facetiously wondered why the news judgment of the *Indianapolis Star* viewed this story to be as big as the first landing on Mars.

The story played one day and was gone. The staff ordered Wagner a T-shirt with an inscription on the back reading, "Dirty Bob."

Overcoming the hostility of the Indianapolis newspapers was the greatest problem facing the campaign. If sufficient money were raised, it would be no problem. Television ads would more than offset the tactics of the newspaper editors. But with no money for paid media it was essential to "earn" media in the press, particularly the *Star*. The gatekeeper to that was the *Star*'s chief political reporter, Robert P. (Bob) Mooney.

Mooney was a gaunt, elongated figure with a wide smile and sorrowful eyes. But his personal experiences seemed to soften his view of men and women in public life. He had lived enough of the human tragedy to automatically understand the conflicts, doubts, and foibles of those all-too-human political leaders.

Mooney genuinely liked Larry Conrad. He thought he would make an outstanding governor. And he understood that the Indianapolis newspapers, particularly the *News*, had done everything possible to stain his career. Mooney loved the old adage in Indianapolis that "you have to play to the *Star*." And he knew Conrad was in a bruising, uphill battle against Bowen. If Mooney was to give space to Conrad's campaign, he needed a constant flow of newsworthy items, and he didn't think he was getting them. "Goddamn it, I want Larry to win," he said repeatedly to me, late at night in my office after his next-day stories were filed. "But you've got to give me something to write." He complained to Wagner that the reporters gathered at the Indianapolis Press Club were laughing at the Conrad campaign for "lack of substance" and being populated only by neophytes.

Wagner exploded. With his feral stride he entered my office—the "research shop." He screamed at the seven of us—all at our desks typing speeches and releases: "Goddamn it, did I hire idiots? Our candidate is out here talking—talking—talking, and nobody's hearing him. Why? Because of you! Do I have to write everything myself? I don't ever want to see a goddamn release out of here that says only one thing. Larry's got a story to tell—he's got a message—and I want that message in everything you write!" With a final flailing of arms, he pivoted and left.

Stunned, we all slowly turned our heads to one another. I finally said, "That's Wags. He's lost his temper again. Let him cool down."

The next day Wagner and I met. I knew Mooney had been talking to him. We agreed we needed a newsperson on board who could hang around the Statehouse and gladhand the reporters at the Press Club. A week later Wagner hired Virgil Napier, a former radio reporter. Napier immediately began eating lunch at the Press Club. The rest of us went back to writing the releases and speeches. Only now the first question we asked was: "Where's Larry's story in here?"

In late June and early July the statewide political campaigns ground to a halt. Aside from parades, there was not much to be done. It was the 200th birthday of America, and every community was having its celebration, culminating in the extravaganza on the Mall in Washington. Moreover, the Democratic National Convention was scheduled to open in New York on July 12, and Larry and Mary Lou would be attending. The hiatus in the campaign provided the opportunity to plan ahead.[94]

It was now that Wagner made a fateful decision, one that would be roundly criticized for years thereafter. Facing a well-funded and very popular opponent, Wagner decided to spend his scarce dollars on staff. Maybe, just maybe, all these energetic, bright people moving everywhere in Indiana could whip up a Democratic whirlwind. This calculated gamble was intended to produce a surge in voter turnout. If the newly registered voters, and the marginal Democrats who seldom voted, could be energized, there just might be an outside shot for an upset. As Wagner hired more and more people, he turned them loose on the road with instructions to attend every meeting—of whatever nature—they could find.

Charles (Chuck) Gaddy joined the headquarters staff in Indianapolis, bringing with him an old offset press which he set up in the back room, next to the freight elevator. Wagner purchased thousands of reams of paper and cans of ink and told Gaddy to work twenty-four hours a day printing leaflets and brochures. Maureen Minnemayer, a recent Ball State University graduate, was hired to write material for Gaddy and the printing press.

Charles (Chuck) Deppert and Duke Oliver came on board as labor coordinators. State Representative William A. (Bill) Crawford joined the staff as the liaison with the black community and other Democratic state legislators. Steve Mong, who had been on board before the primary, continued to live in the basement of the Conrad house and travel with Larry. Affectionately nicknamed "the mole," Mong had long legs and wiry hair. He was seldom seen in headquarters; everyone knew he was either on the road with Larry or asleep in the Meridian Street basement. Don Michael, the Cass County chairman, joined the staff as a district coordinator, working with Malcolm and McCarty. Mike Pannos came on board to handle Lake County. Other district coordinators were recruited, both paid and unpaid. Ruth Adams was hired to support Mary Lou and the children in their campaign appearances. Suzanne Ross, a recent Indiana University graduate, was hired to write for Tom Teague. Bettie Cadue, who had joined the staff prior to the primary, continued as a writer of news releases. Dane Newman was the volunteer coordinator. He slept in his sleeping bag in the front office, awaiting the arrival of the morning volunteers. E. C. Walker, Pat Dugan, and John Blair were hired to help with research and photography. Donna Shaw was hired to run the "robo-typewriters"; Carolyn MacAvoy provided secretarial support for Gigerich. Sue Baker was the office coordinator, making sure everyone got to work, had coffee, and stayed in his or her "box."

David Bochnowski made plans to join the staff as political director, immediately under Wagner. Bill Bannon returned from Ohio to help with finances, and Bob Boxell arranged for a leave of absence from his engineering firm to become the finance director. Cathy Henneke moved from the secretary of state's office to campaign headquarters to help coordinate fund-raising events. Diane Grauel took vacation time and lunch hours from Senator Bayh's staff to help raise money.[95]

Wagner and Prosser centralized scheduling. Hartke's scheduler worked in Prosser's office and other staff members were hired to assist with the schedules of the other candidates.

The staff kept growing and growing. More people joined Hartke's staff, and the Carter campaign assigned two people to Indiana, one of whom was Hillary Rodham Clinton. She would periodically appear in headquarters to coordinate appearances by Carter or his family members. Virtually every day there would be someone new on board. There were not enough desks. Long tables were placed in the middle of the rooms and the new staffers would quickly claim a space, like squatters in the Old West.

From this assemblage of bright young people came creative—and sometimes loony—ideas. In an attempt to boost Conrad's name recognition, a "pet billboard" program was set in motion. Gaddy found an abandoned warehouse in Indianapolis and hired a crew to paint "Conrad for Governor" on plywood sheets cut 18 inches by 4 feet. Hundreds were painted and sold for five dollars each to supporters who were instructed to "personally care for the pet billboard by placing it in a conspicuous location and attending to it on a regular basis." The pet billboards started appearing everywhere. They were on the side of barns and on fence posts along the highways. They were in front yards, on trees, and on the sides of old trucks. Early one morning a phone call came in to headquarters from the Indiana State Police. The officer said that signs reading "Conrad for Governor" had appeared overnight on all the highway overpasses on Interstate 65 between Lebanon and Lafayette. Since this was a violation of state law, he expected those signs to be removed by the end of the day. When Wagner was informed, he said: "That goddamn Gaddy. He's loose again. Find him and tell him to get his crew up on 65 and take those signs down." When Gaddy came in, he sheepishly admitted that "it seemed like a good idea at the time." By nightfall, the pet billboards were gone.

Much of the staff's attention was not focused on pet billboards, however. Something much more serious was coming up; the endorsement of the Indiana State Teachers Association (ISTA). The group was holding its Leadership Conference in French Lick in late July. ISTA was, and remains, one of the strongest interest groups in the state. An affiliate of the National Education Association, ISTA represented over 35,000 teachers throughout the state, and their Political Action Committee (PAC) made endorsements, which meant money and manpower.[96] Nancy Papas, a long-time Conrad supporter and former staff member with Birch Bayh, was serving as the director of political education for ISTA and provided data and information to Conrad's staff concerning the issues most important to ISTA. On the basis of issues, Conrad's endorsement by ISTA should have been automatic. He supported increased funding for public schools and set forth a goal of bringing Indiana from thirtieth nationally in public school support into the top ten. He supported "open-scope" collective bargaining for teachers, which would allow them to negotiate non-salary items in their contracts with local school boards. Moreover, Tom Teague had received an award from ISTA for being one of their best supporters in the state legislature.

But ISTA, like many interest groups, always seeks to have it both ways. The leadership of ISTA knew the Democrats were their allies on issues, but they also read the polls. They understood that Bowen and Orr were way ahead.

Conrad and Teague attended the ISTA meeting on July 31 in French Lick and reminded the teachers of their long-standing support for public education. But it wasn't enough. Wagner received word the next week that the ISTA Political Action Committee was going to endorse Bowen. They explained that they had to protect themselves by being with the probable winner. Conrad, Teague, and Wagner were irate. They saw it as a betrayal, and they were going to fight back.[97]

They decided to take the fight directly to each of the officers belonging to the ISTA PAC. Claudia Prosser chartered an aircraft and constructed a schedule for Tom Teague to visit all committee members personally, flying directly to their hometowns and going directly to their houses. In the meantime, Conrad worked the telephones, calling his long-time supporters in ISTA and alerting them to the Bowen endorsement. He asked that they contact ISTA leaders and the members of the PAC.

The pressure was building. Teague was no longer polite in making his case to the committee members. He told them that he would still be a state senator even if the Democrats lost the election, and he could turn against ISTA just as quickly as ISTA turned against its friends.

The tactic worked. ISTA was in a box. The word had circulated among politicians of both parties that the Bowen-Orr ticket was to be endorsed. If they withdrew that endorsement it would severely damage the credibility of the leadership, not only with Bowen and the Republicans, but with their own membership. They had to find a way to wiggle out. But there was nowhere to go without bringing ridicule down on them. The decision was finally made to live with the embarrassment and endorse both tickets. Conrad attended the news conference with the chairman of ISTA's PAC on Tuesday, August 31. The chairman tried to explain the unprecedented endorsement by saying, "We would rather endorse both, thereby encouraging our teachers to become involved, than to withdraw from the race altogether."[98] In an editorial cartoon in the *Indianapolis News* on September 2, a caricature of an ISTA leader, wearing a dunce cap, announced to the audience: "Our Choice For Governor—Otis Conrad."[99]

When Conrad received word that ISTA had blinked, he ordered a case of champagne sent to campaign headquarters. The staff members left their desks and typewriters for the biggest celebration of the campaign.

The campaign needed something to celebrate. In mid-August, the Republican national convention was under way and William D. Ruckelshaus was mentioned as a possible running mate with President Ford. The selection of the native Hoosier would surely sink the Democrats in Indiana. The rumors of a Ruckelshaus candidacy had been rampant for days, and Gerald Ford did nothing to quash them.[100] On Wednesday, August 18, Conrad met with Democratic mayors from throughout the state. During his remarks, he received a phone call from Senator Bayh's office, informing him that Ruckelshaus was still a finalist for the nomination. When Conrad returned to the room, he reported the news to the mayors. Clearly acknowledging the massive problems Ruckelshaus's selection would create, Conrad urged the mayors to step forward to help. Robert Rock, now the mayor of Anderson, was the first to speak up. He knew the pressures of a Democratic gubernatorial campaign when the presidential ticket runs badly in Indiana. He pledged to host a fund-raiser immediately in Anderson for Conrad and promised he would raise at least $15,000. The other mayors also made pledges, but when the meeting adjourned there were few smiles and no applause.

The growing campaign staff was causing internal problems. Wagner's calculated gamble of hiring more and more staff members was maddening to many. Jim Coyle drafted an organization chart of the campaign on poster board and facetiously labeled it "General Command Staff of the 4th Reich." Wagner loved it. But Dave Bochnowski, a black-haired veteran of several statewide campaigns, was a true believer in rigid internal organization. Quickly nicknamed "Mighty Mouse," he strolled through headquarters appearing unperturbed—as though ice water flowed through his short physique. Bochnowski was actually deeply troubled by the chaos. He insisted that some internal organization be imposed on all these staffers. He pleaded and cajoled. Wagner relented. There would be a staff meeting, the first week of September.[101]

But first there was to be the annual gathering of the Indiana Democratic Editorial Association (IDEA) in French Lick. Of the hundreds of Democratic events Larry and Mary Lou Conrad had attended in their lives, French Lick was their favorite. The staff members arrived early at the hotel, and "Conrad for Governor" posters were placed everywhere—in the lobby, the corridors, and even the swimming pool area. The Saturday night banquet was to be keynoted by Governor Jerry Brown of California. In the late afternoon, while Conrad, Teague, and Hartke drove to Indianapolis to meet Governor Brown's plane, Wagner and I remained at the French Lick Hotel to meet with Brown's advance man. When he arrived, I met him in the lobby. I showed him through the banquet hall and informed him of how the head table would be arranged. He said: "That's not how the governor does things. Everybody will be introduced and seated on the dais when Governor Brown is introduced. The lights will be cut. He will enter from the rear of the hall and walk down the main aisle, with a spotlight on him. He will then move onto the dais and take a seat next to the podium. The lights will come up and all the members of the head table will rise and applaud." I looked at him incredulously. I walked away, into the lobby, where I picked up the house phone and called Wagner.

"Wagner, we've got a problem here," I said.

"What's that?" he asked.

"This Jerry Brown staffer thinks this party is for Jerry. You'd better talk to him."

"Bring him up," Wagner said.

We walked up two flights to Wagner's room. When we entered, the advance man started reiterating his demands regarding the banquet.

"Just wait one goddamn minute," Wagner said, his voice rising and his finger pointing. "Your boss is a guest here. He's a guest of Larry Conrad and the Democratic Party of Indiana. And he's going to act like a guest. He's going to do what he's told. And if he doesn't want to do it, he can take his goddamn suitcase and get back on the next plane back to L.A."

While Wagner was lecturing, the man's eyes grew larger and larger. He finally looked down. Then he replied: "Well, I'm sure everything will be fine. We'll do it your way."

Wagner opened the door and motioned for him to leave. When the door closed behind him, Wagner was still hot: "They think they're the only goddamn state in this country. Well, they've just been welcomed to Indiana." That evening Governor Brown was introduced along with the other members of the head table. He politely took his seat, as instructed.[102]

After the meal and the speeches, it was time for the "Conrad Sing-along." Since the summer of 1970, Larry and Mary Lou had hosted a sing-along on Saturday nights, following the IDEA banquet. In a room on the mezzanine, with Mary Lou at the keys, Larry would lead with "When Irish Eyes Are Smiling," and the entire crowd would raise their beer cups and join in. It was the same party Larry and Mary Lou used to host in their younger days in Maryland when Larry would "tub-thump" in accompaniment to Mary Lou. Now the "sing-along" was an IDEA tradition. The Conrad staff provided mimeographed sheets of lyrics to dozens of songs and the partying and the singing continued until the wee hours.

The tired staff members dragged themselves back to Indianapolis the next afternoon and prepared for the staff organizational meeting. In a large meeting room at a downtown hotel, nearly sixty people attended. Conrad spoke first, making it clear that Wagner was in charge of the campaign. He stressed how vital it was for each person to be fully informed about what everybody else was doing. Then Bochnowski took over. He presented an "official" organizational chart and asked each of the division directors for a synopsis of how their division operated. Wagner said nothing. The grand organizational meeting adjourned and everybody went back to doing what they did before, but now, at least, everybody knew their co-workers.

Wagner was convinced that his approach was the right one. "Do you win with organization or television?" he still asks. "We got through the primary with organization, and I took a calculated risk in investing in more organization for the fall. A lot of people were mad at me. Was I wrong? Well, would we have lost by more votes if we did not go the way we did? The complainers always have an easier time when the last gun is fired."[103]

But there was some order in all the chaos of the campaign. Throughout the summer the field representatives and the researchers had been preparing for the sixty-day "sprint to the finish." On September 7, Conrad held a major news conference in which he set forth a plan to lower residential electricity rates in Indiana. Calling Indiana utility companies "among the most profitable in the country," he called for adopting a "fair share" rate for all residences, where the median amount of electrical usage would be billed at a flat, fixed rate. He proposed eliminating the "fuel adjustment charge," claiming that citizens should "know what [electricity] costs before using it."[104]

While returning to the "number one issue" of the campaign, there were other programs working, as well. On September 11, Conrad issued a news release claiming that "over 100,000" new voters were now registered through the registration drive and the goal in the last week of field registration was to add at least another 50,000.[105]

While Bowen's television ads were running statewide, Conrad continued to try to draw attention to himself by meeting people and holding news conferences. On September 15, he was down on the Ohio River, in Clark County, blasting Bowen's taxing plan. By late afternoon he was back in Indianapolis and issued a release asking Bowen "why he allowed income tax deductions for Indiana renters to expire." The next evening five USAC drivers, led by Johnny Rutherford, the 1974 and 1976 Indianapolis 500 winner, hosted a fund-raiser for Conrad at the Indiana State Fairgrounds. On Friday, September 17, Conrad was in Lake County, riding the South Shore Line commuter train and calling for state involvement in Lake County's transportation problem. Later that day, he issued a statement calling the Indiana state tax system one of "the most inequitable in the nation." That evening, he spoke to a group of state employees and claimed that there "is a sense of a 'stockade' in the Statehouse—where employees cannot meet with their governor." He accused Bowen of breaking his 1972 campaign slogan: "He hears you."[106]

On the previous day a bridge over the White River on Indiana State Road 358, between Daviess and Knox counties, had collapsed under the weight of a truck, throwing the vehicle and the driver into the river. Conrad immediately reacted: "While Governor Bowen is out cutting ribbons opening the new interstates, we have bridges on our state highways collapsing." Pointing out that 6,500 rural bridges in Indiana were unsafe for conventional use, Conrad pledged that his administration would give the highest priority to maintaining bridges and state highways.[107] The next day Conrad drove to the site of the collapsed bridge outside of Washington, Indiana, and "tied a ribbon" to close off access to it.[108]

To further refine his message, a new standard speech was drafted. It was designed to help correct a major problem: in spite of Conrad's campaign schedule, Democratic voters were not committed to him. Polling data showed that Bowen was cutting heavily into the base Democratic vote. The speech was directed at Democrats. The intention was to remind these voters why they were Democrats. The speech was a frontal attack on the record of the Republican administration, and Conrad memorized it. Over the remaining weeks of the campaign, he was going to deliver it time and time again.

Previous attempts to get Conrad to attack Bowen's record directly were only semi-successful. He wanted to draw the "big picture" for audiences. He wanted to uplift, to inspire. Data and statistics were not Conrad's way of inspiring. He would tick off a listing of where Indiana ranked, then move on to "this great spaceship called planet earth on which we all ride," and extend his arms as though all who heard would be lifted onto a higher plane.

Conrad was to deliver the new speech first in South Bend at the annual meeting of The Associated Press Managing Editors Association on Sunday, September 18. Wagner met Conrad in the lobby of the hotel and asked him if he had memorized the speech. "Yeah, I've got it," Conrad answered.

"You've got to stay with it," Wagner said. "This is the most important speech of the campaign. Don't leave the text."

"I understand," Conrad said.

Conrad walked across the lobby and into the room. After his introduction, he said:

> There are serious problems in Indiana today. These problems are caused by the way our government is being run. Our state is adrift. Our government is growing in all directions and is directed nowhere. Indiana needs a governor for a change.
>
> Today, Otis Bowen is asking to be returned for four more years as governor. But I ask: At what price?
>
> What is the cost in human needs not met?
>
> What is the cost in services not provided?
>
> And what does government cost the people while promises are not kept?
>
> We should remember Governor Otis Bowen has had political control of the governor's office and the state legislature for over half his tenure as Governor. The Republicans have had the ultimate opportunity for action

and change. And Otis Bowen has promised many things in his political career.

He promised utility regulation reform. Did he deliver? No.

He promised a statewide energy plan. Did he deliver? No.

He promised an ethics code for the Public Service Commission. Did he deliver? No.

He promised to reform the rates we pay for gas and electricity. Did he deliver? No.

He promised to repeal the business inventory tax. Did he deliver? No.

He promised a reorganization of the government bureaucracy. Did he deliver? No.

Conrad then moved to the centerpiece of the Bowen reign, property tax relief:

The Bowen tax package is a package wrapped with Christmas ribbon. The ribbon makes the package pretty. When you cut the ribbon to get inside the package, the instructions say that what you see is easy to assemble. What is inside the package can't be put together. Even when you follow the instructions, it still doesn't work. You can try to return it, but you can't retie the ribbon.

What is inside this package is one of the most inequitable taxing structures in the country:

One large corporation gets more property tax relief than the people in 93 percent of Indiana's counties; more tax relief than all retirees combined. Non-farm business pays only 25 percent of the taxes going into the Property Tax Relief Fund—but gets 55 percent of the benefits.

Who makes up the difference? You and I. We are the ones paying the doubled sales tax. We are the ones paying the tax-on-the-tax every time we buy gasoline.

Conrad then proceeded to lambast the "taxing plan" for being based on politics instead of economics, and criticized Bowen for refusing to debate. He then listed where Indiana ranked in unemployment, business closings, and crime. He mentioned the numerous scandals that had erupted in state agencies in Bowen's first term, contending that "The Governor is not in control of our government."

The speech was finished. But Conrad was not:

Now the actuarial people tell us that somebody like me—a white Presbyterian male who likes to eat—is going to live 72 point 6 years, give or take a few.

You all remember that comet that came around last year. Kohoutek. The best guess of the astronomers is that the Comet Kohoutek was spun out by our Maker of the universe millions of years ago. Millions of years. And we're going to be here about 72 point 6 years.

That's not much time on this great spaceship called planet earth. We don't have time to sit and wait for others to solve problems and make changes. We don't have time because many of our fellow Americans are engaging in that great challenge that faces them every night: prime-time viewing.

Well I know when the Good Lord calls me home I'm not going to be watching the third episode of the fourth rerun of Bonanza. When I'm going to be called home I'm going to be in full stride with both guns blazing . . . now, I hope I get a chance to debate with Him at the time. And it won't be the same type of debate I keep asking for with Otis Bowen.[109]

Then Conrad quoted Oliver Wendell Holmes. He was finally finished. And he still managed to talk about the comet and the great spaceship called earth. The editors loved it. His ending—in his own words—was designed to uplift and to inspire; to reach out and connect people on a higher level.

This new speech, taking direct aim at Bowen's major accomplishment of property tax relief, finally got some attention from the newspaper editors. The speech received coverage in virtually every newspaper. But after two days the coverage stopped. As the newsroom editors frequently say when posting assignments, "If there is nothing new, don't cover it." The speech was a standard speech, and once delivered, it was old.

To Republican leaders, the new speech only added to their impression that Conrad was shrill, a visceral politician who lacked substance.[110] The Bowen polling numbers showed a substantial lead. The governor and his men continued to ignore Conrad.

Conrad's endless press conferences and speeches failed to resonate with the voters. Bowen's speaking style was no match for Conrad's, so the governor carefully avoided direct contact. For the many statewide groups that invited both candidates to speak, Bowen's schedulers always demanded that they not appear together on the dais. Bowen would usually speak first, then leave. One reporter captured the contrast in speaking styles: "Conrad, in fascinating contrast to the nearly laconic, down-home presentation of Gov. Bowen, came on with a swiftly paced, erudite and thoroughly partisan speech."[111] Bowen attempted to restrict himself to carefully structured events, such as ribbon-cutting ceremonies and Republican gatherings.[112]

But there was one blockbuster issue that was assured of receiving statewide coverage: gambling. After several weeks of debating both sides of the issue, Conrad gave the go-ahead to draft a statement pledging his support, as governor, for pari-mutuel racehorse betting in Indiana. He viewed pari-mutuel wagering as an economic measure which would create jobs and stimulate the horse breeding industry. Perhaps comforted by his memories of riding "Old Blacky" through the "hills and hollers" of southern Indiana, he was not morally repulsed by the issue. Governor Bowen's opposition was clear. He had vetoed two bills permitting pari-mutuel betting in Indiana.

Conrad knew the danger of the issue. The conservative side of Indiana was staunchly against any form of gambling. Protestant church groups, in particular, were vehemently opposed. But Conrad had risked the wrath of the opponents before. In his 1974 race he had broached the idea of a state lottery in Indiana—and it was the only stand he took in that race that attracted statewide attention.

On September 30, at a news conference in his headquarters, Conrad said he was "in favor of legalizing pari-mutuel racing in Indiana." He linked his support to the need for more state revenue without raising taxes. He indicated that thousands of jobs would be created and pointed out that Indiana was one of the leading states in breeding standardbred horses. He called for local voters to decide whether or not they wanted a race track built in their community.[113]

Pari-mutuel betting was a high-visibility issue that clearly separated the candidates. Mail poured in to the campaign headquarters, both in support and in opposition to Conrad's position. One typewritten postcard received in late October was from William Edwards in Frankfort. He wrote: "Because of your SUPPORT of pari-mutuel betting, I intend to do everything POSSIBLE to assure YOUR defeat on November 2nd."[114]

Conrad followed up his endorsement of pari-mutuel betting by calling for a total reorganization of state government, a move he predicted could save 10 percent of the costs of state administration.[115]

Conrad now had his answers for questions about state revenue. He could advocate better highways, better school funding, pension reform, a college student loan program, increased funding for mental health, and he could pay for them with revenue from pari-mutuel betting and savings by streamlining state government.

In a strategy meeting at Conrad's headquarters in late September— after it was decided to endorse pari-mutuel wagering—Wagner determined that Bowen's avoidance of the voters and his opposition to pari-mutuel betting and government reorganization should become the central theme in the last weeks of the campaign. Conrad had repeatedly criticized Bowen for being aloof, inaccessible, and hidebound on the issues. Now this theme would be woven into all of his statements and a paid media campaign would be designed to get the message to the voters.

A few days later, Wagner met with Conrad and the finance people of the campaign. Ed Lewis was there, along with Herb Simon, Bob Boxell, and Stu Grauel. Everyone agreed to the general principle that campaigns should not go into debt. But this campaign had absolutely no chance of winning without additional dollars for media. Jimmy Carter's presidential campaign was falling in the polls and this made fund-raising even more difficult for Conrad. The men in the room finally decided to borrow $120,000. The six of them agreed to personally guarantee the note, with each person responsible for $20,000. They agreed that if Conrad lost, they would do everything possible immediately after the election to erase the debt by hosting a fund-raiser. They borrowed the money from Merchants National Bank in Indianapolis.[116]

Wagner tried to squeeze additional money, as well. He instructed Bochnowski to talk with all the staff members and those who could afford it would forego their last two paychecks in order to supplement the media buy.

One county literally gushed money to the Conrad campaign. The local party in Delaware County, Conrad's "home" county, controlled most of the county and city offices and these were used by the county chairman, Jerry Thornburg, and his finance director, Ira (Rip) Nelson, to raise funds for their old high school friend. Wagner would call Thornburg, screaming for more money. Thornburg would then call Nelson. As Nelson described it: "He would just call me up and tell me that the governor's campaign needed another $20,000. I'd go out and get it. We'd drive it down the interstate and meet somebody halfway and give them the briefcase. There was so much money going through that receipts didn't always get written. That ain't no crime."[117]

But whatever was borrowed and raised was not enough. The Republicans were far outpacing the Democrats in dollars. By late September, Bowen had already purchased $228,000 worth of television time and had reserved another $200,000. He was supplementing his television ads with a $60,000 radio buy. Conrad himself said that Bowen's television ads were "more numerous than hair on a dog's back."[118] The minuscule amount of dollars available to Conrad would be swamped by the Republican budget.

Wagner gave up on television. "While we are going to do some TV, it will not be the amount we initially contemplated," he told a reporter. "We simply do not have that type of money."[119]

Wagner devised a strategy to run radio ads urging people to look for Conrad's message in newspaper ads. He brought John Anthony ("a media genius," according to Wagner) on board to produce the radio spots and distribute them statewide. Wagner then reserved space in all the major newspapers of the state for the last week of the campaign.[120]

As October opened, the pace of the campaign quickened even more. Larry and Mary Lou were on the road constantly, as were Tom Teague and Virginia McCarty. The newspaper and television reporters were now focusing on the race, assuring more coverage. There was a sense that Conrad was building momentum by solidifying the Democratic base vote. And his message was clear.

But the *Indianapolis News* was there to slow him down. On October 7, Conrad spoke in Vincennes before the Indiana Broadcasters Association. He renewed his attack on Bowen's record. He claimed that the administration had ignored "one state government scandal after another," citing turmoil in the Real Estate Commission, the Employment Security Division and the Medical Licensing Board; he called on the broadcasters to "crack the barrier protecting the Republican governor."[121]

The next day, the *News* carried a picture of Conrad addressing the Broadcaster's convention. In the upper right-hand corner of page-one, Conrad was in profile, with his tongue sticking out and his hand at his neck. The cropping of the photo suggested spittle flying from his mouth.[122] I brought the newspaper in that afternoon and laid it down in front of Claudia Prosser. Claudia cried. Conrad saw the photo the next day. Staring at it, he just shook his head. In that same newspaper, Ed Ziegner wrote a long article profiling Conrad's campaign. Based on a lengthy interview with Conrad, Ziegner again resuscitated the Master Plan, asking if the "well publicized" event is a "liability." Conrad replied: "I've been asked about it . . . twice in the campaign. It may be there, but if it is, I'm not aware of it."[123]

Indeed, the Master Plan was not an issue in the campaign. The outcome was to be determined by political trends and Republican dollars. The Conrad campaign had been well planned and fully recognized the constraints. Try as he would, Conrad simply could not shake hands with the millions of Hoosiers who would elect the next governor. His schedule was no match for the hundreds of thousands of dollars Bowen was able to spend on television, reaching all Hoosier households. But his personal style of campaigning represented what he was—a man taking politics back to the people, a man who did not believe that leaders should be separate from the people.

A final blow was delivered to the Democratic ticket in the last week of the campaign. Eugene Pulliam personally decided that his newspapers would not print the Conrad newspaper ad. Conrad and Wagner were incensed. The meager dollars they had borrowed and begged had been spent on a small television and radio campaign alerting viewers and listeners to watch for the newspaper ads. The ads were accepted and printed by all other newspapers in Indiana. But the ad would not appear in the state's largest newspaper.

On Friday, October 29, Conrad held a news conference in front of the Star-News Building on North Pennsylvania Street in downtown Indianapolis. Holding up a copy of the rejected ad, he said:

> In accepting the nomination of my party at the Democratic State Convention, I announced that the people of Indiana will know how I will govern by seeing how I run my campaign. I pledged that our message will be delivered to all Hoosiers.
>
> I have pointed to what is right in Indiana. And I have been pointing out what is wrong after eight years of Republican rule. I have raised questions about the unfair Republican taxing plan, the skyrocketing costs of gas and electricity, the property tax relief that was calculated to last barely through this election, the 4-percent sales tax, the sad condition of our highways, the unemployment in Indiana, and the lack of leadership over the past eight years.
>
> When you raise these kinds of questions, your campaign is not going to generate the big contributions from special interest groups. These questions have not been asked in the news stories or on the editorial pages of the Indianapolis papers. But these questions must be raised before the people can fulfill their duty to cast a responsible ballot.
>
> In order to raise these questions, I decided to use most of our advertising funds for newspaper ads. We purchased TV and radio advertisements to ask the people to watch for our newspaper ads. These ads raise the questions which are the real issues in this campaign.
>
> Yesterday, the *Indianapolis Star* refused to print this ad. The people in the largest city in Indiana, the 11th largest city in the nation, are prohibited from reading about these issues in their newspaper. The *Star* has a policy unto itself. It will not accept ads referring to the record of my opponent. This kind of policy is trying to draw a picture with a pen having no ink.
>
> If the newspaper does not raise the questions; if they refuse to allow me to purchase ads to ask these questions, then how are the people supposed to be informed?
>
> The newspaper owners have the prerogative of any businessman: to turn down a paying customer. The *Indianapolis Star* also has the right to endorse my opponent, as they did earlier this week.
>
> But the people also have a right—a right to know about the real issues affecting them and their government.

> It is the responsibility of the candidates to raise the issues in a campaign.
>
> It is the responsibility of a newspaper to inform the people of the issues.
>
> It is the responsibility of the people to cast their ballots based on their evaluation of the issues.
>
> I am fulfilling my responsibility. The people would like the opportunity to fulfill theirs.[124]

Conrad's courageous act—a frontal criticism of Indiana's largest newspaper company—invigorated the tried and true Democrats. For generations they had had to live with a brazenly partisan newspaper that enjoyed a virtual monopoly on news coverage in most of Indiana. Now they had a leader holding a mirror up the face of the Pulliam empire.

Four days later was election day, Tuesday, November 2, 1976. The Conrad family was up early. While Marshall and Ruby tended to the children, Larry and Mary Lou went to the polls to vote. Conrad and Mong then drove to the Indianapolis airport where a chartered flight was waiting. The weather was bright and clear. I met them at the aircraft and we flew over the harvested cornfields to Kokomo, South Bend, and Muncie, visiting precincts and shaking hands. When the aircraft landed in Muncie, we were met by Steve Caldemeyer, who drove us to a precinct headquarters where Conrad shook hands with the workers. While he was occupied, I dashed down the street to the county courthouse where I voted for Larry A. Conrad for governor.

We then drove to Daleville, where Larry stood outside the doors of the Daleville elementary school and shook hands with his old neighbors. The former Conrad residence in Daleville was directly across the street. The plane flew from Muncie to the Chesterfield airport, just outside Anderson, where we met it and flew back to Indianapolis. When we were airborne, Conrad leaned over to me and asked, "Have you got what I'm supposed to say tonight?" I replied, "I've got your victory speech here with me." I handed it to him. "I don't write concession speeches. If you lose, you're on your own."

He laughed and said, "It's moving. I can feel it. I just don't know if we had enough time or money."

Back in Indianapolis, Conrad went home to await the returns. The entire Conrad family was there, and so was Birch Bayh. By 7 P.M. it was clear. Conrad was losing, and losing big. He called his children together and told them he was beat. "You did what I wanted you to do for the last year, and you've been great about it. We did the best we could."[125]

The Democratic state ticket gathered at the Howard Johnson's on West Washington Street and by 8 P.M. Conrad and his family had arrived for the concession speech. "Some late figures are coming in," he told the noisy crowd, "but we're a little disappointed with what they show." He thanked his supporters for their tireless efforts. In a later interview he said he was "perfectly at ease and at rest" with his effort, and said he wanted to "thank our neighbors who tolerated our going in and out of our driveway at all hours of the day and night." He said he did not have any specific plans for the future, but indicated he hoped "to have some influence on the Indiana political scene."

The final results showed Conrad carrying only sixteen of the ninety-two counties. He lost by 309,312 votes out of 2,163,798 cast. Bowen received 57.14 percent of the vote to Conrad's 42.86 percent. He ran behind Jimmy Carter, who received 46.15 percent of the two-party vote in Indiana, but he was substantially ahead of Senator Hartke, who received only 40.77 percent of the two-party vote, carrying only 9 counties against Richard Lugar. The rest of the Democratic state ticket ran better, losing by approximately 40,000 votes.

Political scientists define a landslide as any election in which the victor receives more than 55 percent of the vote. In 1976, Larry Conrad was caught in such a landslide. But there was one great silver lining that day for the Democrats. Carter won the White House. And in Indiana, the Conrad campaign had set in motion a new formula that would forever change the state Democratic party.

Wagner views it as a watershed for Hoosier Democrats: "The 1976 campaign was unique. It contributed greatly to changing the Democrat party. It was the first time organized labor got involved at the gubernatorial level and was fully accepted. People were very accepting of everybody. Larry accommodated people who were historically the tried and true Democrats who were never really part of the old structure. He brought them out and he brought them together. Many of those that started with Larry are now in the positions of power in the party, and they retain their sense of openness and participation."[126]

Conrad frequently commented that a person is lucky to have three statewide campaigns in him. In six years he had campaigned statewide four times. He reached for the brass ring in 1976 and it was beyond his grasp. But he had known he was going to run for governor when he was a schoolboy, and the next gubernatorial election was only forty-eight months away.

Three guys were sitting in front of a brickmaking establishment, taking clay and straw and putting it in a mold. A man walked up and asked, "What are you doing?" The first guy said, "I'm filling this mold." He asked the second guy and he said, "I'm making a brick." He asked the third guy and he replied, "I'm building a cathedral."

—*Larry A. Conrad*

CONRAD HAD HOPED against hope to be governor. He had exhausted himself, his family, and his staff. But their efforts fell far short. Conrad himself recovered quickly. There was no personal devastation, as there had been when the Democratic establishment assaulted him with the Master Plan. In fact, there was a great deal of personal satisfaction and vindication. He was now the titular leader of the Indiana Democratic party, a sitting secretary of state, and a personal friend of Jimmy Carter and Walter Mondale.

After the election, Larry and Mary Lou took a short trip to Florida. Upon returning, Conrad settled into the calmest year of his turbulent career as secretary of state. Once again, his main job was to "make sure nobody steals the state seal."

For the first time in seven years, he turned his attention to the legislative process. The Democrats, in spite of Conrad's defeat, had gained control of the Indiana State Senate. Conrad, in looking out for some of his campaign staffers, prevailed upon his old primary election opponent and new Senate president pro-tem, Robert Fair, to hire Bill Gigerich, E. C. Walker, and Jim Coyle on the majority staff. Knowing that Democratic legislation would find a friendly reception in the Senate, Conrad asked John Livengood to update his research and findings for the reform of election laws and lobbying.

Conrad had supported such legislation in the past, attempting to strengthen reporting requirements for state lobbyists and to clarify certain provisions of the election laws, but these bills had been easily defeated by the Republican legislature. Now he had a chance at least to get some bills through one house.

Edwin J. Simcox, who was then serving as the secretary to the Republican State Committee and would, in 1978, be elected secretary of state, remembers Conrad's legislative proposals. "On election law reform, he was ahead of his time. Of course some of his proposals were from the Democrat agenda and from organized labor, particularly liberalizing voter registration. But he also proposed limiting campaign finances—and now I agree with this—limiting campaign finances—because they are poisoning the system."[1]

Conrad and Livengood worked the 1977 General Assembly for their proposals. They achieved only limited success, obtaining passage of laws concerning the political makeup of the state election board, changing procedures for declaring a candidacy for public office, and clarifying and extending the definition of a "security" in Indiana. Bills to reform campaign finance failed.

Conrad also now had time to return to one of his true loves: Indiana history. For years, going back to his days with Senator Bayh, he had been disturbed by an incident that occurred in Marion, Indiana, in August of 1930: the lynching of two young black men. The mayor of Marion in that month and year was Jack Edwards. Conrad knew Edwards well, and whenever he saw him, the conversation turned to that night of terror. Conrad transcribed many of his conversations with Edwards and began reading the newspapers of the period. He decided to write a book about the incident, and Claudia Prosser began typing his dictation.[2] Conrad found himself occupied with other tasks, however, and the book was never completed.

One task involved the City of Indianapolis. "We ran into trouble with the Department of Housing and Urban Development," Deputy Mayor David Frick recalls, "because we changed our boundaries under Unigov and we no longer automatically qualified for grants. With President Carter in the White House, Larry was a natural contact to try and help us with HUD." Conrad contacted Senator Bayh and the two of them arranged, through the White House, for a Washington meeting with the top officials in HUD. "The HUD officials certainly did not want to be there, talking about Indianapolis," Frick continues, "but we brought our maps and our charts, and we laid them out on the floor, and before long Larry and I and all the HUD officials were on our hands and knees, looking at the old and new city boundaries. We got our status as a qualified city."[3]

This was the first time David Frick had met Larry Conrad, and like most other people, Frick was immediately struck by his easy demeanor, his energy, and his insights. "I had viewed him as being politically motivated, not policy oriented. My perception was wrong, and I saw that after I became involved in government and started working with people, regardless of their politics, race, or religion. Larry was an incredible man. Very warm."[4]

As is usual in Indiana, the politicians were now turning their attention to the next campaign, the off-year 1978 election. There was no U.S. Senate seat up that year, so the "head of the ticket" would be the nominee for secretary of state. Conrad, of course, was prohibited by the Indiana Constitution from seeking a third term. But his commitment to public service and his exhausting schedule over the past fifteen years demanded that he continue to play a role in the Democratic party.

As the 1978 primary election approached, Conrad's former staff members were deeply involved in doing something many wished had been done in 1976. They were going to seize control of the Democratic party. They were going to remove Bill Trisler as chairman of the Democratic State Central Committee. The man who stepped forward to make the all-out effort was Don Michael, the Cass County Democratic chairman who had worked for Conrad in 1976 and had wanted to replace Trisler after Conrad's huge primary election victory. Richard (Dick) Malcolm, one of the statewide field coordinators from the 1976 campaign, and Stan Nice, who was the 2nd district coordinator for Congressman Floyd Fithian, became the unofficial campaign managers for Michael. They looked for support among all the Conrad people, and they didn't have to look far. Bob Wagner was with them. So was Chuck Deppert. Bun Gallahan was on board early. The leaders of the UAW joined them. But the remnants of the old establishment were still in place in many of the counties and districts. There had to be several new county chairmen if they were to win.

Michael, a bald, mustachioed man with a round face and flaccid cheeks, was taking the chance of his life. He had quit his job in Logansport to join Conrad's campaign staff in 1976. Now he was going to take on the leadership of the Democratic Party of Indiana. In terms of determination and drive, he was the equal of his mentor, Larry Conrad. He had no money, but he knew his mission. The UAW gave Michael $1,000. Michael had to borrow more, and he, Malcolm, and Nice signed notes. The three men never really stopped campaigning after November 1976. They merely changed their aim. They continued to drive from county to county, meeting with precinct committeemen, elected officials, and county chairman. They preached that Trisler had to go. And slowly but surely they were winning converts.[5]

Following the May 2, 1978, primary, the county political parties reorganized, followed by the election of the district officers. It was clear the Michael-Trisler race was going to be close. Michael had to make some deals to obtain the majority of the twenty-two members of the state committee. One of the offices they were going to have to deal was the secretary of the State Central Committee. Strangely enough, it was the only party office held by a former Conrad supporter, Bill Gigerich.

Gigerich remembers those days well. "I had suffered some because I took the secretary's job to begin with. Some of Larry's people, I think, never did trust me totally after that, because I was then part of the same State Committee that had always opposed Larry. But I was there because it was part of Wagner's strategy for us to get something out of 1976."[6]

Gigerich contends he volunteered to step aside if that was what was needed for Michael to win. But he never heard back from Michael, and as different party organization people contacted him, he told them he wanted to stay and was planning on running. A few days before the state reorganization, Stan Nice finally called him and said: "I thought you were getting out. You're screwing this up. We have to go up north for the secretary in order to get the votes we need."

Gigerich said he was staying in. "I told him 'No.' I had made commitments to people when they never got back to me."[7]

Conrad was under pressure from his ex-staffers and leaders of the UAW to get involved on Michael's behalf. They argued that now was the time to take over the party organization. Conrad's message throughout the 1970s was to open the party, and Trisler's removal would be a significant step in that direction. Moreover, organizational change in an off-year would mean minimum disruption for the statewide campaigns. Conrad agreed to help Michael.

The day after Gigerich had spoken with Nice, Gigerich reported to work in his Statehouse office. He received a call from Conrad: "Get out, and I don't want to hear any more about it."

"I felt like a kid who was caught by his father coming home late," Gigerich says. "I was stunned." For the next two days he vacillated. He thought he had the votes to stay, but he realized the only reason he was there was because of Conrad. Finally, on the morning of the reorganization meeting, he made up his mind. "I decided that if I stayed I would only get hurt more, so I stepped aside."[8]

Later that day Don Michael was elected chairman. Ed Ziegner was the first to pop a question to the new leader of the party: "The story is you owe all your support to Birch Bayh, Dallas Sells, and Larry Conrad. If they come to you, how could you turn them down?" Michael remembers saying, "If it's not in the best interest of the Democratic party, I wouldn't do it." Ziegner followed up: "Well, what makes you think you could turn them down?" Michael answered, "My soul is not for sale to anyone at any price." Ziegner looked down, and Michael walked away.[9]

The "Conrad Crazies" were now in charge of the Indiana Democratic party.

Following Michael's election, Conrad refocused on his own career. He had been on the public payroll almost continuously since 1963. Now he had to make plans for his livelihood after he left office in December of 1978. He would be forty-three years old and unemployed.

Many people are motivated primarily by money. They measure their career advancement in dollars. Not Conrad. He had always lived on his paycheck, supplemented by Mary Lou's part-time jobs. It wasn't much. As a lawyer he would have made much more, even if he had stayed in Muncie. But money was not his major motivation. He was activated by people.[10]

Of course, he had his law degree. But his appreciation of the law did not extend to the courtroom practice. His legal education had disciplined his mind, but such discipline never extinguished that mental flame that licked at the edges of grand thoughts and accomplishments. The pedantry of the law was not his love. He thought briefly about teaching. Perhaps he could obtain a position on the law school faculty at IUPUI. He was devoted to education. But after making a few discreet inquiries, it was clear there would be no permanent openings for him.

He also considered lobbying. Such a venture would utilize his experience in both the legislative and executive departments. His vast number of friends and supporters throughout the state provided a network of contacts that few others in Indianapolis could match. But these brief flirtations with other career choices foundered on the thought that he wanted to be his own boss. He wanted the mobility and the freedom to use his experience and rely upon his contacts to chart a new course. He decided to start his own law firm. He and the securities commissioner in his office, Raymond J. Hafsten, Jr., made plans to open a law firm in Indianapolis: Conrad and Hafsten. Claudia Prosser also would join the firm as the chief administrator and secretary.

But first he had to assist in the transition. The 1978 election results were a disaster for the Democrats. President Carter was at midterm, and the Republicans took advantage of the election cycle. Running on the slogan of "The Bowen Team," the Hoosier Republicans elected all their statewide candidates, retained control of the Indiana House of Representatives, and regained control of the Indiana State Senate.

A Biography

Republican Edwin J. Simcox was elected secretary of state. Only thirty-two years old, Simcox had worked his way up through the Republican organization, starting in LaPorte County. He found his way to Indianapolis when he was elected secretary of the Republican State Committee. From there he launched his race for secretary of state. In planning his own tenure in office, he was unprepared for what he was to experience when he came face to face with Larry Conrad. "I came up through the Republican Party organization and, like any organizational politician, it's ingrained in you that the enemy is any member of the other party. You think everything is black and white," Simcox says.

Immediately after Simcox's victory, Larry called him and scheduled a meeting. He thoroughly explained the operations of the office and how he had organized them. He was frank in telling about his successes and his failures as secretary of state.

"What first endeared me to Larry was how gracious he was to me when I won the office. I met with him frequently between my election and swearing-in. We had breakfast or lunch frequently, and we got to know one another. He would call me and say, 'Ed, I have a staff member leaving and the slot is open. Why don't I hire your person now and they will have a head start in the job by the time you're sworn in.' And he called me once and told me that the meeting of the National Association of Secretaries of State was scheduled and he had money in his office budget to attend. But he said he thought I should attend instead, even though I would not yet be in office. He said he had talked to the budget agency and they had approved spending the money for my travel. He was a class guy. I made up my mind that I wanted to emulate Larry by being a good loser, if I would ever lose, and by being right by the person coming next."[11]

Eight years later, Simcox passed the reins of office to Evan Bayh. When he did so, he emulated Larry Conrad.

Simcox found the office "in good shape." There were some processes and procedures that he wanted to change, "but my proclivity was administration, anyway, and Larry was an idea man. He was a 'rush of ideas.' As secretary of state I was naturally going to focus more on administration and procedures." When Simcox took his oath of office, he asked Larry to be on the podium. "We had became so close that I wanted him to be with me during my swearing-in. I was proud to have him with me."[12]

Conrad was now on his own. When he and Hafsten first opened the doors of the law office in December 1978 on the sixth floor of the old Merchants National Bank building on the corner of Washington and Meridian in downtown Indianapolis, many people thought it was an imperfect equation. The idea of Larry practicing law appeared to be a mismatch. His friends knew he was not suited to those churlish chores a practicing attorney must undertake. But Larry Conrad and Raymond Hafsten recognized this fact. "Conrad was not a legal advocate," Hafsten says, "and we talked a lot about that. He was to make rain, and with Carter in the White House, he had big contacts even in Washington. But he wasn't a lawyer. He didn't know how to be mean. He wasn't an advocate; he didn't have that toughness; he cared too deeply for all people."[13]

Initially, they were pinching pennies. Larry had the big office, decorated with dozens of pictures of himself with federal and state officeholders and friends. Hafsten's office was down the corridor. To save money on parking, Conrad and Claudia would often drive together to work. "We finally started making a little money," Hafsten recalls.[14]

During the summer of 1979, there was another gubernatorial election on the horizon. Governor Bowen was prohibited from seeking a third term, and Senator Bayh was preparing to run for his fourth term. Was Conrad going to run again?

When he left office, he left the door open for another run at governor. He had to consider it. There was no doubt he could win another primary. But he would still be plagued by his perennial problem: lack of money. The Republican party was still united, and Bowen's heir apparent was Lieutenant Governor Robert Orr. Reluctantly, but without remorse, Conrad put aside his childhood dream of being governor.

There were two Democrats wanting to succeed Conrad as the party's nominee. John A. Hillenbrand II, a long-time financial supporter of the party, started hitting the J-J circuit, telling the partisans that he intended to run in 1980. State Senator Wayne Townsend also viewed 1980 as his turn to reach for the brass ring.

One by one during the summer and fall of 1979, the Conrad Crazies trooped into Larry's law office to get their marching orders. If he ran again, they would be with him. But Conrad was edging out of the race and leaning toward Hillenbrand. He personally liked Hillenbrand's friendly and outgoing manner. Moreover, Hillenbrand had the personal wealth to substantially fund the campaign, something Larry never had. Hillenbrand had a sterling business background with his family-owned firm, Hillenbrand Industries, Inc., a company that manufactured caskets and hospital beds. Moreover, if the Democrats were ever to win the governorship again, they had not only to hold on to their base voters, such as members of organized labor and minorities, but also to broaden their appeal. That could be done only by a clear message, and a message without money is doomed to die.

Bill Gigerich had already signed on as Hillenbrand's campaign manager. He in turn approached other veterans of the Conrad campaign, offering them positions. It wasn't long before Larry was hinting to his political friends that Hillenbrand was his choice. Finally, in December of 1979, Conrad made it official. He endorsed John Hillenbrand for governor.[15]

A Biography

When Larry moved, most of the party organization moved with him. But there were problems with organized labor. Union leaders remembered a vicious strike at Hillenbrand Industries years before, and they feared that Hillenbrand's big business background would shut them out of the inner circles of the party. After Larry's public endorsement, labor leaders called him at the office and at home, berating him for going with Hillenbrand. Larry patiently explained to his old friends that their fears were unfounded; Hillenbrand was not anti-labor, and his background promised a wider appeal for the party. He provided his judgment that the best chance of winning was with Hillenbrand. But the labor leaders were not mollified. Larry's explanation was taken as a personal statement, which they respected from their old ally and friend. But they were going with Townsend.

While Robert Orr was uncontested for the Republican nomination, the Democratic party was engulfed in one of the most divisive primaries in modern history. It was the torso of the party organization fighting against its own strong right arm, organized labor. On Tuesday, May 6, 1980, the organization won, but just barely. Hillenbrand received a little more than 52 percent of the statewide vote, winning the nomination by 26,403 votes.[16]

Hillenbrand's narrow victory was not a good omen for November. The party was divided. The dollars that should have been available for the general election had been spent in May. Moreover, Senator Bayh's reelection campaign also was sputtering, owing to the late start necessitated by Marvella's death only a year before.[17]

Conrad fully expected his political time to be spent on President Carter's reelection campaign in Indiana. But by midsummer John Hillenbrand prevailed upon him for a further commitment. The divisive primary had paralyzed the gubernatorial campaign. Weeks went by with few statements from Hillenbrand or his running mate, State Senator Robert Peterson. The energies of the candidates and staff members were expended on trying to bring organized labor back into the fold.

Hillenbrand called, and Conrad answered. Along with Bob Boxell and David McFall, a former staffer for Congressman Lee Hamilton, Larry agreed to take over the management of the Hillenbrand campaign. They called a staff meeting at the campaign headquarters on 16th Street in Indianapolis.

"I don't have to tell you the position we're in," Larry said to the workers. "When we are involved in the political process, we have a duty to our party. And we want everyone in this room to do their duty. Of course, we expect to have a lot of fun doing it. Some of you will probably be eating and sleeping here in headquarters. Some of you may even sleep together. So we're going to have fun in this serious business, and if lightning strikes, John Hillenbrand will be our governor."

But lightning did not strike. On November 4, 1980, Hoosiers voted overwhelmingly Republican. Robert Orr received more votes than Otis Bowen had garnered in 1976. Senator Birch Bayh lost to Congressman J. Danforth Quayle. Ronald Reagan won Indiana and the nation.

Following the Democratic disaster, Conrad was finally freed from politics. In February 1981, at the age of forty-six, he could turn his time and attention to his family, his business, and his city.

The Conrads' oldest son, Jeb, was now a student at Indiana University–Bloomington. Amy, their daughter, was soon to graduate from high school and enroll at Indiana University, as was Andrew. Jody, the youngest, was just entering high school. Conrad at last was able to spend time with the children, attending soccer games and school events. He also took to bread-making. On Saturday mornings he would be the first one in the kitchen, kneading dough, setting it to rise, and eventually removing the fragrant loaves from the oven. Mary Lou and a friend, Judy Laikin, meanwhile, were spending more and more time with their small business, Personal Shoppers, which sold advertising specialties and corporate gifts. In 1976 the women had ordered some gifts for Larry to give his staff members in the secretary of state's office. From that first order came the idea of marketing such specialty items to other companies and organizations.[18]

And Conrad decided to start a newspaper. Throughout his political years he had grown to love the dozens of weekly newspapers in Indiana's small towns. As he traveled Indiana he would always stop at the offices of these weeklies, and came to know the publishers and the reporters by their first names. During his 1976 campaign he had a special column, "My Indiana," that was mailed to all the weeklies. It was not a political column; it was a column on Indiana history. Many of the weeklies— especially those affiliated with IDEA—published the pieces verbatim.

Conrad's new paper was a genuine "family newspaper" called the *Rooksby Reunion.* He got the entire extended family of Conrads and Rooksbys involved. His cousins in California wrote articles about their activities and experiences. His mother Ruby, wrote several columns about her father, the huckster, and the old homesteads in Harrison County.

The newspaper appeared only periodically, usually just before and just after the July Fourth holiday. It was over Independence Day that the extended family would convene in Harrison County for a reunion. The aunts, uncles, cousins, nieces, and nephews would come to the "red clay country" to eat, drink, and tell stories. Pictures were taken, which would appear in the next issue of the *Rooksby Reunion.*

The men of the family started another tradition: the Conrad Family Open. Larry, his three sons, Bob Rooksby, and other males of the family would gather at one of Larry's favorite places, French Lick, where they would spend an August weekend playing golf.

Larry's immediate family always had room for others, and his involvement with the Simons deepened. Following Herb and Diane's marriage in 1981, Larry and Mary Lou and Herb and Diane frequently vacationed together in Florida and Mexico. Indeed, the big client Conrad had for his law practice was Melvin Simon and Associates.

By the mid-1970s the Simon interests had already reached that "take-off" plateau in business where work and shrewd investments start paying compound dividends. Melvin Simon was mustered out of the service at Fort Benjamin Harrison in the late 1950s. Born and raised in the boroughs of New York, he decided to make Indianapolis his home. He leased space at a local shopping center and began laying the foundation for his business. In 1960, his younger brother, Herbert, joined him, and Melvin Simon and Associates was formed. Within five years they had developed enclosed shopping malls throughout central Indiana and had undertaken similar projects in other states. Melvin Simon's keen business sense had catapulted the company onto a new plane. He knew merchants had to have people—and the people were at those thousands of intersections in America where interstate highways and bypasses force them to be. By the late 1970s, this company, started only some twenty years before, was enjoying breathtaking profits, and there was more to come.

The Simon headquarters were located at 1800 North Meridian Street. Herb Simon was functioning as the chief operations officer as Melvin increasingly split his time between southern California and Indianapolis. But the firm had started in Indianapolis, and the Simons had planted roots in central Indiana. They had profitable malls in Anderson, Bloomington, and Muncie, and were developing a "consumer mall" on the east side of Indianapolis—their first major incursion into their own city. They were taking on the behemoth of shopping center developers, Edward J. DeBartolo, headquartered in Ohio.[19]

The friendship between Herb Simon and Larry Conrad was solidified even more by Diane Meyer. In a sense, Diane was devoted to two men, Herb and Larry. Her affection for Larry was a sibling love, an attachment that a man and woman can have that melds commitments, experiences, and minds. "He was the brother I never had," she says.[20] His spontaneity and grandeur of dreams and thoughts had captivated her early, in 1968. And when someone was hooked on Larry, they became a Conrad Crazy.

After Diane's devastation over Robert Kennedy's death, she became politically devoted to Birch Bayh. But Larry Conrad won her ultimate political—and sibling—heart.

And Larry delighted in her dedication, spontaneity, and tenacity. She made things happen. She called him constantly about her immediate notions and thoughts. By now he knew her so well he could disarm her or inflame her. It was a special relationship: Larry and Mary Lou, Herb and Diane. And their ambitions and desires merged in those high-flying years of dollars and dreams in the late '70s and early '80s.

The Simon money was becoming a major force in Indiana, and the banks recognized it. Here was a native-born empire that was adroitly expanding everywhere. A loan to the Simons—a few million dollars here or there—was backed by the land and the malls and the cash flow of this privately held company. The Simons could not buy or build fast enough.

"Larry was spending about 90 percent of his time with the Simons," Hafsten says.[21] Others in Indianapolis began viewing him as the avenue to the seemingly bottomless Simon pockets. John Krauss, who served as director of metropolitan development under Mayor Hudnut and later was to become deputy mayor, remembers those days well. "It became known that if you wanted to get the Simons involved you had to talk to Larry."[22]

And there were some people who wanted to get the Simons involved. They were people deeply concerned about Indianapolis and its future. And they had reasons for their concern.

For decades Americans—including Hoosiers—had made fun of Indiana's capital city. It was "India-no-place" or "Naptown," where everything closed at dark and you couldn't get anything to eat until dawn. Some people described Indianapolis as a "cornfield with lights." In fact, its location is reputed to have been a mistake. When the Indiana General Assembly sent the surveyors north from Corydon in 1820 to find a site for a new state capitol, they came upon the confluence of Fall Creek and the White River. It was spring and the rivers were roaring, fed by the melting snow and the spring rains. Clearly, they thought, these waterways are navigable, and this site, virtually in the middle of the state, should be the capital. Navigation on the White River would assure commerce. But they were wrong. Today, Indianapolis is one of the largest cities in the world not on a navigable waterway.[23]

The city is largely white and overwhelmingly Protestant. It is jokingly referred to as the largest city in the world where everybody went to the same high school.[24] In the middle of the twentieth century, the city was going the way of other midwestern and eastern cities; the downtown area deteriorated and the people continued to move out in droves. Between 1950 and 1970, over forty thousand people left Indianapolis.[25] The investment in the new interstate highway system promised only further flight. The outer loop, I–465, allows a driver to drive around Indianapolis, never seeing the state capitol building. But there wasn't much to see in the way of government buildings, anyway. Although the historical plaque in front of the Statehouse brags about the building costing only $1 million in 1889, not much was spent on the "copper dome" for the next hundred years. In 1959 a "high-rise" state office building was constructed across the street to the west for the various state offices, but this building was criticized so much for the cost that nobody has even named it after a public official, living or dead. It's simply the State Office Building, or SOB.[26]

In the post–World War II years there was little to attract business and people to Indianapolis. Of course, it was the state capital and the geographical center of the state. But other midwestern cities, such as Columbus, Ohio, and Springfield, Illinois, had these same advantages and they were anchored in adjacent states, each of which had twice the population of Indiana. Former mayor William H. Hudnut III provided a description of Indianapolis in those years:

> Growing suburbanization began to tighten a noose around the midwestern industrial city by limiting its spatial growth and bleeding off a disproportionate share of the affluent population. The population inside the noose was becoming increasingly composed of minorities and poor people. This process set up the dichotomy that most older cities faced . . . : between suburbs and inner city, which is to say, between white and black, rich and poor.[27]

The "noose" that was strangling Indianapolis was clearly seen by city leaders. As early as the fall of 1964, Democratic mayor John J. Barton appointed an advisory committee to draft a "program of progress" for the city. Within a year this committee became the Greater Indianapolis Progress Committee (GIPC), a not-for-profit organization funded by foundation grants and private dollars. One of the first tasks undertaken by GIPC was to propose organizational changes in the structure of both city and county government.[28]

Mayor Richard Lugar not only continued the commitment to the progress of Greater Indianapolis, but personally extended it. The consolidated city-county government (Unigov) was a singular achievement, but Lugar also personally sought out people who had left Indiana to pursue careers in other states, and encouraged them to return to Indianapolis. One such person was David Frick. Frick had attended high school in Indianapolis and had gone on to Indiana University and Harvard Law. He was working in Washington, D.C., for a Chicago-based law firm when he was introduced to Mayor Lugar by an old college friend, Jim Morris. "I was scheduled to be rotated back to the Chicago office, and I wasn't keen on going," he recalls. Lugar asked Frick to "look at Indianapolis, because things are changing in our town." Frick viewed Indianapolis "as a pretty sleepy town," but he heeded the mayor's advice and flew to Indianapolis. He liked what he heard and saw. He quit his law firm and joined the law offices of Baker and Daniels in downtown Indianapolis.[29]

Following the 1975 election, William H. Hudnut III took over City Hall from Lugar. He clearly saw the problems confronting the city, and he attempted to move quickly. "I had a proactive philosophy of government, not a caretaker one. I believed that it was not always true that government is best which governs least," he wrote, stressing that his sense of leadership was to "make good things happen for the community."[30]

Very early in his administration, Hudnut called together prominent business and civic leaders for a "visioning" meeting, where "new visions, new themes, and new projects" were discussed, focusing on how to "overcome people's commitments to private gain with a commitment to the public good."[31]

While the inchoate "visioning" was taking place elsewhere in Indianapolis, the man who always saw the big picture in human events was sitting in his Statehouse office working on minor legislation and outlines of his book.

The Indianapolis City Fathers finally got a wake-up call. In 1977, officials of the U.S. Clay Court Tournament—in search of better facilities—threatened to abandon Indianapolis and move the annual tennis tournament to Chicago. Michael G. Browning, a real-estate developer, was shocked. "How can we expect to have this community grow and attract people from outside when we can't keep the things that we already have?"[32]

A "private-public partnership" was forged under the pressure of losing the week-long tennis tournament. The cost to build a new state-of-the-art facility was $7 million. The Hudnut administration floated a $4 million bond, the Lilly Endowment kicked in $1.5 million, and the private sector matched Lilly with another $1.5 million. The twenty-four-court tennis complex was built on the eastern edge of the IUPUI campus, within walking distance of downtown.[33]

The coming together of private and public sector leaders to save the tennis tournament was a defining moment in the history of Indianapolis. The self-confidence of those involved soared. They now knew that a major project could be undertaken for the city, with cooperation from all sectors.

By the end of Conrad's first year in private law practice, the tennis courts were open and a direction had been determined for the renaissance of Indianapolis. The city leaders had agreed on a theme that would weave together the various strengths of Indianapolis: sports.

> Sports! What a way to build on the inherent advantages our city possessed and the base laid for us by the 500-mile race. With their galvanizing effect on the human spirit, sports offered an attractive way to draw people's attention and enlist their cooperation in a partnership across the lines that so easily and often divide them. We would use sports to promote job growth, attract new business, enhance our image, transform us from a branch town to a destination city, and propel us toward major league status. Sports could motivate people to rally round. They have an energizing effect that other causes—such as building a steel mill or making us the insurance capital of the country or improving city housing—just do not possess. How about becoming the "amateur sports capital of the country"?[34]

The vision of making amateur sports the centerpiece of the renaissance was refined by a number of younger civic leaders who, somewhat remarkably, agreed that private gain had to be set aside for the public good. This small group of men had no official status. They casually referred to themselves as the "City Committee," and they met regularly for lunch or in the evening at one of their homes to discuss and dream about the future of Indianapolis. Whatever expenses they incurred were paid for from their own pockets. "The city administration, Lilly Endowment, and several members of the business sector were groping for what would put Indianapolis in the forefront of public perception," Sidney Weedman, a member of the City Committee, recalls. "Jim Morris at the Endowment was the initiator, along with Tom King at the Chamber of Commerce. They pulled together men who were second or third in command of their companies, thinking that the presidents and CEOs were too busy. But the number twos and threes could influence the number ones. So the City Committee was carefully selected."[35]

Conrad's initial selection to the City Committee was because he represented the Simon interests. The Downtown Merchants Association, a for-profit organization, was developing a downtown building at 2 West Washington Street, and the Simons were chief investors in the rehabilitation. Jim Kittle and Al Fernandes were in charge of the Association and Sidney Weedman worked closely with them as Executive Director of the Commission for Downtown. Weedman remembers when he first met Conrad. "I was called to Kittle's office and Larry was there. Jim said, 'I want you to meet Larry Conrad, who represents the Simons. You must know him.'"

After one introduction to Larry Conrad, a connection was made. Conrad's innovative thinking and political skills were now turned to business. "A couple of days later, Conrad called me," Weedman remembers, "and that was followed by a flurry of notes and memos he would send saying, 'Weedman! We ought to look into this.'"[36]

Within months, Larry was in the center of this group, and his reputation as being a civic "mover and shaker" among the business and professional elite was growing.

What made it possible for this small group of people to coalesce so quickly and fuel the resurgence of this "rustbelt city"? There were several factors, the first being the absolute unselfishness of the men involved. Indeed, their "private gain" was independent of their notion of civic progress. Each had an innate understanding that the Indianapolis "boat" they were all in was sinking, and the mentality of "every man for himself" would result in the death of all. Bankers, developers, lawyers, and political leaders came to understand that revitalizing downtown Indianapolis would open a plethora of financial opportunities for themselves and others, but without a clear and sustained focus, there would be continual decay.[37]

A second factor was having money available for civic projects—lots of money. The Lilly Endowment had decided to fuel the rebuilding of Indianapolis by digging into its own deep pockets to fully or partially fund new facilities. The key player in Lilly's commitment was James T. Morris, who had worked his way up to the presidency of the Endowment.

A friendly, round-faced, self-effacing man, Morris was eight years younger than Conrad. After college, Morris took a position with an Indianapolis bank, and in 1967 he volunteered for the Lugar for Mayor Campaign. He ended up driving Lugar and acting as his press spokesman. After Lugar's victory, he joined his administration as chief of staff. Six years later, he moved to Lilly Endowment as the director of metropolitan area programs.[38] As he was promoted to vice-president and then president, the uniting theme of "sports" for Indianapolis was at the forefront of his thinking.

In 1979, Morris granted $200,000 to fund the Indiana Sports Corporation, an entity devoted to identifying and bringing sporting events to the city. Sandy Knapp, an employee of the Indiana Pacers, was hired as the first executive director, and set about detailing the dreams and ideas of the City Committee. That same year, the Lilly Endowment provided $5 million—and the state government threw in another $10 million—to launch the White River Park Development Commission which was to create a 250-acre urban park adjacent to the river.[39] Immediately, plans were made to use the park and adjacent facilities (such as the planned renovation of the field track and the new natatorium on the IUPUI campus—which the endowment helped fund with a $14.7 million grant) for statewide amateur athletic events, to be called "The White River Park State Games."[40]

Everywhere in the downtown there was private money being leveraged with government dollars and Lilly Endowment grants. The burden on the taxpayers of the $95 million Hoosier Dome was eased when the Endowment kicked in $25 million, and a second Indianapolis foundation provided another $5 million. And this financing of the new stadium was committed and spent without a professional football team as a tenant.[41]

Conrad became the major "idea man" for the City Committee, the vast majority of whom were solid, white-collar, Hoosier Republicans. Each of them began seeing the dimensions of Larry Conrad. He was not the shrill liberal Democrat they had stereotyped in their minds. One of the many Republicans who saw the other sides of Conrad was Mayor Hudnut. "He had an ability to transcend partisanship. He was a convener, a facilitator. He was protagonistic, not antagonistic."[42]

For his part, Conrad could disarm these blueblooded Republicans and gently chide their partisanship with his self-deprecating remarks. He would regale them with his stories. He told them of how he once drove to southern Indiana in his state car, with the "Star–3" license plate. "The third best car in the state, after the governor's 'Star-1' and the lieutenant governor's 'Star–2.' Well, we stopped to get gas and the service station guy looked at the license plate and said, 'Boy, you must be somebody important. Are you a deputy sheriff?'"

And he would often remind them that he had once run for governor, "but I kept it pretty much of a secret at the time." Sid Weedman remembers another City Committee member responding, "Well, if we had known you back then, you just might have been governor."[43]

By the fall of 1981, the leadership of Indianapolis had coalesced around sports. And the sporting event they had their eyes on was the National Sports Festival. The United States Olympic Committee had launched the festival to preview Olympic athletes two years before the big games. The significance of hosting the 1982 event went beyond merely showcasing Indianapolis. It was part of a larger strategy which was clearly grasped by members of the City Committee. In 1978, Congress had passed the Amateur Sports Act of 1978, which required that each Olympic sport had to have its own national governing board. One of the City Committee members, Theodore (Ted) Boehm, described the law as one requiring "an instant creation of a whole new national industry."[44]

It was up to the Indiana Sports Corporation to spearhead efforts to land this new "national industry" in Indianapolis. Sandy Knapp's focus was on winning the first big prize, the National Sports Festival.

When the U.S. Olympic Committee announced in February 1981 that the 1982 festival would be held in Indianapolis, Conrad and the other City Committee members were ecstatic. Their vision was now coming true. A successful festival in Indianapolis would only promise more successes. A few months later, Conrad sent a "news release" to other members of the City Committee:

FOR IMMEDIATE RELEASE
OCTOBER 9, 1981

Brussels (Reuters)—Indianapolis, capital city of one of the United States of America, will be the host city for the 1985 NATO War Games, a spokesman for the international treaty group announced today.

The games will bring well-armed military contingents from 14 North American and West European nations to Indianapolis in August, 1985, for eight days of competitions and conflicts.

The armed forces will compete for gold medals in a full range of modern warfare events, including close order drill, pillage, motor pool, marksmanship, holocaust, and military courtesy.

A highlight of the annual games is the modern military pentagon, a grueling test of competitors' career stamina in coat-tailing, perquisites, budgeting, memos and memoires, and doom-saying.

West German Brigadier General Horst Wesel, chairman of the NATO committee responsible for the selection of sites and targets, said that Indianapolis was chosen on the basis of superior transportation facilities, local support for parades, terrain suitable for armored and airborne operations, and available hotel and motel facilities.

General Wesel said that members of his committee were especially impressed by the field fortifications already built by the city government and the University of Indiana along several of the city's principal thoroughfares. He said this civilian support was consistent with the trend toward urban devastation now popular in international conflict.

Other cities to reach the final selection state were Amsterdam, Coventry, and Dresden. This year's NATO War Games were held in Paris, the former City of Light.[45]

Under the aegis of the Indiana Sports Corporation, every detail of the festival was organized and planned. One or more persons were assigned to specific events. Larry Conrad and Herb Simon were in charge of the opening ceremonies.

From his sixth-floor law office, Conrad started making contacts with hundreds of people, soliciting ideas and identifying people who had expertise in all the areas required for an extravaganza. He needed music. He needed balloons. He needed refreshments. He needed the perfect location. He needed crowd control experts. He needed national media coverage. Most of all, he needed to meld all these together into his picture of the perfect opening ceremony.

There was nobody more suited for the task. Larry Conrad could reach back through the decades and pull on all his experience and organizing abilities—and all the lessons he had learned from his high school and college days, and the state and national conventions he had attended, to guarantee a show that would be the envy of the Summer of '82.

Calls kept pouring in and going out of his office. Volunteers were located. Vendors were identified. And suggestions kept coming. One man called to tell Larry that he had a friend who could approach Frank Sinatra to sing at the opening ceremony. Conrad laughed. "Can't we find a Hoosier with a good voice?" he asked.

Obviously, the festival would attract national celebrities, but Conrad was intent on using Hoosiers. The exposure of Indianapolis to the nation provided an opportunity for Hoosiers to display their talents—to show the country that somebody other than rubes lived between the lake and the river. He insisted on Indiana residents being at the heart of the organizing.

Conrad decided the site for the opening ceremonies would be the state-owned American Legion Mall. Stretching five blocks north from New York

A Biography

Street, between Meridian and Pennsylvania streets, the grassy expanse was interrupted only by the World War Memorial, sited between Vermont and Michigan streets. The northern end of the mall was anchored by the state and national headquarters of the American Legion.

At 3:30 P.M. on Thursday, July 22, over 6,000 people crowded on the mall to see the opening ceremonies of the National Sports Festival. Television sportscaster—and Hoosier native—Chris Schenkel served as master of ceremonies. When he introduced the Ben Davis marching band, Conrad's sense of irony was satisfied. What he remembered most about the Ben Davis band was when they marched onto the floor of the 1972 Democratic state convention playing "Happy Days Are Here Again" in support of Matthew E. Welsh's gubernatorial nomination.

Conrad had promised that the opening ceremonies would "be something this city had never seen before." They were. Along with the marching bands of Ben Davis and three other high schools, there were World War I biplanes twirling in the air while the young women champions of the United State Twirling Association performed on the ground. Hot-air balloons were launched as more than 2,600 athletes paraded from the War Memorial to the American Legion headquarters. White homing pigeons—350 of them—were released, along with thousands of small helium-filled balloons. Immediately following the ceremonies on the mall, seventy-nine-year-old comedian Bob Hope opened the celebration at Market Square Arena, where he sang a medley of tunes, including "Back Home Again in Indiana."[46]

Everyone was awed by the opening. The only minor complaint was that the helicopters used by the television network flew so low and were so loud that people could not hear the invocation, prompting Chris Schenkel to say, "The ABC affiliate must get a longer lens and stop spoiling the beauty of this ceremony."[47]

The wonder that was the opening ceremony was not surprising to members of the organizing committee. Nor were the men and women who knew Larry and had worked previously for him stunned by the success. Terry Straub, who worked for Larry in the secretary of state's office and served as a campaign coordinator in 1972, expected the extravaganza to be first-rate. After working in the White House for President Carter, Straub joined the public affairs staff of U.S. Steel in Washington. "I managed many campaigns after 1972. We had some spectacular lessons from that state convention. We all learned how to blow the roof off a place. We saw with our own eyes the amount of energy that music can add to an event. And visual movement is key. Larry had all of this experience from his political days. He knew how to organize an event on a grand scale."[48]

Larry himself acknowledged the connection between his political campaigns and his civic duties. Four years after the National Sports Festival, he spoke to a group of employees of Melvin Simon and Associates on the importance of volunteering:

> You cannot run the entire show the first time you start out. In every campaign I was ever in, at the volunteer level, there were usually three or four people who were heavily credentialed, strongly recommended, who failed miserably. They weren't worth their salt or their reputation. On the other hand, in every campaign I was ever in, there were one or two people who walked in off the street, who nobody knew—and Mayor Daley of Chicago used to have a statement that you "don't talk to nobody that nobody sent." Well, that's not necessarily a good axiom, because in every campaign there are a couple of people who just walk in and say, "I've never been involved and I want something to do." And I always had two people who ended up being probably the most influential people in the campaign because they had the raw ability—the organizational ability—they had the dependability—they had the integrity. So other volunteers are the same kind of way. People assess you, and you can move right up in the same kind of way.[49]

These days were proving to be some of the most productive of Larry's life. His extensive political contacts throughout the state and the nation, coupled with his new acquaintances among the business elite of Indianapolis, provided a critical mass of talent that could be called upon to realize his ideas. As the Simons began preliminary plans for a Mall of America in Minnesota, Larry could pick up the phone and call Walter Mondale to obtain information on local officials. When the Indiana state legislature was considering appropriations for the White River State Park Commission, or cross-county banking, Larry knew who and when to call. B. Patrick Bauer, a veteran Democratic state legislator from South Bend who served on the House Ways and Means Committee, remembered his technique. "He never stood around the legislative halls trying to button-hole legislators. He would call instead. He called me at a crucial time when we were considering cross-county banking. He explained the problems the Simons were having with financing in Indiana because of the inability of our banks to provide complete financial services of such magnitude. It was the first time anybody could actually explain to me what was at stake."[50]

Former state representative Hurley Goodall, who served fourteen years, retiring in 1992, ranked 173 lobbyists he had come to know. On a scale of one to ten, with ten being the best, only two lobbyists were judged as tens. One was Larry Conrad.[51]

Conrad's relentless political pace in the 1960s and 1970s did not allow much time for charitable work. He became a life member of the NAACP in the 1960s, and was particularly interested in the fight against sickle cell anemia. In 1974 he served as the honorary chairman of the Indiana March of Dimes. Now that he was out of office and recognized as a organizer and idea man, the requests continually came for him to spend time on various boards and special projects. In 1979 he became president of Hemophilia of Indiana and established a fund-raising program to fight the disease. For some causes he could only lend his name, but some held special interest for him. His interest in history prompted him to join the Historic Landmarks Foundation and to serve as chairman of the board of directors of the Museum of Indian Heritage. His fondness for his old high school team, the Muncie Central Bearcats, led him to be an associate director of the Indiana Basketball Hall of Fame. But most of his "special interests" involved his adopted city of Indianapolis. He served on the board of directors of the Indianapolis Convention and Visitors Bureau and became a leader in raising funds for the Indianapolis Zoo's move to White River State Park.

"We can do something with this downtown," he constantly stressed in his remarks to downtown groups. "We can do something that will make the people of other cities, like those in Muncie, actually want to come to downtown Indianapolis. But they need to be attracted. They aren't going to naturally come to a place they call Naptown."

Aside from his work with the unofficial City Committee, he became active in the Indianapolis Urban League. He was appointed to the advisory board of Winona Memorial Hospital Foundation. He agreed to serve on the board of directors of the Downtown Promotion Council and joined the Greater Indianapolis Progress Committee. Mayor Hudnut appointed him to the Mayor's Community Council, and he joined the board of directors of the U.S. Clay Court Championships.

He recognized that the cultural life of the city required constant encouragement and nourishment. He joined the board of directors of Dance Kaleidoscope, a local dance repertory company, and helped raise money for the Indianapolis Symphony Orchestra. He loved telling this story:

> You can't have a great city without having a great orchestra. When we decided we had to rehabilitate the old Circle Theatre and make it an orchestra hall, we planned special concerts to help raise money. One evening I talked to one of the young oboe players. He said he didn't like playing all the modern music that we thought was good for fundraisers. He wanted to play Liszt. I told him he had to play some rockabilly if we were going get everybody involved in this project. I told him that once it opened he'd be able to play Liszt in one of the finest halls in the land. He didn't seem convinced. So I told him that a lot of people were like me; they would say, "Yeah, I support the orchestra, but by God, just don't make me go." That seemed to do it. He laughed. He said he'd play some rockabilly.

One day he was asked, "How do you decide which group you are going to help?" He replied, "I ask one question: Is Gordon St. Angelo on this committee? If the answer is 'Yes,' I decline." Then he laughed. That was the most disparaging remark one ever heard from Larry Conrad.

In fact, he even took the initiative in getting together with his old nemesis, Ed Ziegner. One spring day Larry was strolling through the downtown when he encountered Ziegner. He told Ziegner they had to get together. Ziegner was amenable. A few days later Larry called and scheduled lunch. "I did have lunch with him," Ziegner later recalled. "We didn't do it frequently, but we did talk. He was a skillful public servant. It took a while for Larry to cool down from all that about the Master Plan. But some of it may have been my fault, too. Indiana politics can get vicious, but I made up my mind a long time ago that there's no permanent hostility or damage. I don't let disputes like this go on forever, but I'm better at that now than I used to be."[52]

Conrad's delight in bringing diverse people together found its fullest expression in these years when he hosted his annual "Holiday Party" in his law offices on the sixth floor of the Merchants Bank Building sometime about the second week of December. Claudia Prosser would spend weeks developing the statewide mailing list, ensuring that all of Larry's old political staff members and supporters received invitations, along with members of the chamber of commerce, the business elite of Indianapolis, and state officials. Democrats, Republicans, and Independents were there. It was a "command performance" for everyone. A person had to attend, just to find out who else was there. From late afternoon into the evening hours, lines of men and women snaked their way into the front door of Conrad and Hafsten. They were greeted by large tables of hors d'oeuvres and an animated, smiling Larry Conrad, who was always in the middle of a story:

> I was down in southern Indiana, and I had just wound up another speech for governor. I jumped off the back of the flatbed after telling everybody how I was goin' to fix their roads and cure their arthritis. A good ol' boy runs up, grabs me, and says, "I like what you say, but there's one thing I want to ask. Where do you stand on the United Nations?" I cleared my throat, and said, "Well, what do you think is the problem?" He looked at me right down the old gunsights and said, "Well, I've got nothin' against them having it, the problem is there's too goddamn many foreigners in it."

When the laughter died down, he had another:

> After I lost the 1976 race, a couple of little gray-haired ladies came into my Statehouse office. They had been great supporters of mine. They said they wanted to see me, because they had a present for me. Well, they came in the office and told me they felt so bad because I lost. I told them "I appreciate that, but I'm sure you don't feel as bad as I do." They said they wanted to give me something they had made, and they unfurled a large wall-hanging. They had embroidered a saying on it: "I don't go to sleep at night until I have disturbed somebody."

> I laughed. They said they remembered me saying that at some speech I'd given down by the river. I thanked them, and said, "I know right where I'm going to hang this," and they started looking around at the walls of the office. I said, "No, No. I'm taking this home and hanging it on Mary Lou's side of the bed."

Conrad's sense of revelry was the balm that soothed the raw suspicions of the businessmen and the politicians. "We all had fun together," John Krauss remembers, "and when people have fun together the level of trust increases, regardless of the diverse backgrounds of the individuals. That's what happened to Indianapolis in the 80s."[53]

In 1983, an entirely new dimension was added to Conrad's life: the Indiana Pacers basketball team. The NBA franchise had a stormy history. In the previous eight years, the Pacers had had three separate owners, and there were continuing rumors and threats that the franchise would be moved to another city. When the 1982–83 season ended, the Pacers had won only twenty games and were awash in red ink.

Mayor Hudnut led the effort to find a buyer who would pledge to keep the team in Indianapolis. One of the first persons he approached was Herb Simon.

> After weeks of negotiations, I ended up one day in Herb Simon's office, accompanied by two or three civic leaders. Herb looked me in the eye and said, with that great grin of his, "Well, I've got to do it, don't I?" To which I replied, "Yes, Herb, you've got to do it . . . for civic pride."[54]

Herb and Melvin Simon purchased the Pacers, and Larry Conrad had a new assignment: to figure out how to fill the nearly 17,000 seats available for each home game. An entire schedule of special promotions was planned, and every business guest who was in town to do business with Melvin Simon and Associates got a Pacers ticket.

Not since his days as the student manager of the Muncie Central Bearcats had Larry Conrad walked the basketball floor before a game. Now he was a fixture at Market Square Arena, strolling around the court, shaking hands and greeting the fans as they took their courtside seats. At halftime he would shepherd the special guests down the runway to the Simon suite, where hot hors d'oeuvres and liquid refreshments were abundant. Mary Lou and all the Conrad kids made the Pacers games part of their regular routine.

Conrad was doing very little except assignments for Melvin Simon and Associates. His schedule no longer permitted much direct political involvement. When an old friend would call, he would agree to give a Jefferson-Jackson Day speech in his or her county, and he always had time to talk with his old staff members and political allies when they dropped by the office. But his time was consumed by business.

In 1982, his old friend Don Michael was defeated for reelection as chairman of the Democratic State Committee by Jerry Miller, the former mayor of South Bend and ally of Gordon St. Angelo. The next year, at the annual gridiron dinner sponsored by the Indianapolis Press Club, Conrad was the "roastmaster." In commenting on Mike Phillips, the Democratic leader in the Indiana House of Representatives, Conrad said: "He is credited with laying the plans last year for seizing control of the State Democratic Committee—which is like stealing a junk car abandoned on the street."[55]

Actually, Conrad was disappointed in the party. He realized that Don Michael was in charge of a party apparatus that was poorly funded and rent with factionalism. The old organization people were picking on the bones of a dead carcass. In 1980, when county chairs complained to Conrad about Michael's leadership, he would retort that one "should not rush to judge until you have walked a mile in his moccasins."

After the 1984 May primaries, John Livengood met with Conrad and told him he had decided to challenge Jerry Miller for the state chairmanship. Livengood was serving as the chairman of the Marion County Democratic Central Committee, and thought he could put together enough votes to be state chairman. Conrad asked him the standard question he asked everyone who sought his advice about running for office: "Why do you want to do this?" Livengood answered, "I want to be the state chairman when we elect the next governor." Conrad shot back, "Then what?" Livengood said, "Then I don't care. If the governor doesn't want me to stay on as state chairman, I'll resign." Conrad looked directly into his eyes and said, "If you really mean that, you'll be the best state chairman Indiana has ever had." Livengood always remembered his remark. "All Larry had seen were state chairmen who wanted the job for themselves, not for the party." Livengood was elected chairman of the Indiana Democratic party that year, and was still in office when Evan Bayh won the governorship in 1988—the first Democrat elected in twenty-four years.[56]

It was inevitable that Conrad would fold his law practice and go on the payroll of Melvin Simon and Associates. Throughout the summer of 1983, Herb Simon and Larry talked about his moving directly into the corporate headquarters. Herb finally made a formal offer to name him vice-president of corporate affairs. The Conrad and Hafsten law practice was dissolved, and Larry and Claudia moved into the corporate suites of Melvin Simon and Associates, Inc., which had recently relocated from North Meridian to Merchants Plaza on Washington Street.

Finally, Conrad was making money. His schedule was even more hectic. He now was responsible for a corporate division, and additional people were hired. Shortly after moving into his new office, he read an article about a group headquartered in Washington, D.C., called Partners for Livable Places. The article made reference to John Krauss. "Larry had read something about Partners, and I served on their Board of Directors. He wanted more information, and I called Washington and had them send all the material to him. A few weeks later Larry called back and said, "I'm interested and maybe would like to go on their Board of Directors." I recommended him to Robert McNulty, who was president of Partners. Mayor Hudnut had just gone on the Board the previous year."[57]

In April 1985, Partners for Livable Places held an international forum in Indianapolis on "city assets." Conrad had just joined the Board of Directors, and he and Mayor Hudnut had secured private money to bring the conference to Indianapolis. "It was a very large event," Robert McNulty explains. "Over 400 attended, including many from Europe, and Lady Bird Johnson spoke at the luncheon. Between Larry and Bill Hudnut, we had the perfect combination of political and business experience."[58]

Partners for Livable Places was a perfect match for Conrad. Having established a network of over one thousand organizations, Partners' mission was to help solve local problems. "These are the vexing problems of cities and towns," McNulty explains, "like race, and enduring social problems. We offer ourselves as an outside friend and we establish an agenda for change that involves long-term strategic planning. We seek to overcome barriers and create a new frame of social equity. We are a long-term collaborator."[59] If Larry Conrad were to write a mission statement for an organization he wanted to lead, it would have been identical to the mission of Partners for Livable Places.

Another aspect of Partners was particularly appealing to Conrad. The organization had an international vision. The German Marshall Plan of the United States had provided funding to Partners to foster international cooperation at the local level, and study tours were frequently conducted on which Americans could see first hand some of the innovative efforts being tried in European communities. It wasn't long before Conrad had Herb Simon interested in Partners, and they were off to Paris and Strasbourg, touring the great cities of Europe. Everything seemed to be booming in Indiana's capital city. In 1983, the U.S. Gymnastics Federation moved their national headquarters to Indianapolis, spurred by a $300,000 grant from Lilly Endowment. Another $150,000 from Lilly enticed the U.S. Synchronized Swimming organization to relocate from Colorado.

Indianapolis hit the big leagues again early in 1984 when Robert Irsay moved his NFL team from Baltimore to Indianapolis. After weeks of secret and delicate negotiations, Irsay packed the team's belongings into Mayflower vans and, under the cover of darkness, moved to the Hoosier Dome. That summer, about two weeks before the first exhibition game in the Dome, Conrad spoke to a group of restaurant owners in downtown Indianapolis. "They weren't sure about this, but I told them we were going to be a big city, and there would actually be people downtown on Sunday afternoon, and they should be prepared. They were used to going down South Meridian. It was so quiet that a wino could sleep all week and never be disturbed. I told them now it was going to be nothing but wall-to-wall people."[60]

And more plans were underway. Throughout the summer of 1984, Conrad and the other leaders went to work on bringing the next sporting event to Indianapolis, the 1987 Pan American Games.

On December 18, 1984, the movers and shakers of Indianapolis were ecstatic. The 1987 Pan Am Games had been awarded to the Circle City. Indianapolis was vaulting into the big time. The games would bring international exposure. The city leaders were sure they were up to the task. The National Sports Festival had come off with very few hitches, and actually turned a profit for the first time in the history of the games. With more publicity and more people, the same could be done with the Pan Am Games. And afterwards? There was always the Olympics.

The local organizing committee constituted themselves as PAX-I (Pan American Ten—Indianapolis), and Theodore R. (Ted) Boehm agreed to serve as chairman of the board. The board hired thirty-three-year-old Mark D. Miles as the president and chief operating officer. Miles was in charge of the staff and supervised all activities relating to the games. The organizing committee assigned specific tasks to various members. Conrad and Herb Simon were again in charge of the opening and closing ceremonies.

As Conrad began brainstorming the events, another ceremony was being planned behind his back. On February 8, 1985, Larry Conrad would be fifty years old. In a silent conspiracy with Claudia Prosser, Jim Morris, Sid Weedman, and others, Mary Lou began plotting a surprise birthday party. Invitations were mailed to over five hundred people throughout the state, and each person was pledged to secrecy. The event was to be held in the ballroom of the Athenaeum at 401 E. Michigan the week after Larry's birthday.[61] Jim Morris agreed to make sure Larry was occupied at dinner while the crowd gathered in the ballroom. After dinner, Morris suggested they stop by the Athenaeum for an after-dinner drink. When they entered, Morris started walking up the stairs toward the ballroom. Conrad asked him where he was going. Morris said, "Just come on up here for minute, there's something I want to look at." They walked through the ballroom doors, shoulder to shoulder, and the crowd erupted. Conrad, dressed in a light brown overcoat and a cap, appeared stunned. His eyes reflected awe as his fleshy face reddened in embarrassment. Everyone joined in the singing of "Happy Birthday."[62]

"Last year I turned fifty," Conrad said the next summer when he spoke to a business luncheon, "and my wife threw a surprise party for me. She invited all the free world."

Conrad loved a party. And he saw the upcoming Pan Am Games as being the biggest party Indianapolis had ever thrown. He decided Indianapolis needed publicity to let the whole world know what was happening in "Naptown."

With the success of the National Sports Festival in 1983, the arrival of the

Colts in 1984, the opening of the remodeled Union Station in 1986, and the landing of the Pan Am Games for 1987, Conrad knew Indianapolis was ready for "prime time." What was needed was for the media to showcase the city and its renaissance.

A fellow board member with Partners for Livable Places, Wilbur E. (Bill) Garrett, was on the board of the National Geographic Society, publisher of the *National Geographic.* Conrad decided Garrett's magazine should showcase Indianapolis.

He prevailed upon Garrett to visit Indianapolis, then pressed his friends into action to ensure that Garrett was suitably impressed. In a 1988 speech to a service club in Indianapolis, Larry described the elaborate efforts they took to guarantee a *National Geographic* article:

> I thought we should show Bill Garrett not only our new buildings, but our people. I called the secretary who was handling the logistics of his visit and I said, "I don't know where this person is, but somewhere in Indiana there is a man or a woman who knows Bill very well. They are close personal friends. Let's find that person, and have him sitting with Bill. And another thing, Bill has to have a special hobby or interest that has nothing to do with his work. Let's find out what that hobby is, and find a Hoosier who is an expert in it."

> Well, a couple of days later, she called back. She was stumped. "How do I find out these things?" she asked. I told her to call Garrett's secretary, swear her to secrecy, and start asking questions. She did. She called me back the next day and said, "You'll never believe this. His best man in his wedding is a journalism professor at IU. And his two hobbies are tennis and wine-making."

> No problem. When Bill got off the plane, his best man was waiting to drive him downtown. He was stunned. That night, at dinner, we had the president of Oliver Winery sitting at his table, next to the former president of the U.S. Clay Courts tennis tournament.

> When I took Bill back to the airport he said, "I can't figure this out. I saw my oldest friend—he was the best man in my wedding. And I love tennis, and seated at my table was the head guy for the Clay Courts. And my hobby is wine-making, and the president of one of your wineries was there." I looked at him and said, "Well, isn't that strange. But there's a lot of good people in Indiana."

In the August 1987 issue of *National Geographic*—the same month the Pan Am Games opened in Indianapolis—there was a thirty-page spread on the city entitled "Indianapolis On The Rebound."[63]

But while some ideas were working well, Conrad and the other members of the PAX-I committee faced some major obstacles.

One of the biggest hurdles was to find sufficient housing in Indianapolis for over six thousand athletes. In 1985, Mayor Hudnut proposed a $47 million general obligation bond issue to build a "Pan Am Village" in the downtown area which could be converted to permanent housing stock for the city after the games concluded. Tied to the bond issue were neighborhood revitalization projects, which promised construction activity elsewhere in the city.

But this bond issue would raise taxes, and tax increases are anathema to Hoosiers. A group calling themselves the Indianapolis Taxpayers Association immediately came out against the bond issue and collected thousands of signatures in opposition. The city leaders attempted to secure enough signatures in support, but they fell short. The bond issue was defeated.[64]

Taken aback by the reaction of the citizens, the organizing committee scrambled. Finally, they reached an agreement with the U.S. Army command that Fort Benjamin Harrison, on the northwest side of the city, would be vacated by service personnel and converted into "Pan Am Village" for the games.

The members of PAX-I were slowly coming to the realization that hosting the Pan Am Games was not just one step up from the National Sports Festival. It was a mammoth leap. They were now dealing with a $33 million budget, which required selling nearly $6.5 million worth of tickets and recruiting nearly 38,000 volunteers. They ran into problems with the bond issue and housing. Their budgetary projections for specific events were also running into trouble, and negotiations with television networks for coverage were laborious and tedious. Even Ted Boehm had to admit—a few days before the games opened—that "I don't think we quite realized the magnitude of this thing."[65] Years later, Mayor Hudnut wrote that the Pan Am Games "stretched us to the limits."[66]

Conrad's schedule was devoted almost exclusively to the games. Although technically in charge of the opening and closing ceremonies, he was deeply involved in nearly all the planning. His perspective was the optimistic one, the one that continually urged the staff members and organizers to reach out and find the talent to solve the problems. Where are we to find translators for the Spanish-speaking athletes and officials? From the foreign language departments of the colleges and universities, and from the Hispanic population of Indiana. How are we to communicate with the tens of thousands of volunteers? We are going to have regular mailings to them and every senior citizens' group will be asked to address and stuff envelopes.

Conrad's organizing principle for the opening and closing ceremonies was the same one that guided him during his planning of the National Sports Festival. The Pan Am Games were at a much higher level, but the heightened interest only promised more attention for Indiana and the men and women from throughout the state who would organize and execute the ceremonies. Conrad, again, wanted the events to be all Hoosier.

But these were the Pan Am Games, and the eyes of others were on Indianapolis. Two men in the marketing division of the Disney corporation were ex-Hoosiers, and they saw a potential for Disney to receive international exposure by being in charge of the opening ceremonies. They contacted Mark Miles.

Unbeknownst to Larry or Herb, Miles invited the Disney representatives to Indianapolis, where he entered negotiations for Disney to take over the opening ceremonies, which were to be held at the Indianapolis Motor Speedway.

"Larry was disappointed and disgusted when he heard of Disney's involvement," Prosser says.[67] Sid Weedman concurs: "Larry was very upset about it."[68] David Frick remembers that "we debated a lot" about the opening ceremony, and Frick laughingly accused Larry of "provincial thinking" because he thought the ceremony "was in our hands and we could do it." Larry finally relented.[69]

Certainly Larry should have been involved from the beginning in any contacts with Disney. But he was never one to look back, and certainly he held no personal grudge against Mark Miles. Miles was young, and this was a new experience for him. Later, when others criticized Miles for being "arrogant and eager to stand in the spotlight," Larry came to his defense. "It would be a rare person who wouldn't fall prey once in a while to all the attention being given to you in a pressurized situation," he said, and explained that when Miles took on an egotistical air, "I thump him on the ear." He told a reporter that Miles was a "rare species" who "can write his own ticket."[70]

Conrad had no quarrel with Disney's ability to stage such a live show. He recognized the Disney organization as being the world's top show business promoter. They could do it. They could make the Speedway sing. Conrad merely thought Indiana could do it as well. Now, however, it was Disney's show.

Larry backed away from active involvement with the opening ceremonies. He turned most of the coordinating duties over to Claudia Prosser, and he only occasionally met with the Disney representatives. "Larry liked the Disney people," Claudia says, "but they were now in charge and he saw no reason to interfere."[71] His attention turned to the closing ceremonies, which he decided would be held on the American Legion Mall.

As spring came to Indiana in 1987, the PAX-I organizers had identified and begun solving the major problems and were at work on the hundreds of minor logistical details that remained. But the smooth operation of the organizing committee was soon interrupted by new controversies. These were of a different nature. They were political. They involved Cuba.

A centerpiece of President Reagan's foreign policy was for the United States to be actively engaged against left-wing movements in Latin America, such as those in El Salvador and Nicaragua. And always there was an administrator's eye cocked toward Castro.

When the PAX-I organizing committee announced plans to visit Cuba to discuss with Cuban officials—including Castro—the plans for the games and the role of Cuba in the sporting events and closing ceremonies, the Reagan State Department interceded.

From the beginning Conrad and the other organizers considered themselves compelled to coordinate closely with Cuba. Cuba's presence would heighten interest in the games, spur ticket sales, and guarantee television coverage throughout the hemisphere. Also, Cuba was to be the host country for the 1991 games, and it was a tradition at the closing ceremonies to raise the flag of the next host country and play their national anthem.

Elliott Abrams, an assistant secretary of state for Latin American Affairs, was incensed by this. "The government of Cuba is trying to use these games for its political purpose," he proclaimed, and then insisted that the PAX-I delegation going to Cuba be cut in half, from twenty-six to thirteen delegates.[72] Abrams warned delegates that even local government officials could be exploited by Castro. He warned that the government of Cuba was not officially recognized and that such a visit would allow Castro to claim recognition, if not by the U.S. government, at least by local officials. Above all, Abrams and others feared that the Hoosiers might, of all things, actually invite Castro to Indianapolis. The position of the Reagan administration was reinforced by U.S. senators Richard Lugar and Dan Quayle. Quayle said he was reluctant to get involved in the dispute, but thought "it was in everyone's best interest that I put my foot in it."[73] Quayle said he was disturbed by the size of the original delegation and warned the PAX-I members not to "capitalize on the infamy and notoriety of Fidel Castro."[74] In effect, Quayle accused Mark Miles of "courting" Castro.[75]

The organizing committee was to leave for Cuba on April 15. The day before, John Krauss, the deputy mayor, was in his office when the phone rang. It was Mark Miles. "John, what are you doing in two hours?" he asked. "We've got to go to Washington and meet with Elliott Abrams at the State Department. He is putting the kibosh on our delegation going to Cuba." Two hours later, Miles, Krauss, Boehm, Sandy Knapp, and David Gogol, head of intergovernmental relations for PAX-I, were on their way to Washington.[76]

When they arrived at the State Department, Krauss remembers that Abrams "preached to us. He rambled on about human rights and Castro. He said the delegation going to Havana would look like we were recognizing Cuba. Finally, he looked at the list of our delegation and he picked me out as the highest ranking government official and scratched me from the list. And I was just the deputy mayor."[77]

The organizing committee was in an untenable position. The delegation was to fly on an American Trans Air flight to Grenada, where they would board a commuter plane for Cuba. Abrams had cancelled their landing rights in Grenada. With the entire Washington establishment, including the U.S. senators, applying pressure, the PAX-I officials had to capitulate. They agreed they would not invite Castro to the games. They agreed that the delegation would be cut in half. All persons with official government status, such as senior deputy mayor Joseph Slash, deputy mayor Krauss, city-county councilman Glenn Howard, and R. Mark Lubbers, executive assistant to Governor Orr, were to stay behind. The only public official remaining on the list was Paul Annee, chief of the Indianapolis Police Department and head of security for the games.

With the government officials scratched from the list, others decided not to go. Theodore (Ted) Boehm, chairman of the organizing committee, removed himself from the list, later saying that "we decided that people should go who really had central work to do, and I really wasn't one of them."[78] Sidney Weedman, co-chairman for media, publicity, and public relations, also backed off, as did David Gogol. The final roster consisted of thirteen delegates and at least as many journalists. Larry Conrad—having no "official government status"—was one of the thirteen.

While the organizers were engaged in negotiations with Abrams and others—and just a few days prior to their trip to Washington—the American Legion decided to jump into the fray. Conrad had outlined the plans for the closing ceremony in the newspapers on Wednesday, April 1. He promised the celebration on the mall would be "awesome, self-fulfilling, and spiritual" and "as spectacular" as the opening ceremony directed by the Disney organization. The reason it would be as spectacular? Because Hoosiers will have created it "out of our own hands. . . ." Then Conrad explained that the Cuban flag would be raised, and the Cuban national anthem played. This event would be the traditional symbol of the passing of the games to Havana in 1991. "I suppose if you were looking over the Cold War years of America you would not have thought the flag of a non-democratic country would be raised here. I see it as an acceptance of the premise that . . . in this day and age of high military technology, we have to use other methods than armament to persuade people that living is very important."[79]

The officers of the Indiana American Legion read Conrad's statements and erupted. On Sunday, April 5, the executive committee of the Indiana American Legion unanimously passed a resolution opposing the use of the downtown American Legion Mall for the closing ceremonies. The public relations director for the Legion said, "[We feel] that the area is consecrated ground. It is dedicated to those who lost their lives defending this nation."[80] The Legion contended that they had not been informed what a prominent role Cuba would play in the ceremonies, and pointed out that a Legion commander had been executed in Cuba in 1961.

Twenty-five years before, in the closing days of Birch Bayh's first campaign for the U.S. Senate, Cuba had concentrated Conrad's mind. Now Castro was back. Unlike in 1962, Conrad quickly grasped the essence of the concern over Cuba. His innate understanding of ideological rigidity and political posturing led him to clearly define the position of the Pan Am organizers. He knew where "home plate" was in this controversy. The games were an international sporting event, not an international political convention. The organizers had to keep their own counsel and refuse to be lured into a political trap. If the Reagan administration, the American Legion, Senators Lugar and Quayle, and others wanted to shoot down the games to further their positions and political careers, the PAX-I officials should not provide them with the ammunition. What came from the PAX-I offices were measured statements designed to defuse the inflammatory rhetoric and keep negotiations moving.

In response to the Legion's resolution opposing the use of the mall, Mark Miles said: "We'll just have to get with them and hear what their concerns are and see if there's anything we can say that will change their mind."[81] Sandy Knapp, in commenting on the Cuban trip, said, "You don't have to like someone or agree with him to want to meet him."[82]

Conrad himself said little publicly. Privately, he wondered if the American Legion would pass a resolution renaming the War Memorial, which sat in the middle of the mall, the "Peace Memorial." He was disturbed that the Legion had picked the fight and polarized the argument without meeting with the organizing committee. When he heard that Legion officials had sworn that the Cuban flag would never fly over the mall, he and Sid Weedman jokingly planned on sneaking onto the mall at 5 A.M., planting the Cuban flag, and calling the news media.[83]

Whatever wiggle room was left in the negotiations with the Legion was removed on April 6 when Mayor Hudnut spoke out. "If there are serious concerns and legitimate objections about the . . . Mall being used for the closing ceremonies, as I think there are, it probably would make sense to look for another site, and city hall will be happy to work with PAX-I toward that end."[84]

The PAX-I organizers were backed into a corner. And it was becoming increasingly difficult to maintain the schedule that was being thrust upon them. The next week was the planned trip to Cuba where they were to sort out the myriad problems surrounding Cuba's participation. Boehm, Conrad, and Miles hurriedly huddled and suggested options to the Legion, including moving part of the ceremony across the street from the mall—especially that portion of the event requiring the raising of the Cuban flag. They discussed among themselves and others moving the closing ceremonies to the Hoosier Dome or the IUPUI track field.

On Monday, April 20, the American Legion rejected the option of moving the Cuban portion of the ceremony across the street, calling the compromise "cosmetic." Then the Indiana Civil Liberties Union waded in against the Legion, pointing out the mall and the War Memorial belonged to the state, not to the American Legion. The ICLU offered free legal services to PAX-I.[85]

The controversy stirred up by the Legion evoked an opinion from an editor at the *Indianapolis Star*. In a courageous effort at fence-straddling, the editor wrote that the newspaper "respects the Legion's position and shares its convictions about Castro. . . . But the recognition of Cuba at the close of the 1987 Games is in no way a tribute or deferential treatment. It is routine and traditional, part of the protocol of the Games, to introduce the flag and anthem of the next host country." Finally, the editors urged Governor Orr to "persuade Legion officials that there is nothing in the ceremony to warrant giving or taking offense."[86]

There had to be satisfaction on Conrad's face when he read the editorial. Aside from his success with the opening ceremonies for the National Sports Festival, he had never had the support of the Pulliam papers. Now, at least, they halfway agreed with him.[87]

But Conrad and the other organizers knew that any hopes for negotiating with the Legion had collapsed. The closing ceremonies would have to be moved. "We agreed that the whole idea of the games was to be a positive experience for everyone," Weedman says, and "when agitation came from the Legion, we decided it was not worth it. The fight was likely to overcome the event and cast a pall over the games. It was not worth the battle."[88] Conrad concurred. "What we are really here for, after all, is to see who runs the fastest, jumps the highest, and tumbles the best," he told a reporter.[89]

So where should the closing ceremonies take place? The problem with the IUPUI track was a lack of seating, and the physical configuration ruled out fireworks. And Larry wanted fireworks. It was decided the Hoosier Dome would be the venue. "Larry still insisted on using fireworks in the Dome and all I could see was the problems—like the Dome roof catching on fire," Frick recalls. A compromise was reached. There would be a ninety-minute extravaganza inside the Dome, and thirty minutes later the fireworks would take place outside. But Conrad didn't give up on indoor fireworks. He contracted with several balloon companies to create a 500-foot curtain of 27,000 balloons inside the Dome which would explode in a span of fifteen seconds. Electronic detonators would achieve the result, being fired from three separate locations within the Dome.[90]

Sandwiched between the compromise suggestion to the Legion and the final decision to move the closing ceremonies to the Hoosier Dome was the Cuban trip. The PAX-I delegation landed at Jose Marti Habana Airport on Wednesday, April 15, 1987. The thirteen delegates and fourteen journalists were greeted by the vice-president of Cuba's Council of Ministers, the third-highest ranking official in Cuba. Meetings with representatives of several Cuban sports organizations consumed the next two days. Agreement was reached on security arrangements for Cuban athletes, visa arrangements, and drug testing procedures. Cuban officials had threatened to boycott the games if their athletes could not fly on a chartered Cuban aircraft. The PAX-I delegates had no authority to speak about landing rights in the United States, and previous inquiries to the State Department about this problem had gone unanswered. It was finally agreed that both parties would work cooperatively to try to get the Cuban athletes to Indiana on their own plane. "One way or another, we will resolve this transportation problem," Miles told a reporter.[91]

The big agreement came on Friday. Cuba agreed to purchase 220 hours of television and radio coverage. This breakthrough assured the organizers of $350,000 and protected the PAX-I contract with CBS Sports, which had a provision for renegotiating the coverage if Cuba boycotted the event. Accompanying the Cuban agreement, Miles announced that over 45 million viewers in twenty nations would be viewing the games.[92]

Friday evening, following a cocktail reception and dinner, the delegation wondered if they would ever meet Fidel Castro. Cuban officials had hinted that he would attend the reception, but he never showed up. Shortly before midnight, as Conrad and the others were settling into their hotel rooms, there was a knock on the doors. Several security men told the delegates to collect their papers. They were going to the presidential palace to meet Fidel Castro.

In his wood-paneled office, Castro was dressed in "freshly pressed green army fatigues and just-shined black boots." He was in a jovial mood. He autographed baseballs and accepted a baseball cap autographed by major-league pitcher Nolan Ryan.[93]

Most of the discussion centered on baseball, but the delegation posed some substantive questions, as did Castro. When asked if he planned on attending the games, Castro replied through an interpreter, "You'd better ask the chief of police in Indianapolis if it would be too much trouble. I think it wouldn't be so good for him if I go there to multiply his work." He then explained that he expected to be on vacation during the games and would listen to the broadcasts to stay abreast of the Cuban athletes. Then he asked about the controversy over the Cuban flag being displayed on the mall. Everyone turned to Conrad for the response, but Larry was busy taking photographs and at first did not realize the question was posed to him. When he recovered, he gave assurances that the final ceremonies would properly acknowledge Cuba's position as the host of the 1991 games. Castro replied, "It seems to me that controversy doesn't make much sense since we're living in a civilized world. I don't think in Indianapolis you would have such prejudices." He noted that the United States flag is flown in Cuba when American athletes are participating.[94]

When the delegation arrived back in Indianapolis, Conrad was asked about the meeting with Castro. "It was just a bunch of human beings sitting around a table talking about sports. It happens all the time, everywhere in the world."

Mark Miles described the meeting as "remarkably cordial and constructive."[95]

A Biography

But the optimism faded. And again, it was Conrad who was at the center of the controversy. Conrad had decided that the grand finale to the closing ceremony in the Dome would be a series of songs by Gloria Estefan and her band, the Miami Sound Machine. Officials of the Castro government, however, knew of Gloria Estefan and her husband. They were Cuban exiles. Estefan's father had been a bodyguard for the wife of Cuban president Fulgencio Batista, who was overthrown by Castro's guerrillas in 1959.

"If the band plays, we won't go," threatened Manuel Gonzalez Guerra, the head of the Cuban Olympic Committee. He jokingly said he would have to miss the closing ceremony because of a "stomachache." Conrad tried to keep the focus on the purpose of the closing ceremony, which should be "a time for rejoicing," because all the athletes, judges, and officials would be together.[96]

Conrad was still negotiating the seemingly implacable positions taken by the Cuban officials when the Indianapolis Pan American Games opened Saturday, August 8, 1987, at the track. Two Disney executives were in the production booth, coordinating the events with CBS Television—which had sixteen cameras and the Goodyear blimp—to air the opening ceremony for an international audience. Vice-President George Bush opened the games with a one-sentence statement: "I do solemnly proclaim as open the Tenth Pan American Games in Indianapolis, Indiana, United States of America." Then followed the Disney-produced two-hour extravaganza called "The Magic That Is America."[97] But there was trouble in the sky. As the Disney producers were directing the camera shots, an airplane flew over the Speedway towing a banner urging Cubans to defect. A Miami-based organization of Cuban exiles, calling themselves *Cuba Independiente y Democratica* (CID) had chartered the plane and had promised demonstrations against the Cuban team.[98]

But the show must go on, and for the next fifteen days nearly 6,000 officials and athletes would participate in thirty-one sports at venues throughout Indiana. The yachting competition was held on Lake Michigan. The shooting competitions were at Camp Atterbury, outside of Columbus, Indiana. The cycling road races were held in Brown County State Park and the table tennis events were at the Carmel Racquet Club, just north of Indianapolis.

Wherever Cuban athletes were performing, security was tight. During the boxing matches at the Indiana Convention Center, several Cuban fighters swarmed into the stands to confront anti-Castro demonstrators who were stomping on the Cuban flag and jeering the Cuban team. On the last day of the games, a fight broke out at Bush Stadium, where the Cuban baseball team was playing Puerto Rico.[99]

Conrad and the other organizers were working virtually around the clock. But he did pause during the games for something special. On

Wednesday, August 12, 1987, just four days into the games, Larry Conrad became a grandfather. Bennett Allyn Conrad—a beautiful grandson—was born that day in Indianapolis to Jeb and his wife, and Larry and Mary Lou were brimming with the pride that only first-time grandparents truly understand.

But he was back to work within hours. When he awoke on Saturday morning, August 22, he would not go back to bed for over forty-eight hours. He was putting the final touches on the ceremony. The rehearsal for the Sunday gala took place Saturday, and many pieces "just didn't seem to fit," Conrad told a reporter. At 2 A.M. Sunday, Conrad convened a meeting "to straighten them out."[100]

One of the problems was with Gloria Estefan and her band. Their concert schedule did not allow them to arrive in Indianapolis until the wee hours of Sunday morning. Prosser had arranged a private plane to fly them to Indianapolis and they immediately drove to a studio to record all the songs they would sing that evening. One of the things that "just didn't seem to fit" was the amplification within the Hoosier Dome. The solution was to prerecord the songs and have Estefan lip-sync the concert.[101]

The closing ceremony was to begin at 8 that night. But the downtown streets were festive hours before, with church bells and carillons ringing, calliopes playing, and Conrad's ever-present baton twirlers parading in front of the Hoosier Dome.

The Cuban boycott of the ceremony did not materialize, and the number three official in Castro's government did appear for the closing ceremony. The Cuban athletes, however, made their position clear when they remained in their seats on the floor of the Dome while Gloria Estefan cranked up the crowd with her hit songs. The other athletes went wild. They swarmed the stage and some even manhandled women who were working backstage. When security forces finally drove everybody back to the main floor, they danced in the aisles and formed a moving human chain, winding around the chairs.

Cuba's minister of education and sport had the honor of raising the Cuban flag on stage while the Cuban national anthem played. In his speech he proclaimed that "these games will go down in history as the best games to date." The protesters from the CID were under close scrutiny by security agents. They were escorted out of the Dome moments before the Cuban flag was raised.[102]

Conrad and the other organizers were exhausted. "We have to get back to our real lives," Sid Weedman told a reporter. "Monday is a work day." When asked what he planned next, Mark Miles said, "If I had my druthers, I'd just sleep."[103]

The games had ended, and Indianapolis was now recognized as the amateur sports capital of America. Six years after the games, the Indianapolis Chamber of Commerce released the results of a $150,000 study on the impact of amateur sports on the city. Total investment in the sport strategy had amounted to $164 million since 1977. This total included city, state, and federal government contributions, as well as private dollars from corporations, foundations, and individuals. The investment yielded a return of 64 percent for each of the fifteen years, for a total financial impact of $1.89 billion. Over 500 permanent full-time jobs were created.

The sports strategy had persuaded the public. The study showed that 93 percent of the people thought the city "should continue its efforts to attract amateur sports events."[104]

Conrad was not around when the results of the study were released. But he had known years before that Indianapolis was on a roll. Whereas the movement was propelled by the idea of amateur sports, Conrad knew other powers were present.

> We are here right now. We are in Indianapolis, Indiana, deep in the interior of this thing known as the United States. And how are we going to be assessed? Not next year—but fifty years—a hundred years—from now. What kind of people were they? Let them say about us, "There were people on the cutting edge. They were everywhere. Education? They were there. Medical research? They were there. Amateur athletics? They were there. Professional sports? They were there."[105]

His mind would not let him rest. Only a month after the closing of the Pan Am Games, Conrad was in the parking lot of the new downtown location for the Indianapolis Zoo, dressed in his tuxedo and wearing brand-new sneakers. The occasion was a formal dance and a "sneak preview" of the new zoo. The partygoers had paid to come in black tie and sneakers to raise money for the final move of the zoo downtown, scheduled for June 1988. A raffle was held and Larry's name was selected as the winner of an all-paid trip to Kenya in 1988.[106]

Whether it was a fund-raiser for the zoo or the symphony, there simply was too much to do if the historians of the next century were to judge Hoosiers as being "on the cutting edge." In Conrad's mind, a person's lot in life was not frozen in ice or etched in stone. He knew that from his own experience. And a person must struggle with and understand the wondrous events of life in the wondrous invention called the United States.

> Nobody has ever tried to do it like we have tried to do it. We have only been trying this for two hundred years. Two hundred years is nothing in the history of the universe. And we said we were going to make certain guarantees, and we did that governmentally, and it has been difficult. We have been drug from pillar to post. And our Constitution says everybody. Not just menfolk, not everybody but white folk, not everybody but Baptists, not everybody but old folks . . . it just says everybody. It has taken us two hundred years to grind that down to make us—if we are the highest primates, and sometimes I wonder if we are—understand that

philosophy. And when we see your niche against the progress of civilization, you see how wondrous it is. It was just a short period of time ago we were sending folk over the battlefield to stick pikes in the masks of the dead . . . not long at all. Think of that advance of civilization—and we Americans are in the vanguard.[107]

For an individual to add his effort to this "advance of civilization" required constant struggle against the force of inertia—or, in human terms, habit.

The sociologists tell us we are pretty much creatures of habit. We know pretty much what we are going to do every morning. We set the alarm for 6 A.M. You don't change that. She gets out on her side of the bed and he gets out on his side of the bed. Hair comes first and lipstick second, or shave first and brush teeth second. It's all laid out. You watch yourself. It's a pattern because you are used to it, you're comfortable with it and it cuts down on the brain processes of making decisions, which we don't like to do. So they tell us we go through these same routines. We go down the same corridors and descend the same stairs and into the same breakfast area and see the same mate and say the same thing: "How's it going today?" And we don't really care, and we have the same thing to eat in the morning and go out the same door and get in the same car and go out the same drive and we go down the same streets in the same pattern in the same parking lot into the same parking space and take the same route into the same building and sit at the same desk in the same sort of way and at lunch we have about the same things with the same people and we go out the same door and down the same walkway to the same parking space and into the same car and we go out the same parking garage and take the same route home and pull up in the same drive and go in the same house in the same door and see the same person and say the same thing: "How did it go today?"

And then we sit down and do the same things. Normally, she gets the dinner and he's supposed to make conversation or read the paper. And then they eat and then about 7 o'clock a strange thing happens. They convene before the unusual opportunity to enjoy what we call "prime time viewing." He wants to watch channel 13 and she wants to see what's on 6 and as a compromise they watch 8. And then we do that until 10 o'clock and when that same person says that same phrase, "that's all the news, weather and sports for today"—and then all over America they turn out the lights. They go up the same stairs and down the same corridors into the same bedrooms with the same people. And the sociologists tell us we pretty much perform there on the same basis.[108]

His prodding of himself and others extended to all aspects of his life. And politics and government were never far from the center.

In the history of America our two great political parties have come to the defense of our Republic many times. Now, we happen to be Democrats.

And we respect those with whom we disagree. But we are Democrats because we see how our party has defended our Republic. We see it in Thomas Jefferson. We see it in Andy Jackson. We see it in Woodrow Wilson and Franklin D. Roosevelt and in Harry Truman and in John F. Kennedy. It is these men of our party that make us Democrats and have prepared us to come to the defense of our Republic in our time.[109]

Another Democrat—thirty-year-old Birch Evans Bayh III, son of former senator Birch Bayh—began planning his own political career. Bayh's natural assets, including his name, had appeal for every Hoosier Democrat. He had been approached in 1984 to be on the state ticket as attorney general, and declined. Now he set his sights on the office of secretary of state, and Larry Conrad was there to help. Joe Hogsett, Evan Bayh's campaign manager, describes Conrad's role:

> Larry dominated Democratic politics in Indiana during the 1970s and into the 80s. These were his years, in spite of having two Democratic U.S. senators for part of the time. He totally dominated the party. I called on Larry in 1985 when Evan was seeking advice about running for secretary of state. Larry was still the titular head of the party, although he had not run since 1976. Otis Cox was in office, but he was far down the ballot as state auditor and did not have near the following Larry did. Larry was the leader because Birch Bayh, after having lost in 1980, stayed in Washington, so seven years after he left office as secretary of state, Larry was still the party leader. This was the first time I met Larry. He impressed on Evan and me the need to go to the party organizations and the need to raise money.[110]

On Tuesday, January 21, 1986, Larry hosted a fund-raising reception for Evan Bayh at the Embassy Suites Hotel, which had been built on the site of the old Claypool Hotel. He had made several phone calls to contributors and mailed more than 300 letters over his signature. Hogsett remembers the events of that evening and the significance of Conrad hosting the reception.

> He literally called in the old "Conrad Group" of supporters, emphasizing it was to raise dollars for Evan. About 100 people showed up and Larry told the guests: "Look, this is the beginning of the resurgence of the Democratic Party in Indiana and it begins with Evan Bayh." He made it clear that Evan was the leader of the ticket. That was very important to us. It was one of the most significant events that took place. It is where it all began. Sally Kirkpatrick was there, and she became our finance person. It was a coalescing of people who had been behind Conrad and now were with Evan. Larry did not really think this was as significant as it turned out to be. Prior to that fundraiser, a candidate for secretary of state had never raised much money. Ed Simcox, in his reelection in 1982, had raised between $150,000 and $200,000. He led the state ticket—and that was a phenomenal amount of money. Because of Larry's initiative, Evan

raised $650,000. Rob Bowen, his opponent, raised between $550,000 and $600,000. That race was exponentially more important than any other secretary of state's race in recent history.[111]

At the Democratic state convention in June 1986, Larry Conrad delivered the nominating speech for Evan Bayh for secretary of state:

Hemingway tells us about Mount Kilimanjaro, where way up above the tree line, in the snow, they found this stiffened body of a leopard. No one could ever explain why the leopard was at such an altitude. What would possess this powerful animal to go beyond the limit? Well, in the short lives for all of us, there is that time and that place where we choose to take the risk . . . we choose to face the danger. And in that time and in that place we ask ourselves, "If not now, when? If not here, where? If not him, who?" Is this party going to survive or not? This is our last, best, hope.

That summer, Conrad squeezed more political events into his schedule to campaign for Evan Bayh. In mid-August, he had these lines about the young Bayh:

Some of you may not know this, but I am the last living Democrat in the State of Indiana. No. That's not quite true. There's Evan Bayh and me. Well, that's not quite right either. There's Evan and me and six old men who belong to the IDEA. The eight of us get together every August in French Lick. We go there because it sounds a lot sexier than it is.[112]

That fall, Evan Bayh was elected, and a new political career was born. Hogsett summed up the Bayh victory: "Without Larry, it could not have been done."[113]

When new leaders appear they do not necessarily think as their fathers thought before. This was certainly true of Evan Bayh. Larry's affection for the young Bayh was deep. When Bayh spoke to a group that included Conrad, he would always stop at Larry's table and ask for a critique of his speech. In 1990, Larry explained to former senator Birch Bayh what he once told young Evan, "I know you well, Evan, and that is because I knew your mother and your father so well. And you have the best of both of them. You have the perfectionism of your mother—and it comes through in your speeches, where it is clear that you have memorized virtually every word and gesture. And you have the savvy and the quick-mindedness of your father."[114]

But Evan and Larry did not always see eye to eye. One of Evan's first decisions as secretary of state was to cancel a Conrad tradition: the dinner for the drivers in the Indianapolis 500. When Larry entered office, he decided to host an annual dinner just for the drivers. During the month of May there were many balls and receptions, but the only event exclusively for drivers was the banquet the night after the race, at which the prize money was disbursed. Conrad thought the drivers should be featured before the race. He used some of his office budget for mailings and also solicited corporate and labor contributions to pay for the dinner. It became known as the "Drivers Dinner sponsored by the Secretary of State." Ed Simcox liked the idea and continued the tradition through his eight years in office. Evan ended it. Hogsett explains, "Evan did not think the cost was justified and ended it in May of 1987. Both Conrad and Simcox said it did not cost that much. That illustrates the different philosophy of Evan and Larry. Neither one was right or wrong, they just viewed some things differently."[115]

The real tension between Larry and Evan was not over the drivers' dinner. It was over Evan's decision to seek the Democratic nomination for governor in 1988.

Throughout his years as a public official and civic leader, Conrad's respect for State Senator Frank O'Bannon had steadily increased. They came from the same red clay county, Harrison County. O'Bannon's family owned the local newspaper in Corydon, Indiana, and Frank—like Larry—was a fervent supporter of the IDEA. O'Bannon was elected leader of the Democratic caucus in the State Senate when Bob Fair retired. A low-key, friendly, but quiet man, O'Bannon earned the respect of everyone in the Statehouse. His lack of effusion masked his brilliance in fashioning compromises out of the most difficult political battles, whether they were between members of his own party or between the two parties. O'Bannon's leadership position had connected him with many of the business leaders in Indianapolis, and Conrad often spoke with him about issues that would affect Melvin Simon and Associates. When O'Bannon decided to run for governor in 1988, Conrad quickly agreed to serve on his committee. "I talked with Larry more than anyone else," O'Bannon says. "He was my closest confidant."[116]

Then Evan Bayh decided he wanted to make the race.

"Evan went to see Larry," Hogsett explains, "and Larry told him he had already committed to O'Bannon. He said he thought Evan was moving too quickly and making a grave mistake by pushing it too fast."[117]

Sixteen years before, it had been a thirty-seven-year-old Larry Conrad who heard similar advice from the older party leaders when he made the rounds seeking counsel on whether or not to run against Matthew Welsh in 1972. Now the generations had changed, and Larry Conrad was advising thirty-two-year-old Evan Bayh to wait.

"Larry sent me a letter," Hogsett remembers, "saying that Evan should serve one term as secretary of state and Larry would do everything to introduce Evan into the business circles so that after one term they would know him. Then he should look at higher office. He contended that Frank was already respected and well-known. He was a mature politician."[118]

The clear impression that Hogsett gleaned from his communications with Conrad was that Larry had fallen victim to an old myth of Indiana politics: Hoosiers would not elect a dynamic young man as governor. They might send such a man to Washington as a congressman or senator, but not to the governor's chair. Bayh and Hogsett rejected that myth. But their respect for Conrad, and their knowledge of his immense popularity in the party, led them to stay in touch with him.

O'Bannon's campaign suffered a major blow when campaign finance reports for 1987 were released. Evan Bayh had raised nearly a million dollars for his war chest. "We raised an incredible amount of money," Hogsett says. "At the end of 1987 Frank reported only about $250,000 to $300,000, and he had spent some of that. Our polls showed that Evan would win."[119]

Evan's formidable lead in dollars and in the polls convinced most of the insiders that the battle for the nomination was over. Even Conrad was convinced. He knew the power of money in politics and he realized that O'Bannon's name recognition was not high enough for him to be competitive against Bayh when he would be outspent four to one. Still, most of the businessmen in Indianapolis preferred O'Bannon, and Conrad sensed that something had to be done. His access to O'Bannon became a major asset to Evan Bayh.

"At that point, Larry played a role in urging Frank to go for lieutenant governor. He urged Frank to be realistic, and once Evan and Frank came together, the ticket was set," Hogsett says. O'Bannon agrees: "Larry contacted us and I talked to him about combining the ticket in order to make sure we could win in November."[120]

Conrad abandoned the notion that Bayh was too young to be governor. He started telling his friends that "Evan is the most mature thirty-two-year-old fifty-year-old I have ever met."

The Bayh-O'Bannon victory on November 8, 1988, brought the Democratic party back into power in Indiana. The party had a new leader, Governor Evan Bayh. Conrad's role as party leader was now gone forever. The transition from the old party that was chained to patronage and hatched schemes in back rooms and brokered all the nominations and money to a new party that communicated in new ways with all the people was now complete. Larry Conrad and the many men and women who worked for him and were inspired by him had led that transition.

Conrad's attention now turned away from politics and back to business. He described Melvin Simon and Associates in a speech he delivered in the late 1980s.

> I represent one of the world's largest shopping center developers. We have about 130 shopping centers in approximately 28 states, running from Framingham, Massachusetts, to El Paso, Texas. We need a lot of shopping centers so we can lose a lot of money on the Indiana Pacers.[121]

Since 1983, Conrad had been subjected to the management and organizational constraints of American business. The control mechanisms conceived by organizational theorists and executed by accountants and MBAs channel and order human behavior to produce one product: profit. Commercial developers can generate massive profits, but to do so requires massive investment. The amount of money needed for some of the projects they were undertaking was staggering to Larry Conrad, and he admitted it:

> We recently opened a $360 million mall in St. Louis. It's one of the first new things that have happened in St. Louis in years, and people are coming from 50 or 60 miles away. But it takes people to belly up to the bar and open their wallets for these things to happen. In 1979 I had my first meeting on the downtown Indianapolis mall. When we go into downtowns, the numbers just don't work because you've got high land costs and demolition costs.

> Let's just look at them in Indianapolis, and let me explain how this works. There's The Indiana Roof, which we hope to renovate, and the IRT, and the Claypool site. When we started this, we knew Indianapolis was going the way of Detroit and Philadelphia—about ready to pass over into total urban decline. We were approached by the city and we began putting down a plan. We got a $12.8 million Urban Development Action Grant to close the gap. The government takes a lump sum of money and gives it to the city and the city works out a deal to give the money to the developer when he needs it, and it is usually on the front end. There are three private dollars to one public dollar. Our firm has about $38 million in the Embassy site, and $12 million of UDAG money in that. We have about $10 million in 2 W. Washington. Between Phil Duke and us and the merchants association we have another $25 million in One North Capitol. The Indiana Repertory Theater, nobody expects to make money on. We just thought that was a damn good thing to have in our community, and we put about $600,000 in it. The total is leveraged against that $12 million in government money. Downstream, the city will recapture those dollars and reinvest in housing or commercial development.

> When you look at these things, the money becomes almost funny at times. When you're used to worrying about the price of bread or beer, it was a little tough for me to get acclimated to the size. When they say we need two retention ponds in Austin, Texas, and they are going to cost four million dollars, lets just get it done. I wasn't used to that for a while. But that's what developers have to deal with in these monstrous projects. We personally have about $75 million in downtown Indianapolis. Lilly Endowment has probably put twice that amount in downtown. I would say that all the other people have put about that same amount. And what do we have? Most people think that the largest medical complex in the world is in Kansas City. It's not. It's right here, with the IU Medical School and the seven hospitals surrounding the school. Next to that is IUPUI,

one of the largest commuter campuses in the country. It's larger than the University of Kentucky. And it has world-class athletic facilities. The swimmers and divers from all over the world come here to train and set their records. Why is this important? I used to open the New York Times and never see Indianapolis. Now I open the newspapers of the world and I read every day that there is a swimming meet in Indianapolis or a diving record has been set in our city.

He could go on and on about what was happening in his adopted city.

Then there is White River Park. The zoo is there. And to the north is the Conference Center going in on the IUPUI campus. And right over here is Union Station. On the other side, we are looking at a major theme park. I spent last Labor Day in Copenhagen, Denmark, looking at Tivoli Gardens—which is about 400 years old. And we're looking for ideas that will stop people as they are traveling from New York to Los Angeles. And it will be distinctive to Indianapolis. And that is just the start of the complex. The state government campus is going in, and then we are doing something with conventions. We built the Hoosier Dome, and it makes all the difference in the world. The symphony has a new $9 million home. And they sell out, whether it's at noon or night. We recognize the diversity of interest and it is important to fortify each and every segment of the community. We've got people looking for downtown housing, and we've got a new modern grocery store downtown. Now we have on the agenda air rights—something that only the largest cities of the world had to worry about.[122]

But it wasn't only in his hundreds of speeches to civic clubs, employer luncheons, and chamber of commerce dinners that he bragged about Indianapolis. He still delighted in "pressing the flesh" and "walking the streets." As soon as the weather turned warm in April, Larry Conrad would be seen strolling around the downtown streets, buttonholing friends and talking about the projects that were making Indianapolis a new city. By now he was sporting a pure white beard, and his portly frame would amble around Monument Circle. "Sometimes I think it would take him two hours to get back to his office," Dave Allen says. Allen, whose office window overlooks the Circle, often saw Conrad on the sidewalk, many stories below. "He couldn't get ten feet without somebody stopping him and then there would be a long conversation, with Conrad pointing up to one building or gesturing toward the Statehouse. I swear, everybody who worked downtown knew and loved Larry Conrad."[123]

Most of his energies were invested in Indianapolis, but his affection for the entire state often got him out of Marion County and into the other cities. Conrad hatched an idea that the mission of Partners for Livable Places should not be directed just nationally. In addition, each state should have an affiliated program to define problems and work on long-term solutions. Conrad worked with Michael Carroll, who had joined the Lilly

Endowment to work on metropolitan programs, and secured Lilly funding for more than a million dollars to establish the international division of Partners in Indianapolis. The grant money would also support Partners for Livable Indiana, the first state affiliate of the national organization.[124]

Now he consciously sought out opportunities to speak in other Indiana cities, calling on business leaders to find a common theme to use in reigniting urban growth and pride. And he found himself in demand throughout the country. The political and business leaders of Greeley, Colorado, Memphis, Tennessee, Dallas, Texas, and scores of others called him to schedule speeches to their civic groups.

> I had a call from a businessman in Greeley, Colorado. He said he had heard about all the great things going on in Indianapolis and wondered if I could drop down in Greeley and speak to some of the city leaders about how we did it back here in Indiana. I said, "What do you mean, drop down?" "Well," he said, "I know you travel all the time, and I thought maybe when you are passing over Colorado you could simply lay over for a day or so." I told him I couldn't do that. "How do you expect me to light a fire under the civic leaders of Greeley when they are not even willing to open their wallets for a couple of hundred bucks to fly me out there?" He said he understood. A couple of days later he called back and said he had raised enough for my plane ticket and wondered what day I could be there. I told him, "Now we're talking. You've got somebody taking a risk. I'll come."[125]

The majority of Conrad's trips involved solving problems in the far-flung operations of Melvin Simon and Associates. His corporate division was becoming the lightning rod for hundreds of small and large problems relating to government regulations in the scores of communities where Simon and Associates had property and commercial operations. Conrad became the policy operative for solving many of the development problems for the corporation, such as requests for special tax abatements or zones, or government commitments for infrastructure improvements, or special permits. And these policy problems were becoming more complex as the boom years of the 1980s turned to bust.

In the fall of 1987 the stock markets of the world plummeted. That was the first major signal that the borrow, build, and spend years were over. The owners of Melvin Simon and Associates, Inc. began to realize that they were overextended in some of their developments. The Mall of America in Minnesota, for example, had required years of planning and hundreds of millions of dollars. Cutbacks had to be made.

Conrad increasingly felt he was in a corporate straightjacket. The internal accountants began demanding that budgets of all divisions be slashed. Larry Conrad never was one to deliver bad news. His inveterate optimism was too naive for the inner intrigues that accompany corporate downsizing. He was well aware that other officials were beginning to question the necessity for a vice-presidential division devoted to "corporate affairs." When he was informed—not by Herb Simon—that massive layoffs were required in his division, Conrad began planning his departure from Melvin Simon and Associates.[126]

Throughout 1989 he shared some of his thoughts with Robert McNulty, president of Partners for Livable Places. McNulty remembers their conversations. "Larry was increasingly unhappy. The constant pressure to solve all the policy problems with the developments began to erode his spirit. When he lost much of key staff—and they were all loyal to Larry—the final corrosion had set in."[127]

In November of 1989, more trouble came the way of Conrad and the other "movers and shakers" of Indianapolis. On Monday, November 13, the *Indianapolis News* published the first of a seven-part series purportedly looking into the "Lilly Endowment and its impact on the city." The City Committee came in for severe criticism, with allegations that women were excluded from the private meetings and that many of the decisions made by the committee furthered the economic interests of the members. In an editorial concluding the series, the *News* opined: "The series explored the role the endowment had in creating a kind of city government outside the government—the informal and influential City Committee—that had tremendous influence over the city's priorities and policies."[128]

The newspaper series marked the end of the days when, as Conrad himself expressed it, "No place in the country can boast about having so many people moving in the same direction regardless of race, sex, creed or political affiliation. Whether you talk about sports, the arts, education or something else, there is just a feeling here that we can do damn near anything we want to."[129]

Conrad's thoughts increasingly turned back to the days of Conrad and Hafsten. The complete freedom he had to engage in those activities that most interested him had to appear as some of the best times of his adult life. He did not have the huge salary that came with being the vice-president of one of the world's leading development companies, but he also did not have to abide by orders to change his schedule at the last moment to fly to New Jersey or Minneapolis or St. Louis to solve a technical problem. He decided he would leave the Simons and launch a new firm, specializing in governmental relations and corporate consulting. The name would be The Conrad Group. He would be working for himself once again.

Discreet inquiries were made to the principals in some of the leading law firms in the city, and finally it was arranged that The Conrad Group would move into the offices of a local attorney, Jim Smith. Smith had served in the governor's office under Otis Bowen, and his law practice specialized in government relations. It was agreed that the two firms would be in a position to refer clients to one another. In November 1989,

The Conrad Group, consisting of Larry and Claudia, set up shop in the Smith law firm offices in the Indiana National Bank Building. As usual, their primary client was Melvin Simon and Associates, whose interests they would continue to represent.[130]

Conrad's enthusiasm for this new venture was dampened by several factors. Whereas he would not be taking a major cut in pay, he would be starting over again to build a business. And he was now fifty-four years old. In recent months he seemed to lack the energy he had in his younger years. When he caught a cold, it seemed to hang on longer. Yet even longer hours would be required to build a new client base for his new business. His eternal optimism assuaged his doubts, however. He always preached optimism, and now he could recall some of the many lines in the many speeches he had delivered to others:

> In the fast and swift course of life, victory does not always go to the fastest nor the swiftest. Victory always goes to the sure.

> I've seen rain and I've seen fire in my life. I've seen sunny days you thought would never end. But they always do. And they always come back again.

One of his first ideas was to return to his commitment to Partners for Livable Places and spend more time invigorating the Indiana affiliate. "We talked a lot about his taking over Indiana Partners," Bob McNulty explains. "He wanted to become the head of this. We had some problems with the Indiana group. Larry always supported it, but because he was on the national board of directors, we had placed the seed money under the control of others in Indiana, and some of these people saw Indiana Partners as a potential rival to their own groups. They were dragging their feet."[131]

Conrad and McNulty had discussed the possibility that Conrad might resign from the national board and take charge of Indiana Partners. It was agreed that Conrad should discuss this with Michael Carroll at Lilly Endowment and see if they would approve Larry's controlling the remaining $750,000 in seed money. "Larry talked about hiring a couple of people to help him champion the cause," McNulty says. They agreed to discuss it in more detail while they were traveling together in Europe in a few months, in June of 1990.[132]

*I've already led three lives. In 1962, I had the
opportunity to go to work for Senator Birch Bayh
in Washington, where I became the youngest Chief
Counsel in the history of the Subcommittee on
Constitutional Amendments—and wrote the 25th
Amendment to our Constitution. Now that's a
high honor for any citizen, and particularly for any
lawyer. That was my first life. Then I came back
here to Indiana and was elected Secretary of
State—and then I ran for Governor. Now not
many of you know that because I kept it pretty
much a secret at the time. I'm one of only 416
people who have ever stood for the Office of
Governor of our state—and that was like a second
life. Now, in my third life, I'm in business with
Melvin Simon and Associates, one of the largest
shopping center developers in the world. I travel
here and there—all over the world—and I meet
great people and see wonders everywhere. So I have
no regrets, but I sure don't expect to quit soon. We
have too much to do, even right here in Indiana.
But when the Good Lord calls me—and he will call
me—as he will all of us, I hope to be in my boots,
in full stride, with both guns a-blazing. Of course,
I hope to engage Him in a little dialogue first.*

—Larry A. Conrad

Larry Conrad's dialogue with the Good Lord began on June 4, 1990, when he and Mary Lou left on a European tour for Partners for Livable Places. The first stop was to be Strasbourg, France, where the Council of Europe was meeting.

For several months Larry had not been feeling well. He was lethargic and often short of breath. The previous winter he had checked into the hospital for tests. He was diagnosed as having a respiratory infection. In early December of 1989, Mary Lou and Larry spent a week on the warm beaches of the Cayman Islands.

Upon their return, Larry still commented about his lack of energy. One day in early spring, he was scheduled to have lunch with Bob Boxell, but called that morning and cancelled, saying he was not feeling well.[1]

He had never before experienced major health problems. Mary Lou always insisted on his having regular physical exams. In the early summer of 1973, he had experienced excruciating pain, which he attributed to indigestion, and which was diagnosed as a gall bladder attack. Conrad underwent surgery to have his gall bladder removed. His recovery was normal, but he did experience difficulty with the incision, which split open and required another visit to the hospital. Mary Lou remembers it well: "I had him go back to the hospital because the scar split open. The doctor joked about it, saying 'it had to heal too much fat.'"[2]

Mary Lou was always concerned about his health. Yet: "His health was good, considering the way he abused himself. He never had headaches and suffered from only four or five colds all the time we were married. He had a little arthritis in his knees and occasional bouts of indigestion, but that was understandable. I worried about his not getting enough sleep, but my biggest worry was his weight. That is what I really got angry about."[3] Mary Lou always had taken extraordinary steps to control Larry's diet, to no avail.

During the early morning hours of Monday, June 4, Larry and Mary Lou were at home, doing last-minute packing. At 10:30 A.M. Larry drove to his mother's house and picked her up to spend the next few hours with her. Ruby had been living in Indianapolis since Marshall passed away in 1987. Amy drove them to the airport, dropping Ruby off at her house. The TWA flight from Indianapolis to New York departed on time at 1:40 P.M.

The Air France transatlantic flight was to leave from the international terminal at JFK at 7 P.M., with arrival in Paris at 7:45 the next morning. When Larry and Mary Lou landed at JFK, they caught a crowded shuttle bus to the international terminal. Larry was standing, facing Mary Lou, who was seated. He was jostled several times by a man holding a cloth bag. When they arrived at the international terminal Larry discovered that his wallet was missing. In all likelihood, the man on the shuttle with the cloth bag had lifted his billfold. He did have dollars in his money clip in his side pocket, but all his credit cards and other valuables were gone. He placed a call to his secretary in Indianapolis to begin cancelling his credit cards. The long trip to Europe was not off to a propitious start.

Once airborne, Larry immediately ordered two gin cocktails for himself and champagne for Mary Lou. The meal was ordered from "a good menu," as Larry wrote in his diary, and he had a salmon and beef entree. Larry could not sleep on the flight, but Mary Lou managed to doze.[4]

The plane arrived on time in Paris and Larry and Mary Lou had to "chase over the airport to the B station for the Inter Air flight to Strasbourg," due to depart at 2:50 P.M. "We're very tired," Larry wrote in his diary. They sprawled out on a bench in the terminal and dozed. The plane finally departed at 3:30 P.M., and this time Larry managed to sleep. When the plane touched down in Strasbourg, there was "a real bang on landing." The brakes locked and squealed and the plane veered to the right as the pilot shut down the engines. The plane rolled to a stop on the main runway and a steward rushed "down the aisle wiping his forehead in jest." The pilot finally announced that the hydraulics had malfunctioned and the plane would have to be towed. Fire trucks had surrounded the plane. When the tow truck arrived the plane was pulled to a hangar and Larry and Mary Lou walked with the other passengers "all the way back to the terminal."[5]

At 6:30 P.M. Larry and Mary Lou were finally in their Strasbourg hotel room, enjoying "the beautiful view of the cathedral and canal." That evening they joined some of the other trustees, including John Krauss and Ellen Hornbeck. Later, Larry wrote in his diary that they drank beer and wine and ate "sausage, blood pudding, bacon, ham and sauerkraut, and boiled potatoes." Larry topped off his meal with "fromage." They took an after-dinner stroll and were back at the hotel and in bed at 9 P.M. The wake-up call came at 8 A.M. Larry wrote that he felt "drugged and still have virus, but not too much a problem." After breakfast, Larry and several others caught a taxi to the Palace of the European Congress where they attended a session on "spacial planning." After lunch the delegation took a boat tour on the city canal and Larry noted in his diary that they had passed a "restaurant where Herb and I ate years ago."

That evening for dinner, Larry indulged in "jugs of wine, a cheese salad, bread, pig knuckles, hot potato salad and strudel." The dinner conversation was "lots of fun." Larry was doing his best to eat his way through France.

He took extensive notes on the various sessions he attended, punctuating his notes with observations about Indianapolis, writing, "Mike Carroll—need International Center like Council of Europe Chamber to *meet* and *exchange*"; and "high speed trains: Indianapolis–St. Louis–Louisville–Columbus–Chicago–Fort Wayne– Cincinnati."[6]

On June 9 the delegation was to proceed by train to Geneva, Switzerland, making an interim stop at a medieval village. Before touring the village, Bob McNulty joined Larry and Mary Lou for lunch. They all enjoyed the fabulous food and wine, and the luncheon conversation continued for three hours. Conrad informed McNulty of his hectic schedule and the pressures he faced in attempting to consolidate clients for The Conrad Group, describing it as a "hurly-burly" process. They discussed the obstacles in the way of rejuvenating Partners in Indiana. Finally, they decided to walk through the village and McNulty, with a flourish, picked up the luncheon tab because "poor Larry" didn't have his wallet.[7]

The rail connection to Geneva involved a change of trains. When they arrived at the transfer station, the Geneva train was already waiting. The delegates had no time to spare. Larry and Mary Lou were sitting with two female Partners trustees. Larry grabbed his and Mary Lou's luggage, then offered to take some of their companions' suitcases. Hurriedly carrying and dragging luggage for four people, Larry managed to get on board, tossing the suitcases on the overhead racks just as the doors closed and the train began moving. He collapsed in his seat, flushed and panting, and remarked to Mary Lou that he was really "strained."

A resident of Geneva who had recently become a Partners trustee had made arrangements with the mayor of Geneva to host a dinner party for the American delegation. The mayor rolled out the red carpet. The evening began with a visit to a vineyard where the private reserves were tapped and the glasses were kept filled. From there they went to a hunting lodge for dinner and more wine. The fine food and the fruit of the vine restored Conrad's exuberance, and he regaled the party with his "picture stories" of his days "working for the guvment."

The next morning the delegation boarded a bus for the trip to Lyon, whose mayor, Michel Rivoire, was president of Partners Europe. The bus stopped at an abbey where lunch was served and more wine was consumed. The next stop was a chateau just outside Belley which was owned by Rivoire's close friend, Charles Millon. Millon was mayor of Belley and had served as vice-chairman of the French National Assembly in 1986. The delegation, after imbibing more wine, toured his estate.

Bob McNulty clearly remembers Larry saying, as he sipped his wine, "I don't feel very well." John Krauss recalls walking through the courtyard and asking, "Where's Larry?" Somebody said, "he's sitting over there." He was sitting on a bench in the courtyard. Krauss looked at him and thought, "Larry's not looking well at all."[8]

Larry got up and started walking toward the bus. Mary Lou caught up with him. "He could barely walk," Mary Lou later wrote in her diary.[9] She took the camera case from him and helped him onto the bus. He sat in a seat directly behind the driver and Mary Lou sat next to him. As others got on the bus they expressed their concern, and he replied, "I'll be O.K., I just don't feel very well." He told Mary Lou that he had a sharp pain, "front and center between my lungs." He described it as a "toothache," never ceasing nor decreasing. Then he closed his eyes and leaned his head back as the bus pulled away, heading for Lyon.

It was nearly two hours before the bus arrived in front of the Concorde Hotel in Lyon. As Larry and Mary Lou got off, he said: "Mary, get me to the room. I must lie down." They immediately checked into room 404, "the most depressing old room we'd ever stayed in," Mary Lou wrote in her diary. It was 8:30 P.M. and the pain continued.

Mary Lou propped him up in bed; the pain was so intense he could not lie down. For the next hour there was no improvement and Mary Lou's concern was growing. A little before ten o'clock, she called a physician. He arrived at the room at 10:30 and quickly checked Larry, diagnosing extreme gastritis caused by all the wine and food. He gave Larry three nitro pills, a sleeping pill, and an injection for pain.

The doctor left briefly, returning at 11:30 with a portable EKG machine. Larry told him the pain had not subsided, and the doctor recommended that they get to a hospital quickly. "We were both terrified," Mary Lou wrote.[10]

At 1 A.M. the ambulance pulled up to the emergency room at the Grand Blanch Hospital. Mary Lou's worry deepened when she saw the hospital. "It was an old, old, socialized medical facility," she wrote. "It was a depressing place, and nobody spoke English." An intern examined him first, then brought in a physician who said that he needed an entire battery of internal tests, but the hospital had no open beds. It was clear to the doctor that Larry belonged in a cardiology hospital, and he ordered an ambulance to take him to the Hopital Cardiovasculaire et Pneumologique Louis Pradel.[11]

The ambulance arrived at the cardiology hospital's emergency room at 5:30 A.M. and the physicians immediately began tests. Within an hour Larry was moved to room 662, where the tests continued. For the first time in over twelve hours Mary Lou felt some relief. "I could tell that the doctors knew what they were doing," she wrote. The head of the cardiology unit was the physician in charge; he ordered several EKG and ultrasound tests. By mid-afternoon the diagnosis was certain: Larry's aorta was ruptured. Surgery was required immediately. Mary Lou was in a daze. She knew there was no chance for a second diagnosis; there was no alternative. "We had to rely on a lot of faith," she wrote.[12]

As Larry was being prepared for surgery, Amy was finally able to get a telephone call through to the room, where she talked to her father. At 9 P.M. he was moved to surgery. "I kissed Larry goodbye," Mary Lou wrote. "It was the most difficult moment of my life. He did not feel confident, nor did I."[13]

The surgeon estimated that the procedure would last about three hours, and Mary Lou located a telephone and called all the children. She then began the long wait.

Around midnight Michel Rivoire and Margo Wellington, another member of Partners, came to the hospital and waited with Mary Lou. At 1:30 A.M. the surgeon finally appeared and told Mary Lou there were many complications. A second surgery was needed to halt hemorrhaging in the thorax. Rivoire and Wellington arranged for the hospital to provide Mary Lou a room to get some sleep.

At 7:30 A.M. the surgeon called Mary Lou and then came to her room. He informed her that Larry's condition was very serious and that the surgery had been difficult. The surgical team had to reinforce all the arteries on one side of the brain, as well as arteries to the kidneys. Larry was suffering from a type-one aortic dissection.

Like a piece of delaminating plywood, an artery can split apart in layers. When the dissection occurs, the blood continues pumping between the layers, in the false channels, forcing the artery apart. The dissection spreads. Of the various types of aortic dissections, this is the most severe. A type-one dissection occurs above the aortic valve and can spread quickly to the carotid artery, which supplies blood to the brain. This had happened to Larry, but the rupturing also had spread to his renal artery.

During the first three and one-half hours of surgery, the doctors had removed the dissected section of the aorta and replaced it with an artificial lining. Then it became clear that the dissection had spread to both the carotid and renal arteries and these in turn had to be repaired with artificial linings. That took another six and one-half hours in the operating room. There was over a 90-percent risk factor in such cases. Larry was in very critical condition. For the time being, however, he was stable. All that could be done now was to wait.

Michel Rivoire made arrangements to transfer the Conrads' luggage to the 140-room Hotel Ibis Lyon Bron Montchat, located immediately east of the hospital. Like many other European tourist hotels, it had a small registration area, with a restaurant off the lobby. During the spring, summer, and fall, sliding glass doors opened off the restaurant onto a shaded terrace, with umbrella tables, surrounded by grass and a waist-high hedge. This hotel was to be home for Mary Lou for the next month. The Conrad children and their spouses, as they came and left, also stayed at the Ibis, as did Claudia Prosser and her niece, Sara. The death watch had begun.

When Larry was first stricken, Claudia Prosser and Sara were in London. This was Prosser's first trip to Europe, and her niece was accompanying her. They were to visit England, stop in Paris, then join the Conrads in Lyon. Prosser learned of Larry's attack and immediately called Lyon. "My French was not very good then," she recalls, "and all I could find out was that Larry was still alive." She finally got through to Amy in Indianapolis. They decided Claudia and Sara should continue with their travel plans since Amy, her husband, John, and Jody were booking a flight to Lyon.[14]

But on Tuesday, June 12, Prosser talked with a nurse at the hospital and learned of the extended surgery and the hemorrhaging. She immediately booked a British Airways flight to Lyon leaving that afternoon. Mary Lou made arrangements for Michel Rivoire and John Krauss to meet Claudia and Sara at the airport. When they arrived at the hospital, Mary Lou was waiting in the lobby. She had been expecting Claudia and her niece, as well as Amy, John, and Jody.

Mary Lou, Claudia, Sara, Michel, and John Krauss immediately went up to see Larry, and found Amy, John, and Jody outside Larry's door. They had mistakenly first gone to the hospital next door, and missed Mary Lou when they proceeded, finally, to Larry's room. They could see Larry through the glass partition; he was on a respirator, in a large circular room. "We could see the back of his head," Prosser remembers, "and we had an intercom to talk to him. I saw immediately he had no movement on his right side." They took turns talking to Larry. John Krauss remembers Larry responding to Amy's and Claudia's voices, but not to his.[15]

That evening everyone ate at the hotel and Mary Lou attempted to relate all the developments of the past two days—the lengthy surgery, the loss of oxygen to the brain, the acute kidney failure, and the partial paralysis. There was continuing concern about infection.

The next day Michel arranged for a translator to meet with Mary Lou and the doctors. They indicated that Larry would need to be moved to another room for dialysis. They were also going to test for any brain damage. That evening the Conrad clan dined again at the hotel and then played a game of euchre.

Mary Lou finally got a respite the next day when she and Amy went to a local pub for lunch. They walked through the winding streets of Lyon, talking for hours. "We walked and walked and walked," Mary Lou wrote. That afternoon the doctor reported that it would take two to three weeks of dialysis, and they were looking for gradual but steady improvement. They reassured the family that the procedure was not endangering Larry and explained that his slow reflexes were due to the lack of blood flow to the brain during the surgery. They also pointed out that he was heavily sedated and they should not expect immediate responses from him. There were continuing complications. Larry's potassium level was elevated and they had to make several changes in his medication.

Slowly Mary Lou and the others began establishing a routine. Visiting hours in the intensive care unit were restricted to two hours a day, from 2 to 4 P.M. Visitors entering the room were required to dress in white hats, blue gowns, and white booties.

On Sunday, Michel and his wife invited Mary Lou and family to their house for lunch. By now everyone had mastered the Lyon bus system and they took the No. 28 route downtown, where they strolled along the Rhone before lunch. They were back at the hospital by 2 P.M. and Mary Lou, Amy, and John visited Larry. She wrote in her diary: "He responded to us and showed some improvement over yesterday. His eyes met mine for the first time. He was pleading for my help. I feel so helpless! I told him I loved him and would take care of him forever. He truly heard me."[16]

The next day Amy, John, and Jody returned to Indiana. Mary Lou had to summon all of her strength to say goodbye, but she knew they could not remain indefinitely.

The waiting was wearing Mary Lou down. She had run out of her blood pressure medication and was experiencing palpitations. When she looked at herself in the mirror she saw bulging, bloodshot eyes. She finally made arrangements to see a French doctor. Her blood pressure was 175 / 105. He immediately replenished her medication.

On Tuesday, June 19, Andy and his wife, Patty, arrived in Lyon, along with Diane Simon and her three children. Another visitor from Indiana that day was a specialist in interventional cardiology.[17]

In her search for answers about Larry's illness, Mary Lou had called an old family friend, Dr. Edward Steinmetz, an Indianapolis cardiologist. As luck would have it, one of Steinmetz's partners, Dr. Thomas J. Linnemeier, was then in France, attending an international medical conference in Nice.

The conference invitation had provided Linnemeier an opportunity to combine a family vacation with continuing education. Scratching three weeks from his Indianapolis calendar, Tom Linnemeier and his wife, Georgiann, their three daughters, Tom's mother, and Georgiann's mother and father had all rented a villa in Saint Tropez, outside of Nice. As they were checking in at the villa, the phone rang. It was Stan Hollis, another partner.

Linnemeier remembers the call well. "Stan said Larry had an attack and was in the hospital in Lyon, and with the language problems Mary Lou had no idea what was going on. He asked me if there was any way I could get to Lyon. I told him I would leave first thing in the morning." Alice Hollis then called Mary Lou and told her to expect Tom the next day.

At that time, Tom Linnemeier had no idea where Lyon was. Since both he and his father-in-law were pilots, they initially considered renting an airplane and flying there. The next morning they set out in their rental car, searching for an airport. But a plane was not immediately available. They turned the car north, through the Alps, toward Lyon—a four-and-a-half-hour drive.

At the hospital, after discussing Larry's condition with the attending physician in the intensive care unit, Linnemeier examined the patient. "His pupils were dilated. He had only cortical reflexes, but it appeared the operation was holding. But the rest of his body was going."[18]

When Linnemeier looked at the angiogram X-rays "I saw an unbelievable split. It was not subtle. It was horrendous. The inner lining of the aorta was literally flapping in the bloodstream. Often it is very difficult to detect where the split is occurring, but not in this case. It would have been an excellent photo illustration for medical students."[19]

Linnemeier was well aware of the grave situation facing Larry. He knew the terrible pain associated with an aortic dissection and the severe risk that occurs when the dissection has spread to the carotid artery. "It was very serious. The dissection had nearly amputated the artery, depriving the brain of its blood supply. It is a huge operation to try to save somebody from this."[20]

Later, at the Hotel Ibis, Linnemeier told Mary Lou that he could not believe Larry had survived. A type-one aortic dissection is extremely dangerous and survival rates during surgery are low. He explained that the type of surgery performed on Larry "had to be done very quickly after the diagnosis and unless the timing was perfect, surgeons would not normally perform this operation, even in Indianapolis." He reassured Mary Lou that the paralysis was temporary and his brain damage was confined to some motor skills. He then said Larry had a little less than a 50–50 chance of surviving. Mary Lou thanked him. He gave her his phone number at the villa, and he and his father-in-law left for the return trip to Saint Tropez.[21]

That evening Larry was able to move his right side. Mary Lou's spirits soared.

Diane Simon had rented two limousines. Now they were able to venture out beyond the bus routes for lunch and dinner. On Friday, June 22, all of France began a celebration of music, culminating in a fireworks party on June 24, the Night of St. Jean. Bands were playing in the parks and plazas. People were dancing in the streets of Lyon. Mary Lou wrote in her diary: "We struggled with the limo in the tiny streets filled with people." That morning Larry had suffered a seizure, but the doctors stabilized him quickly. The next afternoon Mary Lou was in the room with Larry. "He focused his eyes on me and cried a tear," she wrote. "He knows! He's so afraid."

Diane and her children returned to Indiana on Monday, June 25, and the next day Jeb and his wife, Sam, arrived. By now, Larry's kidneys were functioning again and he was off dialysis. On Thursday of that week Andy and Patty Conrad left for the states.

The doctors had detected internal bleeding—referring to it as "a small leak"—and ordered another battery of tests to determine the exact location. A physical therapist was working with Larry every day and there was more movement evident on his right side.

But another problem was confronting the doctors: infection. A bacteriologist had been treating Larry's lung infection and had finally determined that it was fungal in origin. On Saturday, June 30, he called Mary Lou and requested a meeting. He said he did not know what type of fungus was involved, and asked Mary Lou and Claudia where Larry had been during the last two or three years. They started naming the trips. The Cayman Islands. Cuba. Kenya. He told them he would continue his tests to determine the exact nature of the infection. It was dangerous because the infection could attach itself to the artificial linings. That would be fatal.

Two days later the bacteriologist had the answer: histoplasmosis. Claudia remembers thinking: "A good old Midwest fungus from pigeon shit."[22]

During the first three days of July, Larry showed slow but steady progress. He was still heavily sedated. "Those were the best days he had," Claudia remembers. "He was heavily drugged because they did not want him to move and break loose the artificial parts in the arteries. Larry would squeeze my hand but he could not speak."[23]

On July 3 Claudia took her niece to Paris where they visited Notre Dame and lit candles for Larry.

That night was the beginning of the end. Larry's temperature soared. The high fever destroyed his hearing. The doctor thought the impairment could be temporary, but the setback was devastating. Mary Lou was very discouraged. She placed a call to Tom Linnemeier, who, by now, had returned to Indianapolis. "Mary Lou told me they had found a fungus growing in his blood. I knew immediately that when you get those bad infections, the patient is terminal. I consoled Mary Lou, and told her I could not say what she should do, but it was close to the time to turn the machines off and end the agony."[24]

Claudia kept telling Mary Lou that Larry's fighting spirit and energy were not gone. But Claudia also knew that she was not confronting the facts. Larry no longer responded with a squeeze when Claudia took his hand. On Thursday, July 5, his breathing was erratic. His heartbeat was irregular. By that night he was stable again. On Friday, Claudia remembers him being "absolutely peaceful." All vital signs were O.K.

The next morning Claudia and Mary Lou met in the hotel restaurant for their morning coffee. Suddenly, Mary Lou received a page from the hospital. She went to the phone, then returned to the table and said: "Let's go. This is it."[25]

They walked to the hospital, paged the doctor, and waited, holding hands, for about twenty minutes until the doctor came in. He said: "In the night his temperature went way up." Claudia interrupted: "Is he alive or is he gone?"

"He's gone." Mary and Claudia cried.

The doctor gently asked if they wanted to see Larry. Mary Lou said "Yes." The doctor left them alone for a few minutes; a nurse then entered and escorted them into a narrow room. Mary Lou and Claudia joined hands and walked, each on one side of the bed, with their joined hands over Larry's body. His eyes were open. Claudia backed away. Then each of them felt his naked shoulder. He was warm. "We both talked to him," Claudia says. "We each told him we loved him."

When they left, the doctor asked them if they could perform an autopsy. Mary Lou was in a daze. She looked at the doctor, but could not speak. Claudia finally replied: "No." She now wonders if that was the best decision. "He was in one of the best hospitals in the world. Maybe they could have learned something in that autopsy."[26]

Now, in all their sorrow, they had to make funeral and travel arrangements. They returned to the hotel about 11 A.M. and Claudia called Michel Rivoire's friend, who left immediately to join them. She then called the American consulate in Lyon, where a Dr. Stafford was the envoy. Then she tried the American Embassy in Paris and finally got an operator who said the embassy was "closed until Monday, but I'll try to get the message to somebody." Claudia never heard back from the embassy.

Mary Lou and Claudia met with Rivoire's friend in the hotel lobby, where he assured them that he would take care of all arrangements. They went back upstairs to Mary Lou's room and she called the children, informing each of them that "Daddy passed away." Claudia then called Indianapolis and talked to Lisa, the secretary at The Conrad Group. She also spoke with Jim Smith, and then she called her sister. The next call went to Diane Simon, and then Mary Lou called her brother.

After the calls, Claudia told Mary Lou she was going to order some drinks sent up to the room. "As Larry would have said," Claudia notes, "we needed some 'fresh horses' at that point."

The next day they attended an art fair in downtown Lyon, and Rivoire took them to the Lyon Rose Garden. On Monday, the envoy, Dr. Stafford, an African-American woman, came to the hotel and gave Larry's cancelled passport to Claudia. She then said to Mary Lou: "Regardless of the circumstances, I hope your stay in Lyon has been enjoyable. I find the people to be kind, but because I am the representative of President Bush, I'm treated differently."[27]

Mary Lou had been informed that during the flight back the body would have to be held in New York for twenty-four hours. They both agreed that they did not want to stay overnight in New York, but they were not going to leave the body there while they flew on to Indianapolis. In discussing their itinerary, Claudia finally said, "Mary Lou, we know a lot of people. Why don't we get in touch with them?" She pointed out that Vice-President Dan Quayle had faxed her when he learned of Larry's death. Then Claudia remembered that the Health Commissioner for New York City was Woody Myers, former Health Commissioner for the State of Indiana. Claudia suggested they get in touch with Myers. "Now you're thinking again," Mary Lou responded.[28]

Claudia called Lisa in Indianapolis and had her track down Woody Myers. Myers was shocked at the news about Larry. He told Lisa that he would take care of everything. There would be no twenty-four-hour wait. He gave Lisa the name of a contact who would be available the day the flight landed at JFK.

A Biography

Both Air France and TWA upgraded their tickets. When they arrived at JFK, there was about a two-hour layover and they were then on their way to Indiana. It had been five days since Larry's death.

Mary Lou had already decided that the funeral service would be private. The children had made the arrangements through Max Nelson at Aaron-Ruben-Nelson Funeral Home, and had selected Larry's final resting place, at Crown Hill Cemetery. The private service was scheduled for Monday, July 16.

After that, the rest of the week was consumed with planning the public memorial service. For the family it was a diversion from their devastation. They had to make decisions about music, speakers, and ushers.

The public memorial service was set for Sunday, July 22. Diane Simon had suggested that it be held at Eagle's Crest, a special preserve within Eagle Creek Park on the northwest side of Indianapolis. After Claudia inspected the area and the park, Mary Lou agreed.

On Sunday, in a light mist of rain, hundreds of people came to console Mary Lou, the family, and themselves. They came to mourn—and to celebrate—Larry Conrad, a man who had touched each of them in such profound ways, and who was now physically gone from their lives.

Each person received a cream-colored card on which was printed:

I find the great thing in this world is not so much where we stand, as in the direction we're moving . . . we must sail sometimes with the wind and sometimes against it—but we *must* sail, and not drift, or lie at anchor.

OLIVER WENDELL HOLMES

LARRY A. CONRAD LIVED HIS LIFE BY THESE WORDS AND SPOKE THEM OFTEN. THEY ARE HIS LEGACY TO ALL WHOSE LIVES WERE TOUCHED BY HIM.

July 22, 1990

NOTES

1

1. Douglas S. Freeman, *R. E. Lee: A Biography,* vol. 1 (New York: Charles Scribners, 1934), p. 436.

2. See Douglas Waitley, *Portrait of the Midwest: From the Ice Age to the Industrial Era* (New York: Abelard-Schuman, 1963), ch. 5.

3. Accounts differ as to the exact size of Morgan's force. The captain of the steamboat *T. J. McCombs* reportedly said that 4,800 men and 5,000 horses landed in Indiana. See Edison H. Thomas, *John Hunt Morgan and His Raiders* (Lexington: University Press of Kentucky, 1975), p. 78. Also see W. Fred Conway, *Corydon: The Forgotten Battle of the Civil War* (New Albany, Ind.: FBH Publishers, 1991).

4. Some of the facts on the river crossing are based on a senior term paper by Larry A. Conrad from Ball State Teachers College entitled "Morgan's Ohio Raid" (undated, probably 1957), in possession of the author. Conrad relied both on scholarly works and interviews with his relatives and "an old resident of Corydon."

5. Conrad, "Morgan's Ohio Raid," p. 11. After crossing the Ohio on the two steamboats, Morgan set fire to one, the *Alice Dean,* which sank about 100 yards off the Indiana shoreline. When the river was low, her cypress hull was often visible. In 1966, during the construction of the Matthew E. Welsh toll bridge at Mauckport, the wreckage of the *Alice Dean* was raised by several residents of Harrison County. They intended to start a local museum, but it was never built. Many artifacts from the steamboat were sold at flea markets and auctions. Larry Conrad obtained a small piece of cypress from the *Alice Dean* and had it mounted as a wall plaque.

6. Mary Jane Mynett interview with author, June 30, 1994. Mynett is a first cousin to Larry A. Conrad and a great-granddaughter of Harvey Huffman.

7. Howard H. Peckham, *Indiana: A Bicentennial History* (New York: W. W. Norton & Company, 1978), pp. 72–74.

8. The following account of the Rooksby family relies heavily on Ruby Rooksby Conrad, "The Rooksby Heritage," in *The Rooksby Reunion,* vol. 1:2 (Summer 1981), in possession of author.

9. Ibid.

10. Central Normal College was a private normal school. When it closed in 1951, the school claimed that nearly one-third of the teachers in Indiana had taken

courses there. See James H. Madison, *Indiana Through Tradition and Change: A History of the Hoosier State and Its People, 1920–1945* (Indianapolis: Indiana Historical Society, 1982), pp. 284–285.

11. Harry Jackson interview with author, April 20, 1993. A few weeks later, Jackson was killed in a traffic accident on Route 60. He was alone in his pickup truck when another vehicle crossed the center line and hit him head on. State Senator James Lewis (D-Charlestown), introduced Senate Bill 107 in the 1993 Indiana General Assembly. It passed and took effect July 1, 1993. It allows towns with less than 500 people to change the town name by petition rather than election.

12. Larry Lee Johnson interview with author, May 13, 1993.

13. Remarks of Mary Lou Conrad at funeral service for Ruby Rooksby Conrad, July 27, 1994, Corydon, Indiana.

14. Larry Lee Johnson interview with author, May 13, 1993.

15. Edward J. (Joe) Beck interview with author, February 14, 1996.

16. Larry Lee Johnson interview with author, May 13, 1993.

17. Letter from Larry Conrad to Larry Lee Johnson, dated March 19, 1963, in possession of author.

18. Charles Hiatt interview with author, March 9, 1994. Hiatt attended high school with Conrad. Coach Lawrence "Jay" McCreary left Muncie Central after the 1957 season to take the head basketball coaching position at Louisiana State University. He died April 17, 1995, at age 77. See "Jay McCreary dies; coached 'Cats vs. Milan," *Muncie Evening Press,* April 17, 1995, p. 1.

19. Jerry Thornburg interview with author, October 19, 1993. Thornburg attended high school with Conrad.

20. In a letter to Larry Lee Johnson, dated September 26, 1951, Conrad wrote: "We are having class elections here and I have to give a speech, which I truly hate." Tom Raisor, now an attorney in Muncie, declined to be interviewed for this book.

21. Larry Lee Johnson interview with author, May 13, 1993.

22. Letter from Larry Conrad to Larry Lee Johnson, dated March 19, 1963, in possession of author.

23. Letter from Larry Conrad to Larry Lee Johnson, dated May 5, 1949, in possession of author.

24. Letter from Larry Conrad to Larry Lee Johnson, dated April 19, 1953, in possession of author.

25. The story of the 1954 Milan Indians is told in Greg Guffey, *The Greatest Basketball Story Ever Told: The Milan Miracle, Then and Now* (Bloomington: Indiana University Press, 1993).

26. Larry Lee Johnson interview with author, May 13, 1993.

27. Ibid. Johnson did not make his grades that first year. He returned to Borden where he got a job at the cabinet company. He returned to Ball State in 1960, by which time he was married and had a young daughter. Living in married student housing and working part-time as a barber—a job Marshall Conrad helped him find—he finally graduated in 1964 and took a teaching position in Borden, where he also coached.

28. Mary Lou Conrad interview with author, October 22, 1993.

29. Ibid.

30. Ibid.

31. Letter from Larry Conrad to Larry Lee Johnson, dated March 12, 1960, in possession of author.

32. Letter from Larry Conrad to Larry Lee Johnson, dated February 2, 1960, in possession of author.

33. Birch Bayh had failed his first bar exam by one point. Many Indiana Democrats, including his wife, Marvella, thought the grading of the exam could have been rigged by Republicans to embarrass him. See Marvella Bayh, *Marvella: A Personal Journey*, with Mary Lynn Kotz (New York: Harcourt Brace Jovanovich, 1979), pp. 70–71.

2

1. Marvella Bayh, *Marvella: A Personal Journey*, with Mary Lynn Kotz (New York: Harcourt Brace Jovanovich, 1979), pp. 73–74.

2. William B. Pickett, *Homer E. Capehart: A Senator's Life, 1897–1979* (Indianapolis: Indiana Historical Society, 1990), pp. 163–164; also see Edward H. Ziegner, "Indiana in National Politics," in Donald F. Carmony, ed., *Indiana: A Self-Appraisal* (Bloomington: Indiana University Press, 1966), pp. 53–54.

3. Ziegner, "Indiana in National Politics," p. 42.

4. Pickett, *Homer E. Capehart*, pp. 166–167.

5. Bayh thinks he and Conrad were first introduced at the Delaware County YD dinner the previous fall, but does not specifically remember meeting him until the Bar Association refresher course. Bayh recalls that when they met at the course, Conrad seemed to know him already. Birch E. Bayh, Jr. interview with author, April 20, 1995.

6. Charlie Richmond interview with author, June 22, 1993.

7. Robert Boxell interview with author, March 9, 1993; Robert Pastrick interview with author, October 5, 1993.

8. Robert Boxell interview with author, March 9, 1993.

9. Larry Conrad letter to Larry Johnson, May 26, 1961.

10. See Marvella Bayh, *Marvella: A Personal Journey*, pp. 75–76.

11. Ibid., p. 77.

12. Robert Hinshaw interview with author, May 20, 1994.

13. Birch E. Bayh, Jr. interview with author, April 20, 1995.

14. Ibid.

15. Robert Boxell interview with author, May 19, 1993.

16. Larry Cummings interview with author, January 4, 1994. Bayh acknowledges that all major decisions were thoroughly discussed with Boxell, Conrad, and Hinshaw. He, however, had final say. Birch E. Bayh, Jr. interview with author, April 20, 1995.

17. It was not until 1976 that the Indiana General Assembly moved the nominations for the U.S. Senate from the state conventions to the direct primary. That legislation also moved the nominations for governor and lieutenant governor to the primary. Following the 1980 elections, the nomination for lieutenant governor was moved back to the state conventions.

18. Larry Conrad interview with William B. Pickett, conducted November 14, 1969, Indiana University Oral History Project (IUOHP), accession number 69–35, p. 12.

19. Ibid., p. 1.

20. Ibid., p. 12.

21. Jack New interview with author, August 19, 1994.

22. Matthew E. Welsh, *View from the State House* (Indianapolis: Indiana Historical Bureau, 1981; reprinted 1992), p. 19.

23. David J. Allen interview with author, June 8, 1994.

24. Ibid.

25. Marvella Bayh, *Marvella: A Personal Journey*, p. 78.

26. Robert Boxell interview with author, May 19, 1993.

27. Jack New interview with author, August 19, 1994. According to New, this is the first time he ever heard of Larry Conrad.

28. Conrad interview with Pickett, IUOHP, p. 2.

29. Ibid., p. 14.

30. Robert J. McNeill, *Democratic Campaign Financing in Indiana, 1964* (Bloomington: Institute of Public Administration, Indiana University; Citizens' Research Foundation, 1966), p. 28. The party controlling the governorship expected all state employees to contribute 2% of their salary to the state central committee.

31. Pickett, *Homer E. Capehart*, pp. 172–173.

32. Robert Boxell interview with author, May 19, 1993.

33. Robert Hinshaw interview with author, May 20, 1994. The labor brochure is the one with the parenthetical comment "Bayh pronounced By." A copy is in possession of the author.

34. Birch E. Bayh, Jr. interview with author, April 20, 1995.

35. Ibid.

36. Robert Hinshaw interview with author, May 20, 1994.

37. Birch E. Bayh, Jr. interview with author, April 20, 1995.

38. Robert Boxell interview with author, May 19, 1993; Birch E. Bayh, Jr. interview with author, April 20, 1995.

39. Robert Hinshaw interview with author, May 20, 1994.

40. Bill Colbert interview with author, May 8, 1994; Robert Boxell interview with author, May 19, 1993; Larry Cummings interview with author, January 4, 1994.

41. Robert Boxell interview with author, May 19, 1993.

42. Bill Colbert interview with author, May 8, 1994.

43. Robert Boxell interview with author, May 19, 1993.

44. Robert Hinshaw interview with author, May 20, 1994.

45. Larry Cummings interview with author, January 4, 1994. The jingle won the first-place award for the best political commercial of 1962.

46. Robert Boxell interview with author, February 10, 1994.

47. Robert Boxell interview with author. See *Muncie Star*, October 21, 1962, p. 1.

48. Conrad interview with Pickett, IUOHP, p. 8.

49. Ibid., p. 9.

50. United Press International (UPI) wire story, in possession of author.

51. Conrad interview with Pickett, IUOHP, p. 22.

52. Marvella Bayh, *Marvella: A Personal Journey*, p. 91. Birch Bayh took Johnson's advice to heart, but he disagreed about staffers not being from Indiana. Birch E. Bayh, Jr. interview with author, April 20, 1995.

53. Robert Boxell interview with author, May 19, 1993.

54. Robert Boxell interview with author, March 9, 1993.

55. Birch E. Bayh, Jr. interview with author, April 20, 1995.

56. Robert Hinshaw interview with author, May 20, 1994.

57. Diary of Mary Lou Conrad, in possession of author.

58. Ibid.

59. Jerry Udell interview with author, August 16, 1994.

60. Marvella Bayh, *Marvella: A Personal Journey*, p. 140.

61. Birch E. Bayh, Jr. interview with author, April 20, 1995.

62. Larry Cummings interview with author, January 4, 1994.

63. Stephan Lesher interview with author, April 8, 1994.

64. Robert Boxell interview with author, May 19, 1993.

3

1. Fred Graham later was to become a news correspondent for CBS.

2. Birch E. Bayh, Jr. interview with author, April 20, 1995.

3. Birch Bayh, *One Heartbeat Away* (Indianapolis: Bobbs-Merrill, 1968), p. 29.

4. John D. Feerick, *The Twenty-fifth Amendment: Its Complete History and Earliest Applications* (New York: Fordham University Press, 1976), p. 65; quoted in Richard B. Bernstein, with Jerome Agel, *Amending America* (New York: Random House, 1993), p. 164.

5. Stephan Lesher interview with author, April 11, 1994.

6. Birch Bayh, *One Heartbeat Away*, p. 37.

7. Mary Lou Conrad interview with author, November 23, 1992.

8. Birch Bayh, *One Heartbeat Away*, p. 129.

9. Marvella Bayh, *Marvella: A Personal Journey*, with Mary Lynn Kotz (New York: Harcourt Brace Jovanovich, 1979), pp. 126–130; Birch Bayh, *One Heartbeat Away*, p. 129.

10. Robert Boxell interview with author, February 10, 1994.

11. Ibid.

12. Ibid.

13. Robert Boxell interview with author, May 19, 1993.

14. Stephan Lesher interview with author, April 8, 1994.

15. Ibid.

16. Birch Bayh, *One Heartbeat Away*, p. 133.

17. Marvella Bayh, *Marvella: A Personal Journey*, p. 137.

18. Conrad played a key role in arranging convention schedules for noted personalities, including Robert Redford.

19. Birch Bayh, *One Heartbeat Away*, p. 162.

20. Birch E. Bayh, Jr. interview with author, April 20, 1995.

21. Jerry Udell interview with author, August 16, 1994.

22. Birch Bayh, *One Heartbeat Away*, pp. 239–240.

23. Ibid., p. 276.

24. Ibid., p. 288.

25. Ibid., pp. 303–304.

26. Ibid., p. 333.

27. Untitled six-page manuscript by Larry A. Conrad, dated 1973, in possession of author.

28. Marvella Bayh, *Marvella: A Personal Journey*, pp. 88–89.

29. Ibid., pp. 159–160.

30. Ibid., pp. 160–161.

31. Ibid., p. 160.

32. Robert Boxell interviews with author, January 18, 1994 and May 8, 1994.

33. Marvella Bayh, *Marvella: A Personal Journey,* p. 161.

34. Jeffrey Lewis interview with author, March 5, 1993.

35. "Campaign 68" manual for Birch Bayh, in possession of author, pp. 5–6.

36. James P. Carey interview with author, February 25, 1994; Wiley Spurgeon interview with author, February 25, 1994.

37. "Statement by Senator Robert F. Kennedy on the Death of the Reverend Martin Luther King, Rally in Indianapolis, April 4, 1968." Transcript provided by the John Fitzgerald Kennedy Library, Boston, Mass.

38. On Saturday, May 14, 1994, President Bill Clinton, along with Senator Edward Kennedy, Mrs. Ethel Kennedy, Martin Luther King III, and Dexter Scott King, picked up shovels and broke ground at 17th and Broadway in Indianapolis for a monument to the Rev. Martin Luther King, Jr. and Senator Robert F. Kennedy. See *Indianapolis Star,* Sunday, May 15, 1994, p. 1 and p. A–8. For many years, Larry Conrad had suggested that the site of Robert Kennedy's speech be dedicated to the two men. Several speakers at the ceremony referred to Conrad as being the inspiration for the dedication. See Andrew Levy, "The Big Nap: Indianapolis as City of the Future," *Dissent,* Fall 1994, p. 496.

39. Friedrich Nietzsche, *Beyond Good and Evil: Prelude to a Philosophy of the Future,* translated by Walter Kaufmann (New York: Random House, Vintage Books ed., 1966).

40. Theodore H. White, *The Making of the President, 1968* (New York: Atheneum, 1969), pp. 208, 209.

41. Quoted in "Clinton Visit Spurs Memories," *Indianapolis News,* Friday, May 13, 1994, p. 1.

42. Diane Meyer Simon transcript of remarks at memorial service for Larry Conrad, Indianapolis, July 22, 1990.

43. Jerry Udell interview with author, August 16, 1994.

44. Robert Boxell interview with author, May 19, 1993. L. Keith Bulen remembers that the Republican State Central Committee purchased an option on the rights to the song for political use. "We jumped at it early," Bulen says. "We did not know if Bayh was going to use it or not. But I believe in failsafe." L. Keith Bulen interview with author, June 28, 1994.

45. Birch E. Bayh, Jr., interview with author, April 20, 1995.

46. Alan Rachels interview with author, September 14, 1994.

47. Ibid.

48. Article by Gil Neal, reporter for the *Louisville Courier-Journal,* reprinted in Conrad for Governor newspaper handout (April 1972?), in possession of author.

49. Jerry Udell interview with author, August 16, 1994.

50. Larry A. Conrad conversation with author, December 1975.

51. Robert Boxell interview with author, May 19, 1993.

52. Mary Lou Conrad interview with author, October 22, 1993.

53. Robert Rock interview with author, June 7, 1993.

54. Jeffrey Lewis interview with author, March 5, 1993.

55. Mary Lou Conrad interview with author, October 22, 1993.

56. Jeffrey Lewis interview with author, March 5, 1993.

4

1. Theodore H. White, *The Making of the President, 1968* (New York: Atheneum, 1969), p. 198.

2. See Raymond H. Scheele, "Political Parties in Indiana," in William P. Hojnacki, *Politics and Public Policy in Indiana: Prospects for Change in State and Local Government* (Dubuque, Iowa: Kendall/Hunt, 1983), p. 29.

3. For the story of Unigov see C. James Owen and York Wilbern, *Governing Metropolitan Indianapolis: The Politics of Unigov* (Berkeley: University of California Press, 1985).

4. Two other amendments also were approved. One permitted the Indiana General Assembly to move from biennial to annual sessions. The other replaced the judicial article (Article 7) with a new section that changed the selection method for appellate and supreme court judges. See the annotated version of the Constitution of Indiana, 1851, in *Here Is Your Indiana Government* (Indianapolis: Indiana State Chamber of Commerce, 1991), 25th ed., particularly pp. 143 and 145–146.

5. Robert Rock interview with author, June 7, 1993.

6. Quoted in Robert J. McNeill, *Democratic Campaign Financing in Indiana, 1964* (Bloomington: Institute of Public Administration, Indiana University; Citizens' Research Foundation, 1966), p. 11.

7. For an analysis of electoral turnover in Indiana during this period see Gary L. Crawley, "Turnover in American State Houses: 1952–1978" (Ph.D. diss., Michigan State University, 1982).

8. Gordon St. Angelo interview with author, September 10, 1993.

9. Ibid.

10. Alan Rachels interview with author, September 14, 1994.

11. Ibid.

12. Robert Boxell interview with author, November 16, 1994.

13. Robert Rock interview with author, June 7, 1993.

14. Ibid.

15. Jack New interview with author, August 17, 1994.

16. *New York Times*, March 6, 1970, p. 1.

17. Birch E. Bayh, Jr. interview with author, April 20, 1995.

18. See *New York Times*, March 6, 1970, p. 1, and *Indianapolis Star*, March 6, 1970, p. 3.

19. Birch E. Bayh, Jr. interview with author, April 20, 1995.

20. Robert Boxell interview with author, March 9, 1993; Larry Cummings interview with author, January 4, 1994.

21. St. Angelo acknowledges that "it makes sense that the Bayh contingent was for Bobby, since Bayh was close to the Kennedys, but it was not real apparent as I recall." Gordon St. Angelo interview with author, September 13, 1993. Actually, Bayh had provided information to Kennedy prior to Humphrey's entry into the race, but Bayh considered himself friends with all the presidential candidates and

adopted a public stance of neutrality. See Marvella Bayh, *Marvella: A Personal Journey,* with Mary Lynn Kotz (New York: Harcourt Brace Jovanovich, 1979), pp. 180–181.

22. Robert Boxell interview with author, March 9, 1993.

23. N. Stuart Grauel interview with author, June 11, 1993.

24. Robert Boxell interview with author, March 9, 1993. On Bayh's presidential ambitions see Marvella Bayh, *Marvella: A Personal Journey,* pp. 191ff.

25. Gordon St. Angelo interview with author, September 10, 1993.

26. Stephan Lesher interview with author, April 6, 1994.

27. The U.S. Senate rejected Haynsworth's nomination on November 21, 1969, by a vote of 55–45.

28. Gordon St. Angelo interview with author, September 10, 1993.

29. Michael Barone, Grant Ujifusa, and Douglas Mathews, *Almanac of American Politics, 1978* (New York: E. P. Dutton, 1977), p. 263.

30. See Gordon Englehart, "Hartke and Bayh: From Cool to Cold," *Louisville Courier Journal and Times,* May 17, 1970, p. 1.

31. Gordon St. Angelo interview with author, September 10, 1993.

32. Bayh called some county chairs asking about possible candidates. Byron Klute interview with author, March 18, 1993.

33. Ken Cragen interview with author, May 5, 1993.

34. See Englehart, "Hartke and Bayh: From Cool to Cold"; Claudia Prosser interview with author, February 10, 1993; Alan Rachels interview with author, September 14, 1994.

35. See Englehart, "Hartke and Bayh: From Cool to Cold."

36. Robert P. Mooney, "Bayh Suffers Setback in Demo District Vote, *Indianapolis Star,* May 14, 1970, p. 1.

37. Gordon St. Angelo interview with author, September 10, 1993.

38. Birch E. Bayh, Jr. interview with author, April 20, 1995.

39. Jeffrey Lewis interview with author, March 5, 1993.

40. Campaign brochure, "Larry Conrad: Secretary of State," undated. In possession of author.

41. Gordon St. Angelo interview with author, September 10, 1993; Bill Colbert interview with author, February 4, 1994.

42. Claudia Prosser interview with author, February 10, 1993.

43. William Gigerich interview with author, September 24, 1993.

44. Conrad had strongly encouraged John Loughlin to run, thinking the state ticket needed someone from South Bend. Conrad did not publicly support Loughlin because of his own race, but was pleased that Loughlin won the nomination. Jeffrey Lewis interview with author, March 5, 1993.

45. Ed Simcox interview with author, September 17, 1993.

46. Incumbent Trudy Etherton was unopposed for the nomination for state auditor, and Richard Wells of Valparaiso defeated Harold Negley for the nomination for state superintendent of public instruction.

47. Robert F. Wagner interview with author, June 10, 1993.

48. Ibid.

49. An elaborate walking schedule was designed and all the candidates would participate on different days in different locations.

50. Ed Tracey interview with author, October 4, 1993.

51. Robert F. Wagner interview with author, January 16, 1993.

52. Ibid.

53. Ibid.

54. Oral History Interview with Vance Hartke, recorded by Charles T. Morrissey for "Former Members of Congress, Inc.," pp. 10–11. Transcript provided by the Indiana State Library.

55. "Hartke's Offices Here Allegedly 'Bugged,'" *Indianapolis Star,* August 18, 1975, p. 1.

56. "'Bug' Allegedly Planted On Chair In Office Of Hartke Confidant," *Indianapolis Star,* August 19, 1975, p. 1. Wilcox's private detective firm apparently engaged in such activities even after the 1970 elections. In 1971, his firm received a $500-per-month contract from L. Keith Bulen to provide "security" for the Marion County license branches. That same year, Wilcox and his firm were accused of trying to "bug" the campaign headquarters of Democratic mayoral nominee John F. Neff, who was running against Bulen's man, Richard G. Lugar. See copyrighted story, "Wilcox and Bulen Aide Reportedly Tried to 'Bug' '71 Demo Mayor HQ," *Indianapolis Star,* August 20, 1975, p. 1.

57. C. Timothy Wilcox interview with author, December 13, 1995.

58. Oral History Interview with Vance Hartke, p. 11. The out-of-court settlement was on the condition that the details would not be revealed. Off-the-record comments by several people familiar with the case indicate that the settlement was for $240,000 and the defendants included one of the largest investor-owned utilities in Indiana and an attorney with one of Indiana's leading law firms.

59. C. Timothy Wilcox interview with author, December 13, 1995.

60. Jeffrey Lewis interview with author, May 3, 1993.

61. Ibid.

62. "Assets Listed By Candidate," *Muncie Evening Press,* July 21, 1970, p. 13.

63. Larry Conrad conversation with author, May, 4, 1990.

64. Raymond J. Hafsten, Jr. interview with author, February 13, 1995.

65. Jeffrey Lewis interview with author, May 3, 1993.

66. Ibid.

67. Diane Simon interview with author, December 5, 1995.

68. Ibid.

69. Stephen Powell interview with author, February 3, 1994.

70. Mary Lou Conrad interview with author, October 22, 1993.

71. Stephen Powell interview with author, February 3, 1994.

72. Column by Bob Barnet, "Show Biz Note: Politico Smash! Tops Billing at Fair Gala," *Muncie Star,* January 10, 1971, p. A–5.

73. Claudia Prosser interview with author, February 10, 1993.

74. Jeffrey Lewis interview with author, March 3, 1993.

75. The "doughnut" consists of the seven counties surrounding Marion County: Boone, Hamilton, Hancock, Shelby, Johnson, Morgan, and Hendricks. In recent decades these counties have experienced increased population growth attributable to relocation of Marion County residents. Like the "collar counties" of Illinois—those surrounding Cook County—they are largely Republican. Democrats always hope for low turnout in the doughnut.

76. Mary Lou Conrad interview with author, October 22, 1993.

77. Jeffrey Lewis interview with author, March 3, 1993. Boxell had phoned the

Daleville house before Conrad left for Indianapolis, telling Larry that "he thought we had it, but couldn't say for sure." Mary Lou Conrad interview with author, October 22, 1993.

78. The vote totals are from the secretary of state race in the *1970 General Election Report of the Secretary of State of the State of Indiana,* p. 4.

5

1. Handwritten inaugural remarks by Larry A. Conrad, undated, in possession of author.

2. In fact, Lewis and several of his college friends, including Powell, had an agreement among themselves that they would participate in several different campaigns and whoever was with a winner would hire the other friends. Lewis, of course, was with Conrad. Powell originally worked for William (Bill) McCarty, who was defeated for the Democratic congressional nomination in the 10th district. Steve Powell interview with author, February 3, 1994.

3. Jeffrey Lewis interview with author, March 5, 1993.

4. N. Stuart Grauel interview with author, June 11, 1993.

5. Vicki Weger interview with author, June 21, 1994.

6. Jeffrey Lewis interview with author, March 5, 1993.

7. N. Stuart Grauel interview with author, June 11, 1993.

8. Jeffrey Lewis interview with author, March 3, 1993.

9. Jeff Lewis memo to Larry Conrad dated January 21, 1971, in possession of author.

10. Jeff Lewis memo to Larry Conrad, dated February 19, 1971, entitled "Notes from Coordinators meeting, February 18, 1971," in possession of author.

11. Bill Bannon memo to Jeff Lewis entitled "Travel Report, Saturday, February 27, 1971," in possession of author.

12. Terry Straub memo to Jeff Lewis, undated, in possession of author.

13. Vicki Weger interview with author, June 21, 1994.

14. Unsigned memo in possession of author.

15. Robert Boxell interview with author, March 9, 1993.

16. John Loughlin interview with author, September 10, 1993.

17. Boxell memo to "LAC, Stuart, Jeff and Vicki" dated May 19, 1971, and Boxell memo to LAC dated May 27, 1971. Both memos in possession of author.

18. Agenda written by Bob Boxell for June 1, 1971, Coordinators Meeting, undated, in possession of author. Emphasis in original.

19. Memo from Jeff Lewis to LAC and Boxell, dated June 14, 1971, entitled "Progress Report on Political Program," in possession of author.

20. Section 1 of Article 5 of the Constitution was finally amended to allow the governor to succeed himself when the voters approved the measure in the general election on November 7, 1972.

21. Governor Welsh's eyesight was failing, and he was undergoing treatment for the condition. Otherwise, his general health was excellent.

22. Robert Boxell interview with author, March 9, 1993.

23. Vicki Weger interview with author, June 21, 1994; Jeffrey Lewis interview with author, March 5, 1993.

24. Memo from David Bochnowski to "LAC," undated but probably written in

mid to late November 1970, entitled "Plans and Thoughts," in possession of author. Emphasis in original.

25. Ibid.

26. Robert P. Mooney, "Welsh Backing Grows After '72 Announcement," *Indianapolis Star*, July 21, 1973, p. 4.

27. The Indiana Democratic Editorial Association (IDEA) and its counterpart, the Indiana Republican Editorial Association (IREA), are throwbacks to the earlier age when newspapers actually admitted their partisan preference. The IDEA annual meeting in French Lick every August attracted the party faithful, the few newspaper editors and publishers still forthright enough to admit their partisanship, and numerous other reporters and lobbyists. The IDEA meetings still occur in August of each year.

28. Robert Boxell memo to "LAC" dated July 24, 1971, entitled "Welsh Announcement." In possession of author.

29. Memo from "Rooker" (Rooksby) to LAC and other staff members, undated, entitled "IDEA Convention," in possession of author.

30. Nick Angel letter "To all District and County Chairmen and their Committees in the State of Indiana," dated August 13, 1971, in possession of author. Grammatical and punctuation errors in original.

31. Memo from R. Boxell to LAC, dated September 7, 1971, in possession of author.

32. Letter in possession of author.

33. Memo from "Rooker" (Rooksby) to LAC, entitled "Trip Report—Jefferson, Switzerland Counties," dated August 14, 1971, in possession of author.

34. Undated brochure entitled "Larry Conrad: Your Secretary of State," in possession of author.

35. Robert Boxell interview with author, March 13, 1995.

36. Ibid.

37. Ibid.

38. Robert Boxell interview with author, April 2, 1993.

39. Gordon St. Angelo interview with author, September 10, 1993.

40. Robert Boxell interview with author, March 9, 1993.

41. Mary Lou Conrad interview with author, May 24, 1994.

42. Robert Boxell memo to "LAC" entitled "Political Posture," dated January 12, 1972, in possession of author.

43. Jeff Lewis memo to "LAC and Boxell," entitled "Announcement Package," dated January 21, 1972, in possession of author.

44. Terry Straub memo to "LAC," entitled "Getting it on with a bang instead of a soft pop!" dated January 18, 1972, in possession of author.

45. Announcement speech in possession of author.

46. Campaign brochure in possession of author.

47. The Chicago television market covered northwest Indiana and the Louisville market covered south-central Indiana.

48. Campaign brochure entitled "A Man with a Stake in Indiana's Future," undated, in possession of author.

49. Chicago mayor Richard J. Daley supposedly told President Lyndon Johnson in the mid–1960s, "Do something with that war. I don't care what it is, but get rid of it. The voters are starting to talk about it."

50. Robert Pastrick interview with author, October 5, 1993.

51. Paul Light, *Baby Boomers* (New York: W. W. Norton & Company, 1988), p. 134.

52. See William J. Watt, *Bowen: The Years as Governor* (Indianapolis: Bierce Associates, 1981), pp. 16–17 and 21–22. Also see Stan Evans, "Tax Hike Issue Surfaces Again," *Indianapolis News*, June 2, 1972, p. 14, and "Democrats Busy Drafting Planks," June 6, 1972, p. 34.

53. Indiana Chamber of Commerce, *Here Is Your Indiana Government*, 25th ed., 1991, p. 147.

54. Robert P. Mooney, "Politics in Perspective," *Indianapolis Star*, Sunday, June 18, 1972, section 2, p. 10.

55. "Democrats Busy Drafting Planks," *Indianapolis News*, June 6, 1972, p. 34.

56. "Democrats Study Platform Proposals," *Indianapolis News*, June 7, 1972, p. 73.

57. Paul M. Doherty, "Welsh Bid Beamed at Delegates," *Indianapolis Star*, June 5, 1972, p. 15.

58. Quotes contained in Conrad brochure, undated, in possession of author.

59. Ibid.

60. Alan Rachels interview with author, September 14, 1994.

61. Birch E. Bayh, Jr. interview with author, April 20, 1995.

62. "Demo Unit Considers Delegate Challenges," *Indianapolis Star*, June 7, 1972, p. 11.

63. "Conrad Denies Any Link With Bolinger-Signed Mail," *Indianapolis Star*, June 14, 1972, p. 4.

64. Robert Mooney, "Welsh Gain Fails to Dismay Conrad," *Indianapolis Star*, June 10, 1972, p. 5.

65. "Welsh Claims Strong Backing in 3d District," *Indianapolis Star*, June 14, 1972, p. 15.

66. "Larry Conrad Lists $32,750 Net Worth," *Indianapolis Star*, June 6, 1972, p. 4.

67. Ibid.

68. Brochure, undated, in possession of author.

69. Paul M. Doherty, "Unorthodoxy Called For In State Government, Larry Conrad Believes," *Indianapolis Star*, June 12, 1972, p. 17.

70. Ibid.

71. Vicki Weger interview with author, June 21, 1994.

72. Mrs. Wallace did not appear in Indianapolis. Her husband underwent surgery on Sunday, June 18, to remove the bullet that struck him on May 15 while he was campaigning in Maryland. The Indiana manager of the Wallace campaign declared that he had been misinformed about her appearance at the state convention. See *Indianapolis Star*, June 21, 1972, p. 10.

73. That morning the *Star* printed a UPI story from Washington stating that James A. McCord, Jr., an employee of Richard Nixon's campaign committee, had been arrested for the break-in at Democratic National Headquarters at Watergate. Democratic National Chairman Lawrence O'Brien called for an FBI investigation. See "Nixon Election Aide Arrested," *Indianapolis Star*, June 19, 1972, p. 2.

74. John S. Mason, "Conrad Backers Fail to Seek Key Panel Posts," *Indianapolis Star*, June 20, 1972, p. 12.

75. Robert P. Mooney, "Welsh, Conrad, Predict Convention Wins," *Indianapolis Star*, June 20, 1972, p. 1.

76. Claudia Prosser interview with author, February 10, 1993. When asked about

the telephone hookups, Gordon St. Angelo said he could not remember "rigging the phones" at the 1972 state convention. St. Angelo interview with author, September 10, 1993.

77. Jeffrey Lewis interview with author, March 5, 1993.

78. Gregory Schenkel interview with author, September 28, 1993; Terrence Straub interview with author, November 28, 1994.

79. Gordon St. Angelo interview with author, September 10, 1993.

80. Robert P. Mooney, "Demos Pick Welsh For Governor," *Indianapolis Star*, June 21, 1972, p. 10.

81. John Livengood interview with author, September 29, 1993.

82. Ibid.

83. Robert P. Mooney, "Trisler Still Favored To Become Interim Democratic State Chairman," *Indianapolis Star*, March 29, 1974. J. Manfred Core was elected Democratic state chairman in August 1960 when Chairman Charles E. Skillen resigned at the IDEA meeting at French Lick after a dispute with gubernatorial nominee Matthew Welsh. Core stayed as chairman through Branigin's election in 1964. Three more chairmen served before Livengood took over in 1984. Evan Bayh was elected governor in 1988.

84. Mooney, "Demos Pick Welsh For Governor."

85. Gregory Schenkel interview with author, September 28, 1993.

86. Terrence Straub interview with author, September 28, 1994.

87. Claudia Prosser interview with author, February 10, 1993.

88. Vicki Weger interview with author, June 21, 1994.

89. Mooney, "Demos Pick Welsh For Governor."

90. Robert P. Mooney, "Bowen, Orr Picked for 1972 GOP Ticket," *Indianapolis Star*, June 24, 1972, p. 1.

91. See Watt, *Bowen*, pp. 17–20.

92. L. Keith Bulen interview with author, June 28, 1994.

93. Ibid.

94. Watt, *Bowen*, p. 21.

95. There was a festering problem in the Democrat party, however. Frank E. McKinney, Sr., an Indianapolis banker and a powerhouse in the state party—who had served as chairman of the Democratic National Committee under President Truman—was not selected as an at-large delegate to the national convention. McKinney claimed that St. Angelo assured him of an at-large delegate post and then reneged. Dallas Sells, the head of the UAW, came out in favor of McKinney's appointment. St. Angelo defended himself: "There never was a commitment made to Mr. McKinney by myself or anyone else under me. It was not within my power to do it." St. Angelo was a national delegate selected by the 8th district caucus and was elected to head the Indiana delegation to the Miami convention. See "UAW Director Comes to McKinney Defense," *Indianapolis Star*, June 22, 1972, p. 1.

96. Bob Boxell memo to "Governor Welsh," entitled "Campaign Personnel," dated June 27, 1972, in possession of author.

97. This event became an annual affair and was renamed "The Conrad Political Reunion." The last one was held August 8, 1976.

98. Vicki Weger interview with author, June 21, 1994

99. Theodore H. White, *The Making of the President, 1972* (New York: Atheneum Publishers, 1973), p. 325.

100. See Watt, *Bowen,* pp. 21–23.
101. L. Keith Bulen interview with author, June 28, 1994.
102. Watt, *Bowen,* pp. 22–23.

6

1. Peter Christen Asbjornsen, *The Three Billy Goats Gruff* (New York: Seabury Press, 1973); illustrated by Paul Galdone.
2. L. Keith Bulen interview with author, June 28, 1994.
3. Edward Ziegner interview with author, June 16, 1993.
4. Jack New interview with author, August 17, 1994.
5. See Theodore H. White, *The Making of the President, 1972* (New York: Atheneum Publishers, 1973), p. 214. Also see Larry J. Sabato, *Feeding Frenzy* (New York: Free Press, 1991), p. 57.
6. Edward Ziegner interview with author, June 16, 1993.
7. N. Stuart Grauel interview with author, September 31, 1993.
8. Three individuals were indicted in March 1974 for failing to deposit $19,559.35 in office funds. Two of these employees, Shelia Plank and Lionel R. Smith, worked for Conrad. The third, Martha Ann Barksdale, had been an employee under Conrad's predecessor, William Salin. See "Pearcy Asks Data On Conrad's Office," *Indianapolis News,* April 16, 1974, p. 1.
9. Mary Lou Conrad interview with author, October 22, 1993.
10. Actually, Governor McCray was convicted in April 1924 on a federal charge of using the mails to defraud creditors. Governor Jackson was put on trial in 1928, and ex-Governor McCray testified at the trial that Jackson and "his Klan associates promised McCray immunity from the charges then pending against the governor and offered him $10,000 in cash." See James H. Madison, *Indiana Through Tradition and Change: A History of the Hoosier State and Its People: 1920–1945* (Indianapolis: Indiana Historical Society, 1982), p. 71. The Klan influence also cost Indianapolis mayor John L. Duvall his job when he was convicted of taking bribes from Klan leader D. C. Stephenson. See entries on John L. Duvall and Claude E. Negley in David J. Bodenhamer and Robert G. Barrows, eds., *Encyclopedia of Indianapolis* (Bloomington: Indiana University Press, 1994), pp. 517 and 1045.
11. Interestingly, the editors of the *Indianapolis News* did not rate the Master Plan as one of the top ten stories of 1973. The number one story, in their judgment, was the passage of Governor Bowen's tax program, followed by the U.S. District Court ruling requiring busing for desegregating public schools in Marion County. The ninth-ranking story was the "Spring meat shortage," and number ten was "Statewide teacher strikes." See *Indianapolis News,* December 18, 1973, p. 6.
12. The newspaper stories, by various reporters, all refer to a 193-page document. This number was apparently derived from adding the 3 pages of front matter (cover sheet, table of contents, and foreword) to the 190 pages of text. A manual count of all the pages, however, shows the document to contain 197 pages. This is verified by a computer count of pages in a computer file prepared by the author. Some of the chapters' cover sheets were not paginated—hence the discrepancy.
13. Gordon St. Angelo interview with author, September 27, 1993.

14. Edward Ziegner, "Conrad for Governor 'Master Plan' Bared," *Indianapolis News,* November 20, 1973, p. 1.

15. Claudia Prosser interview with author, February 10, 1993.

16. Gordon St. Angelo interview with author, September 27, 1993.

17. *Indianapolis News,* November 20, 1993, Home Edition, p. 1.

18. Gordon St. Angelo interview with author, September 10, 1993.

19. Emphasis in original.

20. "Conrad Calls Alleged 'Master Plan' Libel," *Indianapolis Star,* November 21, 1973, p. 5.

21. "Conrad Declares Plan Fraudulent," *Indianapolis News,* November 21, 1973, p. 2.

22. William M. Schreiber interview with author, January 31, 1994.

23. John Livengood interview with author, September 29, 1993.

24. Bill Gigerich interviews with author, May 26, 1993, and September 24, 1993.

25. Claudia Prosser interview with author, February 2, 1993. Segretti was hired by the Nixon White House to perform "dirty tricks" on Nixon's political opponents. See Carl Bernstein and Bob Woodward, *All the President's Men* (New York: Simon and Schuster, 1974), pp. 115–128. Fensterwald was serving as legal counsel to James W. McCord, Jr., one of the six Watergate burglars. See Walter Rugaver, "McCord Tells Senate Unit of New Watergate Names," *New York Times,* March 26, 1973, p. 1.

26. Diary of Mary Lou Conrad, in possession of author.

27. Mary Lou Conrad interview with author, October 22, 1993.

28. "Conrad Rues Barbs in 'Plan,' *Indianapolis News,* November 24, 1973.

29. Mary Lou Conrad interview with author, October 22, 1993.

30. Diary of Mary Lou Conrad, in possession of author.

31. N. Stuart Grauel interview with author, June 11, 1993. Claudia Prosser recalls that a listening device was found in an electrical outlet on the wall in Conrad's office, but this was never made public. Prosser interview with author, February 10, 1993.

32. Bill Gigerich interview with author, May 26, 1993.

33. Gordon St. Angelo interview with author, September 10, 1993.

34. Jack New interview with author, August 17, 1994.

35. Bill Gigerich interview with author, September 24, 1993.

36. John Livengood interview with author, September 29, 1993.

37. Gordon Englehart interview with author, September 10, 1993.

38. Robert Pastrick interview with author, October 5, 1993.

39. William M. Schreiber interview with author, January 31, 1994.

40. Paul Doherty, "Unorthodoxy Called For in State Government, Larry Conrad Believes," *Indianapolis Star,* June 12, 1972.

41. Dr. Otis R. Bowen, in recalling his 1972 campaign, said: "We took the delegate books from the last two or three conventions and discovered that two-thirds of the delegates are repeaters, so we knew who to contact. I made 1,800 house calls that year." Bowen interview with author, April 19, 1993.

42. Edward Ziegner, "'Doomsday Book' Was Kept On Delegates, Conrad Says," *Indianapolis News,* November 30, 1973, p. 1. The Master Plan, section VII, p. 4: "At a meeting such as the IDEA French Lick affair, Larry should have his children and others out in front playing football or somekind [*sic*] of sport that shows together-

ness and male leadership. Even women libers [*sic*] would applaud this type of show."

43. "Police Shelve Conrad Request," *Indianapolis News*, December 10, 1973, p. 1.

44. Edward Ziegner, "Conrad's Staff 'Calls' Political?" *Indianapolis News*, December 11, 1973, p. 1.

45. "State Police Say 'Nay' To Conrad," *Indianapolis News*, December 17, 1973, p. 27.

46. Robert Wagner interview with author, January 16, 1993.

47. Robert Wagner interview with author, June 10, 1993.

48. John Livengood interview with author, September 29, 1993.

49. Mary Lou Conrad interview with author, October 22, 1993.

50. Ibid.

51. Claudia Prosser interview with author, February 10, 1993.

52. Edward Ziegner interview with author, June 16, 1993.

53. L. Keith Bulen interview with author, June 28, 1994.

54. Edward Ziegner interview with author, June 16, 1993.

55. Gordon St. Angelo interview with author, September 10, 1993.

56. Gordon St. Angelo interview with author, September 13, 1993.

57. In the dozens of internal memos by Conrad staffers reviewed by the author, Gordon St. Angelo is never referred to as "Saint," always as either "Gordon" or "St. Angelo." At one point the Master Plan uses the full name: Gordon Lewis St. Angelo.

58. Claudia Prosser interview with author, February 10, 1993.

59. John Livengood interview with author, September 29, 1993.

60. Edward Ziegner, "25 Pass Lie Test On 'Plan': Conrad," *Indianapolis News*, December 19, 1973, p. 1.

61. Vicki Weger interview with author, June 21, 1994.

62. Steve Powell interview with author, February 3, 1994.

63. Ibid.

64. Ibid.

65. Gordon St. Angelo interview with author, September 10, 1993.

66. "Conrad Ready 'to jolt Democrat structure,'" *Muncie Evening Press*, April 9, 1974, p. 15.

67. Steve Powell interview with author, February 3, 1994.

68. Ibid.

69. Ibid.

70. This is most likely the case. In the confidential report to Larry Conrad by the polygraph examiner, Michael E. Beaver, the name of "Jeffrey Stewart Lewis" is typed in a different typeface than the other names and is the last name on the list. The name is initialed "MEB," for Michael E. Beaver. The other twenty-four names on the list are not initialed and are not in alphabetical order, suggesting they were arranged according to the sequence in which they were examined.

71. Edward Ziegner, "State Demos Begin 'Conrad Plan' Probe," *Indianapolis News*, January 7, 1974, p. 1.

72. "Confidential Report of Investigation," by Michael E. Beaver, addressed to Larry A. Conrad, noting the examinations were conducted between December 6, 1973 and December 14, 1973. This report is in the possession of the author.

73. "Report of the Special Committee," dated February 20, 1974, p. 1, in possession of author.

74. Robert F. Wagner interviews with author, January 16, 1993 and November 1, 1995.

75. Gordon St. Angelo interview with author, September 10, 1993.

76. N. Stuart Grauel interview with author, June 11, 1993.

77. Untitled copy of understanding between Secretary of State Larry Conrad and the Indiana Democratic State Committee, undated, in possession of author.

78. Paul Jasper conversation with author, September 17, 1993.

79. Handwritten notes by Robert F. Wagner, dated January 23, 1974, in possession of author.

80. Robert F. Wagner interview with author, November 1, 1995.

81. Diary of Mary Lou Conrad, in possession of author.

82. The foregoing relies on Robert F. Wagner interviews with author, January 16, 1993, January 13, 1995 and November 1, 1995. Gordon St. Angelo does not recall that the topic of Conrad's resignation "even came up." St. Angelo interview with author, September 13, 1993.

83. "Report of the Special Committee," dated February 20, 1974, in possession of author.

84. Robert F. Wagner interview with author, January 16, 1993.

85. Associated Press story, "Dem leaders urge Conrad not to seek reelection," *Gary Post-Tribune*, February 25, 1974, p. LCC 1.

86. "Final Report of the Special Committee," dated March 9, 1974, in possession of author.

87. Jeff Lewis recalls that Gordon St. Angelo had asked him if political work was done on state time in Conrad's office. Lewis said "Yes," and St. Angelo asked him if he would sign a statement, prepared by Michael Phillips, to that effect. Lewis agreed. When Lewis appeared before the Special Committee, Phillips produced the statement and asked if Lewis had signed it. Lewis acknowledged that it was his signature, but when Phillips asked for names of people who performed political work, Lewis terminated his testimony. He thought he had an agreement with Phillips not to name anybody. Jeff Lewis interview with author, December 23, 1993.

88. Paul M. Doherty, "Conrad Defies 'Master Plan' Controversy, Seeks Second Term," *Indianapolis Star*, March 13, 1974, p. 8.

89. "Conrad Urged to Avoid Race," *Indianapolis News*, March 4, 1974, p. 3.

90. Robert P. Mooney, "Lugar Acts to End Corruption Mess," *Indianapolis Star*, March 3, 1974, section 2, p. 6. Prior to this, the Republicans were content to let the Democrats fight among themselves. L. Keith Bulen recalls having lunch in December or January with Gordon St. Angelo and Edward Ziegner. Bulen recalls a discussion of the Master Plan and Conrad. "I read the Master Plan," Bulen remembers, "but I remember very little about it. We [Republicans] didn't do anything with it. I saw it as an intramural fight; it was a free black eye [for the Democrats]." L. Keith Bulen interview with author, June 28, 1994.

91. "Conrad Urged to Run Again at Columbus," *Indianapolis News*, March 8, 1974, p. 5.

92. "Fifth District Demo Chief Defends Conrad," *Indianapolis Star*, March 6, 1974, p. 9.

93. Claudia Prosser interview with author, February 10, 1993.

94. Ibid.

95. "Final Report of the Special Committee appointed by The Indiana Democratic State Central Committee," dated March 9, 1974, in possession of author.

96. Paul M. Doherty, "Conrad Defies 'Master Plan' Controversy, Seeks Second Term," *Indianapolis Star*, March 13, 1974, p. 8.

97. N. Stuart Grauel interview with author, June 11, 1993. While in Washington, Conrad's old friends from his Senate days hosted a fund-raiser for him.

98. Unsigned letter dated March 7, 1974. Copy in possession of author.

99. Robert P. Mooney, "Unseen Letter Caused Demo Stir," in "Politics in Perspective," *Indianapolis Star*, March 17, 1974, section 2, p. 8. Mooney misidentified the Bayh staffer who called Rutherford as Dr. Karl O'Lessker. It was in fact Carl Oleska.

100. Gordon St. Angelo interview with author, September 27, 1993. At the time, St. Angelo admitted that he did "speak with friends in Arizona on Powell's behalf to find him employment," but that help "was asked by Powell's friends, rather than Powell himself." See "Conrad ready 'to jolt Democrat structure.'"

101. Signed and notarized "Affidavit" of James Stephen Powell, dated March 22, 1974. Copy in possession of author. This "Affidavit" is a summary of Powell's sworn statement of June 17, 1974.

102. Charles Deppert interview with author, July 20, 1993. Deppert never found out the name of the person Wagner called, and Wagner does not recall it.

103. Robert P. Mooney, "St. Angelo to Resign Demo Post," *Indianapolis Star*, March 24, 1974, section 2, p. 1.

104. Edward Ziegner, "St. Angelo to Retire April 6 As State Democratic Chief," *Indianapolis News*, March 25, 1974, p. 23.

105. Gordon St. Angelo interview with author, September 10, 1993.

106. Ibid.

107. Edward Ziegner, "Gordon St. Angelo, Hail and Farewell," *Indianapolis News*, March 30, 1974, p. 19.

108. Edward Ziegner interview with author, June 16, 1993.

109. Letter entitled "Dear Democratic Official," dated March 22, 1974, signed by Leo A. Voisard. Copy in possession of author.

110. See Paul M. Doherty, "St. Angelo's Resignation Stirs Up Demo Activity," *Indianapolis Star*, March 26, 1974, and Ed Ziegner, "Welsh Turned Down Job As Interim Demo Chairman," *Indianapolis News*, March 26, 1974.

111. Paul M. Doherty, "Demo Power Fight Shaping Up Over Successor To St. Angelo," *Indianapolis Star*, March 28, 1974, p. 1.

112. Birch E. Bayh, Jr. interview with author, April 20, 1995.

113. Marvella Bayh, *Marvella: A Personal Journey*, with Mary Lynn Kotz (New York: Harcourt Brace Jovanovich, 1979), p. 221.

114. Birch E. Bayh, Jr. interview with author, April 20, 1995.

115. Ibid.

116. Edward Ziegner, "Sen. Bayh Backs Trisler For State Party Chairman," *Indianapolis News*, March 29, 1974, p. 1.

117. Robert P. Mooney, "Trisler Elected, 'Master Plan' Report Blocked," *Indianapolis Star*, March 31, 1974, section 2, p. 1.

118. Ibid.

119. Paul M. Doherty, "Did Conrad 'Turn Tables' On St. Angelo Over Plan?" *Indianapolis Star*, April 5, 1974.

120. Ibid.

121. Edward Ziegner, "Democrats Tell Conrad To Reduce State Staff," *Indianapolis News*, April 8, 1974, p. 1.

122. "Conrad ready 'to jolt Democrat structure, April 9, 1974.'"

123. "Conrad wants Democratic housecleaning," *Peru Daily Tribune*, April 11, 1974, p. 1 and "Schreiber Near Conrad Challenge," *Indianapolis News*, May 17, 1974, p. 6.

124. Art Harris and Skip Hess, "Political Aids [*sic*] On Conrad Payroll," *Indianapolis News*, April 10, 1974, p. 1.

125. Conrad had not released Powell's affidavit at the news conference, although some reporters had copies. The affidavit was finally released by Conrad on Friday, May 3, 1974.

126. Edward Ziegner, "Conrad's 'Tell All' Conference Fizzles," *Indianapolis News*, April 11, 1974, p. 1. Other statewide reporters differed in their assessment. Gordon Englehart in the *Louisville Courier-Journal* wrote, referring to the Master Plan: "Seldom has so much been so over-written about something of so little significance." Calling it a "squalid alley brawl," Englehart contended the only real issue was whether or not some of Conrad's employees devoted their working hours to politics, and he said the solution was to have an investigation of this question by the prosecutor. See "Public's legitimate concern unresolved in brawl over 'Master Plan,' Conrad," *Louisville Courier-Journal*, April 21, 1974. Bob Flynn from the *Evansville Press* concurred; the issue was ghost employees: "once their existence is proven or disproven, the rest of the report, as far as the Average Citizen is concerned, is merely an essay on political skulduggery—real or imagined." See Robert Flynn, "Politics: Kernels from the master plan," *Evansville Press*, April 13, 1974.

127. Gordon St. Angelo interview with author, September 10, 1993.

128. Birch E. Bayh, Jr. interview with author, April 20, 1995.

129. Skip Hess and Art Harris, "Conrad 'Plan' On State Time?" *Indianapolis News*, April 12, 1974, p. 1.

130. N. Stuart Grauel interview with author, June 11, 1993.

131. Draft of letter addressed to Mr. Bill Trisler from Robert Wagner, undated, in possession of author.

132. Copy of letter from Larry A. Conrad to the Honorable Noble Pearcy, dated April 15, 1974, in possession of author.

133. Paul M. Doherty, "'Plan' Dispute Probe Requested By Conrad," *Indianapolis Star*, April 14, 1974, p. 1.

134. The last audit of Conrad's office was completed June 30, 1973. See "Pearcy Asks Data On Conrad's Office," *Indianapolis News*, April 16, 1974, p. 1.

135. Ibid.

136. John C. Nichols refused to return several phone calls from the author in 1993 to request an interview. At the time he was affiliated with an Indianapolis firm, Claridge House Medical Publishing Corp.

137. Edward Ziegner, "Hoosier Demos Look Down From Cloud 9," *Indianapolis News*, April 20, 1974, p. 19. Apparently Ziegner's opinion of St. Angelo's leadership did not take into account the financial condition of the Democratic State Central Committee. Bill Trisler later claimed that when he took over the reins, the party was $51,000 in debt. See Robert P. Mooney, "Demo Leader Trisler's Status In Doubt," in "Politics in Perspective," *Indianapolis Star*, May 9, 1976, section 2, p. 6.

138. "City Desk Memos," *Indianapolis News*, April 26, 1974, p. 6. In all likelihood

this "dart" for the week was written by Ed Ziegner. In previous articles under his byline he had referred to the new Democratic state chairman as "William" Trisler. Trisler's real first name was Bill, not William.

139. Art Harris and Skip Hess, "Political Calls Okd by Conrad," *Indianapolis News*, April 25, 1974, p. 1; Skip Hess and Art Harris, "Conrad Political Calls Crisscrossed The Nation," *Indianapolis News*, April 26, 1974, p. 1.

140. Stephan Lesher interview with author, April 6, 1994.

141. Conrad was well aware of the historical significance of the Amendment; during the summer of 1973 he prepared a detailed "Book Outline" dealing with vacancies in the vice-presidency. He also wrote a six-page introduction in which he said: "If Vice President Spiro Agnew's current problems result in resignation or removal from office, the replacement mechanism of the 25th Amendment would be triggered for the first time. A vacancy in the Vice Presidency would mark the 17th occasion in American history, totaling more than 38 years, when that office was empty." The outline and introduction are in the possession of the author.

142. John Livengood interview with author, September 29, 1993.

143. Art Harris and Skip Hess, "36 Tell City Calls On State Bill," *Indianapolis News*, April 29, 1974, p. 1. The article listed all the phone calls and the cost of each, but did not list the total cost of the 36 calls to Tell City, which was $73.59.

144. Skip Hess and Art Harris, "Audit Begins On Conrad Phone Bills," *Indianapolis News*, April 30, 1974, p. 1.

145. William M. Schreiber interview with author, January 31, 1994.

146. See Robert P. Mooney, "Politics in Perspective," *Indianapolis Star*, April 21, 1974.

147. B. Patrick Bauer interview with author, December 23, 1993.

148. Untitled press release by Larry A. Conrad, in possession of author. See Robert P. Mooney, "Conrad-Schreiber Contest Eyed As Garver Cancels His Candidacy," *Indianapolis Star*, May 4, 1974, p. 17.

149. Mooney, "Conrad-Schreiber Contest Eyed As Garver Cancels His Candidacy."

150. Case Number C74–525, Marion County Circuit Court, May 8, 1974.

151. "Conrad Sued For Libel By Nichols," *Indianapolis Star*, May 7, 1974, p. 26.

152. See "Conrad Sued For Libel By Nichols"; Skip Hess and Art Harris, "$500,000 Libel Suit Filed Against Conrad," *Indianapolis News*, May 6, 1974, p. 25. William B. Olsen filed the suit in the wrong court and on May 8 moved to dismiss without prejudice the case from Superior Court to refile in Circuit Court. Wagner's law partner, Felsom Bowman, represented Conrad and Wagner. On May 28, 1974, he filed a motion for an extension of time of 30 days, which was approved by Circuit Court Judge John Niblack on May 30. On August 20, 1974, Olsen moved to withdraw as Nichols's attorney of record, claiming that he could not locate his client and that to the best of his knowledge, "John C. Nichols no longer resides within the territorial boundaries of the United States." His motion to withdraw was approved. No other action ever took place on the suit. It was finally dismissed without prejudice on March 14, 1975. There was no story in the Indianapolis newspapers about the dismissal.

153. Two Democratic state senators who did not receive congratulatory phone calls were James Plaskett of New Washington and Robert Mahowald of South Bend. These two provided the only Democratic votes in the State Senate in 1973 for

Governor Bowen's property tax control package, which also raised the sales tax. They were both defeated in the primary. They were vigorously opposed by the UAW. Dallas Sells vehemently opposed the tax package because of the shift in the tax burden and the increase in sales taxes. See Paul M. Doherty, "Both Demos Who Backed Taxes Lost," *Indianapolis Star*, May 9, 1974, p. 10.

154. Copy of letter dated May 8, 1974, signed by Jerry Lantz, Chairman, Fourth District Democrat Central Committee, in possession of author. Lantz had the date of the general election wrong. It was to be held November 5.

155. Letter dated May 9, 1974, addressed to "The Honorable Larry Conrad," signed by Emmett W. Eger, Mayor, City of Rensselaer, in possession of author.

156. Art Harris and Skip Hess, "Conrad Home Town Calls 'On State,'" *Indianapolis News*, May 10, 1974, p. 1. Conrad had indeed taken steps in May 1973 to cut back on long distance calls in the office. Indiana Bell had issued new cards in January 1973, replacing the old cards. It is unclear when these new cards were distributed to the secretary of state's office. Stu Grauel admitted that Conrad's attempt to cut back did not mean eliminating all long distance calls, contending there were legitimate reasons for them. Clearly, long distance calls can be charged to a credit card when the person possesses the number of the card. One does not need physical possession of the card. It appears that many of Conrad's staff members had the credit card number even if they were not issued a card. See Art Harris and Skip Hess, "450 Conrad Calls Made After Credit Was 'Stopped,'" *Indianapolis News*, May 4, 1974, p. 1.

157. Skip Hess and Art Harris, "Conrad Phone Bill $67,236 In 39 Months," *Indianapolis News*, May 17, 1974, p. 1. This headline was in the City Edition. When the later Home Edition was released the headline changed to "Conrad Phone Bill $67,236 in 41 Months."

158. Art Harris and Skip Hess, "Conrad Gas Billings High For Single Car," *Indianapolis News*, May 21, 1974, p. 1.

159. "Conrad Credit Card Misuse 'Warning,' *Indianapolis News*, May 24, 1974, p. 9. Governor Bowen does not recall making a public statement on this issue. He does recall speaking to staff aides about Conrad's problems with telephone calls, and thinking the scrutiny given to Conrad was unfair, given the political nature of all elective offices. Otis R. Bowen interview with author, April 19, 1993.

160. Robert Pastrick interview with author, October 5, 1993.

161. Ibid.

162. B. Patrick Bauer interview with author, December 23, 1993.

163. When Conrad's people failed to oust most of the old regulars from their district posts, Wagner met with Trisler and pledged Conrad's support to Trisler's reelection. He reportedly told Trisler "I want to wash off the blood," and said he had no complaints with Trisler as long as the state convention was open, with the delegates in the driver's seat. See Robert P. Mooney, "Conrad Aide Would 'Wash Off Blood,'" in "Politics in Perspective," *Indianapolis Star*, May 19, 1974, section 2, p. 6.

164. Donald Yeagley interview with author, August 19, 1994. In fact, Yeagley remembers that Conrad had been made an "Honorary Member of the UAW," but cannot recall if that was before or after the 1974 state convention.

165. See Robert P. Mooney, "Conrad's Labor Union Backers Band Together," *Indianapolis Star*, June 17, 1974, p. 1.

166. Robert P. Mooney, "AFL-CIO Head Indorses Schreiber," in "Politics in Perspective," *Indianapolis Star*, June 16, 1974, section 2, p. 4. Zagrovich's support for Schreiber did not surprise Wagner. He had accused Zagrovich at the meeting of the Special Committee of launching an investigation of Wagner even though it was Conrad who was the subject of the inquiry. Robert F. Wagner interview with author, January 13, 1995.

167. See Robert P. Mooney, "Conrad, Schreiber Fight Splits Demos in Convention Caucuses," *Indianapolis Star*, June 18, 1974, p. 1. Actually, Bayh's "neutrality statement" favored Conrad, who contended all along that the delegates should make the decision without party officials dictating their choice.

168. Robert F. Wagner interview with author, November 1, 1995.

169. Text of nominating speech for Larry Conrad, in possession of author. Emphasis in original.

170. See Paul M. Doherty, "Bass Drum Punctuates Democratic Convention," *Indianapolis Star*, June 19, 1974, p. 1; Robert P. Mooney, "Secretary of State Conrad Wins Easy Renomination," *Indianapolis Star*, June 19, 1974, p. 1.

171. Diary of Mary Lou Conrad, in possession of author.

172. See Robert P. Mooney, "Conrad Pays Filing Fee, Compromises," *Indianapolis Star*, June 6, 1974, and Mooney, "Secretary of State Conrad Wins Easy Renomination."

173. Diary of Mary Lou Conrad, in possession of author.

174. William M. Schreiber interview with author, January 31, 1994.

175. Aside from Conrad and Senator Bayh, the delegates nominated Jack New for treasurer, Mary Aikens Currie for auditor, and Billie R. McCullough for clerk of the Supreme and Appellate Courts.

176. Thomas R. Keating, "Voting Fun, Lake County-Style," *Indianapolis Star*, June 19, 1974, p. 17.

177. N. Stuart Grauel interview with author, June 11, 1993. The securities division of the secretary of state's office did have tape recorders for recording hearings, but these were never used outside of the division. On rare occasions, Conrad's speeches would be tape recorded, but there was no central file for these tapes. Not until 1976 did the campaign purchase a tape recorder to record all of his speeches. The purpose of such recordings was to have verification of Conrad's quotes on the campaign trail. Many of the 1976 tapes are in possession of the author.

178. As far as it can be determined, reporters never asked Conrad or Grauel about the existence of audio tapes. Nor, apparently, did any members of the Special Committee.

179. Gordon Englehart interview with author, September 10, 1993.

180. "Report of the Special Committee" of the Indiana Democratic State Central Committee, dated February 20, 1974, in possession of author.

181. Edward Ziegner interview with author, June 16, 1993.

182. Gordon St. Angelo interview with author, September 10, 1993.

183. Gordon St. Angelo interview with author, September 27, 1993.

184. Jack New interview with author, August 17, 1994.

185. Several months later, in an interview, Conrad was asked, "What about the Master Plan, did you ever find out who did it?" Conrad said, "No, there was never any proof. I think I have a good idea; some from one side and some of ours, and

money changed hands, broke businesses were bailed out, people left the country." Interview of Larry Conrad by Susan Crittenden, "I Want to Be Governor," *Spectator*, vol. 141, no. 1 (July 19, 1975), p. 7. Conrad was obviously referring to the money provided by St. Angelo to Steve Powell and to the fact that, when the John Nichols libel suit was dismissed, his attorney indicated that he thought Nichols had left the country.

186. Robert Pastrick interview with author, October 5, 1993.

7

1. Robert F. Wagner interview with author, June 10, 1993.

2. Lugar did have token opposition at the convention from U.S. Representative Earl Landgrebe, a staunch supporter of President Nixon. Landgrebe was to lose his congressional seat in November to Democrat Floyd Fithian.

3. See Robert P. Mooney, "GOP Plans 'Peace Pipe' Meeting," in "Politics in Perspective," *Indianapolis Star*, May 26, 1974.

4. "Bowen Urges GOP to Unite," *Indianapolis Star*, June 7, 1974, p. 18.

5. L. Keith Bulen interview with author, June 28, 1994.

6. The mayor of Michigan City, Randall C. Miller, was the candidate for state treasurer. Jean Merritt, from Indianapolis, was nominated for state auditor, and Patsy (Pat) Yoho, from Greene County, was the nominee for clerk of the Indiana Supreme and Appellate Courts. The four Republican state candidates were soon placed on the payroll of the Republican State Central Committee in order to campaign full time. Thomas Milligan, the Republican state chairman, revealed that they were paid at the salary rates of the offices they sought. Richard Lugar was offered a salary supplement, but refused. See "GOP Is Paying Salaries Of 4 State Candidates," *Indianapolis Star*, September 12, 1974, p. A–16. The Democrats did not make an issue of these candidates' being paid to run for office. Twelve years later, however, when the Republicans paid a salary to their candidate for secretary of state, Rob Bowen, it became a major issue in the race. Evan Bayh, the 1986 Democratic nominee for secretary of state, accused the Republican party of using license branch revenue to pay Rob Bowen to run for office.

7. The largest fund-raiser was held on February 6, 1973, at the Indianapolis Athletic Club, where about 400 supporters paid $50 per person. The dinner netted about $25,000. See "400 At $50 Conrad 'Appreciation Dinner,'" *Indianapolis Star*, February 7, 1973, p. 16.

8. Paul M. Doherty, "New Revelations Shock Bowen, Milligan," *Indianapolis Star*, August 7, 1974, p. 10. Not surprisingly, *Star* editorials during this period were silent on whether or not Nixon should resign. Four editorials in late July and early August lambasted the House Judiciary Committee. In one editorial on August 1, 1974, the *Star* commented that "impeachment committee liberals masquerade on television as the champions of the people against totalitarian government." There was no editorial on Nixon during that fateful week of his resignation. The next Watergate-related editorial appeared on August 14, where the *Star* praised the new president, Gerald Ford.

9. Robert F. Wagner interview with author, January 13, 1995.

10. Larry A. Conrad conversation with author, May 5, 1990.

11. See "Idea Of State Lottery Doesn't Upset Conrad," *Indianapolis Star,* August 21, 1974, p. 1; Robert P. Mooney, "Bowen Cool To Idea Of Lottery To Finance Pensions For Policemen," *Indianapolis Star,* August 22, 1974, p. 11.

12. Robert P. Mooney, "Conrad Calls GOP Foe's Campaign 'Negative'," *Indianapolis Star,* August 24, 1974, p. 17.

13. Ibid.

14. See Associate Press stories, "Dean Starts Prison Term Of 1–4 Years," *Indianapolis Star,* September 4, 1974, and "Ford Gives Nixon 'Full Pardon,'" *Indianapolis Star,* September 9, 1974, p. 1. Conrad issued a news release from campaign headquarters in response to President Ford's pardon of Nixon. He was hopeful that the "decision was wise, and will in the long run help mend the wounds caused by the Nixon Administration." But he expressed alarm about the "dual system that seems to be evolving in America," where "each day we see persons in power. . . meted out a different type of justice." Conrad for Secretary of State News Release, September 9, 1974, in possession of author.

15. "Bowen Hunts Answers About Conrad Report," *Indianapolis Star,* September 28, 1974, p. 32.

16. "Conrad Covers Questioned Expenses, Repaying $7,753," *Indianapolis Star,* September 24, 1974, p. 6. Text of Conrad's remarks, September 23, 1974, in possession of author.

17. John Livengood interview with author, September 29, 1993.

18. "Conrad Covers Questioned Expenses, Repaying $7,753," p. 6.

19. Editorial entitled "Plug The Money Holes," *Indianapolis Star,* September 26, 1974, p. 32.

20. Art Harris and Skip Hess, "Jury to Probe Conrad's Office," *Indianapolis News,* October 17, 1974, p. 1. Rehm and Bochnowski, along with Bob Rooksby, signed notarized affidavits which were submitted to the State Board of Accounts in which they swore to their employment dates and affirmed that they "never received any compensation for work . . . not performed." Copies of affidavits in possession of author.

21. See "Bowen Hunts Answers About Conrad Report"; "Conrad Controversy Likely to Die Out," in "Behind Closed Doors," *Indianapolis Star,* September 29, 1974, section 2, p. 6.

22. "Certifying Conrad's Office Audit Unneeded," *Indianapolis Star,* October 1, 1974, p. 1.

23. Art Harris and Skip Hess, "Conrad '72 Campaign Calls Charged To State," *Indianapolis News,* October 9, 1974, p. 1.

24. See "Statement by Bulen," *Indianapolis News,* October 12, 1974, p. 1.

25. L. Keith Bulen interview with author, June 28, 1994.

26. Skip Hess and Art Harris, "Pearcy Raps Board For Inaction On Conrad Case," *Indianapolis News,* October 11, 1974, p. 1.

27. Robert P. Mooney, "Pearcy Board Accusation In Conrad Case Rang Phony," in "Politics in Perspective," *Indianapolis Star,* October 13, 1974, p. 1. Robert Wagner would neither confirm nor deny such a "deal," but agreed that the political timing and the events were "transparent." Wagner interview with author, January 13, 1995.

28. Art Harris and Skip Hess, "Conrad Calls for $, Politics," *Indianapolis News,* October 14, 1974, p. 1.

29. Editorial entitled "Vote Conrad Out," *Indianapolis News,* November 2, 1974, p. 4.

30. Ed Ziegner, "Economy The Key To Vote Tomorrow," *Indianapolis News,* November 4, 1974, p. 1.

31. Jack New, the candidate for treasurer, lost the doughnut by only 5,214 votes. One factor here was his home county of Hancock, which he carried by nearly 2,000 votes, running substantially ahead of the ticket. Currie lost the doughnut by 7,620 and McCullough lost by 6,462.

32. The votes totals are from the *1974 Election Report, State of Indiana* issued by Larry A. Conrad, secretary of state. In some of the counties carried by Conrad and lost by Bayh, the presence of a third party candidate in the U.S. Senate Race, Don E. Lee of the American Party, may have affected the totals. Lee received 49,592 votes statewide.

33. Ed Ziegner, "Election Lessons For Both Parties," *Indianapolis News,* November 6, 1974, p. 21.

34. Diary of Mary Lou Conrad, in possession of author.

35. Ibid.

36. See Neal R. Peirce and John Keefe, *The Great Lakes States of America* (New York: W. W. Norton & Company, 1980), pp. 260–261.

37. See Edward Ziegner, "Larry Conrad Opens Campaign With Income Tax Pledge," *Indianapolis News,* December 15, 1975, p. 7. The *Star* estimated the crowd at 3,400. See Robert Rees, "Conrad 'Tosses Hat' In Governor's Race," December 15, 1975, p. 25.

38. Otis R. Bowen interview with author, April 19, 1993. The 1975 Indiana General Assembly, with Bowen's support, passed the law placing the offices of U.S. senator, governor, and lieutenant governor in the direct primary. The state Republican organization briefly considered a statewide "slating" of candidates, prior to the primary, but abandoned the idea. See "Poll Favors Primary For State Offices," *Indianapolis Star,* September 5, 1975, p. 33.

39. Conrad, quoted in "The Next Governor?" *Spectator,* vol. 141, no. 1 (July 19, 1975), p. 6. In this same article Conrad expressed one reservation about the direct primary: "It will cost a lot more."

40. Robert F. Wagner interview with author, June 10, 1993.

41. Ibid.

42. Ibid.; Robert F. Wagner interview with author, November 1, 1995.

43. William Gigerich interview with author, May 26, 1993. Shortly after Gigerich received permission to join Conrad's campaign, he was appointed by the County Commissioners of Marion County to fill the vacancy created by the death of the Washington Township Trustee. This part-time position went to a Democrat only because of a quirk in the Unigov legislation that allowed three elected county officials to act as County Commissioners in filling vacancies. After the Democrats won most of the county offices in the 1974 election, Gigerich got the nod. Shortly thereafter, the state legislature changed the Unigov statute, giving the right to fill such elected offices to the precinct committeemen of the party of the previous incumbent.

44. News release from the Conrad for Governor Committee, undated, in possession of author.

45. Robert F. Wagner interview with author, January 16, 1993.

46. Russell (Bun) Gallahan interview with author, August 18, 1994.

47. Robert F. Wagner interview with author, June 10, 1993. Actually, the total expenditures amounted to $152,918.09, but this included money raised and expended in 1975.

48. Pat McCarty interview with author, May 26, 1993.

49. Robert F. Wagner interview with author, June 10, 1993.

50. Jane Allen, who had served as Conrad's press secretary in the secretary of state's office, had recently married Bob Rooksby.

51. The first two calls to a Democratic household were pro-Conrad calls, in which the voter was urged to support Larry. The third and final call was scripted as follows: "Larry would like to have the time to call you himself, but he wanted me to tell you that even if you don't vote for Larry Conrad, please vote." The script was agreed to by Conrad and reflected his commitment to political participation, regardless of the outcome. Robert F. Wagner interview with author, November 1, 1995.

52. "Democratics [*sic*] need money, enthusiasm," *Peru Tribune*, April 27, 1976.

53. The statewide survey was conducted by Metropolitan Campaign Services and consisted of 524 total respondents, resulting in an approximate error factor of 4.5%. Cross-tabulated data in possession of author.

54. Interestingly, the Republican polls showed "a strong anti-Conrad reaction within the small percentage of voters who were familiar with him." See William J. Watt, *Bowen: The Years as Governor* (Indianapolis: Bierce Associates, 1981), pp. 159–160. Presumably, these polls were of all likely general election voters, although Watt does explain the sample.

55. A Republican poll in February 1976 confirmed Hartke's poor standing with the electorate. Watt, in *Bowen*, p. 162, reported that the poll show a 41–34% plurality "still disapproved of the way [Hartke] had performed as senator. "

56. Media Release, Conrad for Governor, April 12 and April 14, 1976, in possession of author.

57. Jack New interview with author, August 17, 1994.

58. Ibid.

59. Ibid.

60. Ibid.

61. Ibid.

62. Ibid.

63. Ibid.

64. "Democratics [*sic*] need money, enthusiasm." New did try to convince Democratic leaders that he would be a stronger candidate than Conrad by writing them and comparing his vote totals in the 1974 election with Conrad's. He particularly focused on his margins in Marion County and the doughnut. See "New Notes His Support," *Indianapolis Star*, April 4, 1976, p. 10.

65. Robert Fair interview with author, July 3, 1995.

66. Brochure, "Six reasons Larry Conrad makes good sense for Governor of Indiana," undated, in possession of author; Conrad for Governor media releases dated March 14, 1976, March 20, 1976, and April 8, 1976, in possession of author.

67. Jack New interview with author, August 17, 1994.

68. Robert Fair interview with author, July 3, 1995.

69. Diary of Mary Lou Conrad, in possession of author.

70. Ibid.

71. The final vote totals are from the *1976 Election Report, State of Indiana,* Larry A. Conrad, secretary of state. Conrad's loss of Marshall County was puzzling to Conrad's staff. They finally attributed it to an organizational vote favoring Jack New, led by the Marshall County Chairman, whose spouse was a banker.

72. Robert P. Mooney, "Hayes Won't Concede Race Yet," *Indianapolis Star,* May 5, 1976, p. 1.

73. Diary of Mary Lou Conrad, in possession of author.

74. Robert Wagner interviews with author, June 10, 1993, and November 1, 1995. The Sunday after the election, Robert P. Mooney wrote in his "Politics in Perspective" column that the "two best organized campaigns in the recent direct primary elections were those of Larry Conrad. . . and Richard G. Lugar. [B]oth were tops." See *Indianapolis Star,* May 9, 1976, section 2, p. 6.

75. Mooney, "Hayes Won't Concede Race Yet."

76. Ibid.

77. Governor Otis R. Bowen and Lieutenant Governor Robert Orr were unopposed for the Republican nomination. They had hardly tapped their campaign committees for the primary election, and had money to run television commercials three days after the primary, extolling the accomplishments of their administration.

78. State Senator Tom Teague had won the Democratic nomination for lieutenant governor in the primary. He had been opposed by Mary Aikens Currie, the state auditor. Teague won the election by 1,867 votes out of 472,811 cast. His margin of victory in Vigo County (Terre Haute) was 2,394 votes, and nearly 20% of the Democrat ballots in Vigo County were absentees. It was reported that many absentee ballots were found floating in the Wabash River shortly after the primary. A Vigo County grand jury investigated the absentee voting, but decided it would "need months of investigation to find cause for returning indictments." This episode eventually resulted in changing the state law concerning the return of absentee ballots to the county clerk and the process by which such ballots would be counted. See "Vigo Grand Jury Ends Absentee Voter Probe," *Indianapolis Star,* June 18, 1976.

79. Robert F. Wagner interview with author, June 10, 1993.

80. Robert P. Mooney, "Demo Leader Trisler's Status In Doubt," in "Politics in Perspective," *Indianapolis Star,* May 9, 1976, section 2, p. 6.

81. Don Michael interview with author, August 22, 1995.

82. Robert F. Wagner interview with author, June 10, 1993.

83. Robert F. Wagner interview with author, November 1, 1995.

84. William Gigerich interview with author, May 26, 1993.

85. Robert F. Wagner interview with author, June 10, 1993.

86. Ibid.

87. Conrad for Governor media release, "Conrad's Campaign Manager Says Bowen is Vulnerable," May 31, 1976, in possession of author.

88. Robert F. Wagner interview with author, January 13, 1995.

89. See Robert P. Mooney, "'Bridesmaids' Win 1976 Nominations At Demo Convention," *Indianapolis Star,* June 16, 1976, p. 1. Jonathon Birge and State Representative Gregory Reising were the other candidates for attorney general. Birge and Reising withdrew after the second ballot. In the other races, State Senator

Graham A. Richard from Fort Wayne won the nomination for superintendent of public instruction and Leigh Neuhauser from Scottsburg won the nomination for reporter of the Supreme and Appellate Courts.

90. Text of Keynote Address to the 1976 Democratic State Convention, in possession of author. Also see Robert N. Bell, "Demo Speakers Call For 'New Revolution,'" *Indianapolis Star,* June 16, 1976, p. 13.

91. This problem persisted throughout the campaign. In the last week of the campaign both President Ford and his running mate, Senator Robert Dole, visited Indiana. On both occasions, *Indianapolis News* ran front-page photos of Ford and Dole with Governor Bowen. In Jimmy Carter's visits to Indiana he was frequently photographed with Conrad. None of these photos ever appeared in the Indianapolis papers.

92. "Conrad Charges 'Mismanagement,'" *Indianapolis Star,* June 19, 1976, p. 32.

93. John S. Mason and William M. Shaw, "Conrad Manager, Co-op Linked," *Indianapolis Star,* July 21, 1976, p. 1.

94. During this time the Hartke campaign suffered a major setback. Victor Hoffmann, Hartke's campaign manager, died of a heart attack in his hotel room in Indianapolis at age 60. Hoffmann had been my undergraduate professor at Valparaiso University in the early 1960s, and had encouraged me to go on for a Ph.D. in political science.

95. It was during the summer of 1976 that Diane and Stu Grauel separated. Their divorce was final in September 1976.

96. The next largest group representing teachers was the Indiana Federation of Teachers (IFT), affiliated with the AFL-CIO. The IFT was much smaller than the ISTA and had assured Wagner that they would endorse Conrad and the Democratic ticket.

97. Graham Richard, the nominee for superintendent of public instruction, had assured Wagner before the primary that, with him on the ticket, the ISTA endorsement would be assured. Wagner was "furious" with Richard when the ISTA balked, and in 1980, when Richard sought the nomination for lieutenant governor, Wagner supported his opponent, State Senator Robert (Bob) Peterson, who won the nomination. Robert F. Wagner interview with author, November 1, 1995.

98. See "Bowen, Conrad Get OK Of Teachers," *Indianapolis News,* August 31, 1976, p. 33.

99. Cartoon by Barnett, *Indianapolis News,* September 12, 1976, p. 12.

100. See Gerry LaFollette, "Ruckelshaus On Ford List?" *Indianapolis News,* August 13, 1976, p. 1.

101. The Republican National Convention convened in Kansas City the week of August 16. President Gerald Ford was nominated, beating back a challenge from Ronald Reagan. Senator Robert Dole of Kansas received the vice-presidential nomination.

102. Wagner's irritation with Governor Brown was made worse when Brown landed in Indianapolis and refused to get into the limousine with Conrad and Hartke for the drive back to French Lick. Brown said he would ride only in an older model green Plymouth sedan. An older car was eventually located, and Brown agreed to ride in it. Robert F. Wagner interview with author, November 1, 1995.

103. Robert F. Wagner interview with author, November 1, 1995.

104. Conrad for Governor Media Release, "Conrad Pledges to Cut Residential Electric Bills in Indiana," September 7, 1976, in possession of author.

105. Conrad for Governor Media Release, "Conrad Kicks Off Last Days of Voter Registration," September 11, 1976, in possession of author.

106. Conrad for Governor media releases in possession of author.

107. Conrad for Governor media release, "Conrad Asks Bowen Why State Bridges Are Collapsing," September 17, 1976, in possession of author.

108. Television stations from Evansville and Terre Haute covered the event. Conrad for Governor media release, "Conrad Closes Collapsed Bridge by 'Tying Ribbon,'" September 18, 1976, in possession of author.

109. Conrad had proposed a series of joint broadcast appearances with Governor Bowen, and Tom Teague also challenged Robert Orr. Bowen rejected the proposal, claiming there were already several joint appearances scheduled. See "Teague Wants To Debate Orr," *Indianapolis News*, August 25, 1976, p. 8.

110. David Frick interview with author, September 13, 1974.

111. Bill Pittman, "Hartke, Conrad Give Business Their Views," *Indianapolis News*, October 9, 1976, p. 1.

112. Bowen agreed to only three "joint appearances" with Conrad where they would be together on the dais at the same time. The first, before a group called "Indiana Highways for Survival" was held on October 13, 1976. The second, an appearance before the Society of Professional Journalists (Sigma Delta Chi), was on Monday, October 20. The other appearance was two days later before a group called "Public Action in Correctional Efforts" (PACE). All meetings were in Indianapolis.

113. Conrad for Governor media release, "Conrad Supports Parimutuel Racing," September 30, 1976, in possession of author.

114. Emphasis in original. Postcard in possession of author.

115. Conrad for Governor media release, "Conrad Will Cut State Bureaucracy by 10 Per Cent," October 1, 1976, in possession of author.

116. N. Stuart Grauel interview with author, June 11, 1993.

117. Raymond H. Scheele, "Rip in Middletown," *Texas Journal of Political Studies*, vol. 16:2 (spring–summer 1994), p. 63.

118. "'Change In Thrust' Makes Conrad Drop Ad Agency," *Indianapolis Star*, September 26, 1976, section 4, p. 11, and David Rohn, "Reporters Observe Bowen and Conrad," *Indianapolis News*, October 27, 1976, p. 1.

119. See "'Change In Thrust' Makes Conrad Drop Ad Agency."

120. Robert F. Wagner interview with author, November 1, 1995.

121. Conrad for Governor media release, October 7, 1976, in possession of author.

122. Photograph entitled "Like This," *Indianapolis News*, October 8, 1976, p. 1.

123. Ed Ziegner, "Larry Conrad Not Counting Himself Out by Long Shot," *Indianapolis News*, October 8, 1976, p. 6.

124. Conrad for Governor media release, October 29, 1976, in possession of author.

125. See "Knew It Was Over Early," *Indianapolis News*, November 3, 1976, p. 12.

126. Robert F. Wagner interview with author, January 16, 1993.

8

1. Edwin J. Simcox interview with author, September 17, 1993.

2. Two young black men were lynched that night in Marion. A third black teenager, James Cameron, also was dragged from the Grant County jail to be lynched, but in a miraculous turn of events, the mob released him. These events are described in Cameron's book, *A Time of Terror* (Baltimore: Black Classic Press), 1982.

3. David Frick interview with author, October 3, 1994. The Urban Development Action Grant (UDAG) money was instrumental in many downtown projects, including the restoration of the historic Indiana Theater on Washington Street. See William H. Hudnut III, *The Hudnut Years in Indianapolis, 1976–1991* (Bloomington: Indiana University Press, 1995), p. 88.

4. David Frick interview with author, September 13, 1994.

5. Don Michael interview with author, August 22, 1995.

6. William Gigerich interview with author, May 26, 1993.

7. Don Michael agrees that Gigerich was not kept informed, but that was intentional. "We never told anybody where our support was coming from. Our theory was that if Trisler's people knew our supporters they would begin picking them off. The first time all of our supporters would be in the same room together was at breakfast just a few hours before the reorganization meeting." Don Michael interview with author, August 22, 1995.

8. William Gigerich interview with author, May 26, 1993.

9. Don Michael interview with author, August 22, 1995.

10. One major money problem, of course, was the $120,000 debt left over from the 1976 election. In December 1976, an Indianapolis fund-raiser raised nearly $100,000, leaving a balance of slightly more than $20,000. Conrad became personally responsible for that amount, and he and Mary Lou began making monthly payments to begin retiring the debt.

11. Edwin Simcox interview with author, September 17, 1993.

12. Ibid.

13. Raymond J. Hafsten, Jr. interview with author, February 13, 1995.

14. Ibid.

15. Robert (Bob) Rock and Matthew Welsh joined with Conrad in the endorsement. These last three Democratic gubernatorial nominees urged the primary voters to support Hillenbrand.

16. With 541,961 Democrat votes cast, Hillenbrand received 284,182 to Townsend's 257,779. The vote totals are from Secretary of State Edwin J. Simcox, *1980 Election Report, State of Indiana.*

17. Marvella Bayh passed away on April 24, 1979.

18. Mary Lou Conrad interview with author, August 23, 1995.

19. At the time, DeBartolo owned all the major shopping malls in Indianapolis. Years later, in March 1996, the publicly traded Simon Property Group announced merger plans with DeBartolo Realty Corporation, a public corporation. The Simon Property Group had outgrown DeBartolo, reporting 1995 revenues of over $553 million, compared to DeBartolo's $332.7 million. See Steve Kukolla, "Simon, mall rival plan mega-merger," *Indianapolis Star*, March 27, 1996, p. 1.

20. Diane Simon interview with author, December 5, 1995.

21. Raymond J. Hafsten, Jr. interview with author, February 13, 1995.

22. John Krauss interview with author, September 14, 1994.

23. A great deal of effort was expended to prove that the White River was navigable. In 1831, a steamboat followed the White River northward, hauling materials to build the National Road. The boat succeeded in reaching Indianapolis and several citizens claimed the river was navigable. An effort was made to have the Indiana General Assembly declare it to be so and appropriate money to improve the waterway. Unfortunately, when the steamboat began its return trip, it ran aground. It was stranded in the river for some time. See the entry "Robert Hanna," in David J. Bodenhamer and Robert G. Barrows, eds., *Encyclopedia of Indianapolis* (Bloomington: Indiana University Press, 1994), p. 1202.

24. Racial segregation, however, was the prevailing practice in the Indianapolis public school system. See Hudnut, *The Hudnut Years,* pp. 6–7.

25. For Marion County as a whole, "net out-migration has been prevalent since the 1960s. This out-migration reflects both suburbanization into surrounding counties as well as shifts of population to other states and regions of the country." See Bodenhamer and Barrows, eds., *Encyclopedia of Indianapolis,* note to Figure 7, p. 1510.

26. Finally, in 1987, work began on restoring the Statehouse. In addition, a new "government complex" was built and the old state office building was remodeled.

27. Hudnut, *The Hudnut Years,* p. 7.

28. In 1966, anticipating the 1967 Indiana General Assembly, the GIPC formulated a plan to establish a county-wide police department. During the legislative session, John Mutz, a Republican state representative, introduced a bill giving the city police department county-wide jurisdiction and reducing the county sheriff's powers to administering the county jail. This bill failed when Mayor Barton testified against it, but the groundwork was done for Unigov. See C. James Owen and York Willbern, *Governing Metropolitan Indianapolis: The Politics of Unigov* (Berkeley: University of California Press, 1985), pp. 44–45.

29. David Frick interview with author, October 3, 1994.

30. Hudnut, *The Hudnut Years,* p. xxxiii.

31. Ibid., p. 97.

32. Quoted in "Strategy relied on tax funds," *Indianapolis News,* November 15, 1989, p. 1.

33. Years later, some members of the city-county council criticized the $4 million bond issue, claiming they were mislead by the city administration in claiming that advertising revenue at the new facility would pay for the retirement of the bonds. The major advertising contract was never signed. See "Strategy relied on tax funds."

34. Hudnut, *The Hudnut Years,* p. 97.

35. Sidney Weedman interview with author, November 21, 1995.

36. Ibid.

37. The City Committee consisted of 33 members, most of whom participated actively; others attended some meetings but eventually became inactive due to career changes. For the membership of the City Committee, see "Elite panel avoids spotlight," *Indianapolis News,* November 14, 1989, p. 1.

38. See "Victory? Mayor without license?" *Indianapolis News,* November 14, 1989, p. A-4.

39. See "Sports Corp. key to city strategy," *Indianapolis News,* November 14, 1989, p. A–4; "Business opportunity opened for insiders," *Indianapolis News,* November 16, 1989, p. 1.

40. The first annual White River Park State Games opened on Friday, July 1, 1983, with opening ceremonies held at the IU Track and Field Stadium. See Jeff Swiatek, "Sports kickoff fun and games," *Indianapolis Star,* July 2, 1983, p. 1.

41. See "Elite panel avoids spotlight." In March 1984, it was announced that the Baltimore Colts were moving to the Hoosier Dome. Also see William H. Hudnut III, *Minister/Mayor* (Philadelphia: Westminster Press, 1987), ch. 1.

42. William H. Hudnut III interview with author, June 30, 1995.

43. Sidney Weedman interview with author, November 21, 1995.

44. Quoted in "Elite panel avoids spotlight," *Indianapolis News,* November 14, 1989.

45. Copy of release in possession of author.

46. See Susan Headden, "Food, fireworks to fuel flame of festival fanfare," *Indianapolis Star,* July 22, 1982, p. A–1; Richard D. Walton, "Balloons, pigeons, broad smiles brighten festive-minded downtown," *Indianapolis Star,* July 24, 1982, p. A–1.

47. Quoted in Susan Headden, "Ceremonies a feast for sports fans' eyes, ears," *Indianapolis Star,* July 24, 1982, p. 1.

48. Terrence D. Straub interview with author, September 28, 1994.

49. Remarks of Larry A. Conrad before a group of employees of Melvin Simon and Associates, August 28, 1986. Audio tape in possession of author.

50. B. Patrick Bauer interview with author, December 23, 1993.

51. See Hurley C. Goodall, *Inside the House: My Years in the Indiana Legislature, 1978–1992* (Muncie: Ball State University Press, 1995), p. 92.

52. Ed Ziegner interview with author, June 16, 1993.

53. John Krauss interview with author, September 14, 1994.

54. Hudnut, *The Hudnut Years,* p. 294.

55. Audio tape of remarks by Larry Conrad in possession of author.

56. John Livengood interview with author, September 29, 1993. When Evan Bayh decided he wanted Mike Pannos as the new state chairman, Livengood stepped aside.

57. John Krauss interview with author, September 14, 1994.

58. Robert McNulty interview with author, January 13, 1995.

59. Ibid.

60. Remarks of Larry Conrad to teachers. Undated audio tape in possession of author, likely delivered in 1985.

61. The surprise party could not be held on Friday, February 8, 1985, because the NBA all-star game was being played that weekend at Market Square Arena, and Conrad was immersed in the festivities surrounding the game.

62. Larry later told Claudia that he suspected something was afoot when he and Morris entered the building and Larry saw a large catering truck outside. It was the same catering firm that he always used for his parties. Claudia Prosser interview with author, April 16, 1996.

63. "Indianapolis On The Rebound," *National Geographic,* vol. 172, no. 2 (August 1987), pp. 230–259.

64. See Hudnut, *The Hudnut Years,* pp. 65–66.

65. Quoted in Linda Graham Caleca, "Indy gambles big in quest for gold," *Indianapolis Star*, August 4, 1987, p. 1.

66. Hudnut, *The Hudnut Years*, p. 100.

67. Claudia Prosser interview with author, February 19, 1996.

68. Sidney H. Weedman interview with author, February 20, 1996.

69. David Frick interview with author, October 3, 1994.

70. Linda Graham Caleca, "PAX-I president's life a race to the games' finish," *Indianapolis Star*, August 4, 1987, p. C–1.

71. Claudia Prosser interview with author, February 19, 1996. One of the Disney representatives, Phil Lengyel, was also a graduate of Ball State University, something that endeared him to Conrad.

72. Scott L. Miley and George Stuteville, "Official warns of political focus," *Indianapolis Star*, April 15, 1987, p. 23.

73. Mark Nichols, "Quayle feared Cuba-Castro issue would politicize Pan Am Games," *Indianapolis Star*, April 12, 1987, p. 6-B.

74. Linda Graham Caleca and Scott L. Miley, "Cuba, Castro emphasis riles Indiana Senators," *Indianapolis Star*, April 11, 1987.

75. Linda Graham Caleca, "PAX-I president's life a race to the games' finish," *Indianapolis Star*, August 4, 1987, p. C–1. Ironically, Mark Miles had served as the campaign manager for Dan Quayle in his successful run for the U.S. Senate seat in 1980, when Quayle defeated Senator Birch Bayh.

76. John Krauss interview with author, September 14, 1994.

77. Ibid.

78. "Unassuming games chairman is 'brilliant,'" *Indianapolis Star*, August 4, 1987, p. 4.

79. Susan Hanafee, "Pan Am closing to combine fireworks, diplomacy," *Indianapolis Star*, April 1, 1987, p. 49.

80. John R. O'Neil, "Find other place for ceremony, Legion says," *Indianapolis Star*, April 6, 1987, p. 1.

81. Ibid.

82. Linda Graham Caleca, "PAX-I delegation to travel to Cuba for talks," *Indianapolis Star*, April 9, 1987, p. 21.

83. Sidney H. Weedman interview with author, February 20, 1996.

84. Scott L. Miley and Linda Graham Caleca, "Mayor backs site change for Pan Am ceremony," *Indianapolis Star*, April 7, 1987, p. 1.

85. Susan Hanafee and Linda Graham Caleca, "Pan Am finale site still in limbo," *Indianapolis Star*, April 21, 1987, p. 1.

86. "Cuba On The Mall," *Indianapolis Star* editorial, April 10, 1987, p. 24.

87. The *Star* editorialized in 1982 that "Opening ceremonies chairman Larry Conrad deserves special applause. . . ." See "Festival And Future," editorial, *Indianapolis Star*, July 30, 1982, p. A–10.

88. Sidney H. Weedman interview with author, February 20, 1996.

89. Linda Graham Caleca, "Indy gambles big in quest for gold," *Indianapolis Star*, August 4, 1987, p. 1.

90. David Frick interview with author, October 3, 1994; John R. O'Neill, "40,000 expected for Pan Am Finale," *Indianapolis Star*, August 21, 1987, p. D–2; Susan Hanafee, "Special effects will close Pan Am Games, *Indianapolis Star*, August 23, 1987, p. 1.

91. Linda Graham Caleca, "Cuba buys 220 hours of coverage," *Indianapolis Star,* April 18, 1987, p. 1.

92. Ibid.

93. Linda Graham Caleca, "Gentle, joking Castro assures games group Cuba coming to play," *Indianapolis Star,* April 19, 1987, p. 1.

94. Ibid.; Linda Graham Caleca, "Castro says he'll stay home for games," *Indianapolis Star,* April 18, 1987, p. 1.

95. Linda Graham Caleca, "PAX-I ends visit to Cuba on upbeat note," *Indianapolis Star,* April 20, 1987, p. 1.

96. "No. 3 Cuban may come to finale," *Indianapolis Star,* August 21, 1987, p. 1; O'Neill, "40,000 expected for Pan Am finale."

97. See Susan Hanafee, "Pan Am magic sets stage for games' opening," *Indianapolis Star,* August 8, 1987, p. 1; "Pan Am Games off to a flying start," *Indianapolis Star,* August 9, 1987, p. 1.

98. See George Stuteville, "Group urges Cuban exiles to not harass Cuban teams," *Indianapolis Star,* August 21, 1987, p. D–2.

99. See "Cubans, spectators fight at baseball game," *Indianapolis Star,* August 22, 1987, p. 1.

100. "Games end with fanfare, feelings," *Indianapolis Star,* August 24, 1987, p. 1. One of the many problems encountered was that the person in charge of issuing credentials for the closing ceremony snapped under the pressure and simply left. Others were pressed into service. Claudia Prosser interview with author, February 19, 1996.

101. Claudia Prosser interview with author, February 10, 1993.

102. See "Games end with fanfare, feelings."

103. Ibid.

104. See Jo Ellen Meyers Sharp, "City wins big with amateur sports," *Indianapolis Star,* June 26, 1993, p. B–4; Bill Benner, "Amateur sports is paying off in huge dividends," *Indianapolis Star,* June 26, 1993, p. D–1.

105. Undated and untitled audio tape of speech delivered by Larry Conrad, in possession of author.

106. The next year, when Conrad went to Africa, the Kenyans nicknamed him "Biggie-Babba," meaning "respected father," for the way he would question them about their lives, their families, and their diets. It reminded them of the way a father would inquire about what was going on in the lives of his adult children. Roy Schea interview with author, April 16, 1996. Roy Schea is executive director of the Indianapolis Zoo.

107. Undated and untitled audio tape of speech delivered by Larry Conrad, in possession of author.

108. Ibid.

109. Undated audio tape of speech by Larry Conrad before a J-J dinner, probably delivered the summer of 1986, in possession of author.

110. Joe Hogsett interview with author, October 4, 1993.

111. Ibid.

112. Audio tape of remarks by Larry Conrad, in possession of author.

113. Joe Hogsett interview with author, October 4, 1993.

114. Conversation between Larry Conrad and Birch Bayh, May 4, 1990, witnessed by the author.

115. Joe Hogsett interview with author, October 4, 1993.
116. Frank O'Bannon interview with author, April 16, 1996.
117. Joe Hogsett interview with author, October 4, 1993.
118. Ibid.
119. Ibid.
120. Ibid.; Frank O'Bannon interview with author, April 16, 1996.
121. Audio tape in possession of author. Actually, the NBA franchise was owned not by Melvin Simon and Associates, Inc., but by Melvin and Herb Simon personally.
122. Remarks from audio tapes of Conrad speeches, in possession of author.
123. David Allen interview with author, June 8, 1994.
124. Robert McNulty interview with author, January 13, 1995.
125. Undated audio tape of speech by Larry Conrad entitled "Risk Taking," in possession of author.
126. Claudia Prosser interview with author, March 9, 1994.
127. Robert McNulty interview with author, January 13, 1995.
128. "Lilly and a city's shape," editorial, *Indianapolis News*, November 11, 1989, p. A–4.
129. Quoted in Hudnut, *The Hudnut Years*, pp. 15–16.
130. Fifty-one percent of the Conrad Group was owned by Larry Conrad, with Claudia Prosser owning five percent. The remaining amount was owned by Jim Smith. Smith had been retained by Conrad in previous years to represent some of the Simon interests at the Statehouse. Claudia Prosser interview with author, April 16, 1996.
131. Robert McNulty interview with author, January 13, 1995.
132. Ibid.

9

1. Robert Boxell interview with author, November 16, 1994.
2. Mary Lou Conrad interview with author, October 22, 1993.
3. Ibid.
4. Diary of Larry A. Conrad, in possession of author.
5. Ibid.
6. Ibid., emphasis in original.
7. Robert McNulty interview with author, January 13, 1995.
8. John Krauss interview with author, September 14, 1994.
9. Diary of Mary Lou Conrad, in possession of author.
10. Ibid.
11. The name is actually the name of the medical complex, consisting of two separate facilities located on the east side of Lyon. One ten-story building houses the medical units specializing in cardiovascular medicine. The adjacent building houses the units specializing in pneumology. The hospitals are named in honor of Louis Pradel, a former mayor of Lyon.
12. Diary of Mary Lou Conrad, in possession of author.
13. Ibid.
14. Claudia Prosser interview with author, February 10, 1993.

15. Claudia Prosser interview with author, February 10, 1993; John Krauss interview with author, September 24, 1994.

16. Diary of Mary Lou Conrad, in possession of author.

17. For much of the description of Conrad's medical condition, I am grateful to Dr. Linnemeier.

18. Dr. Thomas Linnemeier interview with author, February 29, 1995.

19. Ibid.

20. Ibid.

21. Ibid.

22. Claudia Prosser interview with author, February 10, 1993.

23. Ibid.

24. Dr. Thomas Linnemeier interview with author, February 29, 1995.

25. Claudia Prosser interview with author, February 10, 1993.

26. Ibid.

27. Claudia Prosser interview with author, February 10, 1993.

28. Ibid.

INDEX

Abrams, Elliott, 240–41
Adams, Ruth, 197
Aetna Insurance, 61, 123
AFL-CIO, 132, 141, 161–62
Agnew, Spiro, 152
Allen County, 73, 89, 104, 105
Allen, David J. (Dave), 24, 254
Allen, Dozier, 159
Allen, Jane, *see* Rooksby, Jane Allen
Allen, William L. III, 169, 172, 173, 176–77
Alum, Johnny, 183
American Legion, 241–43
American Legion Mall, 228–29, 239, 241–42
Anderson, 89, 200, 210, 221
Anderson, Charlie, 22
Anderson, Jack, 112
Anderson, John, 156, 161
Angel, Nick, 82
Annee, Paul, 241
Anthony, John, 207–8
Arlington, Virginia, 1
Associated Press, 130, 145
    managing editors, 203
Atlanta, Georgia, 148

BAID program, 78, 123, 135, 148
Bainbridge, Phillip E., 154
Baker, Sue, 197
Ball Memorial Hospital, 15, 21, 28
Ball State University, 11–13, 15, 44, 76, 182, 197
Baltimore, Maryland, 37, 39, 235
Bannon, Bill, 75, 77, 197
Barton, John J., 223
Batesville, 142–45
Batista, Fulgencio, 245
Bauer, B. Patrick, 154, 159–62, 230,
Bayh, Birch E., Jr., 75, 78, 113, 115, 126, 132, 161, 178–79, 197, 198, 213, 216, 249
    meets Conrad, 16, 19
    1962 announcement for senate, 17
    1962 senate campaign, 21–29
    subcommittee chairman, 35
    airplane crash, 36–38
    1968 reelection campaign, 42–48
    and Diane Simon, 45–46, 221
    advice to Conrad, 48, 95–96
    and St. Angelo, 54–57, 89
    and Trisler, 142–43
    1974 Democratic state convention, 162, 164
    1974 general election, 169–70, 176–77
    1976 general election, 210
    1980 general election, 220
Bayh, Marvella, 17, 21, 36–38 42, 143
Bayh, B. Evans III, 17, 217, 234, 249
Beaver, Michael E., 131
Beck, Joe, 9
Beech Grove, 43, 132
Beesley, Kenneth R., 172, 174, 175–76
Belley, France, 261
Ben Davis High School Marching Band, 100, 229
Benadum, Cecil and McClellan, 21
Blair, John, 197
Bloomington, 4, 113, 221
Bochnowski, David (Dave), 42, 80, 88, 100, 105, 126, 174, 197, 200, 201, 207
Bodine, Richard (Dick), 53, 84, 85, 103, 142, 159, 166, 185
Boehm, Theodore R. (Ted), 227, 236, 238, 240–41
Boggstown, 142
Boonville, 93
Borden, 6–9, 113
Boswell, Charlie, 21–24
Bottorff, John, 139
Bowman, Felsom, 195
Bowen, Otis R., 110, 113, 177, 218, 220
    tax package, 92, 94, 111, 179, 202, 204, 205
    1972 Republican state convention, 103–4
    1972 campaign and election, 107–8, 121
    Master Plan, 115, 116, 122, 158, 173
    reaction to Watergate, 169–71
    on direct primary, 178

record criticized, 186, 187, 202–4
Conrad's view of, 189, 191
Wagner's view of, 192–93
newspaper coverage of, 194–96
ISTA endorsement, 199
1976 TV ads, 202, 207
response to Conrad, 205–6
1976 victory, 211
1978 Bowen Team, 216
Bowen, Rob, 250
Boxell, Peggy, 20
Boxell, Robert (Bob), 47, 137, 259
    meets Conrad, 19
    early life, 19–21
    1962 Bayh campaign, 21–22, 24–29
    joins Bayh's senate staff, 30–33
    Bayhs' airplane crash, 37–38
        1968 Bayh campaign, 41–43, 46–
            47
    advice to Conrad, 48–49, 65
    1972 Conrad campaign manager, 78–
        86, 88, 96–97, 99, 105, 123
    Master Plan, 126, 131
    1976 Conrad campaign finance
        director, 191, 197, 207
    1980 Hillenbrand campaign, 219
Brademas, John, 60
Brand, Calvert, 61
Branigin, Roger, 44–45, 52–55, 116, 142, 185
Bremen, 104
Brighton, Bill, 102
Brown, Clarence J., Sr., 41
Brown County State Park, 24, 245
Brown, Jerry, 200–1
Brown, Robert (Bob), 161, 181
Brown, Thomas, 41
Browning, Michael G., 224
Burton, Judy, 142–44
Bulen, L. Keith
    Marion county GOP leader, 58–59
    1970 Republican state convention, 61
    1972 Republican state convention,
        103–4
    1972 general election, 107
    and Ziegner, 110, 127
    on geographical balance, 169, 176
    1974 Republican state convention,
        169–70
    resigns party post, 175
Bush, George, 245, 268
Bush Stadium, 245
Butler University, 45
Byrum, George W., 74, 117

Cadou, Bettie, 197
Caldemeyer, Steve, 210
California, 45, 151, 220, 221
Callahan, Frank, 100
Camp Atterbury, 245
Capehart, Homer, 17–18, 25, 28–29, 115, 178
Capehart, Jim, 83–84
Carey, James P., 44
Carroll, Michael, 254, 257, 260
Carter, Jimmy, 192, 193, 211, 212, 229
Cass County, 197, 214
Castro, Fidel, 28–29, 240–44

Cayman Islands, 259, 267
CBS Sports, 244, 245
Cellar, Emmanuel, 39
Central Normal College, 6
Charlestown, 8
Chesterfield, 210
Chicago, 2, 27, 90, 91
Chittenden, John, 60
Christian, Darrell, 145
Cincinnati, Ohio, 2
Cincinnati Reds, 9
City Committee, 225, 226, 231, 256
Clark County, 6, 66, 170, 188, 202
Clarksville, 87, 88, 158, 178
Claypool Hotel, 17, 22, 28
Clinton, Hillary Rodham, 198
Cloverdale, 158
Colbert, Bill, 27, 28
College Park, Maryland, 30
Colson, Charles (Chuck), 63
Columbus, Indiana, 171, 245
Commission for Downtown, 225
Conrad and Hafsten, 216, 217–18, 232, 234,
    256
Conrad Crazies, 81, 85, 96, 181, 190, 193, 216,
    218, 221
Conrad Family Picnic, 106
Conrad for Governor Committee, 174, 179–
    80
Conrad, Amy Lou, 21, 188, 220, 259, 263–65
Conrad, Andrew Birch, 28, 220, 265–66
Conrad, Bennett Allyn, 246
Conrad family open, 220
Conrad Group, 256–57, 261, 268
Conrad, Hallie, 8
Conrad, Ida Lou, 74
Conrad, Jeb Allyn, 11, 15, 220, 246, 266
Conrad, Jody McDade, 30, 220, 263–65
Conrad, Larry A.
    birth, family, 4, 5–6, 220
    early schooling, 6–12
    college, 12–14
    law practice, 14, 21, 216–18, 224, 234
    Mary Lou, 12–14
    graduation and law school, 15
    1962 Bayh campaign manager, 16,
        22–29
    joins Bayh's senate staff, 30–33, 35
    25th Amendment, 35–36, 38–41
    moves to Daleville, 48–49
    philosophy of Holmes, 57–58
    1970 campaign for secretary of state,
        49, 58–61, 65–73
    campaign funds, 65–66, 170, 180, 195,
        200, 207–8, 218, 252
    and eating, 67, 260–61
    1970 election as secretary of state, 72–
        75
    office staff and administration, 75–76,
        113
    and Matt Welsh, 78
    1972 announcement for governor, 86–
        88
    1972 campaign, 89–108
    response to Master Plan, 117–19, 124–
        25, 128–29, 131, 133–34, 136, 141–

42, 145, 149–50
office scandals, 152–54, 157–58, 172–74, 176
announcement for secretary of state, 2nd term, 138
campaigning style, 169, 171, 180, 193–94, 205–6, 208
labor support, 176
1976 announcement for governor, 178
name recognition, 183
reaction to 1976 primary victory, 190–92
and ISTA, 198–99
and Democratic mayors, 200
and IDEA, 200–1
on utility rates, 202
on voter registration, 202
on roads and bridges, 202–3
1976 campaign speech, 203–5
on gambling, 171–72, 206–7
on Republican scandals, 208
and Indianapolis newspapers, 208–9
1976 defeat, 210–11, 212
legislation, 213
and Indianapolis, 213–14, 235–36, 247, 253–54
1978 Democratic party reorganization, 214–15
1980 primary and general elections, 218–20
City Committee, 225–26
National Sports Festival, 227–29
on volunteering, 230–31
and lobbying, 230
holiday parties, 232
and Indiana Pacers, 233
joins Simon and Associates, 234
and Partners for Livable Places, 234–35
50th birthday party, 236
Pan Am Games, 236, 238–39, 241, 245–47
Cuba, 240–44
and American Legion, 241–43
on civilization, 247
on habit, 248
on political parties, 248–49
and Evan Bayh, 249–52
and Frank O'Bannon, 251–52
on risk-taking, 253, 255
general health, 259
illness and death, 261–67
Conrad, Marshall, 4, 6, 8–9, 15, 157, 188, 210
Conrad, Mary Lou, 36, 83, 108, 136, 196, 212
on Ruby Conrad, 8
meets Larry, 12–14
graduation and first job, 15
birth of Jeb Conrad, 15
birth of Amy Conrad, 21
Bayh campaign jingle, 27
birth of Andrew Conrad, 28
birth of Jodie Conrad, 30
on the extended Conrad family, 30–31, 105–6, 113
Larry's swearing in, 74
on 1972 gubernatorial race, 80, 85

1972 announcement, 88
concession speech, 101
IDEA and Conrad Sing-along, 82, 200–1
the summer of 1974, 105–6
Master Plan
first learned of, 118
effect on Larry and Mary Lou, 119, 124–25, 133–34, 177
response to, 125, 188
Larry's decision to seek reelection, 137–38
1974 state convention, 163–65
campaigning in 1976, 187–88, 208
1976 primary victory, 189
general election loss, 210
and the Simons, 221, 233
birth of Bennett Allyn Conrad, 246
Larry's illness and death, 259–69
Conrad, Patty, 265–66
Conrad, Ruby, 4–9, 11, 15, 125, 157, 188, 210, 259
Conrad Sing-along, 82, 201
Convention and Visitors Bureau, 231
Cooley, Paul, 83
Cooper, John Sherman, 69
Copenhagen, Denmark, 254
Core, J. Manfred, 24–25, 53, 60, 84, 99, 102, 110, 159, 185
Corydon, 4, 68
Cox, Don, 104
Coyle, Jim, 179–81, 182, 184, 194, 200, 213
Cragen, Ken, 56–57, 142
Craig, George, 115
Crawford, William A. (Bill), 197
Crown Hill Cemetery, 269
Cuba, 28–29, 239–45, 267
Cummings, Larry, 30, 56, 143
Currie, Mary Aikens, 60, 129, 140

D-Day Book, *see* Doomsday Book
Daleville, 9, 48, 65, 72–73, 113, 210
Daley, Richard J., 91
Dance Kaleidoscope, 231
Danville, 6
Daviess County, 202
Davis, Dan, 158
Dayton, Ohio, 96–97
Dean, John W. III, 172
Dearborn County, 2
DeBartolo, Edward J., 221
Delaware County, 19, 73, 89, 165, 207
Delaware Hotel, 19
Delegate Bible, *see* Doomsday Book
Democratic National Convention of 1952, 112
of 1968, 55
of 1972, 91, 106, 141
of 1976, 196
Democratic State Central Committee, 25, 65–66, 79, 83–84, 99, 102, 117, 119, 131–32, 134–38, 142–43, 145–46, 148–50, 155, 159, 161, 164, 170, 182, 192–93, 214–15, 234
Democratic State Convention of 1962, 23–24
of 1968, 53, 185

of 1970, 59–60, 79
of 1972, 96, 99–101, 128, 188, 229
of 1974, 159, 162–65, 167
of 1976, 190, 191, 193–94
of 1986, 250
Deppert, Charles (Chuck), 141, 197, 214
Dilbeck, Abe, 97–98
Dillon, John, 77. 118, 145
Disney Corporation, 239, 241
Doherty, Paul M., 121, 141, 144–45
Doomsday Book, 98, 121
Doughnut counties, 169–70, 177
Dubois County, 52
Dugan, Pat, 197
Duke, Phil, 253

Eagle Creek Park, 269
Eagleton, Thomas, 106, 112
East Chicago, 83, 100, 115
East Gary, 158
Eastland, James, 33, 34–35
Edwards, Jack, 213
Edwards, William, 206
Eger, Emmett W., 156
Elizabeth, Indiana, 5
Elkhart County, 89, 102
Energy crisis, 187
Englehart, Gordon, 120, 166
Equal Rights Amendment, 40, 91
Erlichman, John, 170
Ervin, Sam, 111
Estefan, Gloria, 245–46
Evansville, 18, 85, 87, 95, 104, 158, 170, 178

Fair, Robert (Bob), 150, 166, 179, 183, 185,
    186–87, 189–90, 213, 251
Fairbanks, Charles W., 115
Fall Creek, 222
Framingham, Massachusetts, 252
Fensterwald, Bernard (Bud), 35, 118, 119,
    125, 132, 152
Fernandes, Al, 225
Finnegan, Mary, 187
Fithian, Floyd, 214
Flynn, Robert (Bob), 185
Folz, Richard E., 104
Ford, Gerald, 178, 200
Forestal, Jerome, 179
Fort Benjamin Harrison, 221, 238
Fort Wayne, 3, 13–14, 18, 59, 84, 87, 95, 113,
    178
Fort Wayne News Sentinel, 110, 116
Fort Wayne Snider High School, 13
Frankfort, 206
Fraternal Order of Police, 194
Fremont, 144
French Lick, 82, 121, 198, 199, 200, 220
Frick, David, 213–14, 223, 239, 243
Friedlander, Ezra, 75, 126

Gaddy, Charles (Chuck), 197, 198
Gallahan, Russell (Bun), 115, 137, 143–44,
    156, 161, 191, 214
Gallmeyer, Thomas, 18
Gambling, 171–72, 206
Garrett, Wilbur E. (Bill), 237

Garver, Fred, 142, 154
Gary, 70, 87, 132, 180
General election of 1960, 18
    of 1962, 29
    of 1968, 46–47
    of 1970, 62–73, 188
    of 1972, 107–8
    of 1974, 176–77
    of 1976, 210–11
    of 1978, 216–17
    of 1980, 219–20
    of 1986, 252
Geneva, Switzerland, 260–61
Geshwiler, Elton H., 132–33
Ghost employment, 123, 129, 130, 133, 136,
    145, 147
Gibson County, 97, 186, 189
Gibson, Henri, 143
Gifford, Page, 77, 195
Gigerich, William (Bill), 60, 117, 119, 179, 181,
    184, 191–94, 197, 213, 215, 218
Gogol, David, 240
Goldwater, Barry, 58
Goodall, Hurley, 230
Goshen, 68
Graham, Fred, 34–35
Grauel, N. Stuart (Stu), 65, 106, 113
    joins Conrad's staff, 75–76
    political section, 79
    1972 Democratic state convention,
        100
    Boxell's assessment of, 105
    Master Plan, 116, 117, 110–20, 122
    polygraph results, 131
    supports Larry, 132, 138–39
    special committee, 136
    retains Wagner, 148
    telephone calls, 153, 157–58, 172
    tape recordings, 166
    and Jack New, 167, 185
    1976 campaign, 207
Grauel, Diane Meyer, *see* Simon, Diane
Greater Indianapolis Progress Committee
    (GIPC), 223, 231
Green, Clinton (Clint), 24, 159, 184
Greenfield, 60, 157, 185
Grunden, Russell (Russ), 187
Guerra, Manuel Gonzalez, 245
Gutman, Phillip E., 103, 104

Hafsten, Raymond J., Jr., 66, 216–18, 222
Hagedorn, Walter, 153
Hagedorn, Michael, 153
Haldeman, H. R., 170
Hamilton, Lee, 219
Hammond, 60
Hancock County, 67, 189
Handley, Harold, 18
Harris, Art, 134, 146, 148, 151–53, 157, 158,
    174, 176
Harris, Fred R., 54
Harrison County, 3–5, 10, 16, 66, 165, 220,
    251
Hart, John C., 104
Hartford, Connecticut, 37
Hartke, R. Vance, 18, 24, 53, 55–57, 60–64, 66,

73, 75, 123, 139, 143, 151, 163, 181, 182–83, 191, 195, 211
Hatcher, Richard G., 132, 156, 159
Haubstadt, 97
Hayes, Phil, 183, 191
Haynsworth, Clement, 55
Hebron, 144
Hendricks County, 165
Henneke, Cathy, 197
Henry County, 165
Hess, Skip, 134, 146, 148, 151–53, 157, 158, 174, 176
Hill, W. W., Jr., 103, 104
Hillenbrand, John A. II, 52, 218–19
Hinshaw, Robert, 21–22, 24, 26–28, 30
Hilton Hotel, 162
Hoffmann, Victor, 55
Hogsett, Joe, 249, 251–52
Hollis, Stan, 265
Holmes, Oliver Wendell, 57, 205, 269
Holt, Buford, 176
Hoosier Dome, 226, 235, 242, 243, 245, 246, 254
Hoover, Mary Lou, *see* Conrad, Mary Lou
Hope, Bob, 229
Hornbeck, Ellen, 260
Hotel Ibis, *see* Ibis Hotel
Hotel Roberts, *see* Roberts Hotel
Howard County, 165
Howard, Glenn, 241
Howell, Charles, 156
Hric, Paul, 60
Hudnut, William H., III, 222, 223, 226, 231, 235, 238, 242
Huffman, Harvey, 3–4
Huffman, Louisa, 5
Humphrey, Hubert, 9, 54, 99
Huntington County, 157
Hurt, John, 24, 184

Ibis Hotel, 263, 266
IDEA, 82, 83, 121, 200, 220, 251
Illinois Building, 64, 65, 130, 142, 155, 157
Illinois Glacier, 4–5
Income tax, 93
Indiana American Legion, *see* American Legion
Indiana Broadcasters Association, 139, 208
Indiana Civil Liberties Union (ICLU), 242
Indiana Co-operative Handling Association, 194–95
Indiana Democratic Editorial Association, *see* IDEA
Indiana National Guard, 157
Indiana Pacers, 226, 232, 252
Indianapolis, 15, 17, 21, 47, 60, 72, 87, 88, 118, 121, 170, 201, 210
    Conrad comments on, 43, 231, 235
    Robert Kennedy's speech on King's death, 44–45
    and Unigov, 51, 110, 169, 213
    and Simon and Associates, 221–22, 233
    as Naptown, 222
    amateur sports capital, 224–25, 227, 246

in National Geographic, 236–37
Indianapolis Chamber of Commerce, 246–47
Indianapolis 500, 2, 202, 250
Indianapolis Newspapers, Inc., 175
Indianapolis News, 110, 115, 121, 122, 123, 133, 134, 146, 148–50, 153–54, 157–58, 174–76, 196, 199, 208, 256
Indianapolis Press Club, *see* Press Club
Indianapolis Star, 64, 102, 121, 139, 141, 144, 169, 173, 175, 176, 190, 194–96, 209, 243
Indianapolis Symphony Orchestra, 231, 247
Indianapolis Taxpayers Association, 238
Indianapolis Zoo, 231, 247, 254
Indiana Roof, 253
Indiana Sports Corporation, 226–28
Indiana State Board of Accounts, *see* State Board of Accounts
Indiana State Chamber of Commerce, 93
Indiana State Fairgrounds, 202
Indiana State Police, 119, 123, 198
Indiana State Teachers Association, *see* ISTA
Indiana State University, 6
Indiana Statewide Rural Electric Co-operative, *see* REMC
Indiana Supreme Court, 108
Indiana University–Bloomington, 11, 71, 112, 184, 220, 223
Indiana University Purdue University–Indianapolis, *see* IUPUI
Indiana Young Democrats, *see* Young Democrats
Irish Republican Army, 180
Irsay, Robert, 235
Irwin, John, 44
ISTA, 198–99
IUPUI, 15, 224, 226, 243, 253–54

Jackson County, 191
Jackson, Ed, 115
Jamaica, 47
Jasper, Paul G., 132–33, 144
Jefferson County, 3
Jefferson-Jackson Dinner, 43, 52, 150–51
Jefferson, Thomas, 36
Jeffersonville, 8, 169, 170
Jenner, William Ezra, 17–18
Johnson, Faith, 6–7, 9
Johnson, Lady Bird, 235
Johnson, Larry Lee, 6–12, 14
Johnson, Luci, 38, 42
Johnson, Lynda, 38
Johnson, Lyndon B., 29–30, 35, 42–44
Johnson, Zenos, 6
Judiciary Committee, 33, 34, 36

Kearns, Don, 181
Keefe, Robert (Bob), 30–32, 42, 53, 57, 113
Kefauver, Estes, 11, 14, 34–35
Kelley, James F. (Jim), 117, 162, 176, 193
Kennedy, Edward (Ted), 36, 127
Kennedy, Ethyl, 44
Kennedy, John F., 19, 29, 31, 35
Kennedy, Robert, 37, 43–45, 55, 60, 127, 221
Kent State University, 50

Kentucky, 69
Kentucky Derby, 2
Kenya, 247, 267
King, Martin Luther, Jr., 44, 70–71
King, Tom, 225
Kittle, Jim, 225
Klute, Byron, 97
Knapp, Sandy, 226, 227, 240, 242
Knox County, 202
Kohoutek Comet, 205
Kokomo, 96, 171, 210
Kopechne, Mary Jo, 127
Korean War, 11
Krauss, John, 222, 232, 234–35, 240–41, 260–61, 264
Krupa, John, 159, 160
Ku Klux Klan, 114

Laconia, 4–6, 9, 36, 74
Lafayette, 198
Laikin, Judy, 220
Lake County, 46, 73, 76, 83, 89, 90, 102, 156, 159, 161, 171–72, 177, 184, 187, 197, 202
Lake County Democratic Central Committee, 82, 184
Lantz, Jerry, 144, 156
LaPorte County, 102, 217
Lawrence, Lois, 180
Lawrence Township, 15
Lebamoff, Ivan, 84
Lebanon, 198
Lee, Robert E., 1
Lenin, 45
LeRoy, Jacque, 56, 64
Lesher, Stephan, 32, 35, 37–38, 118, 151–52
Letterman, David (Dave), 76, 106
Lewis, Bowman, St. Clair and Wagner, 124
Lewis, Edward D., 62, 64–65, 113, 123–24, 134, 191–92, 195, 207
Lewis, Jeffrey (Jeff), 42–43, 49, 65–66, 72–73, 75–80, 83–84, 86, 88, 100, 105, 106, 123, 126, 129, 131, 136, 140, 157, 158, 167
Lilly Endowment, 52, 141–42, 224–26, 235, 253–56
Linnemeier, Georgiann, 265
Linnemeier, Thomas J., 265–67
Livengood, John, 101–2, 113, 117, 120, 124, 128, 131, 146, 153, 158, 172–73, 182, 213, 234
Lloyd, Russell, 85, 104
Lloyd, William, 122, 174
Logansport, 214
Long, Robert (Bob), 27
Longworth, Edgar L. (Nick), 64
Lookout Mountain, 14
Lopez, Henry (Babe), 161
Los Angeles, 143
Lottery, *see* Gambling
Loughlin, John, 60, 103
Louisville Courier Journal, 120
Louisville, Kentucky, 3, 6, 8, 90
Lubbers, R. Mark, 241
Lugar, Richard G., 58, 103, 110, 161–62, 169, 170, 175, 223, 225, 240, 242

Lyon, France, 261–62

MacAvoy, Carolyn, 197
Madison, 3, 66, 156
Madison County, 89
Malcolm, Richard (Dick), 180, 197, 214
Mall of America, 230, 255
Marion County, 15, 46–47, 58–59, 73, 77, 88, 89, 96, 102, 104, 117, 120, 133, 151, 157, 161–64, 169, 175–76, 184, 188, 254
Marion, Indiana, 213
Market Square Arena, 229, 233
Marshall County, 189
Marshall, Thomas, 115
Martin County, 184
Martinsville, 81
Mason, Maurice, 144, 156, 161
Mason, John S., 194–95
Master Plan, 163, 232
    foreword, 109
    public disclosure of, 114–16
    contents, 116–17
    authors, 165–68
    political impact of, 176–78, 182–83
    and Jack New, 186
    and Mary Lou, 188
Maukport, 3–4
McCallen, Robert, 144, 154, 156, 160
McCarthy, Eugene, 43–45
McCarthy, Joseph, 18
McCarty, Pat, 180, 197
McCarty, Virginia Dill, 193, 208
McCarty, William (Bill), 75, 77
McCray, Warren T., 115
McCreary, Jay, 10
McFall, David, 219
McGovern, George, 91, 99, 105, 106–7, 112
McLean, Virginia, 42
McNulty, Robert, 235, 256–57, 261
McNutt, Paul V., 115
Media, Inc., 129, 140, 150, 155, 167
Melvin Simon and Associates, *see* Simon and Associates
Merchants National Bank, 207
Merrillville, 171
Meyer, Diane, See Simon, Diane
Miami County, 115, 191
Miami, Florida, 91, 106, 143
Miami Sound Machine, 245
Michael, Don, 156, 161, 191, 197, 214–16, 233–34
Michigan City, 158
Milan, 12
Miles, Mark D., 236, 239–40, 242, 244, 246
Miller, Jerry, 100, 161, 163, 167, 177, 234
Milligan, Thomas S., 137, 170
Millon, Charles, 261
Milwaukee, Wisconsin, 143
Modrowski, Pamela, 148
Mondale, Walter, 212, 230
Mong, Steve, 197, 210
Monroe County, 71
Monument Circle, *see* Soldiers and Sailors Monument
Mooney, Robert (Bob), 110, 139, 141, 162, 175,

190, 196
Morgan County, 56, 57
Moss, Ed, 36
Morgan's Raiders, 3–4, 10
Morris, James T. (Jim), 223, 225–26, 236
Muncie, 9, 10, 13, 15, 19–21, 28, 48, 85, 87, 89, 106, 210, 221, 231
Muncie Central Bearcats, *see* Muncie Central High School
Muncie Central High School, 10–12, 20, 231, 233
Museum of Indian Heritage, 231
Muskie, Edmund, 99
Mutz, John, 61
Myers, Jeanette, 56
Myers, Woody, 268

Napier, Virgil, 196
Nappanee, 45
National Association of Secretaries of State, 195, 217
National Geographic, 237
National Sports Festival, 227, 236, 238, 243
Nelson, Ira F. (Rip), 19, 207
Nelson, Max, 268
New Albany, 5, 6
New Castle, 95
New Deal Coalition, 42
New Hampshire 1968 presidential primary, 43
New, Jack, 23, 24, 53, 54, 60, 110, 120, 128, 150, 167, 179, 183, 184–87, 189–90
New Providence, 7
Newman, Dane, 197
Nichols, John C., 66, 78, 97, 105, 129, 131, 140, 147, 150, 154, 157, 167, 175
Nice, France, 265
Nice, Stanley, 156, 161, 214
Nietzsche, Frederick, 45
Nixon, Richard, 54, 107, 111, 113, 166, 168–72
Noble, Freda, 156
Norton, Clark, 39

O'Bannon, Frank, 251–52
O'Brien, Lawrence (Larry), 54, 56
Old Blacky, 7, 206
Oliver, Duke, 197
Olsen, William B., 154–55
Orange County, 188
Orr, Robert D., 104, 199, 218, 219, 220, 241
Owen County, 92

Packard, Michael M., 169–70
Palmer, Lou, 72
Pan Am Village, 238
Pan American Games, *see* PAX-I
Pan American Ten-Indianapolis, *see* PAX-I
Pannos, Michael (Mike), 197
Papas, Nancy, 59, 198
Pari-mutuel betting, *see* Gambling
Paris, France, 235, 259–60, 267
Partners for Livable Places, 234–35, 237, 254–55, 257, 259, 261
Pastrick, Robert (Bob), 83–84, 90, 97, 102, 115, 118, 120, 137, 156–57, 159, 163,

166, 167, 184, 191
Patronage, 52
Pauley, Jane, 106
PAX-I, 236, 237–40, 242–44, 245–47
Pearcy, Noble R., 133, 148–51, 172, 174, 175–76
Perry Township, 96
Personal Shoppers, 220
Peterson, Robert, 219
Phillips, Michael K., 93–94, 133, 134, 156, 234
Posey County, 95
Powell, Steve, 65, 67, 75, 88, 126, 129–31, 140–41, 144, 147, 150, 154, 158, 167
Press Club, 196, 234
Primary election of 1962, 23
    of 1968, 44–45
    of 1970, 50
    of 1972, 25, 96
    of 1974, 155
    of 1976, 187–90
    of 1978, 215
    of 1980, 219
Princeton, Indiana, 186
Prosser, Claudia, 57, 213
    1970 Conrad volunteer, 57, 59, 71
    1972 campaign, 88, 102
    meets Conrad, 113–14
    Master Plan
        Ziegner reveals, 114–16
        accused of ghost employment, 121, 146, 148
        rumors about, 122
        assessment of, 128
        polygraph results, 131
        Larry informs of candidacy, 137
    1974 campaign staff, 169
    1976 campaign staff, 179, 182, 190, 194, 199, 208
    at Conrad and Hafsten, 216, 218, 232
    at Simon and Associates, 234
        Conrad's 50th birthday party, 236
    Pan Am Games, 239, 246
    at the Conrad Group, 257
    Larry's illness and death, 263–64, 266–69
Public Service Commission, 187, 195
Pulliam, Eugene, 208
Punkin Holler, Kentucky, 69–70

Quayle, J. Danforth (Dan), 115, 220, 240, 242, 268

Rachels, Alan, 47, 53, 57, 96
Raisor, Tom, 10
Reagan, Ronald, 220
Redford, Robert, 78
Reed, Robert (Bob), 44
Rehm, George, 174
REMC, 195
Rensselaer, 156, 158
Republican National Committee, 175
Republican State Central Committee, 46, 59, 137, 169, 217
Republican State Convention of 1970, 61
    of 1972, 92, 103–4
    of 1974, 169–70

of 1976, 194
Richmond, 97, 101, 156
Richmond, Charlie, 19
Rising Sun, 2, 95
Rivoire, Michel, 261, 263, 264
Roberts Hotel, 88
Rochester, 143
Rock, Robert (Bob), 53–55, 58, 110, 185, 200
Roe v. Wade, 111
Rooksby, Jane Allen, 117, 148, 181
Rooksby, Lonnie McDade, 5–6
Rooksby Reunion, 220
Rooksby, Robert (Bob), 65–66, 75, 77, 82, 86,
    88, 105, 106, 117, 122–23, 126, 131, 136,
    148, 158, 220
Rooksby, True Curry Huffman, 5
Rooksby, Violet, 5
Rose Polytechnic Institute, 22
Ross, Suzanne, 197
Rothbard, Billy, 67
Roudebush, Richard, 61, 63–64
Roush, J. Edward, 30
Ruckelshaus, William, 46, 199–200,
Rucker, Warren, 156
Russell, Richard, 9
Rutherford, Bob, 139
Rutherford, Johnny, 202

Salem, 68, 131
Salin, William, 59, 66, 72–73
San Bernardino, California, 20
Schenkel, Chris, 229
Schenkel, Greg, 100, 102
Schreiber, William (Bill), 96, 117, 118, 120,
    129, 154, 157, 159, 160–63, 179, 184
Schricker, Henry, 115
Scifres, Mary, 59, 113
Segretti, Donald, 118
Sells, Dallas, 93, 117, 161–62, 173, 176, 191,
    216
Sharp, William, 92, 103, 104
Shaw, Donna, 197
Shaw, William (Bill), 194–95
Shields, Landrum, 180
Shropshire, Jackie L., 132
Shuee, Charles, 156
Silvia, Jamie, 28
Simcox, Edwin J., 213, 217, 251
Simon and Associates, 180, 221–22, 233, 251,
    252, 255
Simon, Bruce, 148
Simon, Diane, 45–47, 65–67, 75, 106, 181, 197,
    220–21, 265–66, 268, 269
Simon, Herbert (Herb), 260
    1976 campaign treasurer, 180, 207
    friends with Conrads, 220–21
    National Sports Festival, 228
    purchases Indiana Pacers, 233
    Partners for Livable Places, 235
    Pan Am Games, 236
    Larry leaves Simon and Associates,
        256
Simon, Melvin, 221, 233
Sinatra, Frank, 228
Singer, William, 91
Slash, Joseph, 241

Smith, Jim, 256–57, 268
Smith, Ken, 118, 119, 125, 129
Snyder, John, 58
Soldiers and Sailors Monument, 2, 130, 254
South Bend, 60, 87, 100, 141, 163, 178, 186,
    203, 210
Special Committee, 131–32, 133–36, 137–38,
    141, 144–46, 148–49, 166
Speedway, 43
Stapleton, Ed, 142
State Board of Accounts, 150, 153, 157, 172–
    76
Steinmetz, Edward, 265
Stephen, Alan, 143
Stoner, Richard B., 163
St. Angelo, Gordon, 93, 106, 191, 231
    selection as state Democratic chair-
        man, 52
    political allies and enemies, 52–53,
        76, 156, 159, 234
    1968 state convention, 53–54, 185
    campaign for national chairman, 54,
        110
    and Birch Bayh, 54–58, 60, 147–48
    and Conrad's 1970 nomination, 58–59
    1970 campaign and election, 61–63
    opposes Conrad, 62–63, 77–79, 83–84,
        89–90, 130
    1972 state convention, 93, 99–102
    Master Plan, 115–16, 119–20, 127–29,
        130–34, 136, 138–40, 144–48, 166–
        67
    and Ziegner, 123, 147, 151, 177
    resigns as state chairman, 141–43
St. Joseph County, 47, 73, 89, 102, 142, 177
St. Louis, Missouri, 19, 252
Strasbourg, France, 235, 259–60
Straub, Terrence (Terry), 75, 77–78, 86, 88,
    100, 102, 105, 106, 113, 126, 229
Stuart, James Ewell Brown (Jeb), 15
Subcommittee on Constitutional Amend-
    ments, 34–36, 118
Sutherlin, Steve, 75
Svihlik, Charles (Chic), 190
Switzerland County, 3

Teague, Tom, 89, 190, 197, 208
Teamsters, 176
Telephone pyramid, 181, 184, 189
Tell City, 153
Terre Haute, 6, 18, 21, 22, 28, 62, 87, 102, 106,
    121, 178, 184
Today Show, 106
Townsend, Wayne, 218–19
Thornburg, Jerry, 19, 207
Tippecanoe County, 89
Tracey, Ed, 58, 62
Trisler, Bill, 136, 139, 142–43, 144–47, 149,
    151, 156, 163, 190–92
Trixler, Jeanne, 103, 157
Tucker, Ralph, 18, 28, 184

UAW, 66, 93, 117, 137, 161, 165, 173, 176, 181,
    191, 214–15
Udell, Jerry, 31, 46, 48
Unigov, 51, 110, 115, 169, 213, 223

Union Station, 139, 237, 254
United Auto Workers, *see* UAW
United Nations, 232
Urban League, 231
U.S. Clay Court Tournament, 224, 231, 237
U.S. Gymnastics Federation, 235
U.S. Olympic Committee, 227
U.S. Steel, 229

Valparaiso University, 55
Vanderburgh County, 89, 96, 104, 171
Vietnam War, 43, 46, 60, 79, 182
Vigo County, 73, 89, 96, 102, 121, 142
Viking I spacecraft, 194–95
Vincennes, 208
Voisard, Leo, 142

Wabash, 144
Wabash College, 30, 101
Wagner, Patricia, 61
Wagner, Robert F. (Bob)
    birth, early life, family, 61–63
    1970 Hartke campaign manager, 56,
        63–65, 123
    law practice, 123–24
    political instincts, 124
    adviser to Conrad on Master Plan,
        115, 131–36, 138, 140–42, 145–46,
        148–49, 154–55, 172–76
    1974 Conrad campaign manager,
        162–64, 169, 171, 176–77
    in 1976, 178–211
    campaign strategy, 1976 primary,
        180–82
    reaction to 1976 primary victory,
        189–93
    campaign strategy, 1976 general, 196–
        97, 201–2, 206–8
    and ISTA, 199
    and Jerry Brown, 200
    and campaign staff, 200
    assessment of 1976 elections, 211
    and Indianapolis newspapers, 208–9
    reorganization of Democratic party,
        1978, 214–15
Walker, E. C., 197, 213
Wallace, Mrs. George, 99
Walsh, Kenneth (Irish), 37
War Memorial, 242
Warner, Amy, *see* Conrad, Amy Lou
Warner, John, 263–65
Warren Township, 96

Warrick County, 184
Washington, D.C., 136, 139, 141, 151, 183,
    213
Washington, Indiana, 203
Watergate, 41, 111, 113, 118, 120, 137, 168–70,
    172
Wayne County, 97, 101
Weedman, Sidney, 225, 227, 236, 241–43, 246
Weger, Vicki, 75–76, 78, 80, 102, 106, 113, 121,
    126, 131, 158
Welch, Robert V. (Bob), 77, 85, 179
Wellington, Margo, 263
Welsh, Matthew E. (Matt), 60, 80, 115, 121,
    128, 170, 174, 229, 251
    meets Boxell, 19
    endorses Birch Bayh, 23–24
    advice to Rock, 52
    1972 candidacy, 77, 81–85, 92, 95–97
        Democratic state convention, 99–
            105
        general election, 107
        Conrad's view of, 78
        St. Angelo supports, 90
    possible Democratic state chairman,
        142
    and Pastrick, 159
    and Jack New, 184–85
Whitcomb, Edgar D., 58–59, 61, 79, 87, 92,
    103, 104, 185
White River, 63, 222
White River Park Commission, 226, 230
White River Park State Games, 226
White River State Park, 231, 254
White, Theodore H., 45, 50
Whiteland, 56
WIBC, 72
Wilcox, C. Timothy, 64–65
Wilson, Theodore D. (Ted), 103, 193
Wisconsin Glacier, 5
Wolfe, William (Bill), 56, 157, 159–60

Yeagley, Don, 117, 137, 161, 191
Young Democrats, 21, 71, 113, 116–17, 129,
    140, 159

Zagrovich, Willis N., 132, 161–62
Ziegner, Edward H. (Ed), 109–11, 112–18,
    120–23, 125–27, 130, 133, 134, 142–43,
    145, 146, 150, 152, 155, 164, 166–67,
    176, 177, 208, 215–16, 232
Zionsville, 106
Zirkle, Kevin, 187

Raymond H. Scheele is a graduate of Valparaiso University and received his PhD in 1972 from the University of Missouri—Columbia. He has taught at DePaul University and since 1975 has served on the faculty at Ball State University, where he is Professor of Political Science and Chairperson of the department. A specialist in state and local government and political parties and elections, he has published several articles on Indiana government and politics. In 1984 the Indiana Democratic party nominated him for the state office of Superintendent of Public Instruction. He also serves as Vice-President of Waggoner, Irwin, Scheele, and Associates, Inc., a research consulting firm based in Muncie, Indiana.